A Portion of the People

A Portion of the People

Three Hundred Years of Southern Jewish Life

Edited by

Theodore Rosengarten and Dale Rosengarten

with a preface by Eli N. Evans

University of South Carolina Press
in association with McKissick Museum

© 2002 University of South Carolina

Published in Columbia, South Carolina, by the
University of South Carolina Press

Manufactured in Canada

06 05 04 03   5 4 3 2

Library of Congress Cataloging-in-Publication Data

A Portion of the people : three hundred years of southern Jewish life /
    edited by Theodore Rosengarten and Dale Rosengarten ; with a preface by
    Eli N. Evans.
          p. cm.
    Catalog published in conjunction with an exhibition.
Includes bibliographical references and index.
        ISBN 1-57003-445-1 (cloth : alk. paper)
        1. Jews—South Carolina—History—Exhibitions. 2. South Carolina—Ethnic relations—
    Exhibitions. I. Title: Three hundred years of southern Jewish life. II. Rosengarten, Theodore.
    III. Rosengarten, Dale, 1948– IV. McKissick Museum.
    F280.J5 P67 2002
    975.7004'924—dc21   2002005545

This catalogue has been published in conjunction with the exhibition,

A Portion of the People Three Hundred Years of Southern Jewish Life

SPONSORED BY

McKissick Museum, College of Liberal Arts, University of South Carolina
The College of Charleston Library
The Jewish Studies Program at the College of Charleston
The Jewish Historical Society of South Carolina

Contents

Illustrations

A glossary of frequently occurring Hebrew and Yiddish terms is located in the back of the volume; infrequently occurring terms are defined within the text. Terms not in common English usage appear in italics upon first occurrence in the text.

Preface

Eli N. Evans

A Portion of the People chronicles an extraordinary American story. It takes us on a journey of three hundred years of Jewish life in South Carolina. Charleston was the capital of the colony where the American Jewish experiment took root, growing deeply into the soil of a state where Jews, in Isaac Harby's poetic observation, joined other religious groups in "one great political family." Harby, a journalist and playwright who would later become a founder of Reform Judaism, in 1816 wrote a letter to Secretary of State James Monroe protesting the removal of the American consul to Tunis because he was a Jew. Harby reminded the future president, who had incorporated the principle of religious freedom in the Virginia constitution, that Jews and other religious minorities were not sects deserving toleration; rather, he said, "they constitute a portion of the People."

From the very beginning in the seventeenth century, Jews were welcomed in the British colony of Carolina as traders and merchants with connections spanning the Atlantic, and as cultured contributors with Old World tastes. They were elected to office, respected as citizens, recruited to bear arms and serve in the militia. Carolina—not yet differentiated into a South and North—was a fantasy come true. It was a place of dreams where Jews could live free in a kind of promised land, free to worship as they saw fit, free to practice any profession, free to trade and to make partnerships with gentiles, free to vote, free to own property and will it to their heirs.

To describe the new homeland, the Jewish imagination called on the Old Testament for inspiration. Listen to Myer Moses speak of his Charleston home in 1806, with this prayerful oration: "Collect together thy long scattered people and let their gathering place be in this land of milk and honey." Hear the words of Rev. Gustavus Poznanski at a dedication speech for the new Beth Elohim in 1841: "This synagogue is our *temple*, this city is our *Jerusalem*, this happy land our *Palestine*."

This was a new situation in Jewish history. Here in America, in a place called Carolina, Jews were not a despised minority tolerated because they were useful. To the dispersed Jews of Europe and the West Indies, America was different, hospitable, hopeful, accommodating to those talented Sephardim whose ancestors were exiled from Spain and Portugal during the Inquisition that started in the fifteenth century. They and their Ashkenazi cousins, who were part and parcel of the early European migration, could begin anew in Carolina, the nurturing cradle of Jewish life in the American South.

~

For South Carolina's Jewish community in the twenty-first century, *A Portion of the People* signals a new self-confidence and a coming of age. It has been a powerful tenet of southern Jewish life that Jews should not be vocal and call attention to themselves. But here is a public celebration of southern Jewish history, with bold assertions of the vital role played by Jews since the first days of European settlement; here is a willingness to explore the shadows as well as to celebrate the sunlight.

If Carolina was good for the Jews, the Jews were also good for Carolina. The new colony and the struggling seaport needed people with trading skills and imagination, contacts and credibility, and a world view that looked outward to the sea and westward to a vast continent. Jews brought all of this and more. They were active players in the colonial enterprise, skilled artisans and merchants, eager to succeed and wanting to be judged only by their qualifications.

For people conditioned to regard New York City as the center of Jewish life, it will come as a shock to learn that in 1800, Charleston, South Carolina, had the largest Jewish community in America. There were 2,500 Jews in the United States at that time—four hundred in New York and somewhat fewer in Philadelphia—but Charleston had five hundred. Not only was Charleston the major port south of Baltimore, it was a cultural center as well, with two theaters and an opera, frequent concerts by foreign artists, and lectures by leading literary and scientific scholars of the day. This was the cosmopolitan world that Charleston's Jews called home. Just look at the faces in the portraits in the exhibition. These are the intelligent faces of the Jewish merchant class, women as well as men, new Jews in the New World. Yet, there was a price to pay for aspiring to the trappings of gentility and high society, a dark side to the embrace of Jews in a homeland whose economy was founded on racial slavery.

A Portion of the People confronts slavery in an honest and open way. The census tells us that through the early decades of the nineteenth century more than four-fifths of white households in Charleston had slaves and that for Jews the proportion was almost as high. House slaves were common—the average was one to three per household. A handful of Jewish plantation owners, the "Jewish gentry," grew the rice called "Carolina Gold." The exhibition includes domestic, decorative, and ceremonial objects from this little-known corner of Jewish life.

South Carolina made history through the achievements of its Jewish citizens. Francis Salvador, son of an Amsterdam merchant and nephew of an important financier and distinguished member of a Sephardic congregation in London, was elected to the First and Second Provincial Congresses of South Carolina, making him, perhaps, the first professing Jew in the modern world to be placed in office by Christians. Salvador favored independence from Britain even if it meant war.

Less than a month after the adoption of the Declaration of Independence, he was ambushed with a band of patriot militia by a group of British-armed Tories and Indians. Francis Salvador died at the age of twenty-nine, the first Jew to give his life for the American Revolution.

By 1820, Charleston had begun to decline as a trade center, its growth faltering from competition from the newer port towns of Mobile and New Orleans, from a fall in prices paid for its major cash crops, rice and cotton, from the alliance of the Northeast with the Midwest made possible by the Erie Canal, from discriminatory tariffs that favored the manufacturing states, and from steam navigation, which shortened the routes from Europe to Boston and New York.

In response to its crisis of confidence and to the wave of evangelical revivals that were sweeping the South, Charleston became more vigorously Protestant. In this charged environment, it was natural that the city's Jews would generate a more American form of Judaism. In November 1824, Philip Benjamin, the father of Judah P. Benjamin, became one of forty-seven members at Beth Elohim in Charleston to petition the trustees to shorten services, to pray in English as well as in Hebrew, to eliminate Spanish, and to require a sermon of "an Inglish discourse" at each service. When the trustees tabled the request, Philip and twelve other dissenters broke with Beth Elohim and organized the "Reformed Society of Israelites."

For fifteen years divisiveness continued, growing ever more bitter. The installation in the synagogue of an organ to play songs on the Sabbath was a last straw. The traditionalists seceded, bought their own burial ground adjacent to Beth Elohim's, and built a wall to separate Orthodox from Reform.

In the 1840s, a wave of German and Polish Jews merged with the stream of native Jewish Carolinians to open a new chapter in the dynamic Jewish encounter with the South. But the storm clouds of the Civil War were gathering. Charleston's young Judah Benjamin became Louisiana's Senator Judah P. Benjamin, subsequently appointed by President Jefferson Davis as attorney general of the new Confederacy, and later as secretary of war and secretary of state. Thousands of Jews participated in the Civil War as soldiers, and in high positions in the civilian ranks. In Charleston, one hundred and eighty Jewish men joined the Confederate army. The "Jewish Johnny Rebs" appear in *A Portion of the People* in photographs and paintings, sad-eyed soldiers who served with young Simon Baruch, fresh out of medical school. Baruch, from Camden, South Carolina, would become a celebrated surgeon and the father of financier Bernard Baruch. Many Jewish women, daughters of the Confederacy, served their country behind the lines and on the home front.

After the war, Reconstruction radicals with Jewish antecedents paraded across the stage of southern history. Franklin J. Moses Jr., a "scalawag" from Sumter, South Carolina, served two stormy years as governor, from 1872 to 1874. Francis Cardozo, a "free person of color" from Charleston, son of a Jewish father and a woman of mixed race, and second cousin, once removed, to Benjamin Nathan Cardozo, the famed United States Supreme Court justice, was a member of the

South Carolina Constitutional Convention of 1868, a trustee of the University of South Carolina in 1869, secretary of state of South Carolina from 1868 to 1872, and state treasurer from 1872 to 1876. In an era noted for graft and fraud, his record stands untarnished.

The eastern European migration to America in the 1880s swamped everything that came before. The "greenhorns" who went south brought their Orthodoxy and Yiddish language with them, along with an ethic for hard work. What happened in Charleston is typical of Jewish history in many southern cities. Within decades, the children of the late-nineteenth-century immigrants had served in two world wars and become bulwarks of the Jewish communal life they and their children helped build.

South Carolina Jews, the exhibition points out, are still a "portion of the people." They are committed to the idea of community, both the Jewish community and the general community. "Americans to the core," to borrow a phrase from Reform leader Isaac M. Wise on a visit to Charleston in 1850, they believe in pluralism and democracy. They have moved with the times to embrace a wider definition of the common good. South Carolina welcomed them three hundred years ago and they have reciprocated many times over with gratitude and participation in every walk of life.

There is a passion that drives *A Portion of the People*. We sense an abounding energy sustained over years of planning and collecting and assembling the elements of past lives. It could not have happened without the intelligence and commitment of Dale Rosengarten, a New York native who attended Harvard in the 1960s and moved to South Carolina in 1976. Read her essay, "A Call for Candlesticks," about the curator's search for objects that tell stories, and you will experience her tireless investigation and the ardor that fired the dream of this project. McKissick Museum at the University of South Carolina and its director, Lynn Robertson, understood that the telling of the South Carolina Jewish story presented an historic opportunity and a profound responsibility. The Jewish Historical Society of South Carolina, founded through the leadership of state senator Isadore E. Lourie, engaged its members in sharing their family keepsakes, photographs, and stories, in an effort to preserve the state's Jewish cultural legacy. The Jewish Studies Program at the College of Charleston, headed by its innovative director, Martin Perlmutter, provided guidance and staffing to launch the historical society in 1994. The National Endowment for the Humanities, the Bank of America, other foundations and corporations, and dozens of enlightened individuals saw the originality and value of the project and gave it their support.

The result is an impressive exhibition and a beautiful book, a contribution to the future that lends depth and nuance to our understanding of the past. It is about South Carolina, to be sure, but it is also about the Jewish story in America, brought to life through an enormous undertaking of research and imagination, with an almost biblical faith in the power of memory to nourish the roots of future generations. ✌

A Portion of the People

Introduction

Theodore Rosengarten

More than a hundred years have passed between the great Anglo-Jewish Historical Exhibition in London, in 1887, and the more modest endeavor generated by the Jewish community of the small state of South Carolina. Despite the intervention of a cataclysmic century, the two events are allied by the motives of the exhibitors and, speaking immodestly, if the interpretive intentions of *A Portion of the People* are realized, they will be related by a capacity to inspire a fresh understanding of Jewish history.

Like their predecessors in England, organizers of the South Carolina exhibition have wanted to rebuff stereotypes of Jews and to demonstrate that Jews have mingled with the larger community since the first days. They have helped build industries, contributed to culture, and in times of emergency have borne arms in defense of the state. In the South, Jews fought to free the American colonies from Great Britain, and eighty years later, to create an independent southern nation. Contrary to slanders circulated in the national press in the 1880s and '90s, Jews in the South supported the Confederate cause, and Jews in the North the cause of the Union, in numbers far in excess of their ratio in the population.

One of the myths dispelled by *A Portion of the People* is that there were no Jews in the South. A second is that the typical southern Jew came in steerage in 1900; a third is that the Sephardim all settled in New York and Newport. Jews, we learn from this exhibition, have been part of Carolina society since King Charles granted a charter for the colony to his entrepreneurial friends, the eight Lords Proprietors, in the seventeenth century.

The saga of Jewish immigration is customarily divided into three periods that correspond to three different cultural groups: Sephardic, German, and eastern European. Historian Oscar Handlin challenged this formulation more than fifty years ago. The story persists in South Carolina, against evidence that all three strands were woven among Jewish arrivals in every era. The tendency of second- and third-generation Jews, regardless of where their grandparents came from, to choose their relatives and identify with Spanish and Portuguese ancestry—to "Sephardize" themselves, in Jonathan D. Sarna's phrase—has been a recurring path to status and self-esteem.

The Anglo-Jewish Historical Exhibition was a product of Jewish emancipation —the coming out from under discriminatory custom and law, and the adoption by Jews of a modern point of view and a modern aesthetic. The exhibition occurred midway in the era of grand industrial and ethnographic fairs starting with the Great International Exposition in London's Crystal Palace, in 1851—at which, incidentally, rice grown by African American slaves on South Carolina plantations was awarded the gold medal of excellence—and ending when Europe plunged into the First World War.

The movement to collect Jewish ritual objects and display them as public curiosities and relics of culture is dramatically recounted by Grace Cohen Grossman in her 1997 monograph, *Judaica at the Smithsonian: Cultural Politics as Cultural Model.* The Anglo-Jewish Historical Exhibition marked the moment from which Jews, as well as gentiles, regarded it as normal and correct to view the Jewish religion as a product of history, as likely to change under the pressures of circumstance as other aspects of Jewish life, such as costume and language. The "unchanging" faith, it was plain to see, diverged from time to time and place to place. To the chagrin of anti-Semites who advocated Jewish emancipation in the belief that by fully participating in the flow of national life Jews would discard their archaic religion, Jews clung to the rudiments of their faith. Neither the trials of the Inquisition nor the temptations of emancipation significantly loosened the bond.

Freedom was the major test for the Jews of Carolina. Freedom from kings, princes, and rabbis. The freedom to believe or not to believe according to individual conscience. The freedom to move about the country at will, to pursue any occupation, to enter into partnerships with Christians, to testify in court, to vote and to run for public office in elections. This condition of unprecedented liberty was not the gift of Judeophiles; it came with the expectation, expressed in the colony's constitution of 1669, that sooner or later the Jews would convert.

One of the first references to a Jew in Carolina was to a Spanish-speaking "linguister," who shows up in military records in 1695 as a translator for the colonial governor interrogating four captive Indians from Spanish Florida. He was likely Sephardic, as were the majority of early settlers. By the mid-eighteenth century, the Ashkenazim, with roots in the German states, were becoming numerically dominant, but the social and cultural preeminence of the Sephardim continued for another hundred years.

Jews who made Charleston their destination were drawn, in part, by the city's reputation for religious tolerance. The constitution drafted for the province by John Locke, private secretary to Lord Anthony Ashley Cooper, granted people of any religion—except for Catholics—the right, indeed the duty, to form a church. The right to vote was given to any white man who owned fifty acres of land. In actuality this right would be challenged periodically until the era of the Revolution.

At the head of the peninsula formed by the Ashley and Cooper Rivers, Charles Town—the name for Charleston during the period of British rule—developed as a center for the export of deerskins and timber, beef and rice. By the mid-eighteenth century, indigo joined the list of commodities. A plant in the pea family whose leaves were boiled and processed into a blue dye used to color the uniforms of British sailors, indigo could be grown in a variety of terrains, from the lowcountry to the upcountry, though it thrived particularly well in the coastal environs. A Jew from London, Moses Lindo was instrumental in establishing the reputation of Carolina indigo and procuring a subsidy from Parliament for its cultivation. Indigo-sorter and dye-maker, chemist and inventor, entrepreneur and promoter, Lindo served as provincial surveyor and inspector of indigo during its heyday as Carolina's second largest revenue crop.

In the wake of the American Revolution, the market for indigo collapsed. Meanwhile, the agricultural economy was revived by two developments: the transfer of rice plantations from inland swamps to sites along the rivers where the tides could be harnessed to irrigate, fertilize, and weed the fields, and by the success of the state's first commercial cotton crops on the sea islands between Charleston and Savannah. Trade in rice, cotton, and slaves enriched brokers or merchants known as "factors" who sold the plantations' produce and supplied them with everything they did not raise or manufacture for themselves. Luxury goods imported from Europe filled the fine city residences of rural planters. Jewish merchants prospered with the rest.

But prosperity did not last. By the 1820s Charleston's star had begun to fade; contemporaries described the port city as a "place of tombs." In 1830, when the pace of immigration to America picked up, New York surpassed Charleston as the capital of American Jewry. To young Jewish southerners looking for a brisk economy and a career in law or business, the commercial frontier of the Mississippi appeared more promising, as did the rich farmlands of Georgia and Alabama. By 1860, New Orleans counted 2,000 Jews among its residents, while Charleston's Jewish population had hit a plateau of 700.

∽

All the essays in this volume deal with the subject of freedom. Each addresses in one form or another how Jews have coped with so much freedom, but also how they responded to a situation where more than half the population was held in slavery. For while Carolina was the first political entity to treat Jews as equals, it also was the only colony on the American mainland whose charter sanctioned racial slavery. Jews indeed were equal—to other white people. Along with Huguenots and Quakers, Presbyterians and dissenters, they bolstered the number of whites, like sandbags on a levee.

Just how substantial was Jewish involvement in the slave trade? Two recent books dedicated to "setting the record straight" demonstrate convincingly, in my opinion, that Jews played a negligible role in the Atlantic traffic. In colonial days Moses Lindo was the lone Jew in South Carolina known to have owned a ship that carried Africans to America. Of 389 slave cargos advertised for sale in Charleston between 1733 and 1774, according to historian Eli Faber, only five were offered by companies that had Jewish partners. In all, Jewish importers took delivery of less than 1 percent of the more than 1,100 slave cargoes on which South Carolinians paid duties in that period.

Yet the publication of Faber's *Jews, Slaves, and the Slave Trade* and Saul Friedman's *Jews and the American Slave Trade* testifies to the tenacity of the question. It gets posed by reputable scholars who are disheartened by a perceived breakdown in the alliance of blacks and Jews that worked for social change in the 1960s, and by demagogues who, according to Harvard professor Henry Louis Gates Jr., use anti-Jewish rhetoric to position themselves in the power struggle within the black community. The question also plagues progressive Jews who want to find a basis to believe that in the eighteenth and nineteenth centuries Jews secretly opposed slavery.

Faber turns the question on its head. He asks why, with "their careers in commerce; their membership in an ethnoreligious trading network that spanned the Atlantic; their facility with languages," Jews were not more deeply involved in the trade than they were. Their mercantile experience would have given them an edge. Why didn't they use it? Were they shut out of the lucrative trade by their gentile rivals? Were they merely "off-loaders" who sold the cargoes from the holds of ships that did not belong to them? Or did they harbor reservations about buying and selling human beings?

Any wish to identify Jewish hostility to slavery runs aground on evidence from the internal markets. Once the Africans reached the port cities of Charleston and Savannah, New Orleans and Natchez, Jewish merchants bought and sold human chattel as well as every other kind of saleable goods. The designers of *A Portion of the People* struggled over how to display the text of an advertisement for "negroes" placed in the *South-Carolina State Gazette* by Abraham Mendes Seixas, a Jewish vendue master, or auctioneer. At the time the notice appeared, in September 1794, Seixas also was serving as warden of Charleston's workhouse, where criminals, debtors, and runaway slaves were incarcerated. The advertisement, which took the form of a rhymed verse or doggerel, may have been satirical, but its object was deadly earnest: to flaunt the quality and guarantee the submissiveness of the men, women, and children Seixas was offering for sale. How, one wonders, could any reasonable person have found this commerce inoffensive? In the Charleston of that era, however, dealing in slaves did not harm a person's social standing. In fact, at the time of his death five years later, Seixas was a city magistrate and a trustee of the Jewish congregation. A large crowd of admirers attended his funeral.

The bottom line is, Jews subscribed to the dominant morality of the time and place. As a leading scholar on the subject, Bertram Wallace Korn, observes, "Any Jew who could afford to own slaves and had need for their services would do so." Jews accepted slavery along with other distinctively southern institutions and ideas such as a code of honor that sanctioned dueling as a method of settling disputes and the defense of the doctrine of states' rights which held that a state could nullify a federal law deemed harmful to its interests.

The question of how masters treated the people they held as slaves is thorny. It is difficult not to apply today's standards of right and wrong, but the fact is, in those days inequality was not regarded as oppression, nor was prejudice synonymous with immorality. Considering the centuries of persecution Jews had endured, should they not have felt empathy for the enslaved? Did not Jewish law prescribe a certain code for the conversion and emancipation of slaves? The record shows that Jewish slave owners in America embraced the prevailing standards of conduct. Their treatment of slaves is indistinguishable from that of gentiles, ranging from cases of kindred feeling to cold calculation of profit and loss.

~

It is hard to imagine anyone more suited by his background and gifts than Eli N. Evans to write the preface to this catalogue. Evans is the author of *The Provincials*, a coming-of-age memoir that tells the story of the flowering of a hybrid Jewish culture in the startlingly friendly soil of the South. He was born and raised in Durham, North Carolina, where his father, E. J. "Mutt" Evans, served six terms as mayor and schooled him in his love for Tar Heels football and basketball. His mother, Sara Nachamson Evans, helped him ward off his worry about Jesus and feel proud of Jewish accomplishment. Another of Evans's books, *Judah P. Benjamin: The Jewish Confederate*, is required reading for anyone who wants to understand the convergence of private life and historical events in an era of glorious ambition and bitter defeat that defines, to this day, the South's peculiarity.

Deborah Dash Moore is the first scholar, to my knowledge, to link the creation of Reform Judaism in America to the hysteria that gripped Charleston in the wake of the unsuccessful—and possibly fabricated—slave uprising of 1822. "Freedom's Fruits" is thus an ironic title, for not only were Jews free to argue with one another over the appropriateness of their traditional "means of worshipping the true God," but the movement to modernize an old religion emerged in an atmosphere charged by fears that an enslaved majority was plotting to win freedom by annihilating its oppressors. Without taking a stand on the authenticity of the plot attributed to the leadership of a free black carpenter and lay preacher named Denmark Vesey, Moore applies a theme developed in an essay she wrote several years ago for a collection titled *Struggles in the Promised Land*, on the history of black-Jewish relations in the United States. In that piece, "Separate Paths: Blacks and Jews in the Twentieth Century South," she argued that Jews complied with the racial code lest they be seen as the "antithetical other." Turning her gaze to the first half of the nineteenth century, she finds similar anxieties at work. In a society that increasingly viewed itself as Protestant and racially superior, a group of younger Jews in Charleston, saying they wanted to strengthen Judaism and help the ancient faith retain its hold on succeeding generations, proposed changing Jewish ritual and liturgy to mimic the rules of decorum set by their gentile neighbors.

Other forces tending toward reform in Judaism played a large and perhaps a decisive role. The spirit of reform was in the air, in Berlin and Cincinnati, in London and New York. But Charleston was special. It was first, and, as Moore observes, it was there that women stepped forward as participants in the service and creators of the liturgy. They wrote hymns and prayers. They operated Sunday schools for the purposes of building community and instilling "Jewishness" in children who were immersed in American culture.

No one regarded America as a stop on the road to somewhere else. Here the prophesy of a Promised Land was fulfilled. Jews could cease their wandering and put down permanent roots. Not only was the profession of faith in harmony with the spirit of the times, so was the idea of national identity. Jews needed no more mourn for a Zion across the sea than they should wish to restore the age of kings. Reformers rejected the thought that it was the Jewish destiny to reconstitute a separate nation on other soil.

Staunch in their support for the separation of religion and state, they sometimes fused the rhetoric of theology and politics, indicating perhaps that the sources of their thoughts and modes of expression were mixed, drawing on both the lingering idealism of the American Revolution and the enthusiasm of the dominant Protestant revivalistic scene. To Isaac Harby, the Jewish intellectual who spearheaded the movement for reform, the ancient Jewish wish for a homeland was fulfilled by the American reality—specifically, the reality of South Carolina— that in his eyes was a perfect equality of religions one with the other and of individuals one with the other. Harby could embrace rival political doctrines without any feeling of contradiction; he accepted the ideas of Jefferson and Madison as strands of one protective American web.

But the fly in the ointment was the coming struggle over slavery that would divide American identity into sections. Jews and Christians alike had begun to see themselves as southern or northern. Jewish advocates could be found on both sides of the great debate over nullification—a rehearsal for the coming secession movement. Meanwhile southern Jewish opinion was united against abolition and the abolitionists. When the day of secession was at hand, no prominent South Carolina Jews withheld support from the southern cause.

For all their pride in the antiquity of the state's Jewish history and their wistfulness for Sephardic culture, the vast majority Jewish South Carolinians today are descended from people who came here from eastern Europe after 1880. Strangers to America's brand of racial politics and to religious reform, these Yiddish-speaking, quintessential outsiders are the subject of Jenna Weissman Joselit's discerning essay, "Land of Promise."

Why these refugees from poverty and persecution chose to come to America is easy to understand, but why they made South Carolina their destination is a mystery Joselit unravels. Viewed from other sections of the country, South Carolina was the consummate backwater, in retreat from the currents of modern life. But to immigrant men willing to put a pack on their backs and peddle their wares, or to families who ventured to open stores in rural recesses where cash money was as scarce as hens' teeth, South Carolina was a virtual frontier.

So while their predecessors had made a living in the plantation-based commerce of their day, the eastern European Jews filled a different niche. They were peddlers and shopkeepers, cloth and scrap-metal dealers, shoemakers and needleworkers. In the large towns and cities, they could band together in neighborhoods and shuls and carry on traditional life in a new setting. But how could a few solitary Jews living in some small town far from a synagogue or a kosher butcher practice their religion? How could they raise their children in the faith?

The dilemma of how—and whether—to remain Jewish in a free and overwhelmingly gentile environment was complicated by a second thread of identity. Could these people, who by virtue of where they were living were southern Jews—could they become Jewish southerners? Integrating with the state's native Jewish population would take time, if it were to happen at all. Language, custom, and vocation separated the two groups, who self-consciously kept their distance. But the biggest divide, nimbly addressed by Joselit, was the divide of history. South Carolina's established Jews had lived through the crucible of the Civil War and Reconstruction. The newer generation had not. The old guard had fought at Antietam and Gettysburg and called themselves southerners; defeat in war may have hardened their sectional identity more than victory ever could have. The parents of the "greenhorns" had spent the years of the American Civil War fending off anti-Semitic assaults in Poland and Russia. Lacking the memories of a shared past and feeling ethnically different, the natives and the newcomers took longer to unite than did their urban cousins to the north. It was through common responses to current events, in particular to two world wars, that they overcame what Joselit calls "the divide" and merged in synagogue and temple, in marriage, business, and society.

Jack Bass is the lone essayist in the catalogue who claims a South Carolina pedigree. Bass's mother, Esther, came from Poland, and his father, Nathan, from Lithuania. They met in New York in 1917 when Nathan, already living in South Carolina, was on a buying trip for his store. In deference to Esther's mother's belief that a baby's looks are determined by its environment, Bass's mother went back to New York when it was time to deliver her first child, for fear that if she stayed in the South the child would be born black.

Jack, the seventh and last child, was born in Columbia, South Carolina, and grew up in the midlands hamlet of North. More precisely, he spent his boyhood in the back of his father's store. He went to public school and to the University of South Carolina, conveniently located next to the state house, where he could observe, gossip, and write about his first love, politics.

In "Just Like One of Us," Bass recalls the offices Jews have held and the influence they have wielded since the founding of the colony. His heart is in the twentieth century, when the story of Jewish officeholders and policy makers is tied inextricably to the southern preoccupation with race. While the Jewish presence in South Carolina had no more impact on the rise or fall of slavery than it did on the rising and setting of the sun, after Reconstruction Jewish legislators were frequently in the position of brokering the racial compact, of writing its rules and negotiating exceptions, albeit within the range of behaviors consistent with white supremacy.

By 1960 Jewish legislators had become identified with programs to improve the quality of life for African Americans. In turn, they received the strong support of newly enfranchised black voters. Once blacks seized the opportunity to represent themselves, however, these same Jewish legislators became superfluous. Given the choice of being represented by a black person or a white, even a white who knew how to make the system deliver, blacks nominated and voted their color.

Outside the rarefied chambers of the legislature, in the privacy of their dry-goods stores and doctors' offices, Jews discreetly violated the spirit of Jim Crow. The rebellious act of permitting a customer to try on a hat or to use a common bathroom did not shake society to its roots, but it was risky behavior that suggested a vision of normality different from the one enforced by law. "In the halls of justice," wrote Jewish comedian and philosopher Lenny Bruce, "the only justice is in the halls." This useful maxim, which Jack Bass takes as his own, urges us to be on the lookout for history made in mundane places—kitchens and fitting rooms, ballfields and garages, courthouse steps and hunting lodges.

The process of composing the exhibition narrative for *A Portion of the People* was unorthodox and exhilarating. Voices from the past were joined with voices from the present. The curators culled passages from memoirs, journals, and letters and evidence from such eloquent records as mortgages and marriage contracts. They distilled recollections from hundreds of oral histories recorded in seven years of collecting. Some people wrote pieces on demand to describe the history and provenance of objects they were lending to the exhibition. The descendants of families who are stewards of these heirlooms generally were pleased to contribute and grateful for the opportunity to inscribe their parents' and grandparents' names in this big book.

As curator, Dale Rosengarten took on the task of eliciting narratives from the lenders and reading them in light of other documentary evidence. Then she had to take the whole *megillah*—Hebrew for scroll, or any complicated affair—and turn it into a series of chronicles, each connected to what comes before and after. Her research associates, Barbara Karesh Stender and Judith Weil Shanks, discovered and recovered a wealth of objects and paintings. They also provided a southern point of view to balance Dale's natural tendencies as a "come-here" from the North. Stender was born and raised in Charleston. Her father's side of the family has lived in South Carolina since the 1850s, while her mother, a Bamberger from the town of Lichtenfels, Germany, escaped the Nazis in the nick of time. Shanks grew up in Alabama. She is a descendant of Rebecca and Isaiah Moses, who founded one of Charleston's "first families."

Though she knew it would make some people uncomfortable, Dale did not shy from portraying the Jews' full participation in the South's moral and material economies. In both the exhibition and her essay for this volume, she has carved out a radical middle ground between the extremes of condemning and glorifying. "A Call for Candlesticks" is chiefly about the joys and tribulations of collecting, about the cathartic and sometimes hilarious encounters with people she met in every nook and cranny of the state while hunting for objects and stories. With Barbara and Judith supplying leads, the search took Dale "abroad" to Georgia, Mississippi, Texas, Oregon, New York, Massachusetts, and other places the descendants of Jews who had lived in South Carolina went on to call home. She discovered how gratifying it can be to locate glamorous objects such as two-hundred-year-old miniature portraits painted on ivory—and how frustrating not to find a single peddler's pack. Telling the full story despite a dearth of objects from the lower end of the social spectrum is at the heart of the curatorial challenge.

Inevitably, there was an inner dimension to Dale's outer journey. The work of collecting makes a person self-conscious. You go around asking people to lend things they don't want to lend. Many potential lenders are not Jewish—the off-spring of people who were, but who married out of the religion. The Jewish past means something different to them than it does to people who continue to pro-fess Judaism. Dale, who was raised in the idealism of the 1960s, when we dreamed of making the world bend to our principles, has channeled her desire for change into the task of making the cultural wealth of South Carolina's Jewish minority available to every portion of the people. ❧

Freedom's Fruits

Deborah Dash Moore

The Americanization of an Old-time Religion

At the start of the nineteenth century Charleston sparkled with promise. A booming port city, it earned its sobriquet "Capital of the South." Wharves bustled, workshops thrived, construction boomed, and stores flourished along King Street, which retained its name despite the city's firm embrace of republicanism. Prosperity encouraged diverse cultural activities. Newspapers attested to a vigorous intellectual and political life; concerts and theatre attracted large and lively audiences. Drawn by opportunities for work and wealth, immigrants migrated to Charleston and settled down to build new lives. Most quickly adjusted to the South's "peculiar institution" and sanctioned racial slavery as a way of life.

FIGURE 1. *View of Charleston harbor, 1836. Courtesy of the South Caroliniana Library, University of South Carolina.*

Jews, too, formed an integral part of the cosmopolitan city. They came fleeing slave revolts in nearby Caribbean islands or from Europe, the majority from England and the German states, some whose families had been expelled from Iberia centuries before. They discovered a modest but confident community of coreligionists, with roots going back to the colonial era. A native-born generation was growing up in the city—American Jews who spoke English, cherished their political rights, and aspired to make a contribution to society.

By 1830, some 83 percent of the city's Jews owned slaves, just less than the 87 percent of all whites who were slave owners. Jews participated in buying and selling chattel slaves and articulated no critique of slavery, based either on Jewish experience or theology. The state's 1790 constitution guaranteed the free exercise of religion, and Jews participated in elections, even running for office. Their slaveholding as much as their officeholding signified Jews' assimilation into Charleston society and culture. In 1812 when Governor Henry Middleton proclaimed a day of Thanksgiving to be observed by the state's churches, Charleston's congregation Kahal Kadosh Beth Elohim objected to his exclusion of Jews. The governor's admission of his oversight reinforced Jewish understanding of their religious rights and the meaning of toleration. It also emboldened Jews to think of themselves as secure citizens.

In 1820 Charleston's Jewish community still exceeded New York's in size, political integration, and diversity. With an estimated population of over six hundred, Jews formed close to 5 percent of the white population, itself a minority in this southern city. Although they lived scattered in various parts of Charleston, many Jews located their businesses and homes on King Street, the emotional if not geographical center of the city for Jews. As a self-conscious religious and ethnic minority accustomed to assuming responsibility for its collective life, Jews usually gravitated toward one another. However, the wide dispersal of residences of Charleston Jews points to a remarkable degree of acclimation to southern white traditions.

Their numbers and increasing prosperity prompted Jews to build institutions. In 1749 they founded the city's first congregation, Kahal Kadosh Beth Elohim. Charleston Jews acquired several burial grounds, started a Hebrew Benevolent Society (1784), and pioneered in establishing in 1801 the first Hebrew Orphan Society in the United States. The latter innovation illustrates how quickly Charleston Jews learned from their Christian neighbors. Jews and Christians met socially as members of the Masons and in the handful of literary groups that bridged the city's class lines. Jews nonetheless also maintained their religious differences, constructing both a *mikveh* (ritual bath) and a communal oven to bake matzah for Passover. The two-story synagogue on Hasell Street contained a women's gallery as well as a central *bimah* (platform) and followed Sephardic religious traditions of worship.

Charleston's prosperity and promise did not last. Signs of economic and demographic change followed the depression of 1819. Dependent on the cash crops of the agricultural hinterland, Charleston's commerce shriveled as prices for rice and cotton, mainstays of its economy, plummeted. Competition from other southern port cities eroded Charleston's trading preeminence. In 1824 the *City Gazette* noted in despair, "Where scenes of industry, activity and growing prosperity were of late so apparent; where once reigned wealth and happiness, nothing now is to be found, but indolence, apathy, poverty and misery."[1] Isaac Harby, one of Charleston's Jewish intellectuals and an editor of the paper, was likely the author of the anonymous article. His perception of crisis was widely shared. Grass was growing in the streets and houses stood tenantless, complained the city fathers. The 1820 census registered a decline in the city's white inhabitants to less than 42 percent of the total, while the numbers of African Americans, both slave and free, rose. The popularity of manumission contributed to the growing population of Charleston's free blacks. Fearful of the independence of its African Americans, the city forcibly closed down the three-thousand member African Methodist Episcopal church.

CATALOGUE 65.

Kahal Kadosh Beth Elohim exterior, by John Rubens Smith (1775–1849), 1812. Facsimile courtesy of Stephen and Julie Ziff. Original in collection of the Library of Congress.

The 1820 congressional debate on Missouri over the admissibility of extend-
ing slavery into western territories initiated what would become a bitter controversy among proponents and opponents of human slavery. Following the debates,
Charlestonians, both black and white, concluded that the federal government
would not act to abolish slavery. Two years later a massive slave conspiracy reputed
to be led by Denmark Vesey, a free black, rattled Charlestonians' sense of security.
"Like a sharp knife, its memory cut into the conscience of Dixie's town dwellers,"
wrote historian Richard Wade. "More than Nat Turner's rebellion, more than any
rumor of a country uprising, it embodied the fullest range of terror, raised the
most awesome possibilities, and disturbed even the most complacent residents."[2]
For weeks in July, the gallows on "the Line" between the city and the Neck (the
upper peninsula) held swaying black bodies, executed as conspirators. As editor
of the *City Gazette*, Harby approved heartily of the hangings and described the
plot as "a scheme of wildness and of wickedness, enough to make us . . . shudder."[3]
Frightened Charlestonians turned away from the cosmopolitan ideal they had
cultivated only a decade earlier. The Vesey affair generated a sense of crisis com-
pounded by the city's economic decline that was not experienced elsewhere in
the South.

By 1824 young, native-born Jews responded to the city's new parochialism
by seeking to put their own house in order. Uncertain times demanded a greater
degree of external conformity. A dozen men who were energetic supporters of
Jewish philanthropy (especially the Hebrew Orphan Society) and active in Charleston's political and cultural life met to petition the city's only Jewish congregation
for change. Seeing the same "apathy and neglect" manifested toward their "holy
religion" as the town fathers saw in the city itself, these "inheritors of the *true
faith*" sought to solve the riddle of their own lack of interest in the synagogue.[4]
The problem, they concluded, lay not in themselves but in the congregation's
worship services.

The petitioners proposed a "more rational means of worshipping the true
God" as a solution for themselves and their children. This meant in practical
terms that services should include English as well as Hebrew, so that worshipers
could understand the prayers. A sermon on the weekly Torah portion would similarly serve to advance a native-born generation's comprehension. Eliminating the
practice of auctioning the honor of being called to the Torah during the reading
of the weekly portion would make services both shorter and more decorous. Such
services, the petitioners averred, would elicit respect from their white Christian
neighbors.[5]

The petition specifically mentioned Roman Catholic, Lutheran, and French
Protestant churches, all minority faiths in a city with an Episcopalian elite and
growing numbers of Baptists and Methodists. Aware of the inroads of evangelism,
including missions to convert the Jews, the dissidents appealed for "outreach" to
Jews and gentiles alike. Mostly, undoubtedly, they had in mind themselves, since
few were members of the congregation and three had married Christian women,
though all identified as Jews. "We wish not to *overthrow*, but to *rebuild*;" they

explained, "we wish not to *destroy*, but to *reform* . . . we wish not to *abandon* the institutions of Moses, but to *understand and observe them.*" Then, in a concluding stab, the men wrote that they wished "to worship God, not as *slaves of bigotry and priestcraft*, but as the enlightened descendants of that chosen race."[6] The metaphor of slavery surely raised hackles among the congregation's leadership, which did not identify with their black slaves and would have resented a comparison of traditional Jewish religious worship with slavery.

Not unexpectedly, the leaders rejected the petition. Older than the petitioners, well established, with high status based on their wealth and respectability, they were not inclined to entertain suggestions for upsetting the status quo from men young enough to be their sons. In fact, several of them were their sons. The petition highlighted differences between the generations. On one side were immigrants, average age of fifty-six, speaking several languages, married, with children and grandchildren. On the other side were native-born, average age of thirty-three, speaking English as their mother tongue, mostly married, with young children. Civic-minded and philanthropic despite their more modest means, the reformers preferred to participate in Hebrew Orphan Society events than in synagogue observances. Several held jobs rather than owned businesses, and their prospects for improvement had dimmed with Charleston's tarnished future. Yet these younger men, especially their leaders, were also well integrated into the city's intellectual and cultural life. They included Abraham Moïse, who practiced law; Isaac Harby, who ran a school and wrote essays and plays; Jacob Cardozo, who edited the *Southern Patriot*; and Samuel Hart, who owned one of the city's two bookstores.

Two of the most important figures behind the petition and the subsequent establishment of the Reformed Society of Israelites, Moïse and Harby, shared similar backgrounds. Both were born in South Carolina to immigrant parents who had built successful businesses in Charleston. Both received American educations and grew up during the city's cosmopolitan expansion at a time when Charleston was the fifth largest city in North America. Both lost their fathers as children, thus experiencing downward mobility and the need to find their own path to economic security. Both had talented and educated sisters who did not marry and devoted themselves instead to enriching Jewish religious life. Penina Moïse achieved renown as a poet and Caroline de Litchfield Harby did not, but both supported and encouraged their brothers in their endeavors. The cooperation and friendship of Abraham Moïse and Isaac Harby in the early years of the Reformed Society animated and shaped its mission.

Beth Elohim's rejection of their petition galvanized the younger generation to organize the Reformed Society of Israelites. Initially modeled on similar societies formed by Baptists and Methodists, the Jewish society began holding monthly meetings in January 1825, consisting of a blend of cultural and social activities. Its constitution, adopted the following month, allowed any male Jew aged seventeen or older to join, thus eliminating KKBE's restrictions against those who married gentiles. The society attracted a membership of approximately fifty men, who, together with their families probably numbered two hundred—a significant

FIGURE 2. *Silhouette of Isaac Harby. From Charles Reznikoff and Uriah Z. Engleman,* The Jews of Charleston: A History of an American Community, *page 89.*

minority of the city's Jews. By the end of the year the society had incorporated, with Aaron Phillips elected president and Michael Lazarus vice president. Although Harby, one of the most enthusiastic proponents of change, counseled moderation, the society had headed down the path of becoming another congregation.

The desire to transform theory into practice was hard to resist. The Reformed Society started to hold services with a choir, hymns, and instrumental music. Led by Moïse, Harby, and David Carvalho, the society met at Seyle's Masonic Hall on Meeting Street. At their Sabbath services members prayed in English as well as Hebrew, read the Torah portion in both languages, and listened to a sermon in English. The shortened service emphasized decorum and education. Women also appear to have participated by joining the singing in the choir. Caroline Harby contributed to the society's experiment, writing hymns for the Sabbath.

The society's constitution required that each year, on November 21, an anniversary dinner would be organized. No business would be conducted except for the election of officers and the presentation of an oration. Isaac Harby delivered the first anniversary oration, which he subsequently published and mailed to dignitaries across the United States, including former president Thomas Jefferson. It was time, Harby announced, to throw away "Rabbinical interpolations" and return to the Bible as "true legitimate authority." Jews needed to adapt to the "circumstances of the times," he claimed, as well as "the country in which we enjoy our liberties." Harby enthused over America, the "land of promise spoken of in our ancient Scriptures." He advised Jews "if they are wise" to immigrate to this nation where their countrymen were "brethren of the same happy family worshipping the same God."[7]

The following year Abraham Moïse gave the anniversary address. He added a touch of pragmatism to Harby's ideological rhetoric. Moïse described the ritual changes introduced by the society. "We claim, then, to be the advocates of a system of rational religion; of substance, not form," he explained.[8] What mattered was not the antiquity of Jewish rites, but rather their "general utility, their peculiar applicability to the age and country in which we live, to the feelings, sentiments and opinions of Americans."[9] Such individualism and reverence for American norms distinguished reform in Charleston from similar efforts elsewhere.

Social pragmatism and the increasing involvement of women in religion, especially evangelical Protestantism, may also have influenced several innovations in the society's prayer book. The marriage ceremony, for example, gives the normally silent Jewish bride a speaking part. "I accept this ring in token of the bond of marriage," she is allowed to say, moving toward a measure of equality with the bridegroom.[10] David Carvalho's manuscript prayer book includes three additional prayers missing from the other reformed prayer books that undoubtedly reflect his position as a young father: a declaration of Israelite faith, a prayer at circumcision, and, most significantly, a naming ceremony for a daughter. More knowledgeable in Hebrew than other members, Carvalho wanted to give the same recognition to daughters as to sons. The ceremony of naming a daughter at six weeks of age invites the mother or godmother to hold the child. The prayer invokes "O kind Parent of creation!" who makes "the human race the object of thy peculiar care."[11] The same blessings are showered on a daughter as on a son in the circumcision ceremony. Harby's prayer book also contains supplications, such as prayers for the sick, confession for the dying, and a burial prayer for women that begins with the quotation from Proverbs: "Who can find a virtuous woman? for her price is far above rubies."[12] Carvalho's own travails, including the untimely death of his wife, are reflected in a new language of faith. In choosing to include a prayer for the Sabbath written by Caroline Harby, the society took the first steps toward incorporating women's voices into Sabbath worship.

In 1828 Moïse ascended to the presidency of the society, a position he held until its demise roughly a decade later. Under his leadership, the society published its prayer book in 1830. An eminent historian of Reform Judaism, Michael Meyer, calls its handwritten predecessor "the first radical liturgy produced in the Reform movement anywhere," almost twenty years ahead of the 1845 prayer book compiled by the Berlin Reform Congregation.[13] The society's prayer book included such innovations as an individual confirmation ritual that involved the recitation of the society's revised version of Maimonides's articles of faith. This creed reduced thirteen statements of faith to ten—perhaps on the model of the Ten Commandments or the Bill of Rights. The reformers eliminated affirmation of a personal messiah and belief in resurrection of the dead and substituted a rejection of the Christian

CATALOGUE 28

Prayer book manuscript, Isaac Harby, Charleston, S.C., 1825. Temple Sinai Archives.

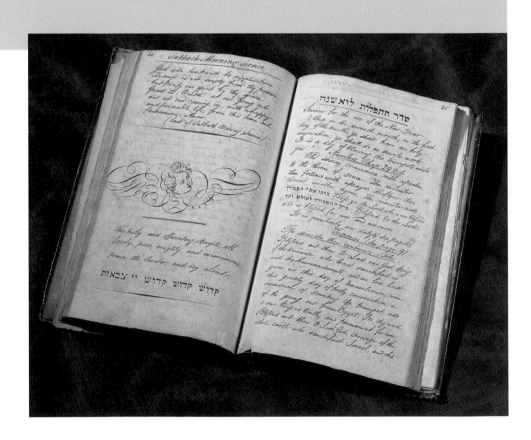

messiah and belief in immortality of the soul. Although modern and American, their theology expressed hostility to Christianity.

The enthusiasm that sustained the society for its first years waned as members left the city, died, or dropped out. Beth Elohim's leaders maintained a steady barrage of criticism. Some young men who might have been tempted to join the society refrained out of respect for their parents. By 1833 the reformers decided to return funds, with interest, to those who had contributed to help build a synagogue. Eventually even Moïse admitted defeat. Unable to change Judaism through an independent society, he rejoined Beth Elohim and discovered the possibilities of reform from within. By helping to write a new constitution for the congregation in 1836, Moïse introduced some of the changes advocated by the reformers. The larger vision disappeared, however, especially the radical liturgy with its intimations of women's equality and its creative personal prayers written by laymen. Instead, authority for innovation passed to established religious leaders who pressed their own theological and aesthetic program.

Most significantly, Beth Elohim decided that their hazzan (religious leader or cantor) should know both Hebrew and English and give a regular "discourse" on the Sabbath. The man chosen to fulfill these new responsibilities was Gustavus Poznanski, an observant Polish Jewish immigrant who was educated in Germany and had worked as a shohet (ritual slaughterer) in New York City.

A fire that destroyed the old synagogue in 1838 created an opening for change. In the process of rebuilding, thirty-eight members petitioned for an organ. Poznanski supported them. A talented musician, he welcomed the opportunity to enrich the worship service with music. Although opposed by the leadership, a narrow majority of the congregation favored the proposal. A minority reacted to their defeat by withdrawing to form a separate, traditional congregation. The new synagogue building with its organ facilitated further changes. Penina Moïse contributed a hymn to the dedication of the synagogue. "Hear, O Supreme! our humble invocation; / Our country, kindred and the stranger bless! / Bless, too, this sanctuary's consecration, / Its hallowed purpose on our hearts impress."[14] It would not be her only contribution. She subsequently wrote sixty of the seventy-four songs for Beth Elohim's hymnal, published in 1842. Later, as Reform became a movement in American Judaism, other congregations adopted some of her hymns, and the editors of the hymnal of the Union of American Hebrew Congregations included over a dozen of them. Several were set to music.

Women's voices would find a place within the synagogue. Penina Moïse's poetry would give expression to the congregation's sacred sentiments during worship. Here is a hymn to brotherly love:

> How beautiful it is to see,
> Brethren unite harmoniously!
> Of kindred sympathies possest,
> By the same joys and woes impress.
> But ah! how every slight a cause,

FIGURE 3. *Penina Moïse, ca. 1830. Courtesy of Anita Moïse Rosefield Rosenberg.*

Hymnal belonging to B. D. Lazarus, Charleston, S.C., 1842. Kahal Kadosh Beth Elohim.

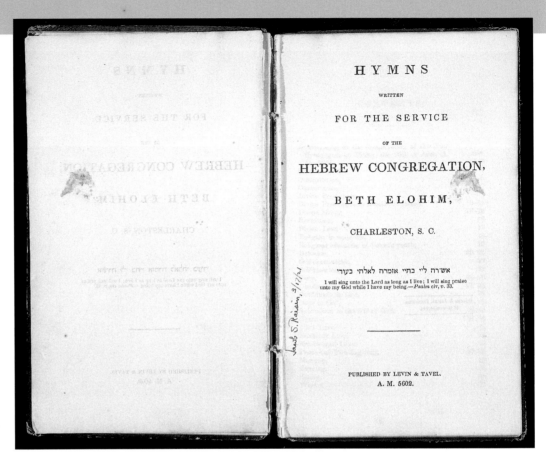

BELOW: FIGURE 4. *Kahal Kadosh Beth Elohim choir book, 1866. Courtesy of Kahal Kadosh Beth Elohim. The melodies used were mostly from the hymnal of the Hamburg Temple or those composed by two of Beth Elohim's organists before 1860, D. A. DaCosta and H. W. Greatorex.*

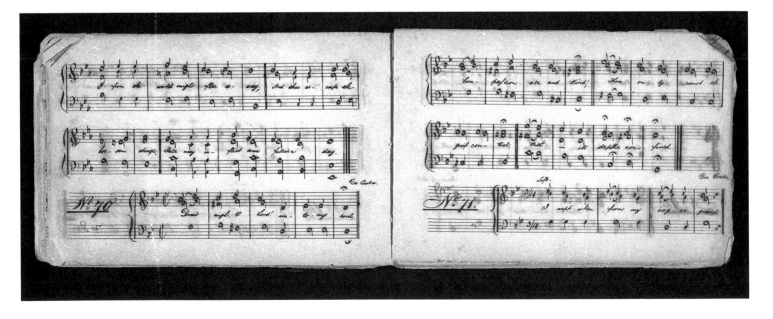

*Will counteract kind nature's laws,
And to that dread estrangement lead,
Against which God and angels plead!"*[15]

Moïse was perhaps the first woman in the annals of American Judaism to contribute to synagogue ritual. As a writer who published in the nation's leading magazines, she accepted a common American understanding that women were more spiritual than men. In a world segregated by gender, religion fell within the sphere of women's legitimate activities. Judaism had relegated women to the margins of public worship. Now, with reform, women began to carve a space for themselves within the synagogue. In 1838 Sally Lopez requested permission to start a Sunday school for boys and girls at Beth Elohim. She followed in the footsteps of Rebecca Gratz in Philadelphia, who shared lessons with her. When Lopez joined the traditionalists who withdrew, Penina Moïse took over leadership of this school—the second Sunday school established in the United States—and guided it for several decades. The establishment of Jewish Sunday schools represented one attempt to counter Protestant missions to convert the Jews.

At the dedication ceremony of the new synagogue building Poznanski celebrated the glories of America. Echoing Harby's anniversary oration he proclaimed: "This synagogue is our *temple*, this city our *Jerusalem*, this happy land our *Palestine*, and as our fathers defended with their lives *that* temple, *that* city and *that* land, so will their sons defend *this* temple, *this* city, and *this* land."[16] Poznanski heralded the arrival of the sons, and, though neglecting to mention it, their sisters. The future belonged to them. The rebellion of reform initiated fifteen years earlier was now reaching its maturity.

The struggle for change did not cease. Proposals for additional innovations triggered more dissent. For three years reformers and traditionalists divided the new synagogue while they argued their case in the South Carolina courts. Finally the courts awarded the synagogue to the reformers. Defeated, the traditionalists built a home for their congregation, Shearit Israel. Thus, Charleston Jews were the first to split on denominational lines. Other cities had more than one congregation, but the additional congregations represented ethnic differences, not ideological ones.

Despite their religious differences, Charleston Jews were unanimous in protesting religious intolerance. In 1844 representatives of both congregations met at the Hebrew Orphan Society building on Broad Street to respond to Governor James Hammond's Thanksgiving Day proclamation. Unlike many such proclamations, Hammond invited "our Citizens of all denominations" to assemble to "offer up their devotions to God the Creator, and his Son Jesus Christ, the redeemer of the world."[17] Undoubtedly, Charleston Jews expected a replay of their earlier, ultimately gratifying, experience with Governor Middleton. Their forceful letter to Hammond demanded an apology. Describing themselves as "a God-serving and prayerful people," over one hundred signatories reminded the governor that the state's constitution guarantees to all "'without discrimination or preference' the free and full enjoyment of every right, civil and religious."[18] Hammond responded

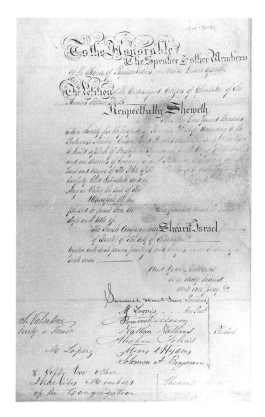

FIGURE 5. *Petition of Act of Incorporation for Shearit Israel, Charleston, S.C., 1840. Courtesy of the South Carolina Department of Archives and History.*

that he "always thought it was a settled matter that [he] lived in a Christian land!" Therefore he made a Christian proclamation, which of necessity united the "name of the Redeemer with that of the Creator."[19] This linkage stunned both traditionalists and reformers. Even as reformers modified Maimonides's belief in a personal messiah, they explicitly rejected Christian beliefs in the divinity of Jesus. Gaining no satisfaction from the governor, an ardent proponent of nullification and secession, Charleston's Jews wrote a response that they published in the newspapers. They trusted public opinion to exonerate them.

This Thanksgiving Day incident, so unlike the one in 1812 and a "notable exception" to a common American pattern, confirms how much the world of Charleston Jews had changed. Between 1812 and 1844 the cosmopolitan society Jews admired and participated in yielded to a narrow, self-defined Christian society, far less tolerant of religious difference or of any deviation from the views of the slaveholding elite. The movement for reform had occurred in response to early intimations of such change, and culminated in the 1840s as evangelicalism transformed the South. By then, wealth and power were concentrating among white planters who had migrated inland to more uniformly Protestant parts of the state dominated by the culture of short-staple cotton.

Within the Jewish world there were many reasons for reform: a generational struggle for authority, the influence of new ideas sweeping across Europe, the presence of a cadre of leaders marginalized by a weakened economy, tremors of political insecurity, perhaps even a desire among young Jews to include their sisters within the synagogue. But Jews lived as well among Christians. A sense of crisis among whites of all religions in Charleston spurred Jews to act there long before their peers elsewhere in the United States. By 1855 congregations with reformed ritual could be found in Baltimore, New York, Albany, and Cincinnati. Beth Elohim and Charleston Jews were no longer alone in their innovations. ❧

Notes

1. Quoted in Richard C. Wade, *Slavery in the Cities* (New York: Oxford University Press, 1964), 11.
2. Ibid., 228.
3. Quoted in Gary Phillip Zola, *Isaac Harby of Charleston 1788–1828* (Tuscaloosa: University of Alabama Press, 1994), 96.
4. Quoted in James W. Hagy, *This Happy Land* (Tuscaloosa: University of Alabama Press, 1992), 129.
5. There is a rich literature on the early reform movement in Charleston. I have relied on the following excellent sources: Hagy, *This Happy Land*; Zola, *Isaac Harby of Charleston*; Michael A. Meyer, *Response to Modernity* (New York: Oxford University Press, 1988); Barnett A. Elzas, *The Reformed Society of Israelites of Charleston, S.C.* (New York: Bloch Publishing Company, 1916); Robert Liberles, "Conflict over Reforms: The Case of Congregation Beth Elohim, Charleston, South Carolina," in *The American Synagogue*, ed. Jack Wertheimer (New York: Cambridge University Press, 1987), 274–96; Leon A. Jick, *The Americanization of the Synagogue, 1820–1870* (Hanover, N.H.: University Press of New England, 1976); Allan Tarshish, "The Charleston Organ Case," *The Jewish Experience in*

America, ed. Abraham J. Karp (New York: KTAV Publishing House, 1969), 281–315;
Gene Waddell, "An Architectural History of Kahal Kadosh Beth Elohim, Charleston,"
South Carolina Historical Magazine 98:1 (January 1997), 6–55.

6. Hagy, *This Happy Land*, 131.

7. Ibid., 146–47.

8. Ibid., 152–53.

9. Quoted in Meyer, *Response to Modernity*, 231.

10. [David Carvalho], *The Sabbath Service and Miscellaneous Prayers Adopted by the Reformed
Society of Israelites*, reprinted by Barnett A. Elzas (New York: Bloch Publishing Company,
1916), 47.

11. Ibid., 38.

12. Ibid., 42.

13. Meyer, *Response to Modernity*, 231.

14. Penina Moïse, *Poems of Penina Moïse* (Charleston, S.C.: Nicholas G. Duffy, 1911), 2.

15. Ibid., 89.

16. Quoted in Meyer, *Response to Modernity*, 234.

17. Morris U. Schappes, ed., *A Documentary History of the Jews in the United States,
1654–1875* (New York: Schocken Books, 1971), 236–37.

18. Ibid., 238–39.

19. Ibid., 240.

Land of Promise

Jenna Weissman Joselit

The Eastern European Jewish Experience in South Carolina

On a balmy spring evening in 1907, August Kohn took to the pulpit of Kahal Kadosh Beth Elohim, the congregation founded more than a century and a half earlier by Charleston's Sephardic Jews, to champion the cause of immigration. At a time when hundreds of thousands of eastern European Jews are calling New York, Boston, and Philadelphia their new home, we in the South would do well to encourage them to put down roots here as well, Kohn told his audience. Their coming would be good for the nation, good for South Carolina, and good for the Jews, too. It would lessen urban congestion and reduce social tension up north while increasing the white population of, and strengthening the Jewish presence in, the South. "The South needs more people, it needs people to develop its wastelands, to build up its industries, and to put new life into the body politic."[1] Why not invite Jewish immigrants to be among those "people"?

For all his apparent enthusiasm for eastern European Jews, Kohn had a distinct kind of immigrant in mind. Not any immigrant would do, only those of an "agricultural type," with an aptitude or inclination for farming. By Kohn's lights, the would-be Jewish farmer rather than the small shopkeeper was best suited to life in the "Southland." Working the land instead of manning a counter, he would not only live among other farmers in the rural heartland of the region, he would also develop an attachment to the soil and, in time, an affinity for the southern way of life. In the process, the Jewish immigrant farmer would boost South Carolina's sluggish economy. South Carolina's farms had not yet turned much of a profit, Kohn conceded. But that had little to do with the land per se and everything to do with those who tilled it. "Remember," he cautioned his listeners, "half of all the farmers are negroes, who are not as persistent and effective in their efforts as others." Hard-working Jewish farmers would succeed where others had failed. A boon to South Carolina, they would also be a boon to American Jewry as a whole, Kohn ringingly concluded. By making a success of themselves, Jewish farmers would "do much to get rid of the twaddle that the Jews as a people are not producers but that they are parasites and live off of others."

Kohn's enthusiasm for farming was of a piece with both American and European Jewry's longstanding belief in the regenerative power of agriculture.

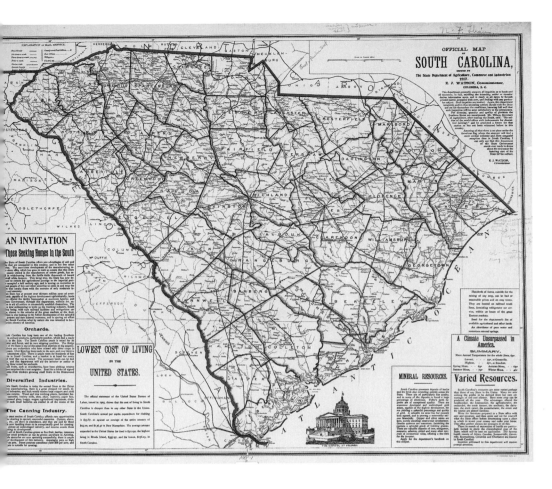

FIGURE 6. *"Official Map of South Carolina,
Issued by the South Carolina Department of
Agriculture, Commerce and Industries," 1912.
Courtesy of the South Caroliniana Library,
University of South Carolina.*

Ever since the protracted battles over the emancipation of the Jews in the late
eighteenth and early nineteenth centuries, tilling the land had come to be seen as
a way to normalize the Jew's traditional economic profile and ease his integration
into European society. Later still, as increasing numbers of eastern European immigrants arrived in the United States, concerned American Jewish leaders also began
to sing the praises of the agricultural life, hoping to accelerate the immigrants'
adaptation to America. What set Kohn apart from his predecessors was his belief
that the South provided an especially welcoming environment. "I, personally, cannot see why the Jewish people cannot come to South Carolina and make a success of their lives" much as previous generations of Jews had done, he declared.
South Carolina, after all, was the "land of promise for the Jewish immigrant," a
place where the "patriotism, valor and conspicuous deeds of our people" were
widely manifest and celebrated.

In the years that followed Kohn's impassioned call for immigrants, several
thousand eastern European Jews established themselves in South Carolina, dou-
bling the state's Jewish population from 2,500 in 1907 to 5,060 by 1920.[2] Some
newcomers took up farming. Inspired perhaps by Kohn's high-minded rhetoric or

the promise of the State Department of Agriculture, Commerce and Immigration that settlers would find in South Carolina a "good and peaceful home," "pleasant" weather, and "help . . . with all problems," they tried their hand at growing fruits and vegetables.[3] Their ranks included twenty-five Russian Jewish families who banded together to form a cooperative agricultural colony on 2,200 acres of land a few miles outside of Aiken. Aptly enough, they called the settlement Happyville, echoing the well-known statement made by the Charleston rabbi Gustav Poznanski in 1841, describing America as "this happy land."

Despite the optimism of its residents, Happyville lasted only two brief years. A series of mishaps, from unusually cold weather to financial miscalculations, cut short the experiment, sending some of the colonists to New York and New Jersey and dispersing others throughout the South.[4] And yet, like so much else associated with modern Jewish history, Happyville endured in memory. Mina Tropp, a longtime resident of Aiken, vividly remembered the visits made to her home by some of Happyville's inhabitants. "I was very little at the time. . . . [But] I recall some of the ladies and men came often to our home. The ladies seemed very dressed up. My mind's eye retains a wide long opalescent green taffeta skirt and very high heels . . . on a very pretty lady. I recall nudging Mama to ask if they could farm or plow, that is, so dressed up. . . . Mama said this dressing up was only for visiting."[5]

Other eastern European settlers, like immigrants everywhere, came down south on the basis of a kindly word or an optimistic turn of phrase they happened upon in a letter from a relative or a landsman (countryman). George Chaplin explained that his father, a native of Bialystok, was "enticed to Columbia" by Max Citron, a fellow Bialystoker. "Max said: 'You can make a living here.'"[6] Still others owed their

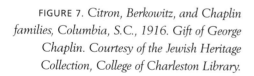

FIGURE 7. *Citron, Berkowitz, and Chaplin families, Columbia, S.C., 1916. Gift of George Chaplin. Courtesy of the Jewish Heritage Collection, College of Charleston Library.*

arrival in the South to happenstance and serendipity, at least if we are to believe the immigrant tales that, like precious keepsakes, descend from one generation to another. "The story is that Sam went to New York's Pennsylvania Station and he said he had so much money, where would it take him, and the fellow said, 'Charleston, South Carolina,' and that's how he ended up here," recalled Dorothy Gelson Cohen and Morris David Rosen of their grandfather Sam Rosen.[7]

Settling in cities such as Charleston and Columbia or in the small towns that peppered the Palmetto State—Beaufort, Latta, and Spartanburg, among them—eastern European Jews swelled South Carolina's Jewish population and altered its rhythms and sensibilities, even its sounds. Renowned among American Jews for their gentility and affability, their courtliness and decorous form of Judaism, South Carolina's Jews had long since assimilated the South's "Anglo-American" ethos.[8] Rabbi Isaac Mayer Wise, visiting Charleston in 1850 from his home in Albany, New York, was smitten by the Jews he met. "Influential merchants, bankers, lawyers, physicians, authors, politicians, political officials, most of them rich, and descended from the old Portuguese families," Charleston Jews, he wrote, were not only "people of culture and refinement." They were "American aristocrats."[9]

The new arrivals were a far cry from aristocrats, at least at first. In the manner of their dress, their gestures, and their language—they spoke Yiddish rather than English—they stood apart from their well-heeled and long-established coreligionists. The various ways they earned a living, as peddlers, small shopkeepers, and, on occasion, as farmers, also set them apart. Filling an economic niche, Jewish peddlers crisscrossed the country, selling pots and pans, blankets and fabric. "My father became a peddler, walking, pack on his back, customers, mostly black, buying on the installment plan, paying thirty-five cents this week, thirty-five cents the next," recalled George Chaplin.[10] Helen Greher Kahn's father peddled from Charleston to Columbia. With his "little merchandise," he stopped at all "those little towns" in between.[11] Eventually, many peddlers set up shop in town. Aspiring entrepreneurs, they transformed Charleston's King Street, for example, into a mecca of "small little stores, clothing stores, furniture stores, notions and that kind of thing," including groceries, shoe stores, and second-hand shops.[12]

Much of the clientele serviced by these "little stores" was African American. At his family's dry-goods store, recalled Henry Yaschik, their "trade at the time would be 75% Blacks and about 25% blue-collar whites." On weekends especially, "Blacks from the nearby sea islands would come in small boats from the islands to the foot of Tradd Street at Adger's Wharf. They would come into town and do their shopping."[13] Both the sea islanders and city residents were drawn to Jewish shops on King Street for a number of reasons. For one thing, merchants like the Yaschiks, explained a local resident, "allowed a black person to try on hats or shoes, which the department stores did not." And, for another, they "extended credit more easily."[14] Sometimes, King Street merchants hired African American help as well. Take Solomon's dry-goods store, which sold merchandise to peddlers on consignment. The clerk with whom most peddlers conducted their business was an African American named Isaac. He "spoke Yiddish like you've never heard in

FIGURE 8. *Goldstein store, 559 King Street, Charleston, S.C., ca. 1927. Courtesy of Alwyn O. Goldstein.*

your life," recollected one Charlestonian. "I mean, you could not tell he wasn't European."[15]

With Yiddish as a common bond, Charleston's newest residents reproduced many of the physical and cultural features commonly associated with the classic immigrant experience of the North and the Midwest. Like their Yankee cousins, they lived among their own kind, in an area of town called "uptown." (In New York City, "uptown" was home to the wealthier members of the community while "downtown" was the site of the "great ghetto." In Charleston, things were reversed.) "Uptown Jews were the ones who came late," recalled a former resident.[16] Added another, "In Charleston, everybody Jewish lived on St. Philip Street," a thoroughfare suffused with the sounds of Yiddish and the aromas of traditional Jewish foods.[17]

Religion, as well as neighborhood, also kept the newcomers apart from the old-timers. While most downtown Jews affiliated with Kahal Kadosh Beth Elohim, its Reform orientation was foreign, and possibly forbidding, to the city's newest Jewish residents. Even the more traditional services at Congregation Brith Sholom, founded back in 1855 by an earlier generation of German and Polish immigrants, was not to everyone's liking. Accordingly, a number of East European Jewish immigrants established their own shul (synagogue)—Beth Israel—whose cadences and rituals kept faith with the Old World rather than the New. What is more, they formed their own network of charitable and recreational organizations: instead of the Masons, they had Anshe Kaluszyn, an organization of men who hailed from Kaluszyn, a small town outside of Warsaw; instead of the Council of Jewish Women, they had the Daughters of Israel, a charitable society that "did things for new and indigent Jewish families."[18]

FIGURE 9. *Brith Sholom Synagogue, St. Philip Street, Charleston, S.C., 1917. Courtesy of Brith Sholom Beth Israel.*

CATALOGUE 162.

Notice of the price of High Holy Day seats at Beth Israel Synagogue, Charleston, S.C., 1933. Collection of Ethel Oberman Katzen.

:-: **BETH ISRAEL CONGREGATION** :-:

145 St. Philip Street

Charleston, S. C., Aug. 28th, 1933

TAKE NOTICE--Passed by our Last Regular Meeting Seats must be paid for in advance.

Men's Seats	$2.00
Ladies' Seats	$1.00
Boys Seats 13 to 18	$1.00

Mr. J. Levin will call on you in the next few days

By order of the President.   I. Oberman, Secretary

The Seat Committee will be in the Synagogue the Last Week before the Holiday From 8:00 to 10:00 P. M.

With the exception of English-language classes run by the Council of Jewish Women, social exchange between uptown and downtown was rare and mutual understanding even rarer. "I'd never seen tallises before," recollected Norman Everett Baum of Camden, referring to the traditional prayer shawl. "We'd never been brought up with tallis. We were so very Reform. . . . Until I went to a cousin's wedding in New York, I'd never even seen a yarmulke."[19] Baum's experience was not unusual. "There were a couple of synagogues uptown where the Orthodox kids went but we really didn't pay them much attention," recalled Dr. Arthur V. Williams, a downtown Charleston resident, who came of age during the inter-war years. "Their families had only been in this country a generation and we were told, 'It takes three generations to make an American.' We were Americans first and Jews second."[20]

Ultimately, it wasn't chronology or even geography so much as history that set one group apart from the other. Put simply, newcomer and old-timer did not have a common history, a shared set of memories of an era when their homes and houses of worship were "prostrated by the ruthless hand of war," their sons killed or maimed and their values mocked and derided.[21] Through an accident of timing, eastern European Jews had escaped all that. From where they sat, the War between the States had little to do with them. To their neighbors, however, it explained everything. As a result of this divide, eastern European Jewish immigrants were placed at a considerable cultural disadvantage. True southernness, it seemed, was destined to elude them.

Eventually, however, distinctions between the old guard and the new faded away. By the time of Kahal Kadosh Beth Elohim's bicentennial in 1950, a week-long

CATALOGUE 163.

Invitation to a circumcision, Charleston, S.C., 1913. Collection of Ethel Oberman Katzen.

event that marked the two-hundredth anniversary of organized Judaism in Charleston—or, as celebrants put it, "two hundred years of growth and happiness" —once-watertight divisions among eastern European, German, and Sephardic Jews seemed to be an artifact of history.[22] The celebration, with its portrait show of Jewish worthies at the Gibbes Art Gallery, "bicentennial banquet," and joint Friday evening service at Kahal Kadosh Beth Elohim in which representatives of all of the city's synagogues participated, was hailed as a "community enterprise . . . a demonstration of goodwill and brotherhood."[23]

Charleston's *News and Courier* took things even further, implicitly contrasting the behavior of Charleston's Jews who were determined to blend in with that of their African American neighbors who, insistently, stood out. "At a time when 'race-consciousness' and 'discrimination' and all the other epithets are hurled by agitators with little understanding and no sympathy, here stands an example of good-will," declared the newspaper. The bicentennial, it continued effusively, carried a "message of tolerance, of good-feeling among men, of mutual respect among people with different backgrounds who have lived together in this city for two centuries in peace and amity and esteem." [24]

Perhaps it took another war—World War II this time—to bring the community together. Virtually everyone had a son or a brother or a cousin who had served in the armed forces. Affluence, no doubt, also had a great deal to do with promoting a collective sense of amity and esteem. The immigrants and their children had prospered in the South, rendering class distinctions increasingly irrelevant. "You could rise from one class to the other," related Henry Yaschik. "The Jews did not have a Saint Cecilia Society or a Society of the Cincinnati where you had to be born into it. In the Jewish society, once you became educated and . . . economically stable, you were automatically included into the upper strata of Jewish society. It was a meritocracy rather than an aristocracy."[25]

More to the point, perhaps, the sons and daughters of eastern European immigrants now laid claim to being southern. Their southernness may not have been as deeply rooted or as unequivocally genteel as that professed by those whose families had lived in South Carolina since the eighteenth century, but it was southern all the same. In a remarkable display of synthesis, eastern European Jews and their descendants developed a distinctive identity, simultaneously like and unlike that of Jews everywhere else. From their accented Yiddish or Hebrew, which they spoke with a southern lilt, and their foodways, which made room for grits as well as gefilte fish, to their abiding affection for the place they called home, the Jews of South Carolina effected an unusual blend of the Old World and the New, of Jewishness and southernness. They had become southern Jews.

In the end, things may not have turned out quite the way August Kohn had envisioned. Farming, after all, never did take hold among Jewish immigrants or their children, for that matter. But Kohn's belief in the South's capacity to do right by its Jewish citizens was generously rewarded. "The history of our Southern States ought to bear ample testimony to the fact that our people as a race have been well received, that they have been encouraged, that they have been given every possible privilege," he wrote in 1907.[26] While much has happened since then, this view of things remains an article of faith among South Carolina's Jews, heartening old-timers and newcomers alike. ℀

Notes

1. August Kohn, *Essay of Mr. August Kohn*, (Charleston, S.C.: n.p., 1907). Quotations are from pages 4, 5, 14, 10, 6, 5, 14, 3. Pamphlet reproduces the essay, titled "The Possibility of Jewish Immigration to the South," read by August Kohn before the annual meeting of the International Order of B'nai B'rith on April 14, 1907.

2. "Jewish Statistics—The United States—Table by States," *American Jewish Year Book* (1906–07), 128; "Jewish Population," *American Jewish Year Book* 27 (1925–26), 382.

3. South Carolina Department of Agriculture, Commerce and Immigration, "South Carolina: The Garden Country of America," (Columbia, S.C.: South Carolina, Department of Agriculture, Commerce and Immigration, [1905]).

4. See, for example, Arnold Shankman, "Happyville, the Forgotten Colony," *American Jewish Archives* 30 (April 1978), 3–19; "Happyville, South Carolina," in Louise Pettus and Ron Chepesiuk, *The Palmetto State: Stories from the Making of South Carolina* (Orangeburg, S.C.: Sandlapper Pub., 1991), 106–9; Carol Woodward, "Montmorenci Colony Enjoyed Two-Year Success," *Aiken (S.C.) Standard*, July 1989, 4–5.

5. Transcript of Mina Tropp Oral History Tape of March 1, 1979, by Arnold Shankman, p. 4, Winthrop University Archives.

6. Interview with George Chaplin, September 27, 1995, Jewish Heritage Collection, College of Charleston Library (hereafter JHC).

7. Interview with Dorothy Gelson Cohen, Mordecai Cohen, and Morris David Rosen, March 5, 1995, JHC.

8. Ludwig Lewisohn, *Up Stream: An American Chronicle* (New York: The Modern Library, 1926), 64.

9. Isaac Mayer Wise, *Reminiscences* [1901], translated and edited by David Phillipson (New York: Central Synagogue of New York, 1945), 143.

10. Interview with George Chaplin.

11. Interview with Helen Greher Kahn, March 5, 1997, JHC.

12. Interview with Solomon Breibart, April 18, 1995, JHC.

13. Henry Yaschik, *From Kaluszyn to Charleston: The Yaschik Family in Poland, Argentina and South Carolina* (Charleston, S.C.: privately published by the author, 1990), 52.

14. Interview with Breibart.

15. Interview with Nathan S. Addlestone, March 13, 1996, JHC.

16. Interview with Abel Banov, April 3–4, 1996, JHC.

17. Interview with Gordan B. Stine, February 19, 1996, JHC.

18. Interview with Karl Karesh, April 22, 1996, JHC.

19. Interview with Norman Everett Baum, May 22, 1995, JHC.

20. Arthur V. Williams, *Tales of Charleston, 1930* (Charleston, S.C.: College of Charleston Library, 1999), 7.

21. "Charleston," *Occident and American Jewish Advocate* 24 (September 1866), 266.

22. Jeanette Felsenthal Pearlstine, "An Editorial," *The Souvenir Book of the Bicentennial (1750–1950): The Story of the Celebration of the Bicentennial of the Charleston Jewish Community, November 19 through November 26, 1950* (Charleston, S.C.: Bicentennial Committee, 1951), 7.

23. Ibid. In the interest of good will, the bicentennial's organizers made sure to honor the religious scruples of all of the participants. As a result, neither the organ nor the choir was heard at the special Friday night service and the wearing of head coverings, in turn, was made optional.

24. "The Jews of Charleston," *Charleston News and Courier*, March 25, 1950, reproduced in *The Souvenir Book of the Bicentennial*, 65.

25. Yaschik, *From Kaluszyn to Charleston*, 46.

26. Kohn, "The Possibility of Jewish Immigration," 16.

Just Like One of Us

Jack Bass

A favorite story told in South Carolina about Jews and the Ku Klux Klan—the story is true—involves a small town Jewish merchant watching a local parade of white-robed, masked, and hooded Klansmen.

As they passed in front of this man's store, he would greet many of them by name. "Hey, Joe," he would yell. "Hey, Bobby." "Hey, Butch." His list grew much longer.

Later, one of the Klansmen asked the merchant how he knew who they were. "I sold you your shoes," he replied.

Growing up in the town of North, South Carolina, as the youngest of seven children of the town's only Jewish family, I had one boyhood memory of the Klan, in the summer and fall of 1950, a year of Klan revival.

Both my parents were immigrants, the only foreign-born people in North. My mother, Esther, came to the United States with her family from Poland when she was two, and my father, Nathan, immigrated alone at age sixteen from a village in Lithuania. The family name there was Bass, a surname the Museum of the Diaspora in Tel Aviv links to a Hebrew word meaning "scribe."

For four years at what then was the whites-only, 110-pupil, North High School, I was both class president and the lightest-weight starter on the football team. After football practice one day in the fall of 1950, I went with several friends to the drugstore soda fountain for milkshakes. A small stack of printed applications for membership in the Ku Klux Klan, listing "white male Christian" as a qualification, lay in front of the cash register. I picked one up and took it to my father, then in his mid-sixties.

After reading it, my father, who generally avoided controversy or confrontation, walked down the street to the drugstore. There he addressed the owner—a fellow Mason—by first name, and asked in a mock serious tone, "Can I join?" I listened to the mumbled response and proudly walked back with my father to his dry-goods store.

Klan motorcades soon drove through North on three successive Saturday nights, and I heard another of his Masonic brothers curse them. My father's customers were mostly poor white and black farmers, many of them landless tenants and sharecroppers dependent on the unpredictable price of cotton and its fall harvest.

When the several dozen cars of mostly out-of-town Klansmen slowly passed in front of Bass Mercantile Company that first Saturday, dozens of frightened black people huddled in the back of the store. A week later, they again sought shelter in my father's store, this time peering out the front door. The third Saturday, most of them remained on the street, standing in front of our store's windows and staring at the cars and their dimly lit occupants.

Intuitively the black community seemed to know that my father's store offered sanctuary.

~

When the eight Lords Proprietors got their land grant for Carolina, the English political philosopher John Locke inspired the original document for governance. Its provision for freedom of religion exceeded that found anywhere in seventeenth-century Europe. Jews arrived soon after the first permanent settlement was established in Charles Town in 1670 and found acceptance quickly.

The election a century later of Francis Salvador to the First Provincial Congress of South Carolina reflected their full participation in social and political life. Jewish historian Abram Vossen Goodman has called this governmental body the first in the modern world "where a Jew was elected to office by his Christian neighbors."[1]

A member of a prominent Jewish family in London that had lost its fortune, Salvador arrived in 1773 to seek prosperity on a large tract of land his uncle had sold to him in South Carolina's Ninety Six District. He developed an indigo plantation and quickly established himself with the backcountry aristocracy. Salvador served on a number of important committees for the First and Second Provincial Congresses and South Carolina's first General Assembly. On August 1, 1776, he

FIGURE 10. *Historical marker commemorating Revolutionary War patriot Francis Salvador, at Coronaca, northeast of Greenwood, S.C., 2000. Photograph by Bill Aron. Courtesy of the Jewish Heritage Collection, College of Charleston Library.*

died at age twenty-nine during an official mission aimed at consolidating back-country support. A force of Indians and Tories ambushed his unit at night. Salvador died after being shot and scalped. His death three weeks after the signing of the Declaration of Independence made him the first Jew to perish for the patriot cause.

A plaque in Charleston's Washington Park was dedicated in 1950 to Salvador's memory:

> *Born an aristocrat he became a democrat,*
> *An Englishman he cast his lot with America;*
> *True to his ancient faith he gave his life*
> *For new hopes of human liberty and understanding.*

Although the Jewish population in the state seldom has exceeded a fraction of one percent of the total, Salvador's service launched a tradition of significant Jewish participation in politics. From the beginning, South Carolina's political, social, and economic fabric was woven around issues of race. In fact, the charter that granted the colony's Jews and Christian dissenters such unusual freedoms called specifically for the establishment of racial slavery. Through their inclusion in political life, Jews have played a continuous role in brokering the state's social compact.

Historians James Hagy and Charles Joyner have documented Jewish acceptance by white elites in Charleston and Georgetown, the state's two earliest communities.[2] Jews called Carolina a "happy land." As late as 1820, Charleston's Jewish population exceeded that of any city in America. Columbia, the state capital, twice elected Jewish intendants, or mayors, before the Civil War.

By 1800, Georgetown's white population of roughly eight hundred included eighty Jews, twice the proportion of Charleston. At least five different Jewish men served as intendant, several for multiple terms, in nineteenth-century Georgetown. Others held a variety of offices, including seats in the legislature. They helped found the Library Society and served as members and officers of the Winyah Indigo Society. The Planters Club, a later and even more prestigious social organization, included a Jewish charter member along with the wealthiest rice planters of the region.

Most Jewish families in Georgetown lived in the town itself and owned a single slave family each, who served primarily as house servants. In this community where a typical large rice planter might own several hundred slaves, apparently only one Jewish slaveowner owned as many as twenty. The Jews engaged primarily in trade and commerce. In addition to dealing in other commodities, several bought and sold slaves.

Jewish individuals in Georgetown contributed local leadership to both sides in the nullification crisis of the 1820s and early 1830s—the debate over whether a state could nullify a federal law. After the Nat Turner insurrection in Virginia in 1832, which had the widespread effect of stamping out political nonconformity in the South, Georgetown's Jews either supported slavery or kept quiet. Five of them died fighting for the Confederacy. Abraham C. Myers, a Georgetown native who grew up in Florida, became quartermaster general of the Confederate army.

This record of Confederate service reflects South Carolina and southern Jewry as a whole. A few Jews went north during the Civil War, including a grandfather of my brother-in-law, Isaac Jacobs of Charleston, who went to Cincinnati and then returned after the war.

South Carolina's antebellum Jewish slaveowners apparently saw no contradiction in celebrating Passover, with its annual seder remembrance of their own history of deliverance from slavery in Egypt. Their Hebrew Bible provided in the Book of Leviticus detailed instructions for the humane treatment of slaves.

A descendant of one of those Georgetown slaves remembered more than four decades later in Oklahoma the Jewish owners (the Sampson family) of her mother. "Dey was mighty sweet to her," eighty-five-year-old Hannah McFarland recalled in the late 1930s to an Oklahoma Writer's Project interviewer. She was there the day the Yankees "captured Mamma's white people's house," she said. "Dey tried to git Mamma to tell dem just what de white folks done to her and all she could say wuz dey was good to her."[3]

Being Jewish, however, did not necessarily mean being benign to slaves. For example, Abraham Mendes Seixas served several years as superintendent of the Charleston workhouse, a facility administered by the city, where plantation owners or overseers sent disobedient slaves to be whipped.

In Georgetown, the Jewish community's political role remained prominent after the Civil War. Before the nineteenth century ended, Sol Emanuel was elected twice as intendant and Louis S. Ehrich three times.

Early in the twentieth century, the financier Bernard Baruch, a relative of several of Georgetown's leading Jewish families, returned to South Carolina from New York and purchased the abandoned rice plantations that made up the original land grant of Hobcaw Barony. Baruch's father, Simon, an immigrant from Prussia who settled in Camden, had served the Confederacy as an army surgeon. He moved to New York after his experience as an attendant at the last fatal duel fought in South Carolina.[4]

Bernard Baruch used his Hobcaw retreat to entertain guests including Franklin D. Roosevelt, Winston Churchill, and Clare Boothe Luce. Hobcaw is now the Baruch Marine Field Laboratory, a marine research facility operated by the University of South Carolina.

Baruch insisted that he never confronted anti-Semitism until after moving north. South Carolina had been so accepting of Jews that even the original Ku Klux Klan took them in. In his autobiography Baruch describes digging in a trunk in the attic and discovering, under his father's Confederate uniform, "a white hood and long robe with a crimson cross on its breast—the regalia of a Knight of the Ku Klux Klan."[5] Originally organized to frighten blacks from voting and to restore white control, the Klan quickly degenerated into a terrorist organization. The federal government had prosecuted it vigorously in South Carolina in the early 1870s.

The Klan's anti-Semitic component emerged following its rebirth in 1915 at Stone Mountain, Georgia, near Atlanta, two months after the lynching of Leo

Frank.[6] A northern-raised Jew charged with murdering a girl who worked at a pencil factory he managed for a relative, Frank was convicted on flimsy evidence in a frenzied trial atmosphere. Governor John Slaton, after reading the trial transcript, commuted Frank's death sentence—a courageous act that the governor correctly predicted would end his political career.

Rather than a nameless lynch mob, the group who by force subsequently removed Frank from jail included men of prominence. They took him to Marietta, the hometown of murder victim Mary Phagan, and hanged him from a tree. Historian John Dittmer, in his *Black Georgians in the Progressive Era*, tells how Tom Watson, the Georgia political leader whose inflammatory editorials for his newspaper, the *Jeffersonian*, had stoked the climate for Frank's lynching, also encouraged a revival of the Klan.[7] Amid flaming torches and a burning cross atop Stone Mountain, the long-dormant organization was reborn. An intensive recruiting campaign spread Klan activity and organization across the South and beyond its borders for well over a decade. This time the Klan extended its nativist message of hate to include Catholics and Jews.

The Frank case received extensive coverage by South Carolina newspapers, whose reportage was informative rather than inflammatory. *The State* vigorously denounced the lynching.[8] But its impact reverberated among Jews throughout the region. Leonard Dinnerstein, an authority on the Leo Frank case, called it "devastating to the assimilated southern Jews. What happened to Frank could have happened to any of them. For the next half century they lived in great apprehension" that other attacks might occur.[9] None did.

Klan-inspired anti-Semitism flared sufficiently in South Carolina in the 1920s that the legislature refused to reelect August Kohn, a man of statewide prominence and influence in commerce and public affairs, to the University of South Carolina Board of Trustees. The university's official historian, Daniel Walker Hollis, wrote that Kohn "had given twenty-four years of loyal, unselfish service."[10] One contemporary observer estimated that as many as thirty-five legislators were members of the Klan.

In 1930, anti-Semitism also helped defeat Solomon Blatt in his first race for the legislature. Blatt overcame it two years later and went on to become South Carolina's dominant Jewish political figure of the twentieth century.[11] An immigrant peddler's son who grew up in Blackville, he completed undergraduate studies and law school at the University of South Carolina, then returned to the county seat of Barnwell as a small-town lawyer. He served thirty-three years as Speaker of the House of Representatives, a record unmatched in any state.

Blatt shared political dominance with fellow townsman Edgar A. Brown, who ruled the state senate as president pro tem and chairman of its powerful finance committee. For a third of the century the "Barnwell Ring" dominated the legislature, which maintained control of state government. Brown would later describe the Barnwell Ring as "two old men who sometimes agree and sometimes disagree."[12] Fiscal conservatism—honed by their experience during the Great Depression of the 1930s—was always a point of agreement.

Once attacked editorially early in his career by the *Anderson Independent* as "the Barnwell Jew," Blatt ruled by a combination of razor-sharp mind, political skill, forceful personality, attention to detail, and devotion to his state. In Barnwell, Blatt also served on the school board during the days of legally mandated racial segregation, displaying a paternalistic interest in improving conditions for black schools. For most blacks in the county seeking legal assistance, the Blatt law firm was the place to go. Much of the work was pro bono.

In that narrow segregationist world, however, Blatt displayed the conservative caution that typified the response of South Carolina Jewry to civil rights. In a 1959 speech to the Charleston Hebrew Benevolent Society, Blatt said it would be "a mistake for the Jewish people to become very active" in the cause of civil rights because "when the time came, those who would be punished as a result of it would be the Jewish people."[13] More than a half dozen synagogues were bombed in the South, though none in South Carolina, where Jewish support for black aspirations was rarely expressed, and where the State Law Enforcement Division had infiltrated the Klan, closely monitoring its activities.

When Rabbi Burton Padoll of Charleston's Kahal Kadosh Beth Elohim spoke out in support of the civil rights movement in the early 1960s, the congregation's elders rebuked him, and his contract was not renewed.[14] An invitation to a black speaker by a congregation in Columbia in the mid-1960s was considered a bold move.

For Jews in the South, the civil rights era presented a problem of how to respond. In the aftermath of the Holocaust, when those who stood by silently would eventually face accountability, cautious silence among southern Jews ultimately left some with unspoken feelings of guilt.

For Sol Blatt, the decline of his leadership began at a moment of high drama in 1966, when the legislature was still all white. The House began debating a bill to restore the state's compulsory school attendance law, which had been repealed a decade earlier as part of "massive resistance" legislation to thwart school integration. Blatt, who rarely spoke on the floor of the House and often became emotional when he did, shed tears in attacking the bill. "You may want a sixteen-year-old so-and-so to sit by your granddaughter," Blatt shouted, "but Sol Blatt will fight and die to prevent it from happening to his granddaughter."[15] When asked whether he would prefer sixteen-year-old illiterates to walk the streets rather than go to school, Blatt answered, "I'd rather have them in the streets. They can be avoided there."

Senator Brown later explained that the reason Blatt had made such an issue on the bill was because "folks back home think he's too much for the Negroes."[16] The 1966 speech, however, led eventually to a move by progressive legislators to replace Blatt as Speaker and left a permanent stain on his image. As his son, U.S. District Judge Sol Blatt Jr., told me, "He made one talk he shouldn't have made."[17]

In 1973, when Blatt, at age seventy-eight, stepped down as Speaker, he noted the presence of black legislators and spoke of a state "where no longer a man's religious views, political affiliations or the color of his skin in any wise prevent him from walking the road of life to a distance far beyond that which he expected in the years gone by."[18]

FIGURE 11. *Jewish legislators and mayors in front of the South Carolina State House, Columbia, 2000. Left to right: Joel Lourie (House 1998–present), Isadore E. Lourie (House 1965–72, Senate 1973–93), Hyman Rubin (Columbia City Council and Mayor Pro Tem 1952–66, Senate 1966–84), Sylvia Dreyfus (House 1976–78), David Taub (mayor of Beaufort, 1990–99), Irene Krugman Rudnick (House 1973–78, 1981–84, 1987–93), Arnold Goodstein (House 1970–74, Senate 1975–80), Richard Moses (mayor of Sumter, 1972–76), Harriet Keyserling (House 1976–92), William Keyserling (House 1993–96), Leonard Krawcheck (House 1967–70). Photograph by Bill Aron. Courtesy of the Jewish Heritage Collection, College of Charleston Library.*

Did this farewell speech by Blatt demonstrate a change of heart? An expression of his true feelings? A recognition of changed circumstances? Or an effort to untarnish his reputation? Perhaps it reflected a mix of them all.

A fellow Jewish legislator, Isadore Lourie of Columbia, had cosponsored the bill to restore the school attendance law and later supported Blatt's successor as Speaker.[19] At the University of South Carolina, Lourie had been student body president. In his first legislative race, younger members of his fraternity, myself among them, distributed handbills door to door. I worked a black neighborhood, where several residents referred to Lourie's being Jewish—always accompanied by a comment or nod of approval. They cited Jewish merchants and housewives as being fair to black customers and domestic workers.

After his election to the senate, the confluence of reapportionment, single-member districts, and the 1965 Voting Rights Act placed Lourie in a majority black district. He survived a challenge by a black female opponent when a third of the African American voters supported him.

"I worked hard and had a good record," he explained.[20] On the floor of the House, he had made the first introduction of an African American sitting in the visitors' gallery, at the time a bold departure from a ritual that long had been reserved for whites. In 1970 Lourie helped recruit two of the twentieth century's first successful black House candidates and actively campaigned with them.

During a legislative career that spanned more than two decades, Lourie aligned himself with a bloc of progressive white reformers who worked to develop and expand state programs in education, health care, and social issues. His son Joel later was elected to the legislature, one of more than a dozen Jews who served there after World War II. Most of them, like the Louries, were progressive.

One of them, Harriet Keyserling of Beaufort, served seventeen years and has written forthrightly in her book, *Against the Tide*, about the tensions of race, especially within the Democratic Party after black Democrats teamed up with Republicans on reapportionment following the 1990 census.[21] This odd coalition created a maximum number of black majority legislative districts. Packing black voters into comfortable majorities in those districts, however, jeopardized progressive white Democrats, including Keyserling and Irene Rudnick, a Jewish representative from Aiken.

After reapportionment removed almost all of the black Democrats from her House district, Rudnick lost reelection in 1994 in what had become a heavily Republican area. Keyserling retired. A decade before, the eighteen-year career of Senator Hyman Rubin (a brother-in-law of Rudnick's husband) ended when a Republican challenger defeated him after Rubin's reapportioned district lost a third of its black Democrats. Earlier, as a Columbia city councilman, Rubin had encouraged voluntary desegregation of downtown eating facilities and the hiring of black clerks in retail stores.

As Keyserling predicted to black Democratic colleagues, they might gain more seats in the House, but would lose power if Republicans became dominant. That is exactly what happened. Keyserling had worked closely with blacks on progressive legislation. She was an early supporter of Governor Richard W. Riley's comprehensive Education Improvement Act and worked to insure black inclusion in her initiatives for expanded state arts programs.

In addition to Jewish legislators, more than a dozen Jews served as mayors in South Carolina towns and cities after World War II. In the county seat of Abbeville, Joe Savitz Sr. served fourteen years as mayor before losing reelection. His son Joe Savitz Jr., a practicing Christian, likewise served fourteen years as mayor until his defeat for reelection in 2000.

In Georgetown, brothers Meyer and Sylvan Rosen served, respectively, as state representative and mayor. By the end of the twentieth century, however, younger South Carolina Jews by and large had abandoned the small towns and either joined the expanding Jewish populations in the state's cities and coastal retirement havens or migrated to larger metropolitan areas. The Jewish sons and daughters of Georgetown have almost all gone—through assimilation and migration. Only the remnant of an organized Jewish community remains.

~

The most serious incident of anti-Semitic intrusion in a South Carolina political campaign happened in the 1978 upcountry congressional race in which twice-elected Greenville mayor Max Heller ran as the Democratic candidate against Republican Carroll Campbell. Heller, who had left Austria as a teenager in 1938 to escape the Nazi threat, led until the closing days of the campaign.

In this race Arthur Finkelstein (who, ironically, would become a consultant for future Israeli prime minister Benjamin Netanyahu), conducted a poll for Campbell that measured voter reaction to such information as whether a candidate was "Jewish" or "a Jewish immigrant." The *New York Times* reported in 1986, when Campbell ran successfully for the first of his two terms as governor, that Finkelstein had told the editor of a political newsletter about a third question posed in the 1978 survey. How would voters react to information that a candidate was "a foreign-born Jew who did not believe in Jesus Christ as the savior?"

The poll indicated that Heller would win if the first two pieces of information were known, but not the third. Campbell was quoted in the *Times* story as calling the newsletter account "inaccurate" and "outrageously wrong."[22]

He acknowledged, however, that his campaign manager had contact with representatives of Don Sprouse, a wrecker-service owner with no political experience who got on the ballot for the same congressional seat by collecting ten thousand names as a petition candidate. Sprouse attacked Heller because he was "not a Christian" and did not "believe in Jesus Christ." Campbell won the election with 53 percent of the vote.

FIGURE 12. *Max and Trude Heller on Main Street, Greenville, S.C., 2000. The street's renovation was accomplished between 1971 and 1979, when Mr. Heller was mayor. Photograph by Bill Aron. Courtesy of the Jewish Heritage Collection, College of Charleston Library.*

~

In South Carolina's turbulent history of race relations, Jews rarely challenged the status quo, but many individuals took small steps to respect personal dignity. My father was among them, allowing black as well as white customers to try on clothes in the dressing room of his store, as did Isadore Lourie's father in St. George. In Beaufort, Dr. Herbert Keyserling, Harriet's husband, provided the requisite two waiting rooms for patients during the days of segregation, but in a radical departure from that period's racial protocol, he refrained from labeling them as "white" and "colored."[23]

Over time the success of the civil rights revolution in pushing forward the ideals of equality and brotherhood made whites more accepting of change after the walls of legally imposed segregation crumbled. The Jewish community became more comfortable in responding. For example, black religious leaders in Charleston participated in 1999 in the two hundred fiftieth anniversary activities of Kahal Kadosh Beth Elohim—as did Rabbi Padoll. In the summer of 2000, a group of African American and Jewish teenagers who belong to an organization called Operation Understanding–Charleston traveled together to civil rights sites across the South. Now in its fifth year, Operation Understanding sponsors such trips annually, as part of its mission to dispel stereotypes and promote dialog, acceptance, and mutual respect.

FIGURE 13. *Operation Understanding: Members of a Jewish and African American youth group at the National Children's Cancer Society Thrift Store, Charleston, S.C., 2000. Photograph by Bill Aron. Courtesy of the Jewish Heritage Collection, College of Charleston Library.*

Under the leadership of Rabbi Anthony Holz, a native of South Africa, the Reform congregation also had begun holding an annual Martin Luther King Jr. memorial event, with biracial participation. The speaker at the 1999 event was Cleveland L. Sellers Jr., a University of South Carolina faculty member who spent seven months in prison after being convicted in 1970 of riotous activity in the tragic episode known as the Orangeburg Massacre.[24]

Then a national officer in the Student Nonviolent Coordinating Committee (SNCC), Sellers was shot on the night of February 8, 1968, in a fusillade of police gunfire on the campus of South Carolina State College. Three students were killed and twenty-seven others were wounded. Sellers ended up spending that night on death row at the state's Central Correctional Institution.

With a master's degree from Harvard and a Ph.D. from the University of North Carolina, Sellers returned to his South Carolina hometown of Denmark, but was unable to obtain a teaching position until after he received a pardon by the state Probation, Pardon, and Parole Board in the summer of 1993.[25]

In July 1999 I traveled with Sellers and Rabbi Holz on a week-long bus trip to civil rights sites across the South sponsored by the College of Charleston. I had coauthored the book, *The Orangeburg Massacre*, and Sellers and I had become friends, a relationship that would not have been possible when we were growing up twenty miles apart in separate black and white worlds. At Beth Elohim, Sellers spoke about the legacy of Dr. King, but what is noteworthy about his appearance is that it marked the first attention given by any Jewish organization in the state to the events at Orangeburg. That event remains so little known that no mention was made of it at either of the South's two major museums of the civil rights era, the National Civil Rights Museum in Memphis and the Birmingham Civil Rights Institute, both of which we visited on our 1999 trip.

The past, however, is beginning to come to light. On February 8, 2001, with Sellers and other survivors of the shootings present, Governor Jim Hodges addressed an overflow audience in the Martin Luther King Jr. Auditorium on the South Carolina State University campus. He referred directly to the "Orangeburg Massacre," a term that itself has remained controversial, and called what happened "a great tragedy for our state."

Historically, the record of South Carolina Jews reflects cautious support for accommodation on racial issues—and sometimes more. The level of acceptance Jews have received from the dominant white community was summed up by a man in North whom I introduced to a nephew visiting from Chicago with his teenage son. The man told my nephew, "We treated your grandfather just like he was one of us." ❧

Notes

1. Abram Vossen Goodman, "South Carolina from Shaftesbury to Salvador," in Leonard Dinnerstein and Mary Pallson, eds., *Jews in the South* (Baton Rouge: Louisiana State University Press, 1973), 32.

2. James W. Hagy, *This Happy Land: The Jews of Colonial and Antebellum Charleston* (Tuscaloosa: University of Alabama Press, 1993); Charles Joyner, *Shared Traditions: Southern History and Folk Culture* (Urbana and Chicago: University of Illinois Press, 1999), chapter 9.

3. George P. Rawick, ed., *The American Slave: A Complete Autobiography*, vol. 7, *Oklahoma and Mississippi Narratives* (Westport, Conn.: Greenwood Publishing Co., 1972), 210–11. Hundreds of such interviews were conducted as part of a Works Progress Administration project across the South, with transcriptions written in dialect.

4. Margaret Coit, *Mr. Baruch* (Boston: Houghton Mifflin, 1957), 30–32.

5. Bernard M. Baruch, *Baruch: My Own Story* (New York: Henry Holt & Co., 1957), 32.

6. Leonard Dinnerstein, *The Leo Frank Case* (Athens: University of Georgia Press, 1987); Albert S. Lindemann, *The Jew Accused: Three Anti-Semitic Affairs (Dreyfus, Beilis, Frank), 1894–1914* (Cambridge and New York: Cambridge University Press, 1991); C. Vann Woodward, *Tom Watson: Agrarian Rebel* (New York: Oxford University Press, 1963).

7. John Dittmer, *Black Georgia in the Progressive Era, 1900–20* (Urbana: University of Illinois Press, 1977), 184–85.

8. *The State*, August 17–20, 1915, cited in Belinda and Richard Gergel, *In Pursuit of the Tree of Life* (Columbia, S.C., 1996), 96 n. 26.

9. Leonard Dinnerstein, *Antisemitism in America* (New York: Oxford University Press, 1994), 184.

10. Daniel Walker Hollis, *University of South Carolina*, vol. 2 (Columbia: University of South Carolina Press, 1956), 321.

11. Solomon Blatt, *The Bridge Builder: Solomon Blatt Reflects on a Lifetime of Service to South Carolina*, ed. George D. Terry and Catherine Wilson Horne (Columbia: McKissick Museum, University of South Carolina, 1986); John K. Cauthen, *Speaker Blatt: His Challenges Were Greater* [1965], reprint with a new foreword by Jack Bass (Columbia: University of South Carolina Press, 1978); Solomon Blatt Papers, 1918–1986, South Caroliniana Library, University of South Carolina; Timothy D. Renick, "Solomon Blatt: An Examination into the Conservative Racial Views of a Jewish Politician in the Deep South 1937–1986," with an accompanying guide to the Solomon Blatt papers, master's thesis, University of South Carolina, 1989.

12. "A Venerable Dixie Legislator Retires," *New York Times*, June 12, 1973, reprinted in Cauthen, *Speaker Blatt*, xv.

13. Quoted in Eli N. Evans, *The Provincials: A Personal History of Jews in the South* (New York: Atheneum, 1973), 148.

14. Interview with Rabbi Burton L. Padoll, October 21, 1999, Jewish Heritage Collection, College of Charleston Library.

15. "Venerable Dixie Legislator," *Speaker Blatt*, xvi–xvii; Evans, *The Provincials*, 144.

16. "Venerable Dixie Legislator," *Speaker Blatt*, xvii.

17. Telephone interview with the author, November 18, 1999.

18. "Venerable Dixie Legislator," *Speaker Blatt*, xvi.

19. N. Louise Bailey, Mary L. Morgan, and Carolyn R. Taylor, *Biographical Directory of the South Carolina Senate, 1776-1985*, vol. 2 (Columbia: University of South Carolina Press, 1986), 953–55; Karen Tannenbaum, *The Louries of South Carolina* (Columbia, S.C.: privately printed, 1991).

20. Telephone interview with the author, May 11, 2000.

21. Harriet Keyserling, *Against the Tide* (Columbia: University of South Carolina Press, 1998), 98–100.

22. Phil Gailey, "Bigotry Issue in Carolina Campaign," *New York Times*, September 24, 1986, p. A28.

23. Herbert Keyserling, *Doctor K* (Beaufort, S.C.: privately printed, 1999), 91.

24. Cleveland Sellers with Robert Terrell, *The River of No Return: The Autobiography of a Black Militant and the Life and Death of SNCC* (1973; reprint, Jackson: University Press of Mississippi, 1990).

25. Ibid.; Jack Bass and Jack Nelson, *The Orangeburg Massacre* (1970, 1984; reprint of 2d ed., with a new afterword, Macon, Ga.: Mercer University Press, 1996), 239–41.

A Call for Candlesticks

Dale Rosengarten

When my husband and I sent out invitations to our son Rafael's bar mitzvah in 1993, friends and family in the North responded with thinly veiled surprise. How could we raise a good Jewish boy in a small southern town where everyone goes to church on Sunday? Where in the wilderness of South Carolina had we managed to find a Hebrew teacher?

Designed in a familiar suburban aesthetic, the sanctuary in Synagogue Emanu-El, where the bar mitzvah took place, comforted our northerner visitors. Still, if they hadn't been sitting, they would have fallen over in shock when Rafe stepped up to the bimah, nodded to the rabbi, and led the service from the opening prayer to the closing kaddish. The ceremonies took longer than usual, to accommodate English translations for the sake of the non–Hebrew-speaking guests. But while from Rafe's mouth the "Hear" in "Hear O Israel" spins out in two syllables, the content and order of the service was distinctly traditional.

At the dinner party afterward, our kinfolk blinked in disbelief when I told them that two hundred years ago Charleston was the cultural capital of Jewish America, and that Carolina claimed many firsts in Jewish history—the first Jew elected to public office in the western world, the first Jewish soldier to die in the American Revolution, the first dissidents to introduce Reform Judaism to the United States. Jewish South Carolinians were making history long before the eastern European forebears of our families had reached these shores.

What I was saying contradicted stereotypes about the South that northerners bring with them. They suspect that southerners are by nature anti-Semitic. Without concrete information, they assume that a society that discriminates against black people is going to dislike Jews. They believe in safety in numbers, and the idea of being part of a tiny minority mingling in a Christian mainstream makes them uneasy.

I spoke with the conviction of the newly converted. The truth is, I had only recently discovered the state's Jewish history myself. McKissick Museum at the University of South Carolina had hired me to draft a prospectus for a long-term research project that would culminate in an exhibition portraying our old and enduring Jewish heritage. South Carolina was playing catch-up. Though we rightly claimed to be the cradle of southern Jewry, we were a decade behind our neighbors in taking a serious look at the South's Jewish past. In 1983, the Mississippi State Historical Museum mounted a show called "Jewish Roots in Mississippi." The Atlanta Jewish Federation had presented "250 Years of Jews and Georgians" and was hard at work on "Creating Community," a history of Atlanta's Jews. "Free to Profess: The First Century of Richmond Jewry" opened in 1986 at the Valentine Museum in Virginia. In 1987, Tennessee's Center for Southern Folklore produced an exhibition on the "Memphis Jewish Community: 1840 to the Present." Two lavish publications had appeared on the history of Texas Jews, and one on Jewish life in Florida. Utica, Mississippi, near Jackson, and now Miami and Atlanta boast handsome new museums dedicated to the southern Jewish experience.

South Carolina's time had come. In fact, there was not a minute to lose. A distinctive cast of characters was rapidly vanishing or had already departed: the peddler and the small town merchant, the Jewish Confederate and the Jewish rum-runner, the itinerant rabbi and the Jewish Episcopalian. Abandoned stores and dwindling congregations mutely expressed the struggle for existence of once vibrant Jewish communities in towns such as Sumter, Camden, Darlington, Dillon, Bishopville, Abbeville, Aiken, and Georgetown. The growing number of Jews in big cities and resort towns concealed the trend toward decline in the rest of the state.

At every step in the pilot project for McKissick, I picked up a sense of urgency. The older generation felt they had stories to tell that had gone untold. They wanted their memories to survive; they wanted their children and their grandchildren to know how they lived and what motivated them. They wanted their achievements recognized. More than anything they wanted to believe that their lives have contributed to Jewish survival.

The results of my survey convinced museum director Lynn Robertson that a larger project was feasible, that there was a significant story to tell, and that from the point of view of collecting life stories and artifacts, South Carolina's Jewish history was a rich vein that reached deep into the foundations of the state. Things got moving in 1994 when former state senator Isadore Lourie and a group of compatriots founded the Jewish Historical Society of South Carolina. An old friendship between Lourie and Alex Sanders, president of the College of Charleston, brought the college into the partnership. Dean of Libraries David J. Cohen offered archival facilities and office space. Charleston's oldest Jewish congregation, Kahal Kadosh Beth Elohim, had recently deposited its manuscript archives at the college. In one fell swoop, the library's special collections department became a nationally significant repository of Jewish materials. It made good sense to build on this beginning.

In January 1995 I embarked on the curatorial trail. As director of the Jewish Heritage Project my job was to record oral histories, collect manuscripts and photographs for the archives, and identify objects for exhibition. My three employers—the historical society, the college, and the museum—ranked these tasks in different order but agreed on the goal of mounting a major show about southern Jewish life.

The historical society provided contacts and introductions. Like Brer Rabbit in the briar patch, I had fallen into a familiar environment: an extensive, well-organized network of people who recognized me as a landsman and welcomed me like family. Though our accents were different, we were the children of people who had come to America from the Russian Pale of Settlement within the last hundred years. Today, in fact, 90 percent of all American Jews descend from the eastern European migration. Once, when asked what his ancestors were doing during the Civil War, Senator Lourie responded: "Which civil war? In 1860 my people were living in Russia."

For the Sephardim who dominated its Jewish culture for the first 120 years, South Carolina had represented the end of the diaspora, a promised land where there was no reason to wish, "Next year in Jerusalem." The theology, as well as the folkways and food ways of the eastern Europeans, encountered a different social reality in the post-Reconstruction South. Slower to assimilate, and slower to be asked to, the eastern Europeans established a new outpost of Jewish exile.

I gave myself a crash course on American Jewish history and began developing a narrative framework for the objects I found. As I traveled about the state, people were eager to show me their things, but not everyone was willing to lend them. Some were hesitant to display their most precious possessions in public. In their sixties, seventies, or eighties in age, they were loath to part for a year or two with objects they valued like limbs—an oil painting of a Confederate ancestor, a hall tree upon which a beloved grandmother had hung her hat, a samovar from Kaluszyn, Poland, no longer used to brew tea but rather to conjure the memory of shtetl life.

A year into the project, we produced a brochure titled "A Call for Candlesticks" and distributed it to households across South Carolina. Why candlesticks? Because they play an essential role in Jewish custom and ceremony, because they were the objects most commonly carried to America, and because they come with such great stories. One particularly eloquent pair was stowed in the corner of a cupboard in Helen Silver's Charleston home. Small brass candlesticks, utterly unassuming, they embodied a past of turmoil and triumph.

What the great French historian Marc Bloch observed about books is true also for objects like Mrs. Silver's candlesticks: their travels are interesting in themselves because they follow the vicissitudes of life. The candlesticks started out in Lithuania in the possession of Helen's aunt, who fled her homeland around the time of World War I. Instead of going west across Europe to try for an Atlantic passage to America, she traveled east, crossed Siberia, and boarded a ship in Japan bound for America. When she landed in California, she weighed eighty pounds—her sister fainted when she saw her. In her knapsack were these two candlesticks, which have since crossed the continent and come to rest in South Carolina.

How could we infuse the show with the emotional power, manifest to Mrs. Silver, of the well-traveled candlesticks? Most people do not go to museums to read. The curator's rule of thumb is, the fewer words the better. Yet every kiddush cup, every certificate of naturalization, every cash register, every miniature painting on ivory has a story behind it. And if an object does not come with a story, setting it in a larger narrative can inspire you to dream up your own.

Consider the destiny, for example, of a silver basket that had been presented to Charleston's Kahal Kadosh Beth Elohim in 1841 and sent along with other valuables to Columbia for safekeeping during the Civil War. Fashioned in 1777 by London silversmith David Bell, the basket began its career as a sugar or sweetmeat bowl with a glass lining, and was purchased perhaps by Joshua Lazarus on one of his trips abroad, or passed down by the family of his English wife Phebe Yates. Lazarus chaired the committee overseeing the commemoration of Beth Elohim's new building and later became the congregation's president. On the basket's cartouche he had engraved his name and the date of the gift, 5601 according to the Hebrew calendar. Likely the basket was used as an *etrog* container, a receptacle for the Sukkot citron.

In February 1865, the basket vanished—the loss blamed, of course, on General William T. Sherman and his troops. In the early 1960s it resurfaced in an antiques

CATALOGUE 83.

Sugar or sweetmeat bowl presented to Congregation Beth Elohim by Joshua Lazarus in 1841 (detail below). Kahal Kadosh Beth Elohim.

store in Connecticut and was purchased by Samuel and Esther Schwartz, collectors from Paterson, New Jersey. In 1964 the Schwartzes visited Charleston to attend a meeting of the American Jewish Historical Society, and there made the acquaintance of Jack Patla, keeper of the Beth Elohim archives and silver expert. Patla identified the basket from a photograph the Schwartzes sent him. Twenty-two years later, in 1986, the couple gave Lazarus's gift back to the congregation.

How had the silver basket spent the missing century? Hidden away in a closet or displayed on some side table in open view? Through whose hands had it passed? Who had called themselves "owner"? The intersection of object and history raises more than questions of provenance and storage. After all, Sherman had a reason for coming to South Carolina. Was the wealth embodied in the silver basket produced by slave labor? Was there such a thing as a Jewish position on slavery? Can displaying the lost and found silver basket fuel a fruitful discussion?

What if the things you are collecting are stories—stories that come without objects, stories that are just words, stories that are memories incarnate?

Stories, no less than things, anthropologist James Deetz might say, are "purposely shaped . . . according to a culturally dictated plan." Stories are not only forms and products of expressive behavior, they are the currency of relationships, a repository of cultural wealth. There may be a universal inventory of themes and motifs, and the reasons people tell stories may vary only within a small range. Yet the stories told by individuals who share a past going back many generations reveal the lineaments of a "plan," which in the case of southern Jews, to paraphrase Moses Maimonides, is a guide to avoid perplexity. "Here is where we are, and here is what we must do, to secure our homes and make a living."

Elderly people I have interviewed appreciate the opportunity to "air" their lives. Some feel compelled to speak, from motives I can only guess. They may be seeking justice or revenge, rehearsing an argument or repairing a broken reputation. They may simply be lonely, happy to have company for the morning or afternoon. And they don't want the interviewer to leave until they are ready for her to go, even if she feels she has heard enough and "collected" what was ripe for the picking. I have noticed that at the start of a recording session, people often dredge up a childhood trauma masquerading in their minds as "a warm memory." At the end of the session, if all goes well, they feel a certain relief, having probed an old wound and made light of the pain.

When I asked Virginia Moïse Rosefield, born in 1909 in Sumter, South Carolina, what she remembered about going to Sunday school, she prefaced her answer by recalling her "happy family" and their "very beautiful home," and then told this story:

> When I was a just a little girl, I had long curls. One of my first memories: I must have been about four years old and Mama was combing my hair, getting me ready to go to Sunday school, and I was crying, it was hurting, I was yelling and she said, "Stop that, Virginia!" She wasn't a patient person. "Stop that yelling."
>
> And I went on, "It's hurting me. You're pulling—" You know how kids do.

FIGURES 14 AND 15. *Virginia Moïse, before and after haircut, Sumter, S.C., ca. 1916. Courtesy of Anita Moïse Rosefield Rosenberg.*

She picked up the scissors and whacked off my hair, and that's the first haircut I ever had. She said, "I'm not going to listen to that another minute."

I was so stunned. I just sat there with my mouth hanging open—between yells. So that was the first thing I remember about going to Sunday school was getting my first haircut.

There is information here, but more important to get across is the sense of a "life lived," of a southern Jewish woman's construction of her self, which is, after all, a historical process, and one that has not stopped with aging. This is wonderfully clear in Mrs. Rosefield's innocent revelation about how a white child in South Carolina in the years before World War I acquired her loyalties.

When my father [Davis DeLeon Moïse] was in the legislature, even before I started kindergarten, mother and I would go to Columbia and we would stay at the Jefferson Hotel for weeks while they were in session. We'd come home occasionally, but we'd stay there, we'd live there. I knew everybody in that hotel: every bellhop, every elevator operator. I had the run of that hotel. Everybody knew me and if I got too near the front door they would snatch me back. It was a wonderful experience for a little girl to have.

I started kindergarten in Columbia. I went to kindergarten every morning to a lady's house who had about a dozen or so kids. The first thing we did every day, and believe me I learned how to do it, we drew a picture of the Confederate flag. Every day. When we got there all these little chairs were pulled up at a table, and in front of each chair was a picture she had drawn. They didn't have copies; we had to fill it in and color it.

Every day for two years that I was in the kindergarten, we did that first. After that, other things might follow, but always that. We could count on it.

The icon of the flag, with its St. Andrew's cross of stars on a field of gray, stirs strong emotions in this part of the world today. The passion comes from the unhealed wounds of racial discrimination, on the one hand, and on the other, from the lingering pain of a lost cause and pride in a distinctive heritage, one perceived to be under attack on a number of fronts. Mrs. Rosefield's story quietly confirms the secret to Jewish acceptance in South Carolina since the days of the Lords Proprietors. Jews are white. In a society that for centuries upheld racial inequality as "a higher law," to quote scholar and jurist Louis Harlan from a 1950s study of school segregation, Jews benefitted from being on the right side—the white side—of the color line. They have enjoyed the same rights and protections under the law as other white people, the same freedom of mobility and access to power and privilege expressly denied African Americans. Even the persecuted and poverty-stricken Jewish immigrants who came to America fleeing conscription, discrimination, and mob violence in eastern Europe could dream of climbing the social ladder. For some the dream proved illusory, but many did indeed manage to move, within three or even two generations, from peddler, to storekeeper, to professional.

My two favorite types of stories are what I call Tales from the Old Country and Store Stories. The former frequently recount how people got their names when they came to America. Edna Ginsberg Banov, born in Charleston in 1908, recalls a story told about her sister Flossie:

> In the Old Country, Flossie was Frumasheina. In Yiddish, *fruma* means religious, and *sheina* means beautiful. That was her name, Frumasheina. Riding on the train from New Jersey to Charleston, Papa was calling "Frumasheinka." Somebody said, "What kind of name is that, mister?"
>
> Papa says, in his English broken but still understandable—Mama didn't understand a word—he says, "That's her name."
>
> He says, "Ooo, and you're going to give her that name in America? She's going to live like that with a name like that. I don't know."
>
> So Papa figured, what could he name her that started with an "F"? Later they're riding past farms and see these huge cows with the big tits hanging, milking cows. And they heard the farmers saying, "Flossie! Flossie!" herding the cows in.
>
> Papa said, "That's a good name, Flossie. Flossie is perfect."
>
> Heavy milking cows—that was the theory they brought over from the Old Country. They didn't have food to eat when they came to this country, they were forced to come here, to seek the *goldene* land.

The storyteller could not have heard this dialogue—she hadn't been born yet. But she probably heard the story told many times and has transmitted a parable of immigrant experience that is found, with variations, in the folklore of Americans of every ethnic origin whose families came "to seek the goldene land." Several years ago, I read at the Jewish Museum in New York this little yarn told by an Italian man: "When I came to America, I thought the streets would be paved with gold. When I got here I discovered three things. Number one, the streets were not paved with gold. Number two, they weren't paved at all. Number three, I was expected to pave them."

The story collector learns that when people start reciting dialogues, you are getting a good story. In its use of such thematic elements as camaraderie among countrymen and the bumpy road toward Americanization, the following store story told by Irving (Itchy) Sonenshine is peculiarly "Jewish" and "South Carolinian" at the same time. Sonny Goldberg, who saves the day and recycles the story for his own profit, was a Charleston retailer of folk dimensions, and one of the last of a historical type.

> Sonny tells a story about the time that Mr. Resnick called him to write a letter for him. Mr. Resnick couldn't speak English too well. So he called Sonny up and says, "Sonny." Sonny says, "Yes, Mr. Resnick?" Mr. Resnick says, "I want you to come by. I want you to write a letter for me." So Sonny goes by. And Mr. Resnick starts dictating to him in Yiddish, telling him that the merchandise he received from the man isn't worth it. "It's junk and it's not worth even looking at." Doesn't want to

keep it in his inventory and he wants to return it and he will keep some of the merchandise to cover the cost of the freight, in and out.

Sonny starts to read the letter back to him. Mr. Resnick was very brutal. Sonny said, "Gentlemen." Right away Mr. Resnick's eyes just perked up. "The merchandise I recently received from your establishment is not the standard quality that my company is used to giving to its customers. Therefore we find it necessary to ask that you allow us to return said merchandise for credit and we will deduct a certain amount of merchandise to cover the cost of handling." Mr. Resnick said, "Sonny, you're the only person in the world that can write a letter exactly like I tell you." Sonny would tell that story half in Yiddish and half in English at the Rotary Club, and the goyim would crack up.

A month into collecting, I followed my curator's instinct to Georgetown, a blue-collar town that used to be the seat of the rice-planting aristocracy, sixty miles north of Charleston. Georgetown was the second place in South Carolina, after Charleston, where Jews settled, and it claims the state's second oldest Jewish cemetery. The town had three Jewish mayors before 1818 and has had several more since then. Of Georgetown's two museums, one is dedicated to rice, the other to the Kaminski family, whose Jewish progenitor, Heiman Kaminski, arrived in Georgetown in 1865. Kaminski was born in Posen (then part of Prussia), came to South Carolina at age fifteen, clerked in a store in Conwayboro, and fought for the Confederacy in the Tenth South Carolina Regiment. At the war's end, legend has it, he came to the port town with two silver dollars in his pocket. Within ten years he was one of its wealthiest and most prominent men, with a hand in a dry-goods store, a hardware store, a medical dispensary, a boat and oar company, a steamship line, the Bank of Georgetown, and the Georgetown Rice Milling Company. His credit report prepared by the R. G. Dun Company in 1875 tersely described him as "rich."

An acrid smell from the town's papermaking plant and red dust from its steel mill waft over grand eighteenth-century houses on the harbor side of town and over treeless mobile home parks and rows of small frame houses on the land side, west of the Wal-Mart. I parked on Front Street across from a dilapidated storefront with the word "Alwyn's" on the brick facade. The last two letters were blown away by Hurricane Hugo so the sign actually read, "Alwy ." Pushing open the door, I walked through a maze of old store cases and racks hung with dresses from 1989, the year of the hurricane, when the store closed for good. At the back I found, as I would almost any day of the week, Alwyn Goldstein and his friend Philip Schneider, whose father, Albert, in partnership with his brother-in-law Harry N. Rosen, had run the New Store down the block.

Mr. Goldstein and Mr. Schneider acted as if they had been waiting for me for years. We talked for two hours, and they would have talked all day. They had a lifetime of stories to tell and all the time in the world to tell them. Alwyn reminisced about his boyhood spent working in his father's store in Charleston ("I was vice president in charge of anything no one else wanted to do") and his move to

FIGURE 16. *Piazza of the Kaminski House, Front Street, Georgetown, S.C., 2000. Photograph by Bill Aron. Courtesy of the Jewish Heritage Collection, College of Charleston Library.*

FIGURE 17. *Alwyn Goldstein and Philip Schneider in Alwyn's, Front Street, Georgetown, S.C., 2000. Photograph by Bill Aron.* Courtesy of the Jewish Heritage Collection, College of Charleston Library.

Georgetown in 1938. Philip recalled his dad, in the depth of the Depression, driving on country roads and log bridges, selling socks and stockings from the back of his Plymouth, taking orders for furniture, stoves, iceboxes, and then refrigerators from people who lived in the back of beyond.

My father traveled the whole county of Georgetown. He traveled to Pawleys Island when you had to go over on a ferry boat. The sand was so deep over on the other side that if you met a car you'd have to jump the rut and maybe help each other back into that rut to go. He was probably better known than any one person in the whole county of Georgetown, including the sheriff, that's right. We traveled all the area around Sampit. We traveled these areas before they had electricity. We put the first refrigerators in these communities.

We used to go over to McClellanville. He used to travel Collins Creek, Tibwin, you name the communities over there. Awendaw, Buck Hall. These were all dirt roads. I mean, these were all primitive places. He never left the store without candy. I mean, all the communities around there knew him because the children would come out and he would give all the children candy, lady-fingers or whatever, boxes of candy.

South Santee right over the bridge—it was a great bridge. It was one of these wooden bridges. And you got on that bridge and rode like this, pop, pop, pop, pop. The bridge was narrow. Two cars would go by. It was a dirt road and off of that bridge, you know how that curve comes down, well, that was clay, that was pure red clay. There was no embankment on the sides there—that was straight off into the wild blue yonder. And we would drive that thing and it would rain and that thing would be as slick as glass. You couldn't see. I am not kidding you, I don't know how my father survived driving that. We came across that bridge one night late and a fuse blew out on our lights in the car. We used to drive a little Plymouth car. I was standing on the running board trying to hold a light so that you could get against the bridge like that; you'd feel the bridge with the car. We came over that bridge without lights and off of that slick road. I mean it was raining. And right off of that to the left was that store, the Thameses ran it at that time. We stopped in there, got a piece of chewing gum or cigarettes, and wrapped the fuse with the tin foil, put it back in, the lights worked and we came on back to Georgetown.

Since the day we met Alwyn has been my most constant correspondent. Every month or so he sends a package of clippings, pamphlets, and papers for the archives. I keep up with Philip through his son, Laz Schneider, an attorney living in Florida. Like the rest of his generation of Jewish Georgetonians, Laz left home for greener pastures, encouraged by his brokenhearted parents to follow his dreams.

Alwyn and Philip are men of regular habits. Every Friday evening, Alwyn leads a short service at Georgetown's Beth Elohim, a congregation formally organized in 1904 as an outpost of its namesake in Charleston. As the last member of his community who can read Hebrew fluently, Alwyn takes his responsibility seriously. He doesn't worry about making a minyan, the ten men required for a Jewish prayer service. The usual crowd, including gentile spouses, numbers eight.

Soon the Georgetown congregation may exist in memory only—memory sustained by conservation activities like those of the Jewish Historical Society. Whether they are objects enshrined behind glass or stories enshrined by the act of recording and transcribing, most of the materials on exhibition in "A Portion of the People" induce in Jewish visitors a feeling of tribal connection that breaks through glass and nurtures self-esteem. Visitors who are not Jewish may be struck by both the strangeness and the sameness of this other culture. A measure of the exhibit's success would be the degree to which they are reminded of the ties that bind them to their own heritage.

There are some objects and stories that Jews would rather not see or hear. One is a tale of a furniture merchant who came by his wealth by overcharging black customers—a minor chord in a body of lore where the dominant refrain is the willingness of Jewish merchants to allow blacks to try on hats and pay on credit and to address them as Mr. and Mrs. When we published the story on the library's web site, I received calls from people worried that documenting the exception supports a dangerous stereotype, a stereotype that within living memory had stoked genocidal terror.

While the image of the usurious Jew makes all Jews cringe, responses to other touchstones vary depending on whether you were born north or south of the Mason-Dixon line. If you come from the South, the most disturbing object in "A Portion of the People" might be a top hat that belonged to Franklin J. Moses Jr., governor of the state from 1872 to 1874, the era white South Carolinians dubbed "Black Rule." Like his mother and his wife, Moses was a practicing Christian. His father, a distinguished attorney and state senator from Sumter, attained the post of chief justice of the state's supreme court. Judge Moses never renounced his Judaism or his son. White southerners in general and Sumter Jews in particular, however, reviled Governor Moses as a "scalawag," a native white who supported the party of Lincoln during Reconstruction. He had been loyal to the Confederacy—he was present when the Confederate flag was raised over Fort Sumter and served as secretary to Governor F. W. Pickens—but after the war his sympathies shifted. Known nationally as the "Robber Governor," he was loathed in his home state as a race traitor. His enemies swore they caught him dancing with "dusky maidens" in the governor's mansion. Family members changed their surnames to DeLeon and Harby; in 1878 his wife divorced him and reverted to her maiden name. Moses fled the state in bankruptcy and disgrace and lived the remaining decades of his life in the North. Arrested various times for a variety of swindles, addicted to morphine and opium, he died in Winthrop, Massachusetts, on December 11, 1906, apparently by his own hand.

One day a young man named Jim Buxton walked into the special collections room at the College of Charleston library with a bound manuscript written by his father. Jim, descendant of an old Episcopalian family from Sumter, had just graduated from Princeton, where he wrote his senior thesis about Wade Hampton, a Civil War hero who "redeemed" South Carolina by reinstating all-white government in 1876. But it was Franklin J. Moses Jr., the subject of the manuscript he had tucked under his arm—his father's senior thesis at Princeton in 1950—that Jim wanted to talk about. At the time it was written, the work had been read and praised by such eminent historians as Francis Butler Simkins and Anne King Gregorie. When Jim's father, Julian, informed his parents he was thinking of revising the essay for publication, they told him that not over their dead bodies would they allow their son to embarrass their friends, including the Moses family of Sumter. Now it was Jim's turn, and he, too, was warned off the subject when he started snooping. In this state, the anger incited by the erratic Franklin J. Moses, a contemporary of Abraham Lincoln and Jefferson Davis, is still too hot to handle.

An object that raises the hackles of northern Jews is a high school football jersey with the words "Jew Boy" on the front, and the initials "J. B. 1" on the back. The jersey was presented to Andy Cohen as part of a "roast" at the banquet of the Darlington High School football team that Andy managed in 1973. That was the same year, nineteen years after Brown v. Board of Education, that black students were admitted to the school, in the north central, or Pee Dee, section of the state. I see the shirt as a schoolboys' attempt to come to grips with ethnic and racial differences. But when I show a slide of the jersey to Elderhostel groups at the College of Charleston, Jewish northerners in the audience gasp, exclaim, get up and walk out. The artifact upsets them. It assaults their sense of security and reminds them of their own encounters with anti-Semitism. "Again," they sigh, "it comes to this!"

It is a measure of how strong the myth and reality of Jewish acceptance are in South Carolina that the epithet "Jew Boy" does not carry the same sting for southerners. I can think of three times in the twenty-five years I have lived here that I have heard the word "Jew" used pejoratively. The first occurred at an oyster roast—a communal dinner at which the bounty of our local waters is cooked on roof tin over a very hot fire—when a neighbor pried open an oyster only to find it filled with mud. "Jewed again," he laughed, tossing the worthless shells on a heap and digging into the cooked pile. "Jewed," in many parts of the world, means "cheated"—and is interchangeable with the equally offensive "gypped," which derives, if you think about it, from gypsy.

The second time I heard the expression was at meeting of the Mount Pleasant Sweetgrass Basketmakers' Association. Myrtle Glascoe, then director of the Avery Research Center for African American History and Culture, wanted to buy a collection of baskets for the center, and I came along to introduce her. Toward the end of the negotiation one of the basket makers stood up and made a fuss: the prices being offered were too low; she was tired of being "Jewed down" all the time. I was pretty sure the diatribe was not aimed at me, but even so my blood ran hot, and when the meeting ended I left in visible distress. On the way out several of the basket makers came up to tell me how sorry they were for the remark, and to assure me it was not intended to cause offense.

The third time the word "Jew" reached my ears was during the struggle to build a public middle school in McClellanville, the coastal village about forty miles from Charleston where my children were born and raised. The town's population is almost all white, while the surrounding school district is mostly black. A majority of town children attend a private school. We chose instead to send our boys to the predominantly black public school with the children of other "come-heres" (newcomers), eccentrics, and poor whites.

The fight over locating the new school in the center of the village was protracted and ugly, one of two events—Hurricane Hugo was the other—that drove away families whose presence had enriched the community. Old friends fell out. Opponents of the plan, primarily private-school parents, felt slapped in the face by people they had welcomed to their village, and tyrannized by outside forces. Supporters of the middle school felt threatened and ostracized. When it became evident that the county school board would win the day, an outspoken foe explained at the town's general store to all who would listen: "The Jews in Charleston promised the niggers in McClellanville a school, and there's not a damn thing we can do about it."

Although the story was a good deal more complicated, there was no escaping the fact that the organizer of the initiative was named Rosengarten, the school attorneys were named Rosen & Rosen, and the architect in charge was Rosenblum. The War of the Roses, as local wags quipped, was a conspiracy of coincidence, for it cannot be said that as a group, Jews in South Carolina acted differently from other white southerners in the desegregation battles of the past.

People on both sides of the McClellanville school struggle who had remained friends filled the sanctuary at Synagogue Emanu-El for our younger son Carlin's bar mitzvah, four years after Rafael's. Senator Lourie marveled over the diversity of the guests. As children came up to recite their parts and share the moment with Carlin, I was less sanguine than the senator. For this bar mitzvah, I knew, would mark a passage in more ways than one. By Jewish law, Carlin assumed responsibility for his actions. I was confident that he knew right from wrong and that he would always be the kind of person for whom the sanctuary would be too small to hold his friends. But I knew that he would be moving on to high school in Charleston, leaving behind the children he had known from birth, who would attend the local school, which we felt was not good enough for Carlin, or for them. Only they did not have access to the alternatives he did. Like his brother before him, he would partake of the historical privilege of his skin color that southern Jews have enjoyed since the seventeenth century. In a moment of family joy, the children making their way to and from the bimah diverted my attention to the social disparities of our times. Here I was, mother of the bar mitzvah boy, an outsider who had become an insider, but only on the outside. ❧

A Portion of the People

Narrative of the Exhibition

CHAPTER ONE

First Families

Collect together thy long scattered people, and let their gathering place
be in this land of milk and honey.

—Myer Moses, *An Oration, Delivered before the Hebrew Orphan
Society, on the 15th Day of October, 1806,* Charleston

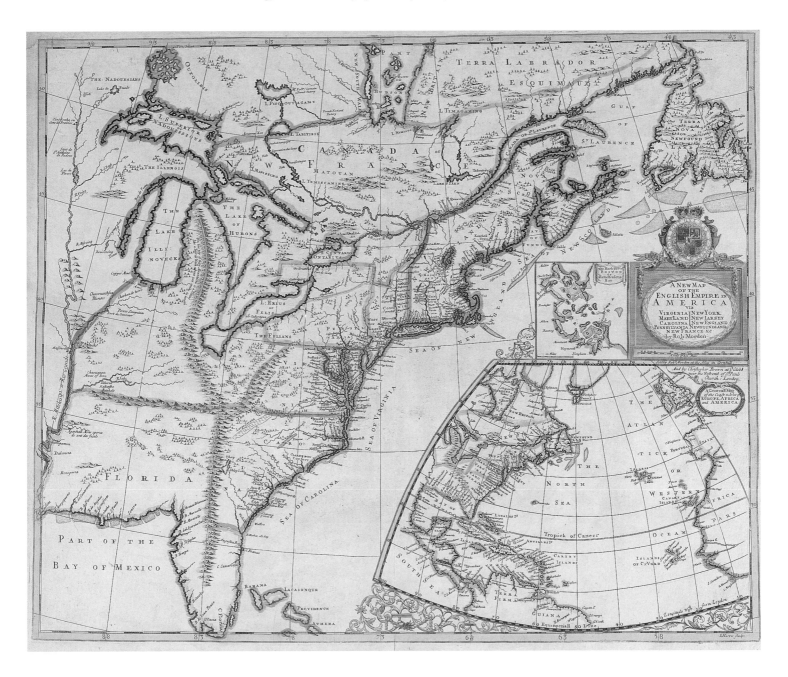

An End to Exile

The unusual provisions for religious tolerance offered by Carolina's Fundamental Constitutions of 1669 were never endorsed by the colonial assembly, but news of an environment friendly to Christian dissenters and Jews spread quickly in Europe and the West Indies. The new British settlement of Charles Town soon earned a reputation as a place where Jews and dissenters could do business and practice their religions without interference.

The first Jewish settlers included people of both Sephardic and Ashkenazic origin, though the Sephardim, whose roots lay in Spain and Portugal, initially outnumbered the Ashkenazim, Jews from the German-speaking lands. The Sephardim had been driven from the Iberian peninsula in a process of separation and expulsion that began in 1391 and peaked in the Inquisition of 1492. The day in August that Columbus was due to lift anchor in the port of Palos, the harbor was clogged with ships taking Spanish Jews and *conversos* to exile. Converso, or new Christian, was the name given to a Jew who had been forced to convert to Catholicism. Converts whose sincerity was suspect were the prime targets of the Inquisitors.

An elite, educated class, the Sephardim gravitated toward commercial centers in the Ottoman empire, the Mediterranean states, central and western Europe, and the West Indies. Wherever they settled the Iberian Jews engaged in a rigorous exchange with the societies that gave them refuge. They founded congregations, added a few Spanish or Portuguese prayers to the traditional Hebrew ones, and conducted business in the local language. The conversos among them either found their way back to Judaism, or did not. By the time the first Jewish settlers arrived in Carolina, their culture was a blend of languages, rituals, folkways, cuisines, philosophies, and arts.

The ancestors of the Ashkenazim were Jews who had migrated to Europe following the Roman conquest of Jerusalem in 70 A.D. They moved from kingdom to kingdom seeking a means to make a living and a place to bury their dead. Restricted over the centuries to certain trades and professions, almost universally prohibited from owning land, and scapegoated in times of plague and war, the Ashkenazim had proved remarkably resilient. They developed strong traditions, a rich body of learning, and a Judeo-German language called Yiddish.

New World settlement by the European powers preceded the general emancipation of Jews in Europe by more than a century. Made worldly by bitter experience, the Jews' fluency in languages, currencies, and legal codes had prepared them to leap into the future. As commerce expanded, cosmopolitan Jewish merchants seized opportunities in European capitals and colonies to play a part in the Atlantic mercantile system.

From London and Amsterdam, Alsace and the Rhineland, Prussia and Poland, St. Croix and Curaçao came merchants, auctioneers, vendue masters, brokers, bakers, butchers, grocers, blacksmiths, shoemakers, tailors, tobacconists, pharmacists, school mistresses, linguisters (interpreters), scriveners (scribes), limners (artists), custom officers, and most common of all, shopkeepers, to seek their fortunes in Charles Town.

In this northernmost outpost of the Gulf-Caribbean plantation region, enterprising Jews became agents of a global trade in American goods, exchanging forest products, deerskins, rice, and indigo for European manufactures and an occasional shipload of African slaves. They furnished the plantations with cloth of all kinds, thread, lace, hats, and shoes; dishes and pots for cooking and baking; ironware, tools, and guns; soap, candles, and medicines; wheat, rum, wine, and olive oil—staples of the European diet. Like their kinsmen who settled in other American port cities, the early Jews of Charles Town functioned as middlemen between the producers and consumers of two worlds. ❧

CATALOGUE 1.

Jonas Phillips (1736–1803), by Charles Willson Peale, ca. 1800. American Jewish Historical Society.

Jonas Phillips, born Jonah Feibush in the German Rhineland, came to Charleston from London in 1756 as an indentured servant and clerk to Moses Lindo, who six years later became the colony's surveyor and inspector-general of indigo. After fulfilling the terms of his servitude, Phillips moved first to Albany, New York, and then to New York City. There, in 1762, he married a Sephardic woman named Rebecca Mendes Machado, a step up on the social ladder for the ambitious Ashkenazi. The early years of the Phillipses' marriage were strained by financial hardship and grief over the deaths of four infant children. In 1764 Jonas was declared an insolvent debtor; the next year he became *shohet* (ritual slaughterer) and *bodek* (examiner of meat) for New York's Shearith Israel congregation.

The Phillipses moved to Philadelphia in 1774, where Rebecca's family joined them after the British army occupied New York. Jonas enlisted in the local militia and worked as a merchant during the Revolution. Tax records show that by 1782 he was the second wealthiest Jew in the city. He has the distinction of being the only nondelegate to send an address, in which he challenged the Test Oath that restricted public office to Christians, to the Constitutional Convention of 1786. In 1793 he was fined for refusing to testify in court on Saturday, the Jewish Sabbath.

Jonas's wife Rebecca, whose father had been the hazzan, or religious leader, of Shearith Israel, was a remarkable person in her own right. Descended from a family of crypto-Jews—Jews who continued to practice their faith in secret during the oppressive days of the Inquisition—Rebecca managed her large household; raised money to buy ritual objects for Mickveh Israel, Philadelphia's new synagogue; helped found the Female Association for the Relief of Women and Children in Reduced Circumstances; and served as the first directress of the Female Hebrew Benevolent Society.

Married at the age of sixteen, she bore twenty-one children in twenty-nine years, a record of fertility among early American Jews. While their sons made their reputations in Philadelphia and New York, the Phillipses kept their ties to South Carolina through their daughter Esther, who moved to Charleston after marrying Myer Moses II. Jonas and Rebecca's grandson, the peripatetic journalist and idealist Mordecai Manuel Noah, spent part of his childhood in Charleston, where his mother died after being abandoned by his father. Noah and his sister Judith were raised by their maternal grandparents in Philadelphia. In 1812, at age twenty-seven, Noah returned to Charleston and embarked on his newspaper career.

The artist Charles Willson Peale was not only a successful painter and engraver but also a museum proprietor, scientist, and inventor. He and his brother James began a dynasty of portrait, miniature, and still life painters. Five of Charles's sons, aptly named Raphaelle, Rembrandt, Rubens, Franklin, and Titian Ramsay (Charles married three times and fathered seventeen children), became well-known artists, and at least five of James's seven children are known to have painted. The American Jewish Historical Society owns two portraits of Jonas Phillips, one attributed to Peale, the other a copy, and two portraits of Rebecca, both thought to be copies of an original by Peale. It was not uncommon in the days before photography for multiple copies of portraits and miniatures to be made, so that likenesses of eminent forebears might hang in the homes of more than one descendant.

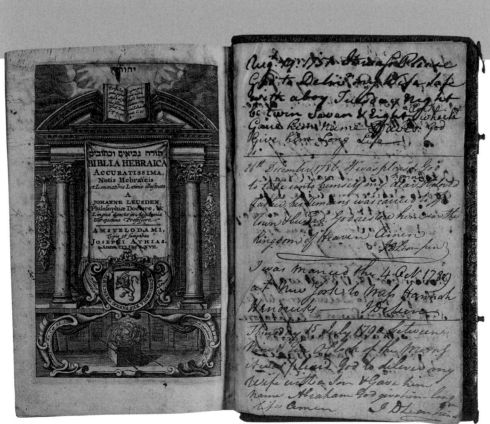

CATALOGUE 29.

Biblia Hebraica, Amsterdam, 1667. Collection of I. Harby and Harriet C. Moses.

The births, marriages, and deaths inscribed in this Hebrew Bible trace a common route the Sephardim followed from the Old World to the New. Presumably it was Jacob DeLeon, grandfather of the South Carolina settler of the same name, who purchased the Bible in Amsterdam. When his son Abraham acquired it, the son recorded the date of his own birth, May 8, 1702, and of his marriage in 1731 in Spanish Town, Jamaica. He then goes on to note the birth of his nine children, beginning with his eldest son, Abraham, born September 21, 1734, and ending with the youngest child, David. Each notation uses the same formal wording:

Atlantic Highway

The Atlantic seaboard was a highway that connected Jewish communities and facilitated family and business alliances up and down the East Coast. Goods and people moved with remarkable ease among the commercial capitals of colonies not yet divided between a North and a South. From Newport, New York, and Philadelphia, to Georgetown, Charleston, and Savannah, to the plantation islands of the Caribbean, a mobile society found shelter, marriage partners, and business prospects among coreligionists chasing similar goals on the American economic frontier. Cousins married cousins to keep real property and other wealth within the family. Multiple marriages among the same families strengthened bonds of affection and commerce.

Jews in the Americas tried to do what Jews everywhere have done: to find ways to sustain their Judaism and maintain Jewish communal life while connecting to the peoples and cultures of the host country. As exiles they tried to blend with the scenery. "Every place you go," instructs a Ladino (Judeo-Spanish) proverb, "act according to the custom of that place." But the Jews' desire to mimic the majority clashed with the duty to obey the arduous rules of their religion. The resulting tension had to be renegotiated in every generation. Crucial to the survival of the community was marrying within the faith. ❧

Aug.t 19, 1751. It was Please God to deliver my wife Safe with a boy Tuesday Night between Seven & eight which Gave him name David—God Give him Long Life

Abraham, the first-born son of Abraham, lived all his life in Jamaica, died at age fifty-two, and was buried at Spanish Town. His death was duly noted in the Bible by his son Jacob.

The next entry, October 4, 1789, finds Jacob in New York, where he married Hannah Hendricks, a member of one of congregation Shearith Israel's most prominent families. (Hannah's brother, industrialist, patriot, and philanthropist Harmon Hendricks, operated the first copper-rolling mill in the country, supplying material to Paul Revere and Robert Fulton, among others.) Hannah and Jacob DeLeon's first child, Abraham, was born in Philadelphia in 1790.

Jacob DeLeon may have fought in the American Revolution in South Carolina, though not as a captain under DeKalb's command, as at least one family chronicler claimed. Certainly by 1796 the DeLeons had settled in Charleston, where they entered the ranks of the Jewish elite. On General Marquis de Lafayette's visit to America in 1825, he presented his Grand Master's Jewel to Jacob's son, Abraham DeLeon, Worshipful Master of Camden's Kershaw Masonic Lodge No. 29. Lafayette had been invited to Camden to help lay the cornerstone of a monument, designed by South Carolina architect Robert Mills, to honor Revolutionary War hero Major General Baron DeKalb. The Marquis was so delighted to be addressed by Brother DeLeon in French, he impetuously removed the jewel and placed it around DeLeon's neck. After DeLeon's death, his son, Harmon Hendricks, gave the jewel to Charleston's Scottish Rite Friendship Lodge No. 9, which retains it to this day.

Jacob DeLeon died in Richland District, near Columbia, South Carolina, on September 29, 1828, at age sixty-four. Ten of his eleven male descendants between the ages of fifteen and sixty served the Confederacy. Two of them worked in civilian capacities; eight joined the army or navy. Four of the eight died in the war.

CATALOGUE 44.

Abraham Moïse (1736–1809), artist unknown, ca. 1790. Collection of Mary Kohn Strasburger.

Born in Strasbourg, Alsace, Abraham Moïse emigrated to Santo Domingo, where he established himself in trade. On the little island of St. Eustatia he met and married Sarah, twenty-six years his junior, the pretty daughter of a noted Jewish family. The couple lived with their four small sons on a plantation in the northwestern corner of Santo Domingo, now part of Haiti. The slave uprising of 1791 sent them fleeing to Charleston. A loyal servant, who later played a conspicuous role in the revolution under the assumed name General Moïse, warned the family of impending danger and escorted them to the port. They carried with them the clothes on their backs and a small trunk of valuables.

According to family historian Harold Moïse, the couple never regained their former affluence; this miniature of Abraham, mounted in gold with the family monogram engraved on back, remains the only relic "to attest his erstwhile prosperity." From their house on Queen Street, three doors from King Street, they sold cloth and tea.

After her arrival in Charleston at age twenty-nine, Sarah bore five more children. All nine Moïse offspring lived to maturity. Among them were the poet, hymnalist, and schoolteacher Penina (1797–1880); and Abraham (1799–1869), first biographer of Isaac Harby and cofounder of the Reformed Society of Israelites. Abraham Moïse Sr. was naturalized the year his namesake was born. Asked by an election manager in 1800, "Did you or did you not possess any and what property . . . before the late election which entitled you to vote?" Abraham replied, "I possessed two negroes." A member of Kahal Kadosh Beth Elohim and a founding member of the Hebrew Orphan Society, he lies buried in the Coming Street Cemetery under the name by which he was known, Moïse Abrams.

CATALOGUE 35.

Abraham Alexander Sr. (1743–1816), attributed to Lawrence Sully, ca. 1795. Carolina Art Association/Gibbes Museum of Art, Charleston, S.C.

London-born Abraham Alexander, the son of Rabbi Joseph Raphael Alexander, sailed to Charleston at age twenty-three, apparently sent by the Sephardic congregation Bevis Marks to become Beth Elohim's second hazzan. For eighteen years he served in that capacity without compensation. Presumably, he returned to England at least once, because his son, Abraham Alexander Jr., naturalized as a citizen of the United States in 1798, was born in England in 1771. The senior Alexander resigned as hazzan in 1784 when he married his second wife, the Huguenot widow Ann Sarah Huguenin Irby, whom he had befriended during the British siege of Charleston.

Alexander's role as one of eleven founders of Scottish Rite Masonry in Charleston was commemorated in a 1959 painting by the Mason and muralist Allyn Cox. The canvas portrays five of the original founders at the corner of Church and Broad Streets, standing outside Mr. Shepheard's Tavern, where Charleston's first Masonic lodge met in 1736, and where the Sublime Grand Lodge of Perfection was organized in 1783. The Mother Supreme Council's first meeting on May 31, 1801 is reputed to have been held in the building Cox depicted. A hatless Abraham Alexander stands second from the left.

A noted Hebrew scholar, scribe, and "calligraphist of the first order," Alexander wrote a *mahzor*, or prayer book for the High Holy Days, in 1805. City directories between 1802 and 1813 list him as clerk and then auditor in the custom house. At the time of his death in 1816 he was collector of the port of Charleston. According to family tradition, he was given a public funeral during which flags of the ships in the harbor and on the custom house were lowered to half-mast. Alexander is buried in the Coming Street cemetery.

Painter Lawrence Sully, the older brother of the more famous Thomas Sully, was born in Ireland and trained in England. He came to America in 1792 and embarked on an itinerant practice as a miniaturist that took him to the southern cities of Richmond, Norfolk, and Charleston.

FIGURE 19. Shepheard's Tavern. Corner of Church and Broad Streets, Charleston, S.C. Birthplace of the Mother Supreme Council, *by Allyn Cox, 1959. Courtesy of the Scottish Rite Temple, Washington, D.C.*

Portraits and Miniatures

In commissioning portraits and miniatures of themselves and family, Jewish Carolinians patronized some of the leading artists of their day, among them James Wesley Jarvis, Charles Willson Peale, and the Sully brothers.

The occasion to have one's portrait painted varied with the individual. A portrait might signify success in business, society, or public life. It might commemorate a rite of passage such as a marriage, an anniversary, or the birth of a child. The most common American portraits are simple half-lengths that focus on the face to achieve a desirable likeness. Paintings of Jewish subjects obey the conventions of pose, dress, background, and demeanor of their time and place.

American miniature portraits, based on English models, reached the height of their popularity early in the nineteenth century. The product of a painstaking technique, miniatures usually were rendered in watercolor on thin sheets of ivory, allowing the artist to explore the delicate translucency of the medium and the interplay of light and color. Images were formed from outline, stippling and hatching, and wash and brush strokes.

Small oval portraits, set in gold frames or jewelry, were succeeded by larger, leather-cased miniatures that emulated styles of full-scale portraiture characteristic of the antebellum period. Mounted with convex glass on the front and backings that sometimes included inlay, decorative designs, and even locks of hair belonging to the sitter, miniatures were a popular way of recalling loved ones. Paintings often were copied so that more than one family member could own a likeness. Wearing a miniature as a locket on a chain around the neck or on a watch fob was a conspicuous expression of sentiment indulged in by the upper classes, even when it stretched their means.

"I have sent you my minature, I hope that you will wear it with as much pleaseur as I doo wereing your hiar [hair] which you sent me," wrote Reuben Simon Krijn in 1818 from Amsterdam to his half-sister Sarah Judith Judah Joseph in South Carolina. Born in Philadelphia, Krijn had moved to Holland as a young man. His letter to Sarah expressed both his wish to see her again and a litany of obligations that kept him from doing so. In his absence, he conveys his affection and longing in the gift of a miniature. "I was quite anxious to send one for my other 2 dear sisters but the limner asks such an extravagant price that I could not think of giving it, you must be satisfied with this untill I can get 2 more. . . . " ❧

CATALOGUE 34.

Leah Lazarus Cohen (1778–1844), by John Canter, ca. 1820. Carolina Art Association/Gibbes Museum of Art, Charleston, S.C.

In this portrait attributed to John Canter, Leah Lazarus wears generous ruffles and lace, attesting to her husband's success. The prized element in her costume is the miniature or pocket watch attached to a chain around her bodice. Long kerchiefs like Leah's sometimes were worn so puffed out in front that the wearer, viewed from the side, was said to resemble a pigeon. Given the date of Canter's death, Leah would have been less than forty-five years old when she sat for the painting.

The daughter of a middle-class shopkeeping family of Sephardic lineage, Leah married a newly made fortune and moved into the planter aristocracy on the coattails of an industrious peddler from Poland. The second of seventeen children of Marks and Richa (Rachel) Lazarus, she was seventeen in 1795 when she wed thirty-two-year-old Mordecai Cohen (see Catalogue 17, page 81). Leah and Mordecai were the parents of eleven children, eight of whom lived to be adults. Cohen and two of the Cohens's sons eventually owned plantations on the Ashley River.

The Lazarus family had been in South Carolina since the 1740s. Leah's father, Marks Lazarus, was a veteran of the American Revolution who rose to the rank of major in Lushington's Company, which came to be known as the Jews' Company because so many Jewish patriots served in its ranks. A man of modest means (in 1790 he owned two slaves), Marks had his wife Rachel declared a sole trader in 1785, assigning her responsibility for running the family's shop. By this time Rachel had given birth to six children, one of whom died as an infant and one as a toddler; she then had eleven more, ten living past childhood. Among Leah's brothers were Joshua, twelve years her junior, and Benjamin Dores Lazarus, whose middle name was a contraction of the Spanish "De Torres."

CATALOGUE 47.

CATALOGUE 61.

Daniel Hart (d. 1811), artist unknown, ca. 1800. Collection of David Hart Crum.

Born in Mannheim, Germany, Daniel Hart emigrated to Charleston in 1783. Arriving on the heels of the American Revolution, he helped revive the Chamber of Commerce and rebuild the war-striken economy. Among the posts he filled was that of consul of the Kingdom of Holland. In 1800, Hart made a substantial contribution to the operating funds for Kahal Kadosh Beth Elohim, which at the time relied largely on voluntary contributions. Though Hart was one of 107 members, his fifty-pound donation amounted to one-sixteenth of the congregation's income. His generous offering followed family tradition: his uncle, Israel Joseph, an early president of KKBE and major contributor to its 1792 building, bequeathed five hundred pounds sterling to the elders of his home congregation in Mannheim.

Dressed in an elegant blue frock coat with gold buttons and a white waistcoat, and with a jabot tied at his neck, Hart looks the typical gentleman of the federal period. This finely painted miniature is encased in a gold locket and backed by blue glass with a memento in the reserve inset in the center. A delicate double column supports a dangling heart minutely inscribed "DH." Perhaps the locket was worn by Daniel's wife, English-born Bella Levy (1762–1851), who had arrived in the port city around the same time as he.

Tea service of Samuel Hart and Esther Ezekiel Hart, by Charles Fox II, ca. 1832. Collection of David Hart Crum.

This ornate tea service was a gift from the Rothschild family to Esther Eudora Ezekiel (1812–1841) and her new husband Samuel Hart upon their marriage in New York on March 27, 1833. Engraved with the monogram "E. E. H.," the silver reflects the social standing of the young couple. Esther was born in Kingston, Jamaica, as was her mother, Leah Levy Ezekiel (b. 1787), and her mother's father, Jacob Levy (b. 1762). Samuel was the son of Daniel and Bella Levy Hart.

Esther died at age twenty-nine. Four years later, her husband Samuel (1805–1896), a publisher and bookseller, issued *The Charleston Book*, an anthology of verse and prose by Charleston writers, edited by William Gilmore

Arabella Solomons Phillips
(1786–1826), artist unknown, ca. 1805.
Collection of Dr. Andrena E. Ray.

Born in Baltimore in 1786 to Myer and Catherine Bush Solomons, Arabella at nineteen married Philadelphia lawyer Zalegman Phillips, son of Jonas and Rebecca Phillips. This elegant miniature, though unattributed, has been described by historian of Jewish portraiture Hannah London as in the style of the Sullys or Henry Inman. Dark curly ringlets surround the fair complexion of Arabella's lovely young face. She wears a simple black dress with the puffed sleeves and high waist of the period, and a lush red wrap about her shoulders. The painting, encased in red leather and lined with white satin, may have been a gift to her husband, a treasured token that Zalegman could have kept on his desk or taken with him on his business travels.

Zalegman Phillips was for many years *parnas*, or president, of Mikveh Israel, Philadelphia's Sephardic synagogue. His brother Napthali held the same post at Shearith Israel in New York. Their sister Zipporah married Manuel Noah, a German-born Charlestonian. She died and was buried in Charleston, leaving her children to be raised by her parents in Philadelphia.

Two of Arabella and Zalegman's eleven offspring married into Carolina Jewish families, thus strengthening ties of kinship across state and regional lines. Catherine Phillips married Montgomery Moses in 1832 and died in Newberry, South Carolina, in 1885. Rebecca Phillips, named for her grandmother, married Jacob Cohen Jr. in 1836 and died four years later in Charleston. Zalegman and Arabella's son, Napthali J., also was in South Carolina, in the Pee Dee town of Marion, at the time of his death in 1864.

CATALOGUE 61 CONTINUED

Simms. Among the contributors were Jewish writers Isaac Harby, Lewis C. Levin, and Penina Moïse. Hart's bookstore was a meeting place for the city's intellectuals. A religious conservative, Hart was among the seceders from Beth Elohim who opposed reform and who, in 1842, petitioned the state to incorporate a new congregation, Shearit Israel, that held to the traditional practices.

CATALOGUE 12.

Caroline "Caro" Agnes Moïse Lopez (1854–1885), by Theodore Sidney Moïse, February 1876. Collection of Mary Kohn Strasburger.

In the Victorian language of flowers, the pansy at the elbow of Caroline Agnes Moïse Lopez symbolizes fond memory, an apt sentiment for the beloved granddaughter of Charleston-born painter Theodore Sidney Moïse. Caro, as Caroline was affectionately called, posed with feathered hat and fine parasol for this stylish portrait painted by her grandfather, while she was visiting him in Louisiana. In 1882 she married Julian Lee Lopez, whose father, David Lopez, was builder of the second sanctuary for Beth Elohim. She died three years later, possibly in childbirth. Her surviving daughter, Theodora Sidney Lopez, born in the first year of her marriage, was reared by the girl's grandmother and namesake, Theodora Sidney Moïse.

CATALOGUE 7.

Mary Olivia Lucas Harby (d. 1834), artist unknown, ca. 1830. Collection of the Moses family.

Born in Louisville, Kentucky, Mary Olivia Lucas was married before the age of twenty to Charleston-born George Washington Harby who, like his older brother Isaac Harby, was a writer and teacher. (George Washington Harby founded a boys' school in New Orleans; Isaac established a co-ed academy in Charleston.) In this portrait Olivia wears a white lace shawl with a repeated design which may or may not be the Hebrew letter ש (*shin*), the initial letter of *Shaddai*, one of the names of God and a talisman for pregnant women. Olivia died of cholera while visiting her parents in Louisville in 1834.

Painters

A center of culture and, in the early nineteenth century, the largest Jewish community in America, Charleston sustained several Jewish artists, notably Joshua and John Canter (sons of Jacob and Rebecca De La Motta Canter), Theodore Sidney Moïse, and Solomon Nunes Carvalho.

Joshua Canter (1767–1826) arrived in Charleston in 1788 from Copenhagen and offered to paint "likenesses from life, designs from fancy or copies [from] nature," and to "teach a few scholars the art of Painting of all its various branches, after academical stile." Among his students was the young Isaac Harby, who, when

CATALOGUE 10 AND 11.

Louis Mann and Mrs. Louis Mann, both attributed to Solomon N. Carvalho (1815–1894), 1865. Collection of Mrs. William Mann Price.

Mr. and Mrs. Louis Mann of Laurens, South Carolina, had their likenesses painted by Solomon Nunes Carvalho in the summer of 1865, shortly after the Civil War ended. The prosperity suggested in the pair of portraits reflects the Manns' success in a dry-goods business during an era that was devastating to many. Born in Lubeck, Germany, Louis Mann and three brothers settled in Pottsville, Pennsylvania, around 1840. Louis, Simon, and Isidore Mann moved to Laurens, South Carolina, sometime before 1860, when they were listed in the census for the upcountry town.

The pendant portraits have been attributed to Solomon N. Carvalho by his biographer, Joan Sturhahn. Mr. Mann's strong nose and Mrs. Mann's flat chest are among the clues Sturhahn cites as evidence of Carvalho's authorship. Dated "15–8–65," followed by a small "c," the canvases bear the imprint of a Charleston artist supply, Jos. W. Harrison, at he opened a private academy in 1817, engaged Joshua as a drawing master (a genteel education customarily included painting in its curriculum).

Artists and intellectuals, as well as tradesmen, abandoned the city in the economic doldrums of the 1820s. Joshua Canter moved to New York shortly after 1822, the year an alleged slave uprising shook Charleston; his friend Isaac Harby followed in 1828. Both died before the end of the decade and are buried near each other and their friend Cherry Moïse, in Shearith Israel's cemetery on Eleventh Street in New York City.

Born in St. Croix in 1782, John Canter came to Charleston some twelve years after his brother Joshua. Employed in 1806 as a drawing master at the College of

62 Queen Street. Carvalho could have painted the Manns in Charleston, or perhaps simply used canvases he had purchased there.

Louis Mann sports a fashionable goatee and mustache. Nothing is known about Mrs. Mann beyond her image—not even her first name. Her dress's high neck and long sleeves, and her jewelry, including four finger rings, befit her position as a merchant's wife. Plain yet well made, the dress denotes a conservative lifestyle typical of a woman of her time and class.

Charleston, he maintained a studio and a practice as a portrait painter in the city from 1809 until his death in 1823. Both Canters exhibited in the 1822 South Carolina Academy of Fine Arts. Very little of their work is identified at present. It appears that John Canter was the man who challenged Mordecai Manuel Noah to a duel. Noah, a journalist, had come to Charleston from New York on unspecified business in 1812 and stirred up the locals by writing satiric "letters" to the *Charleston Times* commenting on fashion, manners, and politics. The showdown with Canter, in which the artist suffered a serious but not fatal wound, was Noah's ticket into Carolina society.

Theodore Sidney Moïse, son of Hyam Moïse and Cecilia Woolf and nephew of the poet Penina Moïse, was born in Charleston in 1808. His formal artistic training is unknown, but his work clearly favors the academic style of the Canters, with whom he may have studied. The city directory of 1829 lists Moïse as an accountant; in 1835 he is identified as a portrait painter, supplementing his income by cleaning and repairing old pictures and practicing calligraphy. Moïse worked as an itinerant artist, traveling through Georgia, Mississippi, and Kentucky before settling in New Orleans, where he painted his most famous portraits, including those of Henry Clay and Andrew Jackson.

Wide-ranging in the breadth of his artistic endeavors and his travels, Solomon Nunes Carvalho (1815–1894) was an accomplished painter, daguerreotypist, explorer, and inventor. Born in Charleston of Sephardic ancestry, he lived at various times on the island of Barbados in the West Indies, where his family had business interests, and in the East Coast cities of Baltimore, Philadelphia, New York, and Charleston. Carvalho epitomized the mobility of South Carolina's early Sephardic families along the "Atlantic Highway." Kept on the move in pursuit of a livelihood, the painter at one time advertised simultaneously in Baltimore and Philadelphia as a portraitist and photographer.

One of Carvalho's earliest and most powerful works is the interior of Kahal Kadosh Beth Elohim, which he painted from memory after the fire of 1838. Though his father, David Nunes Carvalho, was a leading member of the Reformed Society of Israelites, Solomon remained a religious traditionalist. A close friend and admirer of Philadelphia's Rabbi Isaac Leeser, he was a frequent contributor to Leeser's periodical, *The Occident*. He expressed concerns over the high rate of intermarriage, the weakness of Jewish education, and the increasing contentions between tradition and reform. He endorsed certain modifications in traditional practice, particularly the inclusion of English sermons and hymns in services, but cast his lot with the opponents of reform who established Charleston's Shearit Israel.

Through the 1840s and 1850s Carvalho supported himself as a portrait painter and daguerreotypist. He became known for inventing a transparent enamel to protect the fragile surfaces of daguerreotypes. In 1853 Colonel John C. Frémont recruited him to serve as artist and photographer on an expedition from Westport, Missouri, across the Rocky Mountains to the Pacific. Carvalho narrated the western exploration in a successful 1857 volume, *Incidents of Travel and Adventure in the Far West*. In Salt Lake City and Los Angeles, he continued to paint portraits and landscapes and to practice photography. After 1860, Carvalho settled with his family in New York City, but the itinerant nature of his trade took him up and down the Atlantic coast and as far west as New Orleans, executing portrait commissions and exhibiting his work. His best known sitters were Brigham Young and Abraham Lincoln, whom he admired to the point of hero worship. In the early 1870s he underwent surgery for cataracts; diminished eyesight forced him to stop painting, and he focused his energies on inventions. ✣

> *[Jews] are by no means to be considered as a* Religious sect, *tolerated by the government; they constitute a portion of* the People. *They are, in every respect, woven in and compacted with the citizens of the Republic. Quakers and Catholics; Episcopalians and Presbyterians, Baptists and Jews, all constitute one great political family.*
>
> —Isaac Harby, in a letter to Secretary of State James Monroe, Charleston, 1816

"One Great Political Family"

The historic Jewish dream to live free in a promised land and the British drive to colonize a continent converged in the European settlement of Carolina. Like the Huguenots, the French Protestants whose freedom to worship was revoked in 1685 by Louis XIV, Jews were welcomed to the fledgling province by the entrepreneurial Lords Proprietors. In 1696, Huguenots and Jews in Charles Town jointly petitioned Parliament to protect their rights to trade. They allied again the following year and succeeded in securing citizenship for their coreligionists.

The Jews' confidence in the power of petition and their freedom to make partnerships with gentiles point to a new situation in Jewish history. If the nineteenth century would be a long encounter with emancipation for American Jews, then the eighteenth century was a period of rehearsal. Jews in the southern colonies took small steps toward acquiring equal rights and abrupt steps backward when, for example, their rights to vote and hold office were retracted by individual colonial governments.

Jewish support for American independence emerged as part of the mass support for making a break from Britain. Why should Jews side with the patriots? By and large Jews experienced the same rising standard of living and the same allegiance to Britain as their fellow colonials. They were similarly bound to Europe by ties of family and religion, education and commerce. They knew that Jews in England were more free and influential than anywhere else on earth. Furthermore, their inclusion in the American mainstream was challenged in the aftermath of the Great Awakening of the 1760s—the rebellion against established churches and the conversion to evangelical Christianity that swept the southern colonies. The rhetoric of evangelical leaders contained an implicit threat of Jewish exclusion in the theocratic idea that the colonies were Christian territories.

When push came to shove, however, England was perceived as a greater threat to Jewish business interests than America was to religious freedoms. After 1767 the imposition of duties on goods imported to the colonies cut deeply into the profits of American merchants. Gentiles and Jews raised their voices in protest. Meanwhile, the evangelical fervor of the Great Awakening was channeled into

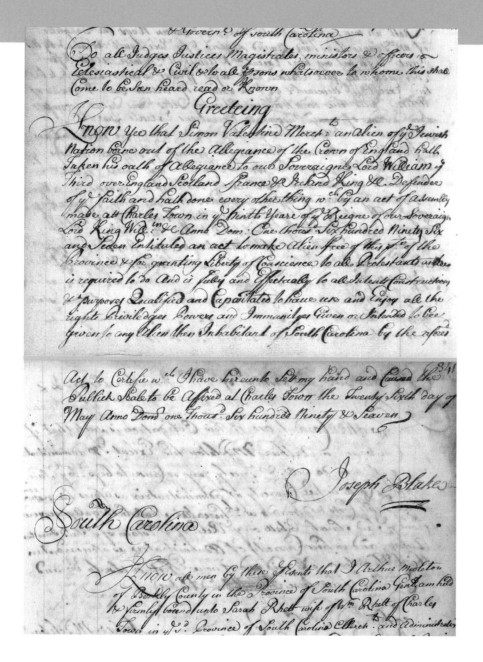

Naturalization of Simon Valentine, Mercht: an alien of the Jewish Nation, May 26, 1697. South Carolina Department of Archives and History.

Simon Valentine was one of four Jewish men who joined sixty Huguenots, or French Protestants, in petitioning Carolina Governor Joseph Blake for citizenship in 1697. Valentine's roots may have been in Vilna, Lithuania, which would have made him the lone Ashkenazi among the four Jews. The governor supported the petition and the colonial assembly granted citizenship to all "aliens," their wives and children, regardless of where they came from. Freedom of conscience and worship was granted to all Christians except Roman Catholics. Though the legislature's wording appeared to exclude Jews, the Jews in practice were grouped with Protestants.

Before coming to Carolina, Valentine had lived in Jamaica and then New York. Well-traveled and thoroughly familiar with the Atlantic mercantile world, his name appears repeatedly in provincial records. In 1682 he pays for his "burgher right" in New York. Two years later he is party to a lawsuit in Albany. In 1696 he signs his name as surety on an administrative bond and records the sale of a slave. In 1698 Abraham Avilah appoints Valentine his "true and lawful attorney." And on July 3, 1701, he is sued for debts owed to Jacob Mears, of Jamaica. Of particular interest, the first documentation of a Jew holding land in Carolina is Valentine's purchase, in partnership with Mordecai Nathan, of a 350-acre plantation, by which the two men met the property qualification for voting. Malcolm Stern, the dean of American Jewish genealogy, calls Valentine South Carolina's first permanent Jewish settler.

politics. The same people who had resisted church authorities became leaders of a revolution that produced unprecedented guarantees of religious freedom.

Though a skeptic himself, revolutionary propagandist Tom Paine appealed to the religious imagination of the Americans. His best-selling pamphlet *Common Sense* is crafted in the form of a secular sermon. Just as the Jews of the Old Testament rejected monarchial government, he wrote, so should Americans—the "chosen people" of the modern world—break free from the British crown.

The majority of Jews cast their lot for independence. Sephardic families, who had been in the New World the longest and were well established in trade, were among the most enthusiastic patriots. The allegiance of the Ashkenazim was more evenly divided, but they too sided chiefly with the Revolution. In the flush of victory, American Jews felt the country owed them a debt; they had earned the right to full equality. A century after allying with the Huguenots for rights of trade and citizenship, Jewish South Carolinians in the post-Revolutionary period forged a strategic alliance with Protestant dissenters intent on disestablishing the Anglican church. Protestant pluralism, not religious liberty, was really the dissenters' goal. The founding fathers went a step further. Influenced by the rational philosophy of the Enlightenment, they insisted upon complete separation of church and state.

"Never before," write historians Jonathan D. Sarna and Jonathan Golden, "had a major nation committed itself so definitively to the principles of freedom and democracy in general and to religious freedom in particular." Charles Pinckney, South Carolina lawyer and delegate to the Constitutional Convention of 1787, introduced a proposition barring religious qualification to any oath for federal office. With Pinckney's approval, the convention amended his proposal to read: "No religious test shall ever be required as a qualification to any office or public trust under the authority of the United States."

During the war, refugees from the occupied port cities of Newport, New York, Savannah, and Charleston swelled Philadelphia's Jewish population to one thousand, or fully half of all American Jews. Undermined by British occupation and the destruction of the waterfront, Newport and Savannah's once-prosperous Jewish commercial classes lost their assets and dispersed. The Jews of Charleston, on the other hand, returned after the war and regrouped, their numbers bolstered by immigrants from Europe and the West Indies, including refugees from the slave rebellion on Santo Domingo. Poised at the brink of technological revolutions in the processing of both the old staple crop of rice and the new staple crop of cotton, South Carolina harbored, for the next thirty years, the largest, wealthiest, and most cultured Jewish community in the nation.

Born the year after the federal Constitution was signed, Charleston intellectual Isaac Harby epitomized his generation's embrace of the new order. No longer would Jews be considered "a religious sect" merely tolerated by the government; rather they comprised, along with other religious groups, "one great political family." These wishful words proclaim the positive legacy of Jewish inclusion in the republic. ❧

CATALOGUE 21.

Sixteenth Degree Prince of Jerusalem Masonic patent, Charleston, S.C., July 20, 1803. Ancient and Accepted Scottish Rite.

The membership of the Masons cut across religion and national origins. Rooted in the artisan guilds of medieval Europe, Freemasonry, though not a secret society, does maintain secrets in regard to obligations, rituals, and modes of recognition. While independent of the tenets of any particular religion, the ancient fraternal order requires belief in God. The Masons' emphasis on brotherhood, charity, and mutual aid appealed to Jews, who in turn were eager to demonstrate social solidarity in any way they could.

One of the first Jewish members of a Charleston lodge was Isaac DaCosta, who joined King Solomon's Lodge No. 1 in 1753 and became its treasurer in 1759. In 1783 he organized the Sublime Grand Lodge of Perfection and, at his death later that year, was deputy inspector-general of Masonry for South Carolina. His successor, Joseph M. Myers, established Charleston's Grand Council of Princes of Jerusalem in 1788. The 1796 minutes of Lodge La Candeur No. 12—kept in French—note twelve Jewish visitors. Several Jewish men, notably David Labat, Israel De Lieben, and Isaac Canter, became officers of Charleston lodges in the eighteenth century.

Of the eleven founders of Charleston's Supreme Council of Scottish Rite Masonry only two were American-born. Men of diverse nationalities, occupations, and religions, they represent a stunning example of assimilation in America's early national period. Four of the founders were Jewish: Emanuel De La Motta, commission merchant and auctioneer, was the Supreme Council's first treasurer general; Abraham Alexander its first secretary general; and merchants Israel De Lieben and Moses Clava Levy its grand inspectors-general. All four

are buried in Kahal Kadosh Beth Elohim's Coming Street Cemetery.

De Lieben and Alexander, the former hazzan of Beth Elohim, were among the signers of this inscribed certificate admitting Thomas Napier as a Prince of Jerusalem, one of the "Sublime Degrees" of Freemasonry. Many basic Masonic symbols are drawn from the stonemason's craft. The triangle symbolizes the supreme being, the compass signifies the circumscription of passions, and the square the need to "square one's actions" by honesty and virtue. The urn on the left with burning incense signifies a pure heart and, on the right, the urn pierced with a sword symbolizes the need to maintain virtue, even when the sacrifice of one's personal desires is required. Masons use the Hebrew dating system and borrow letters from the Hebrew alphabet for symbolic purposes. The letter ה (hey) in the center of the triangle stands for Heredom, a mythical mountain in Scotland. Masonry was so popular in the colonial and early federal periods that its symbols became common decorative motifs; the all-seeing eye, another symbol of the supreme being in Masonic iconography, appears on the American one-dollar bill.

Masons were conspicuous at ceremonies for the laying of cornerstones of synagogues and other important buildings. When construction began on Kahal Kadosh Beth Elohim's first synagogue in September 1792, the eight marble cornerstones were dedicated "by the rules and regulations of the ancient and honorable fraternity of Freemasons." These marble cornerstones are all that remain of the original structure, which burned in the great fire of 1838. When the synagogue was rebuilt in 1840, the cornerstones were set in the vestibule entranceway, where they can be seen today.

CATALOGUE 16.

Grant of arms of the Salvador family, College of Heralds, England, 1745. Special Collections, College of Charleston Library.

Francis Salvador, grandfather of the American patriot by the same name, was a Portuguese Jew who had migrated to England from Amsterdam early in the eighteenth century. His father, Joseph Salvador, had previously secured the right to a coat of arms, perhaps in Portugal or the Netherlands. Once in England, Francis applied for official recognition of the coat of arms he inherited. The document issued by the College of Heralds, while not a patent of nobility, permitted him to call himself "gentleman."

This gray, water-stained parchment, damaged during the South Carolina Inter-State and West Indian Exposition of 1901–1902, can no longer be read; its margins, however, remain remarkably bright with the colors of heraldic devices, canopies, and crowns. Four escutcheons appear on the manuscript. The smallest, in the top margin, is the royal arms of England. The largest, in upper left, is the coat of arms of the Salvador family: "Vert, a Lyon Rampant, between three Flowers de Lys Or." While it is not known who carried the "warrant" to Carolina, it is reasonable to suppose it was a highly prized family possession.

Francis Salvador had two sons, Jacob and Joseph. Jacob's oldest son, Francis, was a child of two when his father died. Born in London in 1747, the younger Francis married his first cousin Sarah, whose father, Joseph, had bought 100,000 acres, known henceforth as the "Jew's Land," in the Carolina Piedmont in 1755. The same year Joseph Salvador acquired a stake in the New World, a devastating earthquake destroyed the family's holdings in Lisbon. The failure of the East India Company further depleted their assets.

THE SALVADOR GRANT OF ARMS FROM THE HERALDS' COLLEGE, LONDON

Original in the possession of the College of Charleston. Irreparably damaged by water during the South Carolina Inter-State and West Indian Exposition in 1902, after the photo was taken from which this plate was made

Late in 1773, young Francis set sail for Charleston, with the intention of recouping the family fortune by planting indigo on seven thousand acres purchased from his uncle. Swept up in the excitement leading to the American Revolution, he identified at once with the patriot cause. In December 1774, at age twenty-seven, he was elected to the First Provincial Congress of South Carolina as one of ten deputies from Ninety Six, the colony's second most populous district, thus becoming the first professing Jew in America to represent the people in a legislative assembly.

He is also the first Jew known to have died in the Revolution. Before daylight on August 1, 1776, his militia troop was ambushed by Indians and Tories hidden behind a split-rail fence near the town of Seneca. Salvador was wounded three times and scalped. According to an eyewitness account, he remained conscious long enough to ask whether his unit had achieved victory, shake hands with the commander, and bid him farewell.

FIGURE 20. *Captain Abraham Mendes Seixas (1750–1799), artist unknown, ca. 1795. Courtesy of the New-York Historical Society.*

New York-born, Abraham Mendes Seixas came to Charleston in June 1774 and fought in the Revolutionary War. His brother, Gershom Mendes Seixas, was the leader of America's first Jewish congregation, New York's Shearith Israel. In 1777, Abraham married Richea, or "Ritcey," Hart, daughter of Joshua Hart. Their marriage notice was the first for a Jewish couple to be published in the Charleston press. It describes her as "a young lady of the most amiable quali-fications." With Philip Minis and Mordecai Sheftall serving as trustees, Seixas agreed to pro-vide his bride with 3,500 pounds, two slaves, and several articles of silver and furniture. The marriage may have been an example of a union between Portuguese and German Jews which, according to Beth Elohim's Rabbi Barnett Elzas, was "by no means uncommon in South Caro-lina in the early days."

Abraham Seixas was the lone Jewish officer in the ranks of the South Carolina patriots. Cap-tain of a Charleston militia company, he fought as a lieutenant of the Continental Line in Geor-gia. Banished from occupied Charleston for refusing to sign an oath of loyalty to the British crown, he settled in Philadelphia in May 1782. There he is listed as one of ten Charleston Jews among the founders of Mikveh Israel, the fifth Sephardic synagogue established in America.

Seixas returned to Charleston when the war ended and made a living as a vendue master, or auctioneer. The city directories alternately describe him as a merchant, tallow chandler (candle supplier), or broker. An advertisement in the South-Carolina State Gazette in 1794 describes the wide variety of goods he handled: Negro slaves, both men and women; land "all o'er the State"; and any articles "of beaux and belles" consigned to him to sell. At the time of his death in April 1799, he was city magistrate, warden of the workhouse, and president and trustee of Kahal Kadosh Beth Elohim.

His son noted in his father's prayer book that Abraham died after an illness of four days. His corpse was taken from the house and "carried to the snogar" (snoga is Portuguese for synagogue). "A greater Number of People never was seen at a Funeral in Charleston before among our Pro-fession."

The oil painting of Captain Seixas, unsigned and undated, pictures him in a patriot's blue coat with the fringed epaulets of an officer, a white waistcoat and white breeches. Holding his sword on his left hip, his round face and portly figure suggest the passage of time. The painting itself has disappeared, preserved only in the pho-tographic plate made by Barnett A. Elzas for his 1905 publication, The Jews of South Carolina.

ABRAHAM SEIXAS
All so gracious,
Once again does offer
His service pure
For to secure
Money in the coffer.

He has for sale
Some negroes, male,
Will suit full well grooms,
He has likewise
Some of their wives
Can make clean, dirty rooms.

For planting, too,
He has a few
To sell, all for the cash,
Of various price,
To work the rice
Or bring them to the lash.

The young ones true,
If that will do,
May some be had of him
To learn your trade
They may be made
Or bring them to your trim.

The boatman great,
Will you elate
They are so brisk and free;
What e'er you say,
They will obey,
If you buy them of me.

Excerpt from an advertisement in *The South-Carolina State Gazette,* Charleston, September 6, 1794.

CATALOGUE 17.

Mordecai Cohen (1763–1848), by
Theodore Sidney Moïse, ca. 1830.
Carolina Art Association/Gibbes
Museum of Art, Charleston, S.C.

Born in Zamosc, Poland, Mordecai Cohen
began life in the New World as a peddler. Rising to shopkeeper, merchant, and planter, he
became one of the wealthiest men in South
Carolina. In 1795 he married Leah Lazarus,
eldest daughter in a prominent Sephardic family (see Catalogue 34, p. 67). Sixteen years later
the couple purchased a grand three-and-a-half
story brick single house on Broad Street, now
the offices of the Roman Catholic Diocese of
Charleston. Cohen amassed extensive holdings
of real estate in and around the city, in the
upstate, and in North Carolina. In addition, he
owned a plantation on the Ashley River; his
sons Marx E. Cohen and David Daniel Cohen
owned estates nearby. During his sixty years
in Charleston, Mordecai served as commissioner of the Poor House (1811–18) and of the
Charleston Orphan House (1838–44); commissioner of markets (1826–32); and director
of the Wilmington and Raleigh Railroad
(1836). When Lafayette visited the city in
1825, the gold plate and silver used at the
banquet in his honor were borrowed from
Mordecai Cohen.

CATALOGUE 18.

Nathan Nathans (1782–1854), by N. F. Wales, 1814. Collection of Judith Tobias Siegel.

Born in England, Nathan Nathans moved to South Carolina before his twentieth birthday. He became a successful merchant and planter, and served as president of Beth Elohim. He left the congregation with the seceders in the 1840s and joined Shearit Israel. In the 1850 census, his household included five other males: Levy Nathans (27), a merchant; David (22), Alexander (18), and Simon (15), clerks; and Jacob (12), too young to work. At the time of his death, Nathan Nathans's estate included eighteen buildings in Charleston.

CATALOGUE 25–28.

Isaac Harby's *Gordian Knot, or Causes and Effects* (1810), *Alberti* (1829), Academy cashbook (1819–1820), and prayer book manuscript (1825). Temple Sinai Archives (plays and prayer book) and collection of Anita Moïse Rosefield Rosenberg (cashbook).

Born in Charleston in 1788, the oldest of seven children, Isaac Harby won respect during his lifetime as an intellectual and political thinker. He is best known today as a pioneer of Reform Judaism. His father, Solomon Harby, had emigrated from England to Jamaica in 1778, at age sixteen, and from there to Charleston after the British pulled out in 1781. He may have come to Carolina to visit his relative, Myer Moses, whose daughter Rebecca he married in 1787. Soon after Isaac's birth the family moved to Georgetown, where Solomon worked as a butcher. Early in 1795 the Harbys returned to Charleston; by 1801 Solomon was an auctioneer and co-owner of a schooner. He died in 1805, leaving Isaac, not yet seventeen, as head of the family.

Harby already had a penchant for writing. In October 1807, he launched *The Quiver*, his first venture in print and likely the first literary magazine published by a Jewish American. The weekly, sixteen-page journal featured poetry, humor, letters to the editor, and Harby's dramatic criticism. It survived for only twelve issues, but its three-month run provided Harby with a bully pulpit to champion the cause of an original American literature and theater.

Harby wrote his first play, *Alexander Severus*, about the same time he was planning *The Quiver*. Apprenticed in a law office, he completed the script "between the drudgery of an attorney's office, and the time allotted to repast and rest," but the manager of the Charleston Theatre declined to produce it. (No copy is known to exist.) Harby struggled to mount his

Let us take a rapid glance at the history of our people since the destruction of the temple, and view the contrast the Jews of the United States now exhibit in opposition to the Jews of Europe—the contrast between a once powerful people, scattered by the Almighty's anger, and bowed in the dust, and humiliated into ignorance, by the petty tyrants of the earth—and the freeborn Jew, the citizen of these enlightened States, raising once more the brow of manhood and proud equality!

—Isaac Harby's *A Discourse . . . before the Reformed Society of Israelites*, delivered on their first anniversary, November 21, 1825, Charleston

second play, *The Gordian Knot*, on the stage. A highly derivative adaptation, the romantic melodrama was the first play written by a Jewish American performed in America. Its debut in April 1810 was something of a fiasco. Playing in front of a sparse audience, the actors botched their lines and mangled the characters. Harby was furious. He tried to rework the play, incorporating three musical numbers into it. Still, a second performance in May fell short of his hopes.

Struggling to make a living, Isaac Harby opened a private academy in Charleston on January 3, 1810, offering instruction in reading, writing, grammar, rhetoric, arithmetic, history, geography, and the Latin and Greek classics.

By the end of July, the academy had enrolled more than fifty pupils, male and female, Christian and Jew. "His love of knowledge was extravagant," friends of Harby recalled. "He might be said almost to devour books." Harby's educational philosophy was Socratic. He believed that teachers should arouse students' instinctive curiosity rather than focus on their deficiencies. "No!" Harby scrawled in margins of Dugald Stewart's *Elements of the Philosophy of the Human Mind*. "Develop & cherish those that are strong and peculiar. Bring nature out."

For three years Harby enjoyed a small measure of economic and emotional stability. Soon after opening his academy, he married Rachael

Mordecai (1782–1827), daughter of Samuel Mordecai of Savannah. His school thrived, moving into new quarters in 1813. The next year, however, Harby's ambitions for a broader audience got the better of him. He purchased a press from Dr. John Mackey, editor of the *Charleston Investigator*, and for several months edited the paper. In July 1814 he changed its name to the *Southern Patriot and Commercial Advertiser* and proclaimed the inaugural issue of a "new" paper.

The venture proved unprofitable, and three years later Harby sold the *Southern Patriot* to his business partner, Colonel Robert Howard. Harby announced his intention to reopen his academy in "Cardozo's Long Room" at

FIGURE 21. The Quiver, *published by Isaac Harby, Charleston, S.C., 1807. Courtesy of the South Caroliniana Library, University of South Carolina.*

47 Tradd Street. His staff would include a full-time assistant and "masters" to teach special subjects, including as drawing master Joshua Canter. By 1819 Harby's academy had about ninety students—sixty-six of whom were Jewish. His pupils included the children of close friends and family, sons and daughters of Charleston's social aristocracy, and a number of indigent youngsters sponsored by the Hebrew Orphan Society. Between January 1819 and May 1820, Harby took in $1,425 in tuition, mainly in cash but also in barter—paper goods, cologne, hats, fine linen.

The academy's initial success allowed Harby more time to write. *Alberti*, his third and last play, opened to public acclaim at the Charleston Theatre on April 27, 1819. A historical romance set in Florence, Italy, the play appealed to audiences on this side of the Atlantic with its themes of liberty and patriotism, wrapped in a twisted tale of mistaken identity. Three nights after the debut, President James Monroe, visiting Charleston, attended its second performance—three years after Harby had written then Secretary of State Monroe his "portion of the people" protest. In the preface to the published edition of *Alberti*, Harby responded to a foreign critic who sardonically called the work a commendable effort for an "American production." "I plead guilty," Harby replied, taking pride in "the accident of birth, which has placed me under the protection of laws that I revere, and in the bosom of a country that I love."

Up to this moment nothing in Harby's career or accomplishments anticipates the bold steps he would take in the cause of reforming Judaism. Late in 1824 he and forty-six other Jewish men signed a petition, addressed to the *adjunta*, or governing council, of Beth Elohim, requesting changes that would make the service shorter, more comprehensible, more decorous, and more in tune with the times. The Judaism of their fathers felt alien and narrow; it could be appreciated as an historical response to centuries of oppression in foreign lands. But now Jews were at home, at the start of a new history in which the challenge to the people and the faith came not from despotism and persecution but from their opposite. "Survival under freedom," historian Jeffrey Gurock notes, "is the fundamental theme underlying Jewish life in the early national period."

Dismissed by the governing council on the technicality that they had failed to follow the provisions of the synagogue's 1820 constitution for addressing their complaint, the petitioners established "The Reformed Society of Israelites" and continued to press their case. In less than two years, having despaired of effecting reform from within, the dissenters decided to build their own house of worship, using their own liturgy. The sanctuary was never built, however, and money raised for its construction was returned with interest.

Three close friends, Isaac Harby, David Nunes Carvalho (1784–1860), and Abraham Moïse Jr. (1799–1869), collaborated in developing the first reform prayer book in America. All three kept their own manuscripts, from which Moïse compiled, edited, and published *The Sabbath Service and Miscellaneous Prayers, Adopted by the Reformed Society of Israelites* in 1830. Two versions of Harby's text have survived, one apparently composed for his youngest sister Caroline de Litchfield Harby. Written in English and Hebrew and illustrated with decorative symbols similar to those found on Masonic documents, Harby's short, simple services exemplify the reformer's creed. Consisting of translations and paraphrases of passages from the old ritual and some original verses, it includes a prayer for the Sabbath written by Caroline. When Harby's wife died in 1827, Caroline accompanied him to New York, cared for his children, and helped him run a school on Howard Street. She became "little mother" to his six orphans when Isaac Harby succumbed to typhoid fever on Sunday, December 14, 1828, just five weeks after his fortieth birthday.

Jewish women could be found behind the counter far more often than on the pedestal.

—James W. Hagy, *This Happy Land: The Jews of Colonial and Antebellum Charleston*, 1993

Women's Work

Working in their husbands' shops and sharing in the endeavors of making a living did not exempt Jewish women from having to perform the tasks required of all women: preparing and preserving foods, making daily meals, washing, sewing, and mending, cleaning the house and attending to the children. Lines written by Frances Sheftall to her husband Mordecai Sheftall on March 3, 1780, reveal a competent and confident partner, conversant with commerce: "I had like to forgot to mention to you that I have received the 2 thousand pounds of Mr. Cape, with which I make exceeding well out by doing a little business."

Four months later, Frances found herself "obliged to take in needle worke to make a living for my family." True, it was a stressful time. Mrs. Sheftall had taken refuge in Charleston during the British assault on Savannah. Now the city was under siege and her "Negroes have every one been at the point of death," stricken by yellow fever and small pox, hence they were "of no use" to her.

From the first days of the colony, free white women normally had servants to assist them. In colonial times, the servants might be enslaved blacks or indentured whites. By the time of independence, slaves were the rule. Regardless of the servants' status, they were people who required food, clothing, and shelter. Training, supervising, and providing for the "help" were jobs which fell to women. The management role of the southern mistresses was not always appreciated outside of the South. Philadelphia educator and social activist Rebecca Gratz wrote to her sister-in-law Maria Gist Gratz in Kentucky on November 11, 1820, "One of the curses of slavery is the entire dependence the poor mistress is reduced to when she is rich enough to have all her wants supplied by numerous servants."

Under South Carolina law, a married woman was a *feme covert*, that is, "covered" by her husband, which meant she could not act legally in her own name and had no property rights except to a dower. For a married woman to conduct business independently, she had to be granted the status of "sole trader" by her husband; this permitted her to own a business, keep the profits, write a will, and, most important, to avoid liability for her husband's debts. In several documented instances a woman was given the rights of a *feme sole*, or single woman, so that property owned by her husband might be transferred to her and removed from the reach of the law. For example, in 1823 Isaac Harby sold all his worldly goods to his younger brother, Henry Jefferson Harby, for one dollar, to hold in trust for Isaac's wife, Rachael, and gave her power over their property "without the intervention, intermedling or controul" of her husband or anyone else.

Philip Benjamin, father of future Confederate statesman Judah P. Benjamin, also found himself in financial straits during the protracted economic recession of the 1820s. Besieged by his creditors, he granted his wife Rebecca DeMendes

Benjamin the status of a sole trader in July 1827. Immediately court actions against him stopped.

Ann Huguenin Alexander, second wife of Abraham Alexander Sr., was a sole trader, very likely operating Alexander's shop while he worked at the custom house. Whether or not she had been designated a sole trader, Rebecca Isaiah Moses had her own listing in the Charleston directory of 1837–1838 under the entry, "Moses, R. I., dry goods." Her daybook indicates she continued to keep accounts for the family, at least until 1863. Her daughter Hannah A. Moses Abrahams shows up in the 1835 directory as a dry-goods merchant, in the 1840 census as head of the household, and between 1845 and 1854 her name appears on a number of transactions involving slaves.

Nuptial documents might secure a woman's rights to property despite her married status. Fanny and Phebe Yates, two sisters from a wealthy family in Liverpool, both married Jewish men from South Carolina. The story of their courtships is unusual. In 1817, Jacob Clavius Levy and Joshua Lazarus traveled to Europe to

LEFT TO RIGHT:
Phebe Yates Lazarus (1794–1870), Joshua Lazarus (1796–1861), and Emma Lazarus (1798–1865), all by Amélie Dautel D'Aubigny, France, ca. 1840. Carolina Art Association/Gibbes Museum of Art, Charleston, S.C.

In October 1835, Phebe Yates of Liverpool married Joshua Lazarus, two years her junior, and sailed with him to Charleston. Some time after the wedding, the couple traveled with Joshua's sister Emma on an extended tour of Europe, where the French artist, Amélie Dautel D'Aubigny, painted their portraits. The wife of the painter Pierre D'Aubigny, Amélie studied with Louis-François Aubry. She excelled in miniature portraits and exhibited at the Paris Salon from 1831 to 1844, where the Lazaruses possibly saw her work. In these finely detailed portraits, Phebe and Emma wear identical décolleté gowns, with their hair drawn up in braids and ringlets. The costumes may have been provided by the artist, or painted after the sitting.

Joshua Lazarus, president of Charleston's Gas Light Company from 1840 to 1856, was instrumental in bringing gas illumination to the city. A man of wealth and property, Lazarus owned twenty pieces of real estate in Charleston and served as the president of the bank in Cheraw. When Beth Elohim's new synagogue was dedicated in 1841, Lazarus, chairman of the building committee, presented the congregation with a silver basket (see Catalogue 83, page 46) likely purchased on one of his trips to England. He became president of the congregation in 1851 and served until his death in Cheraw, South Carolina, in 1861. Emma never married. She died in Sumter in August 1865.

study. The friends both fell in love with Fanny, the seventh and youngest daughter of Samuel Yates. In deference to Levy, Lazarus withdrew his attentions. Fanny and Jacob were married in Liverpool, then returned to live in South Carolina where, according to family lore, "at her first appearance in the dress circle of the Charleston Theatre in Broad Street, the whole house rose in tribute to her matchless beauty."

Almost twenty years later, Joshua Lazarus married Fanny's then forty-one-year-old sister Phebe. Their only child, Edgar Marks, was born two years afterward. A postnuptial agreement, signed in April 1836, put into effect the terms of the antenuptial contract signed the previous October, by which the groom paid $10,000 in trust for Phebe or her children and provided that "notwithstanding her coveture," the bride could name her own trustees or could act for herself. One of the trustees was Joshua's nephew Philip Phillips, who soon would marry Phebe's niece Eugenia Levy. The other trustee was Joshua's younger brother Benjamin Dores Lazarus.

In Pursuit of Gentility

Along with political inclusion came the prospect of acculturation. In physical appearance, dress, and language, Carolina's early Jews were indistinguishable from other Europeans. They shared power and privilege, and they were motivated by the same economic traditions. Free to mingle with their Christian neighbors and unrestrained by rabbinical authority, Jews moved easily in society and married into it, too. Could their ancient faith, used to coping with persecution, survive so much freedom?

Aspiring to higher status, Jewish men and women sought the same marks of social standing that gentiles were seeking. In a twist on the concept of "gentility," many Ashkenazim, who by the time of the American Revolution outnumbered Sephardim in South Carolina, adopted traditional Sephardic practices, called themselves Sephardi, and assumed an aristocratic view of themselves as "earliest-to-arrive."

There were in effect two social ladders, one that German Jewish families might climb to reach the more elite status of Iberian Jews. The second—intermarriage—led out of Judaism altogether. Apparently members of the smaller Jewish community of Savannah more readily ascended to the upper rungs of Protestant society than did Jews in Charleston. When Jacob Levy and his wife, Fanny Yates, moved to Savannah, for example, their single daughters, who in Charleston had been sought for marriage by the "most polished & wealthy young Israelites," were courted by distinguished gentiles and "were all lost to Judaism." In a family history written in 1901, Lucien Wolf contrasts the openness of Savannah's "refined society" to Charleston's "narrow-minded bigotry." In Charleston, Wolf reports, "the higher circles were closed to Jews, while in Savannah, the Minis, Cohen & the Myers families were not only an important part of the best society, but were its acknowledged leaders."

Since the founding of Carolina, no laws have prohibited Jews and Christians from marrying each other. Cultural taboos on the Christian side were relatively weak, while strong personal and commercial ties between Jews and Christians provided motives and opportunities for marrying across religious lines. Especially among elites, intermarriage was a temptation and outright assimilation a possibility. Even the households of congregational leaders were not immune to the threat. Some Jews who chose Christian mates remained Jews, and some Christians converted to the religion of their spouses, yet more than 85 percent of Jews who married Christians before 1840 left the Jewish fold. (At the dawn of the twenty-first century, estimates of the rate at which American Jews are marrying out of their faith range from 41 to 52 percent—up from 3 percent in 1940 and 11 percent in the late 1960s. Compared to the nineteenth century, however, conversion today is more of a two-way street.)

The fate of Ann Sarah Huguenin Irby Alexander suggests that American freedom of conscience and Carolina's cosmopolitanism had not blunted fidelity to Halahkah, or Jewish law. A widow of French Protestant background, she converted to Judaism when she married Abraham Alexander, the Torah reader at Beth Elohim, lived a strictly observant life, and asked to be buried in Kahal Kadosh Beth Elohim's cemetery. Her request was denied, however, because an error had allegedly occurred in her conversion ceremony.

For a people to whom death has great finality, maintaining the purity of the burial ground has been a unifying obsession. David Lopez, builder of the Greek Revival–style temple which replaced Beth Elohim's original synagogue after the fire of 1838, married a Christian woman who never went through conversion. When she died in 1843, Lopez bought his own plot of land next to the burial ground belonging to Shearit Israel, the congregation of Orthodox seceders from Beth Elohim, and there he buried twenty-nine-year-old Catherine Lopez and their infant son.

Columbia's Jewish community apparently suffered a schism over the Burial Society's decision to inter the Christian wife of physician and educator Elias Marks in the Jewish cemetery. Jane Barham Marks died in 1827 and was buried in the graveyard proper. It seems that people afterwards put some distance between her grave and the new ground where they began burying the dead. The older site came to be called "*die geschmadte Beth Haim*," or "the cemetery where converts to Christianity were buried." Elias Marks, founder of a secondary school for women, the South Carolina Female Institute, married another gentile woman and left the faith. ❧

This Happy Land

CHAPTER TWO

Old World Orthodoxy

In 1749 Charleston's Jewish community began meeting formally, taking the name Kahal Kadosh Beth Elohim, Holy Congregation of the House of God. Like congregations in London and Amsterdam, Beth Elohim followed the Sephardic *minhag* (liturgy) of the Spanish-Portuguese Jews. The congregation was strict in its adherence to oral and written law. Violations of the Sabbath or religious holidays were treated with severity. A member who conducted business on a Saturday could be expelled from the synagogue.

By 1764 Beth Elohim had occupied three different meeting houses, each more substantial than the next. Evidence of early tensions between "Portuguese" and "German" Jews points more to cultural differences than to disputes over doctrine. For a time the two groups maintained separate burial grounds and may have worshiped separately. In 1790, the Jews of Charleston put aside their differences and united to support the new state constitution with its guarantees of religious freedom. The following year, when Beth Elohim petitioned for incorporation, the men who signed the document were equally split between Sephardim and Ashkenazim, and all appear to have been born abroad.

It appears that the size of Charleston's Jewish population, rather than its minhag, attracted Jews who were looking for Jewishness. Writing from Petersburg, Virginia, to her parents in Hamburg, Germany, in 1791, Rebecca Samuel expressed an intense desire to settle in Charleston after Passover. "The whole reason why we are leaving this place is because of [lack of] *Yehudishkeit* [Jewishness]," while in Charleston "there is a blessed community of three hundred Jews."

In her assessment of Petersburg as a place for Jews, however, Samuel seems to have been of two minds. "One can make a good living here, and all live at peace. Anyone can do what he wants. There is no rabbi in all of America to excommunicate anyone. This is a blessing here; Jew and Gentile are as one," she noted. On the other hand, Samuel hated the thought of bringing up her children like gentiles: "Here they cannot become anything else. Jewishness is pushed aside here." Petersburg's ten or twelve Jews were "not worthy of being called jews," she claimed. The shohet bought *treyf* meat (that is, the ritual slaughterer bought nonkosher animals). The community had no Torah; no one wore a tallit, or prayer shawl. "We do not know what the Sabbath and the holidays are. On the Sabbath all the Jewish shops are open, except the Samuels'. With us there is still some Sabbath," she demurred. "You must believe me that in our house we all live as Jews as much as we can." ❧

CATALOGUE 66.

Kahal Kadosh Beth Elohim interior, by Solomon N. Carvalho, 1838. Kahal Kadosh Beth Elohim.

Solomon N. Carvalho painted from memory this haunting interior of the synagogue he attended as a child in Charleston, shortly after fire destroyed the sanctuary in 1838. The twenty-three-year-old Carvalho provides a detailed rendering of the 1794 building, with its Gothic windows and traditional Sephardic arrangement of central bimah, or reader's platform, and balconies. The muted tones of the empty interior and the ethereal light pouring through high windows capture a mood of sanctity and loss.

CATALOGUE 68.

Charity box with hinged cover, inscribed in English "This Almsboxe belongeth to the Synagoge of Kahal Kadosh of Charleston in South Carolina," dated 1820 in Hebrew letters, United States, early 19th century. Collection of Michael Jesselson.

On the front of this silver-plated charity box is a gilded cartouche pierced and chased, with two rampant lions, each standing on a scrolled branch, flanking a menorah. "Charity delivers

from death" is inscribed in Hebrew above the cartouche, "A gift in secret pacifieth anger" (Prov. 21:14), below. The sides are each ornamented with a lion's mask with ring handle. The tapering rectangular box has a coin slot and key and sits on four ball supports.

CATALOGUE 86.

Hebrew Benevolent Society seal, by Faith Murray, Charleston, S.C., 1967. Kahal Kadosh Beth Elohim.

Modeled on the benevolent societies of London and Amsterdam, the Hebrew Benevolent Society of Beth Elohim, in Charleston, was founded in 1784 to minister to the sick and bury the dead. The image on the society's seal depicts the Angel of Death holding a scythe in the right hand and an hourglass in the outstretched bony fingers of the left. Engraved in Hebrew is the society's original name, Hebra Gemilut Hasadim (Society for Deeds of Loving Kindness), and its motto, taken from Proverbs 10:2, "Tzadakah Tatzil Mi-Mavet" (Charity delivers from death).

The society first operated as an arm of Congregation Beth Elohim. In 1830, it was incorporated as an independent charitable organization. Besides caring for the needy and

This synagogue is our temple, this city our Jerusalem, this happy land our Palestine, and as our fathers defended with their lives that temple, that city, and that land, so will our sons defend this temple, this city, and this land.

—Rev. Gustavus Poznanski, dedicatory speech at the consecration of the new Kahal Kadosh Beth Elohim, Charleston, March 1841. (Poznanski's son, Gustavus Poznanski Jr., was killed defending his homeland in the Battle of Secessionville on James Island, South Carolina, on June 21, 1862. He was nineteen years old.)

The Birth of Reform

The struggle for reform that began in Charleston in the 1820s was led by young, American-born Jews who had grown up in a climate of tolerance and who wished to emulate the Sunday decorum of their Protestant neighbors. "Americans to the core," in the words of Isaac M. Wise, Jewish Carolinians played a leading role in Americanizing the religion carried here from Europe.

Change was shaped by a people who had exchanged communal self-government for full national citizenship. No towns or cities were barred to Jews. No occupations were restricted. No quotas limited Jewish enrollment in schools. No political office was out of reach, no civic service subjected to the test of religion.

The reformers may have been encouraged in their revolt by the conflict raging across the street at Saint Mary's Catholic Church. Charleston Catholics had

FIGURE 22. *Kahal Kadosh Beth Elohim exterior, Charleston, S.C., ca. 1950. Photograph by Max Furchgott. Courtesy of the Jewish Heritage Collection, College of Charleston Library.*

CATALOGUE 86 CONTINUED

providing material and spiritual assistance to immigrants, the society helped integrate its members into the southern mainstream. In a gesture of civic solidarity, the Hebrew Benevolent Society, along with the Hebrew Orphan Society, marched in the funeral parade of John C. Calhoun in 1850. The full name of the Orphan Society—Abi Yetomin Ubnei Ebyonium, in Hebrew—was "Society for the Relief of Orphans and Children of Indigent Parents." Dating to 1801, when twenty-three Jewish men of varied origin and occupation petitioned the state for a charter, the Orphan Society is the oldest incorporated Jewish charitable organization in America still in existence.

The Hebrew Benevolent Society seal was painted by Faith Murray in 1967. It was commissioned by Thomas J. Tobias, past president of the society and author of a history of the organization that was published in 1965.

challenged the Catholic Church's system for selecting bishops and requested a veto over episcopal appointments. The Unitarians, meanwhile, had denounced all ecclesiastical authority and embraced a deistic theology. Though there is no documentary evidence to support the theory that Harby and the reformers were directly influenced by insurgence in the Christian churches, a spirit of rebellion was in the air. What can be said with certainty is that the Jewish reformers were inspired by the movements for reformation underway in Germany, Prussia, and Holland.

Seeking to modernize Judaism was not the same as aspiring to be Protestant. Reform leaders envisioned a faith true to its essential teachings but compatible with the secular ethic to which, as Americans, they subscribed. They wanted to introduce certain "alterations" into the service, such as shorter ceremonies, a sermon preached on the Sabbath, a more dignified system of offerings, and the use of English in place of Spanish, the "language of a people from whom we have suffered and continue to suffer so much persecution."

The appeal drafted by the Reformed Society of Israelites and presented to the governing council of Beth Elohim in 1824 failed to win approval. The reformers, who on average were half the age of the synagogue elders, withdrew for eight years and worshiped separately. But their day came in 1840 when, with the blessing of the popular minister Gustavus Poznanski, a petition to install an organ in Kahal Kadosh Beth Elohim's new building was adopted by a narrow margin. The traditionalists seceded and formed a second congregation, Shearit Israel (Remnant of Israel), with its own burying ground adjacent to Beth Elohim's Coming Street cemetery. A brick wall was erected between the graveyards, separating the dead of the two congregations.

The question of which faction had exclusive rights to the use of the synagogue went to court in 1843. A jury decided for the reformers and the traditionalists appealed, unsuccessfully. The seceders contended that they had never really left, but the court noted they had stopped paying dues and relinquished their membership. The court refused to tackle the doctrinal dispute, saying that it was up to congregations to resolve issues of religious principle. In retrospect, while the issue of using an organ during services had split the congregation, it was the proposal not to observe the second day of holy days that broke the camel's back and hardened the devout against the cause of reform. ❧

Time fleets—the child, to manhood reared, has left his proud abode,
And royalty's bold protegé has broken Egypt's rod.
The oracle of Israel has set his nation free!
Then sung melodious Miriam, enlightener of the sea.

—Penina Moïse, from "Miriam," in
The Charleston Book: A Miscellany
in Prose and Verse, 1845

From Sunday Schools to Sisterhoods

The first Jewish Sunday school in the South and the second in the nation was founded in Charleston in 1838 by Sally Lopez (1806–1902). Called "The School of Israel" and administered by "The Society for the Religious Instruction of Jewish Youth," the institution was modeled on the Sabbath school begun by Rebecca Gratz in Philadelphia. The two endeavors were closely allied. Gratz would write out lessons in a copybook and forward them to Charleston every week. Lopez would make copies and distribute them to the teachers.

In 1842, Penina Moïse succeeded Lopez as superintendent. With fifty pupils in four classes, Beth Elohim's Sunday school was one of the largest sectarian schools in the city. In 1855 it held its first confirmation exercises. Five boys and one girl were "confirmed" in a ceremony described in a news account as "a novelty" in Reform Judaism. By 1844, Shearit Israel had set up a Sunday school for the Orthodox conducted by "The Society for the Instruction in Jewish Doctrine." Attendance was less robust than across town. Both schools were interrupted by the Civil War. When Beth Elohim and Shearit Israel patched up their differences in 1866, the Reform Sunday school was revived.

Columbia's pioneer in Jewish education came from outside the state. Boanna Wolff was a young Alabama woman who had lived in Philadelphia and whose family was friendly with Rabbi Isaac Leeser. Leeser was the eminent Orthodox leader who had bitterly opposed the introduction of an organ at Beth Elohim, and who had supported the suit brought to court by seceders from the congregation. Wolff went to Columbia in 1843 to visit her sister Elizabeth, wife of city councilman and later intendant (mayor) Henry Lyons. She stayed and organized the Columbia Israelite Sunday School. She found a site, raised money, secured fuel, furniture, and books, and opened the school with thirty students. In later years, the school was led by Julia Mordecai, Charlotte Levin, Louisa Hart Lyons, and Rachel Barnet.

Jewish Sunday schools were a response to some of the same forces which inspired the Sunday school movement in the Protestant churches that spread from England to America in the early 1800s. A woman's place in society was being redefined in the wake of the American and French revolutions with their radical principles of equality, and with the mustering of female workers into the nascent industrial economy. Southern Jewish women who created and took advantage of chances to work and teach outside of the home benefited indirectly from women in the northern states and England who were making names for themselves speaking out against slavery.

CONTINUED ON PAGE 97

CATALOGUE 88.

"Facts for You and Me," an educational card game used by Penina Moïse, ca. 1867. Kahal Kadosh Beth Elohim.

Daughter of Abraham and Sarah Moïse, Penina Moïse (1797–1880) was one of the first female poets published in America. Her poems appeared in newspapers and journals in Charleston, Boston, and New Orleans. A volume of her poetry, *Fancy's Sketchbook*, is dedicated to "The Misses Pinckney," Maria Henrietta and Harriott, daughters of Charles Cotesworth Pinkney, who were Penina's friends, fellow intellectuals, and perhaps patrons. Penina wrote most of the hymns for Beth Elohim's first hymnal, published in 1842, likely the first hymnal composed for a Jewish congregation in America.

Champion of political and social causes, Moïse wrote fervently of the plight of the Irish during the famine of the 1840s and of religious intolerance in England. After the Civil War, she and her sister Rachel and Rachel's only child, Jacqueline, returned to Charleston from refuge in Sumter and opened a school for girls. Her teaching methods were based on a pedagogy known as "Magnall's Questions." She herself taught advanced reading and gestures in elocution—remarkably, even after she lost her eyesight. Every Friday afternoon her classes played the game "Facts for You and Me," drawn from geography, history, antiquities, and Biblical events. To keep physically and mentally fit, Moïse, who suffered from painful neuralgia, exercised daily by walking around her bed. She would choose a letter from the alphabet and name all the cities, mountains, rivers, historical figures, and literary characters whose names began, say, with A. The next day she would take the letter B and walk a mile around and around the bed until she had exhausted her subject.

Humble to the last, her final words were: "Lay no flowers on my grave. They are for those who live in the sun, and I have always lived in the shadow." Recalling Moïse's fondness for life, joyous philosophy, and ethic of service, her friend Charlotte Adams declared, "Penina was, in the finest sense, the mother of her people."

In some Protestant churches ministers and the women who ran the Sunday schools clashed in a struggle over sacred territory. Clergymen complained that the women taught a watered-down doctrine and used their entrée to the classroom as a lectern for advancing claims for women's rights. In the synagogues of South Carolina, however, activism by women was praised from the altar. Jewish Sunday schools, rabbis believed, would be a bulwark against conversion to Christianity. As thirteen-year-old Rachel Lyons, a graduate of Columbia's Israelite Sunday School, remarked in her 1851 graduation address, "We are but few in this town." Jews needed the contributions of every man, woman, and child to keep their faith from dying on the vine.

The experience of raising and administering funds, of working outside the home and running an organization, gave Jewish women the heady feeling of upholding their faith and their people. Sunday school teachers emphasized the domestic and communal duties of Judaism, in effect training the next generation for leadership roles in the powerful sisterhoods and women's federations that would emerge later in the century. ✺

The Polish Synagogue

As the site of the first Reform congregation in America and the birthplace of secession, South Carolina was a major battlefield in the struggle for Jewish identity in the Old South. For southern Jews in the mid-nineteenth century, the question of allegiance was complicated by the tension in their religion between tradition and reform, and by the emerging conflict in the Union between slave states and free. Nowhere were the issues more acute or the antagonists more self-aware than in the old and new Jewish communities of South Carolina.

As early as 1852, a small group of immigrants from eastern Europe began meeting in Charleston under the leadership of Rabbi Hirsch Zvi Margolis Levine, who himself had recently arrived from Poland. The congregation formally organized in 1855 as Berith Shalome (now Brith Sholom) or "Covenant of Peace"—the first Ashkenazic congregation in South Carolina and one of the first in the South. The next year Berith Shalome bought land for a cemetery north of the city. Within a month its president, Nathan I. Rosenband, was buried there, a victim of yellow fever.

The newer Yiddish-speaking immigrants were uncomfortable with both the Sephardic orientation of Shearit Israel and the Anglicized service of Beth Elohim. With membership primarily from Prussia and Poland, Berith Shalome was known as the "German and Polish" or simply the "Polish" synagogue. Its congregants gave Charleston's Jewish population a more foreign appearance than before. People of modest means, including peddlers, artisans, metalworkers, and bakers, Berith Shalome's forty to fifty members quickly became ardent southerners.

Have the kindness to interest yourself in our behalf, by procuring for us a Kazon, Shoukad, & Mole [hazzan, shohet, & mohel]. One man must do the whole business.

—Morris Ehrlick, president of Berith Shalome, Charleston, to Alexander Oelsner, 1858

CONTINUED ON PAGE 99

CATALOGUE 91.

Rabbi Hirsch Zvi (Margolis) Levine's notebook, Charleston, S.C., 1852. Collection of Carol Kaminsky.

Following his brothers-in-law, Samuel, Moses, and Benjamin Winstock, the first of whom had immigrated to Charleston in the late 1830s, Rabbi Hirsch Zvi Margolis made the transatlantic passage in midlife. Upon his arrival he took the more American-sounding name Levine and at once organized a minyan (a quorum of ten men required to hold a public prayer service). The rabbi kept a small notebook in which he recorded such congregational affairs as the English and Hebrew names of the twenty-six members, and the small amounts,

ranging from 12 cents to $1.50, that they donated at the reading of the Torah.

The record book has been passed down from generation to generation. It includes notes for sermons; material for eulogies; instruction for a shohet; the text of blessings for those called to the Torah; the correct procedures for delivering a get, or bill of divorce, and performing a *halizah*, which excuses a childless widow from the obligation of marrying her husband's brother; and an abstract of a sermon Reb Hirsch Margolis's father delivered on Rosh Hashanah.

Born in 1807, son of Chaim Laib and Soreh Margolis, Levine was one of the first trained and ordained rabbis to come to America. His

notebook demonstrates an excellent command of Hebrew and a high degree of learning. Hirsch Zvi was instructed first by his father, a descendant of a long line of rabbis and learned teachers, including Rabbi Yomtov Lipman Heller (1579–1654), the famous "Tosfos Yomtov," who produced a well-known commentary and other works, and led the Jewish communities of Prague, Vienna, and Krakow. Soon after his marriage the young Margolis attended a Lithuanian yeshivah (school for Talmudic study), received his *semikhah* (ordination), and settled in his wife's hometown of Wirballin.

When Reb Hirsch immigrated to America, he left at home his wife, Esther Rachel Winstock, and several children, two of them

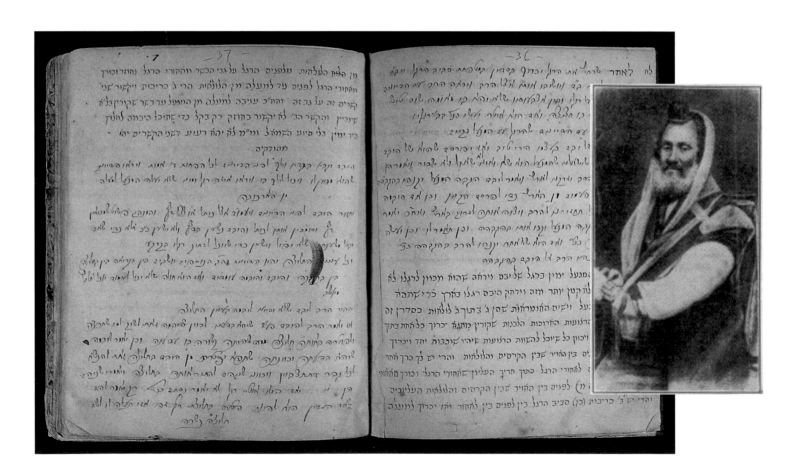

The congregation continued meeting through the Civil War in rented quarters on St. Philip Street, out of range of Union shelling. Congregants Pincus Pinkussohn, Lipman Rich, Jacob Volaski, Simon D. Jacobowski, and others, served in the Confederate army or the home guard.

After the war, Charleston's Beth Elohim and Shearit Israel found themselves too poor and scattered to sustain separate synagogues. The old adversaries agreed to merge. They split the presidency and vice presidency of the congregation, worshiped together in Beth Elohim's Hasell Street sanctuary, and sold Shearit Israel's building on Wentworth Street. The organ had been lost during the war and was not replaced until 1871. Consolidation of the two older congregations left Berith Shalome as the only strictly Orthodox shul in town. By the turn of the century, membership at the "Polish" synagogue, bolstered by Yiddish-speaking immigrants from eastern Europe, had surpassed that of Beth Elohim. ❧

A Polish congregation was organized in Charleston as early as 1857. Though this element of the community now far outnumbers the older element, it has no history, communal or otherwise, worth recording. It has never had a leader and bids fair to continue in its present condition.

—Barnett A. Elzas, rabbi of Kahal Kadosh Beth Elohim, Charleston, 1894–1910, from *The Jews of South Carolina*, 1905

That's hutzpah!

—David J. Radinsky (b. 1940, Seattle, Wash.), rabbi of Brith Sholom Beth Israel, Charleston, 1970–present

---

CATALOGUE 91 CONTINUED

grown with children of their own. He soon sent for Esther and the younger offspring, and met their ship at the dock in the company of Esther's brother Ben. Fourteen-year-old Dora Amelia (Dubra Malkah in Hebrew) was amazed to see the fine clothes and good grooming of her uncle, and to hear his southern speech. After settling briefly in Due West, South Carolina, near Abbeville, where Moses Winstock had moved in 1854 to help his asthma, the Levine family returned to Charleston and Reb Hirsch opened a hoop-skirt factory at 365 King Street.

At age eighteen, Dora Amelia met Harris Levin, a young peddler from Kovno, Russia, and married him in 1859. After the firing on Fort Sumter, they moved to the Confederate capital of Richmond, Virginia, where Dora's uncle, Samuel Winstock, was president of Beth Shalome congregation. Harris enlisted in the home guard; Dora tended the Confederate wounded in a tobacco warehouse turned makeshift hospital at Drewry's Bluff.

After the war, when changing fashions undermined the crinoline business, Reb Hirsch and his wife moved to Baltimore, Maryland. An 1870 city directory lists him as "teacher" and her as "huckstress."

Each year on the eve of Yom Kippur, Reb Hirsch Levin—by this time he had dropped the "e"—gathered his family about him. Garbed in his *kittel*, a white robe worn to symbolize purity on solemn occasions such as the High Holy Days, weddings, and burials, the old man would bless his descendants. One Friday afternoon in November 1887, he was riding home on a horse car and, as dusk approached, became fearful that he might be violating the prohibition against traveling on the Sabbath. He jumped off the vehicle, slipped, and fell under its wheels. Levin lingered several days on his deathbed, praying with his minyan. With his last breath he is said to have obliged a friend who asked, "Reb Hirsch, *kein witz?*" ("What's funny?"), by telling a joke.

Plantation Life

Southern Jews more often than not lived in towns and cities, rather than in the country. Typically they earned their livelihood as shopkeepers, merchants, and tradesmen and women. Most eked out a marginal living at jobs which had low status and high insecurity. Some Jews, however, did acquire the means to buy landed estates. Francis Salvador was developing his family's tract in the Ninety Six District as an indigo plantation with an overseer and thirty slaves, when his life was cut short in 1776 in the infamous ambush at the hands of Tories and Cherokees. Jacob Phillips owned a plantation near the Salvador lands; in the 1790 census he is listed as head of a household, with four males and one female, not in his immediate family. These could have been wage earners or indentured servants. Lizar Joseph's swamplands near Black Mingo Creek, according to family lore, were the staging area for Francis Marion's operations during the War of Independence.

CATALOGUE 92.

Isaiah Moses (1772–1857), by Theodore Sidney Moïse, ca. 1835. Collection of Cecil A. Alexander.

The portrait is undated, but the style of Isaiah Moses's collar and cravat suggests the painting was made in the 1830s, when Theodore Sidney Moïse was in his twenties and Moses about sixty. Father of sixteen children, Isaiah Moses was a religious traditionalist. The sons of his first marriage were among the first Jewish settlers in Cincinnati.

Successful merchants who invested in rural property might maintain their residences in town. Early in the eighteenth century, Simon Valentine and Mordecai Nathan bought a 350-acre plantation, and Nathan acquired a second on his own. A hundred years later, Nathan Nathans, a president of Charleston's Beth Elohim, owned a tract on the Cooper River. Barnet A. Cohen planted cotton, indigo, and provision crops in Barnwell County. At the time of his death, in April 1839, he owned thirty-five Negroes and approximately five hundred acres of land. Charleston city directories and other records list as planters Jacob Barrett, Solomon Cohen, Mordecai Cohen, Marx E. Cohen, David Cohen, Isaac DaCosta, Myer Jacobs, Edward Levy, Isaac Lyons, Samuel Mincks, Isaiah Moses, and Moses Winstock. A somewhat dubious account written in 1884 claims that Jacob Ottolengui of Charleston owned a Savannah River plantation and a thousand slaves. If this is true, Ottolengui would be the only Jewish slaveholder of that scale in the entire South.

CATALOGUE 93.

Rebecca Isaiah Moses, née Phillips (1792–1872), C. W. Uhl, 1843. Collection of Henry A. Alexander Jr.

Rebecca Moses's modest dress is typical of an observant Jewish woman. In the Sephardic tradition, her hair is covered with a transparent lace cap—not the *sheitl* (wig or headdress) worn by married women of eastern European descent. The smocking on the sleeve of her dress demonstrates highly skilled needlework. As a sign of education and refinement, Rebecca is shown reading. The two-column format of the book she is holding suggests a Bible or prayer book. The swatch of crimson upholstery visible at her elbow signifies her well-to-do status. The pearl arrow pin at her neck was passed down in the family and appears again in a twentieth-century portrait of Rebecca's granddaughter, Rebecca Ella Solomons Alexander.

By rice planting standards, the Cohens' Ashley River plantations were under-staffed. Mordecai Cohen worked twenty-seven hands on his estate in St. Andrews Parish. At Clear Springs (a translation of the native Cusabo name of "Tipseeboo" or "Tipboo"), his son Marx E. Cohen employed about twenty-five people on a thousand acres, a modest work force compared to the hundreds and thousands of laborers owned by the Middletons, Heywards, and Balls. Only a portion of Clear Springs was in cultivation. Cohen raised small amounts of rice and corn, and enough potatoes and peas to supply a subsistence for his workers. He kept a variety of livestock, including dairy cattle, sheep, and hogs. His journals, covering the years 1840 to 1868, record purchases of additional bacon and the buying and selling of common and exotic poultry. A more important business at Clear Springs was the manufacture of bricks, which Cohen shipped from his wharf on the river. In May 1853, for example, he sold more than 150,000 hard brown, soft brown, gray, and red bricks. He also sold timber, and his hands were kept busy cutting and hauling oak, loblolly, and yellow pine.

Cohen's journals are rich in the details of ordinary life. Most entries begin with an observation of the weather. What Cohen calls a "Record of Events" is in fact a chronology of slave births and deaths, with a special mention of "lost time" from illnesses and runaways. He regularly records allotments of cloth and shoes and the distribution of food, both of which continue without interruption through the Civil War. His son Marx E. Cohen Jr., a Confederate soldier, was killed at Bentonville in 1865. The elder Cohen moved to Sumter after the war and died there in 1881.

Acquiring a plantation was a step up the social ladder. It also satisfied the property requirement for voting, though owning property in town could suffice. In status-conscious Charleston, tradesmen were looked down upon by the planter aristocracy. "I should think my own father an accomplished knave," remarked a gentile Carolinian in 1818, "if he had at any time made money in the dry-goods line in King Street. They are all Jews and worse than Jews—Yankees, for a Yankee can Jew a Jew directly."

In reality, rural property was often a drain on incomes earned in town. Not only intellectuals like Isaac Harby and tradesmen like Philip Benjamin, but also merchant-planters lived financially precarious lives. If a plantation sank into debt, chances were that the owner could fall back on his urban business. The opposite might also be true: a merchant might sell his country assets to pay his debts in the city.

Isaiah Moses was born near Bremerhaven in the Kingdom of Hanover, on March 18, 1772. Early in the 1790s he moved to England, where he had four sons. Upon his wife's death, sometime before 1800, he came to America with his brother Levi, initially leaving his sons in England. In 1807, at age thirty-five, he married fifteen-year-old Rebecca Phillips. Rebecca had been born in 1792 in the West Indies, possibly on board her father's cargo ship en route to St. Eustatius. Her mother, Hannah Isaacks Phillips, sometimes traveled with her husband, Jacob, to visit family in the West Indies; Hannah herself may have been born in Jamaica, though her parents' main residence was Newport.

For five generations, Rebecca's forebears had lived or sojourned in New York, Newport, Curaçao, London, Martinique, and Jamaica. Her great-grandfather, Abraham Isaacks, an early parnas of Shearith Israel in New York, is buried in the oldest Jewish burying ground in North America. His son, Jacob Isaacks—her grandfather—was a founding member of the famous Touro Synagogue in Newport. Rebecca's grandmother, Hannah Mears Isaacks, was a cousin of Judah Touro's mother. Rebecca's parents moved to a plantation in the South Carolina upcountry, near the vast tract belonging to the Salvador family known as the "Jew's Land." Like Francis Salvador, her father Jacob Phillips served in the militia during the Revolutionary War.

Rebecca, the Phillipses' fourth child, was six years old in 1798 when her mother died in Martinique. After her early marriage, Rebecca lived with Isaiah in Charleston, where he had a store on King Street. The first three of their twelve children were born in Columbia, where Rebecca may have gone to be with family; the rest were born in Charleston.

Between 1801 and 1813 Isaiah progressed from "grocer" to "shopkeeper" to "planter." Seven years after marrying Rebecca, he paid six thousand dollars for 794 acres of land in Goose Creek. The place was called The Oaks, and for twenty-eight years the Moseses cultivated rice there, putting as many as fifty "hands" into the fields to grow the grain known as "Carolina gold." For some if not all of this time, the family kept a house and business in town; in 1837, after more than two decades as mistress of The Oaks, Rebecca Moses was listed in the city directory as running a dry-goods store at 248 King.

Moses used his land for security on several occasions, notably during the Panic of 1837 when he borrowed money from Beth Elohim's charity fund, Karen Kayemet. In 1840 the plantation house burned, and the next year Moses sold the property to C. P. Shier for $3,750—some $2,000 less than he had paid—to satisfy his debt to the congregation. Very possibly some of the enslaved were sold off as well.

Isaiah Moses lived to be eighty-five. When he died in 1857 most of his fortune was tied up in slaves—twenty-one in all, five men, thirteen women, and three small children—valued at eight thousand dollars. Rebecca continued to hire out the workers and to pay taxes on them and on her house on King Street.

For many years Moses sat on the governing board of the synagogue. He vehemently opposed changes in the Sephardic service and, with Abraham Tobias, resisted giving up the Sephardic minhag (the Spanish and Portuguese liturgy). When the bitter struggle over reform went into the courts and the traditionalists lost, Moses and other seceders joined the breakaway congregation Shearit Israel. At the consecration of their new house of worship on Wentworth Street on Friday, August 13, 1847, Isaiah Moses carried one of the three *seferim* (Torah scrolls). He was followed in the procession by his son-in-law, the hazzan Jacob Rosenfeld. Still another family member, Isaiah's son Levy, opened the door, while Reverend Rosenfeld commenced singing in Hebrew, "Open for me the gates of righteousness."

CONTINUED ON PAGE 106

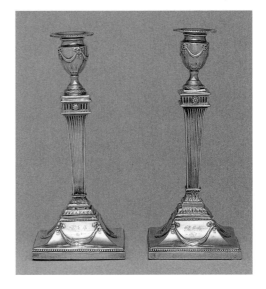

FIGURE 23. *Silver candlesticks belonging to Rebecca Isaiah Moses, made by John Settle, England, 1792. Courtesy of Judith Weil Shanks and Cecil A. Alexander.*

Silversmith John Settle designed these English Sheffield candlesticks in neoclassical style— referred to as "federal" in the young republic. Characteristic elements include decorative parallel ridges, swags, and beads. Made in 1792, the year Rebecca Phillips was born, the candlesticks bear much of their history in inscription. They were given to Rebecca in 1813, the year her husband purchased The Oaks, and inscribed with her married initials, RIM. The initials of subsequent owners are engraved with the dates of acquisition. Rebecca Moses's daughter Cecilia Moses Solomons named her daughter Rebecca, while the older Rebecca was still alive. This naming practice is common among Sephardic Jews but not among the Ashkenazim, who consider it bad luck to name a child after a living relative.

Though their ancestors are not known to have come from Spain or Portugal, the Moses and Alexander families followed Sephardic rituals and considered themselves Sephardim. Both the younger Rebecca and her son Cecil married cousins, as was frequently the case among early American families, Jewish and gentile.

CATALOGUE 94.

Avenue at The Oaks, Goose Creek, pastel on silk by Elizabeth O'Neill Verner, ca. 1940. Carolina Art Association/Gibbes Museum of Art, Charleston, S.C.

Born in 1883 in Charleston, Elizabeth O'Neill Verner studied at the Pennsylvania Academy of Fine Arts and specialized in etching at the Central School of Arts in London, England. In 1937 she traveled to Kyoto, Japan, where she taught etching and studied the brush technique of sumi painting. It may have been this trip that inspired her to work on silk.

Verner began experimenting with pastels in the 1930s, at the height of her powers as a printmaker. The method she developed of layering pastels on a piece of silk stretched over a wooden board was so much her own she called it "Vernercolor." Because the colors could not be blended, the process was especially painstaking and the result luminous. She liked to start a composition in the early morning sunlight, and complete it in one sitting.

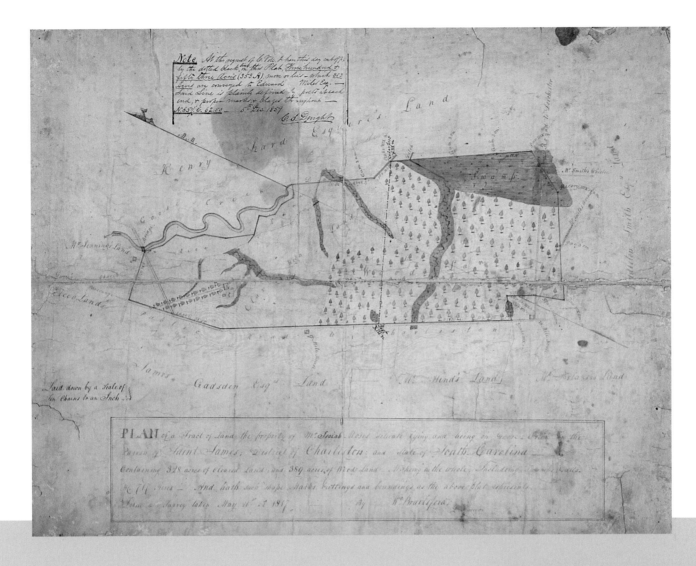

CATALOGUE 95.

Survey plat of The Oaks, South Carolina, 1817. South Carolina Historical Society.

In the plat of The Oaks, based on a survey by William Bradford that Moses commissioned in 1817, the live oaks leading up to the plantation house are represented as cones. In Verner's pastel, the avenue of majestic trees shelters a pastoral road. The Middleton family had owned the plantation for 116 years, beginning in 1678 when Edward Middleton received the original land grant. Situated on the public road seventeen miles from Charleston, The Oaks abutted the property of Saint James Goose Creek Church and parsonage.

According to Bradford's survey, The Oaks contained 328 acres of cleared lands and 389 acres of woods. Along the northeastern edge of the property, on Goose Creek, were sixty acres of rice land, far short of the acreage necessary to justify the expense of building dikes and trunks to facilitate tidal irrigation, a prerequisite for profitable cultivation. By the time Isaiah bought the place, the soil was depleted. Despite the money and labor poured into it, the land never produced a profit.

FIGURE 24. *Advertisement for sale of The Avenue, also known as The Oaks plantation, Charleston Courier, February 26, 1840. Courtesy of the Charleston Library Society.*

F 26   2   T. C. FAY.

PLANTATION AND 50 NEGROES FOR SALE.—The Plantation well known as the AVENUE, adjoining Goose Creek Bridge; it is 16 miles from the city, and contains 750 acres—about 250 acres well fenced, and in a high state of cultivation; about 60 acres Tide Rice Swamp, entirely free from salt; the balance is abundantly wooded with the best of Yellow Pine, Oak and Hickory.

There is a Brick Yard near the Bridge, which has been in operation two years, with a permanent case, a good shed, an inexhaustible supply of water, and every requisite necessary to carry on the Brick making Business, extensively and profitably. Vessels drawing 6 feet water can load at the Brick Yard.

The Mansion, Kitchens and Barns, are extensive brick buildings, which, with the Negro Houses, Stables and Carriage House, are in good order. There is a valuable avenue of Live Oak Trees, leading from the road to the Mansion, one-third of a mile in length, and a fine spring of water, a convenient distance from the house, which has never been known to fail.

ALSO,

A prime gang of fifty NEGROES, accustomed to the culture of Rice and Provisions, as well as the making of Bricks.

The above property, together with the Stock, consisting of Horses, Mules, Cows, Oxen, the Plantation Utensils, and a Charleston built Sloop, capable of carrying 20,000 bricks, or 20 cords of wood, will be sold low, and the terms made to suit the purchaser. For further particulars, apply on the premises, or to   L. I. MOSES,
At the South Western Rail Road Bank, Charleston, S. C.
F 26   wth2 mw8

ONE HUNDRED SLAVES, VALUABLE

In a letter dated January 31, 1927, Hannah M. Moses, a granddaughter of Rebecca and Isaiah, recounted to her cousin Henry Aaron Alexander, the family chronicler, a scene that pokes fun at Isaiah's piety and Rebecca's practicality:

Once when he was Vice President of the Synagogue, he had indigestion, couldn't keep anything on his *breadbasket*, so the doctor told him to eat *raw oysters*—Great Mercy! What! Never! Against all Jewish law. No shell fish. Here our wonderful Grandma spoke up. She said, "take them as medicine, your health requires it to be done." Well in order not to set a wicked example to his family, he went out to the furthest corner of the Oaks with a trusted servant to open the oysters and began to eat the oysters—but alas! At that very corner just over the fence was a lot belonging to the Synagogue property. Just at that time two members came out to inspect it. What did they behold? Mr. Isaiah Moses, that pillar of the Synagogue, eating oysters!!! He was ordered to face the powers of the Congregation, but here again our Grandma came to the front. She brought the Doctor. He was absolved.

CATALOGUE 96.

Israel Solomons (1847–1854), artist unknown, ca. 1850. Collection of Henry A. Alexander Jr.

The fourth child born to Cecilia Moses Solomons and Abraham Alexander Solomons, a boy named Israel, was the first to live beyond infancy. "A loving, charming, beautiful boy of seven," he died at Cecilia's parents' home in Charleston during a yellow-fever epidemic that ravaged the lowcountry. A. A. Solomons was Savannah's leading druggist, hence was delayed in leaving for Charleston when he got word of his son's illness. "Those were the days of slow travel and only by boat from Savannah to Charleston," reported Rebecca Ella Solomons Alexander, who was four months old when her brother died. "My father reached his boy, who he idolized, to find him dead! In all my life I never heard my father call his name and my mother said that even to her he could not speak of his loss which would have comforted her very much."

One of eight children, Eleanor Joseph was born in the hamlet of Black Mingo, South Carolina, in 1794, and grew up in Georgetown. The family was prosperous. Eleanor's mother, Sarah Judith Judah, had come south from Philadelphia. (It was her half-brother, Reuben Simon Krijn, who wrote to her about sending a miniature painting of himself.) Eleanor's father, Lizar Joseph, born in Mannheim, Germany, in 1762, became a salt merchant and wharf owner in the port of Georgetown. By 1800, the Jewish business class dominated civic and cultural life in the town. Appointed clerk of the market, inspector of customs, and later warden and coroner, Joseph was a member of the prestigious Winyah Indigo Society and served as its secretary. At various times the tax collector and clerk of the Court of General Sessions and Common Pleas were Jews, as were the customs inspector, postmaster, and officers of the Winyah Artillery Company and the Winyah Light Dragoons. Georgetown's Jews enjoyed the confidence of their Christian neighbors to a degree unparalleled in North America. Five times in the nineteenth century, Jewish men held the post of intendant or mayor.

In 1814, Eleanor married Israel Solomons in Georgetown. She was nineteen, he forty-four. Born in Amsterdam, Israel had tried to make a living in South America and the West Indies before immigrating to South Carolina. Throughout his career he was plagued by financial difficulties. To raise money to put in trust for his new bride and for a daughter by his first wife, Solomons was forced to mortgage a number of slaves. When he died in 1830, he left Eleanor and their eight surviving children destitute.

Our letters from Miriam are most satisfactory—she writes every week and finds a Carolina winter much to her taste, her last was from a Plantation on the Santee, the residence of her Brother-in-law about 12 miles from Georgetown where the winter foliage of live oak & evergreens strike her as not more beautiful than singular—the presence of flowers in the open air, and all the luxuries of a southern climate have great charms for her—and her heart is attuned to harmonize with everything in her new home for she is still desperately in love, and her husband being the great man of the village, he & everybody around her, pay her homage (she says for his sake) but I have from others, that Miriam for her own sake is valued—and both you & I know her well enough to believe it.

—Rebecca Gratz to her sister-in-law Maria Gist Gratz, January 15, 1837. (Miriam Moses, a niece reared by Rebecca Gratz after Miriam's mother died in 1823, married Solomon Cohen of Georgetown, South Carolina, on November 30, 1836.)

Friendship and kinship linked several generations of the Solomons, Alexander, and Moses families. Eleanor's great-uncle Israel Joseph was parnas of Kahal Kadosh Beth Elohim in Charleston at the time Abraham Alexander Sr. was the congregation's religious leader. In 1815 Eleanor's husband, Israel Solomons, went into partnership with Abraham Alexander Jr., a Charleston hardware merchant, who had married Eleanor's aunt Hannah Aarons. Ties between Eleanor Israel Solomons and Rebecca Isaiah Moses date to their girlhoods, when Eleanor was growing up in Georgetown and Rebecca in Charleston.

Marriages among these clans create a family tree only die-hard genealogists dare tackle. In 1809, two years after Rebecca Phillips married Isaiah Moses, Eleanor's cousin Miriam married Isaiah's brother Levi. In 1822 Eleanor's brother Joseph married his cousin Frances Alexander. In 1836 Aaron Alexander, a brother of Frances, married Sarah Moses, daughter of Rebecca and Isaiah; the next year another Alexander sister named Eleanor married Moses Goldsmith, a nephew of Rebecca and Isaiah. Eleanor Solomons's son Abraham Alexander, named for his great-uncle, later married Isaiah and Rebecca's daughter Cecilia.

This tapestry of relationships has been stitched into a quilt. In the early 1850s, Eleanor moved from Georgetown to Savannah to join her son Lizar and his wife Perla, who were living "allmost next door to Brother A" (Abraham Alexander Solomons). On the occasion of this move, Eleanor's younger sister Charlotte Joseph orchestrated the making of an album quilt to present to Eleanor. Family friends, women and girls, Jews and gentiles, sewed sixty-three blocks, which were then pieced together. The overall pattern is a checkerboard: floral chintz prints alternate with geometric patterns in calico. In each type of block, the colored fabric is appliquéd, or sewn, onto white muslin. The motif of repeating hexagons used in the quilt was popularized by *Godey's Lady's Book*, which promoted the technique of cutting out paper patterns or templates, basting fabric onto the paper, then joining the pieces. Called "template piecing," this technique was suggested by *Godey's* for use by little girls in making patchwork quilts for their doll beds.

Some of the designs in the individual blocks of Eleanor's quilt are trimmed with crocheted braid, some with embroidery. Most of the makers are identified by inscriptions, inked in black by Eleanor, many now too faded to read but legible fifty years ago when they were transcribed and recorded by H. A. Alexander Sr., author of *Notes on the Alexander Family of South Carolina and Georgia*. The sewers who contributed to Eleanor's quilt lived mainly in South Carolina and Georgia, but cousins from as far away as New York also made blocks. The center block, with peacock and eagles, is signed by "C," who might be Charlotte Joseph.

The Cohen women who contributed to the quilt, granddaughters of Solomon Cohen of Georgetown, had initiated a fund-raising campaign in Savannah to pay a hazzan to come to the Georgia port town. The man they hired was Jacob Rosenfeld, who married Leonore Moses, Rebecca and Isaiah's daughter, identified on the quilt as Leonore R.

One block was made by six-year-old Cecilia Solomons, granddaughter of Eleanor Solomons and daughter of Lizar and Perla Solomons. Young Cecilia's aunt, Cecilia Solomons, who lived near Lizar and Perla in Savannah, also contributed, as did her mother Rebecca Moses, still residing in Charleston. "Aunt" Cecilia had shown herself an accomplished needleworker at age fourteen, when she made a large, intricate lace shawl for her mother. As an adult she proved adept at embroidery, stitching a white-on-white baby cap made with needle lace for her sister Sarah's children.

Eleanor's album quilt includes a block sewn by the black woman who nursed the Solomons children. Attributed to "My servant Rinah," the piece is evidence that a bond of affection coexisted with the bond of servitude. As valuable property, Rinah and her children were mortgaged more than once by Eleanor's husband, Israel Solomons. In 1814, the year Eleanor and Israel married, Rinah was among the slaves pledged by the groom to raise money for the bridal trust. Whether

CATALOGUE 97.

Album quilt made for Eleanor Israel
Solomons, née Joseph (1794–1856),
pieced and appliquéd chintz and calico
on muslin, 1851–1854. Collection of
Cecil A. Alexander.

CATALOGUE 98.

Loan document between Israel
Solomons, Abram Alexander, and
Abram Otolengui, Charleston, S.C.,
May 15, 1814. Collection of Henry A.
Alexander Jr.

to protect their investment, or from motives of the heart, the Solomons saw to it that Rinah's children received medical help when they needed it. In 1830, the year Israel died, one of Rinah's daughters was under a doctor's care for almost three weeks. The bill was sixty dollars, or about a year's gross income for a typical slave. Despite her financial distress, Eleanor, as "Administrix" of her husband's estate, paid it.

Deeds and wills, bills of sale and mortgages, tax rolls and census records all show that Jews owned and conveyed slaves in roughly the same proportions as their non-Jewish neighbors, including free people of color. The census of 1850, for example, reports that 51 Jewish Charlestonians, out of a total Jewish population of 500, owned 288 of the 12,000 slaves in the city. In other words, Jews, who made up 2 percent of the white population, owned 2 percent of the bondsmen and women. Among the city's 3,441 free blacks listed in the census, 266 owned a total of 1,087 slaves.

Unlike Quakers, who opposed Negro bondage and left South Carolina when the state made it nearly impossible to emancipate slaves, Jews showed no unity of opinion about slavery based on religious principle. The lone public policy issue to which they responded with one voice was freedom of religion. On questions of states' rights, western expansion, tariffs on manufactured goods, war with Mexico, or the wisdom of secession, Jews could be found on both sides of the debates. When it came to the rights of citizens to govern their slaves according to local practice, no differences can be discerned in the opinions of Jews and non-Jews.

Entries in the daybook kept by Rebecca Moses between 1841 and 1860 disclose the standard range of transactions involving slave property. These include conveyances through sale and gift; the issuance of badges for hands hired out and sent as far away sometimes as Georgia or Alabama; the sale of people who created problems by running away or stealing; the mistress's computations of the value of the family's slaves, increased by births, diminished by illness and death. Nothing demonstrates so clearly how slavery figured in the financial and moral economies of slave-owning families as the litany of births and deaths of the black people, especially the high number of infant deaths.

Rebecca Moses staunchly supported the southern cause, though the feeling in her family was not unanimous. Her daughter Sarah and Sarah's husband, Aaron Alexander, a grandson of Beth Elohim's hazzan Abraham Alexander, were die-hard Unionists. Living in Savannah during the war with another daughter, Cecilia, and her husband, Abraham Alexander Solomons, the son of Israel and Eleanor Solomons, Rebecca endured the humiliation of sharing her daughter's home with the enemy. In December 1864, after General William Tecumseh Sherman's army conquered the city without firing a shot, federal officers were lodged in the Solomons' residence. Five months later Rebecca suffered a stroke when, according to family legend, she heard a newsboy in the street shouting the news of General Robert E. Lee's surrender. ❧

The Moving Frontier

Between 1820 and 1880, some 150,000 Jews joined in the vast "German" migration to America, leaving central and eastern Europe at a rate several times that of non-Jews. Ninety percent of these Jewish immigrants came from families that had made a living in some form of trade. They were shopkeepers who sold dry goods, hardware, or foodstuffs; many peddled in the countryside, returning to their

FIGURE 25. *A. Friedheim & Bro., Rock Hill, S.C., 1902. Courtesy of Rock Hill Economic Development.*

villages and homes for the Sabbath. Not merely dealers in trinkets and notions, peddlers mediated between peasants and urban markets and traded in cattle, horses, and grain. With the consolidation of small farms and the urbanization of the German states, Jews who had lost their livelihoods moved to the cities or booked passage overseas.

Those who came to Carolina aspired to work for themselves. They were attracted initially to Charleston by its established Jewish community, its equality of status, the commerce of a busy port, and news of an opening backcountry. By ones, twos, and fours, Jews fanned out across the state, until there was no market town that was not served by a Jewish-owned shop. A credit system backed by successful Jewish businessmen looked out for ambitious young "drummers," or traveling salesmen, and helped them set up shop wherever one was needed. The Jewish business world was characterized by general stores in small towns, dry-goods stores in the cities, and department stores that grew out of these. To their rural clientele merchants sold seeds and fertilizer as well as cloth and shoes. They extended credit to planters and farmers, wrote mortgages, brokered cotton, and immersed themselves in the staple crop economy.

In towns where there were several Jewish families, Jews organized benevolent societies and acquired land to bury their dead. If they were too few to form a congregation, they observed the High Holy Days in borrowed space: a room above a store, a Masonic lodge, a town hall, or an agricultural society. Desiring both to be embraced by America and to retain their Jewish identity, Jews modeled their self-help institutions on both traditional ideals of communal responsibility and American principles of voluntary association.

In Camden, the second oldest town in South Carolina, Jews acquired land for a "burying ground" in 1792. The Jewish community of merchants and planters grew slowly over a century until, in 1880, Congregation Gemalith Chasodim was formed. Known for their skills at dueling as well as at business, Camden's Jews, like Georgetown's, were readily accepted in politics and even prodded to seek public office. Likewise in Sumter, thirty miles southeast of Camden, the doors to political office were open without prejudice to Jews.

The heads of Sumter's first Jewish families were Charleston-born men who came in the 1820s in search of opportunity. Welcomed into local society, they founded lucrative law practices, won appointment to the bar and election to the state legislature, and fought, when the time came, for the Confederacy. ❧

Of the Jews in the village [of St. Matthews] there were about ten families, all recent immigrants, and so aliens in speech and race and faith. Most of them, moreover, were quite prosperous. Yet between them and these Southern villagers the relations were hearty and pleasant and consolidated by mutual kindness and tolerance. Only one Jew and that was my father, was looked upon with some suspicion by the severer among his Gentile neighbors. The reason was curious and significant; he did not perform the external rites of the Jewish faith and, upon entering a fraternal life insurance order, he smiled and hesitated when asked to affirm categorically his belief in a personal God....

When summer came, we who had no vegetable garden—and would have been just as helpless had we had one—received daily attentions from our Gentile friends: baskets of tomatoes or okra or sweet-corn or bell-pepper. And one friend, a very aged physician who liked and admired my mother and had a dim but steady perception of her profound spiritual isolation, sent her weekly a great basketful of roses.

—Ludwig Lewisohn, *Up Stream:*
An American Chronicle, 1926

CATALOGUE 112.

CATALOGUE 105.

Apothecary bottles, mortar and pestle, and measuring cup from J. J. Klein drugstore, Walterboro, S.C., 1845–1938. Collection of Lucille Finger Powers.

German-born chemist James Jacob Klein (1819–1879) spoke seven languages. In his youth, he worked as an interpreter and played the violin. Settling in Hickory Valley, on the outskirts of Walterboro, in 1845, he erected a small building in his yard, from which he dispensed drugs. Dr. Klein's drugstore was the first pharmacy in Walterboro. After the hurricane of 1879 blew the roof off the family's house, Klein moved the drugstore to the corner of Washington Street and Railroad (now Memorial) Avenue in town and added a second story as living quarters for his wife and children.

Getta Silberman was Klein's second wife. She probably hailed from the Ukraine. In 1856 Klein had divorced his first spouse, Caroline, who was not Jewish. (South Carolina did not permit divorce, so Klein traveled to La Porte, Indiana, to obtain the decree.) Upon her move to Walterboro from upstate New York, his new bride changed her name to Caroline Getta Klein. Her family was so well-to-do, according to Klein family lore, they could set a table for two hundred without borrowing anything. Klein may have met Getta through a matchmaker; one family member calls her a "mailorder bride." Getta's father's name appears on a plaque commemorating the founders of the Reform temple in Syracuse, New York. She died of cancer at age forty-nine.

When J. J. Klein died of heart disease, his son Dr. John Marcus Klein took over the business. John had passed the state examination for pharmacy at age seventeen. During his tenure he had his name blown into all the apothecary bottles. The servants called him "The Boss Man" and his sisters appropriated the title, always referring to him as "The Bossm'n." John supported his mother and sisters and married Lucille McTyeire, twenty years his junior. He built a home in 1926 and died the next year of a stroke.

Toys belonging to Maier Triest, ca. 1910. Collection of Maxine Triest Freudenberg.

A fourth-generation Charlestonian and consummate southerner, Maier Triest had only one regret: that because his mother traveled to see family in New York late in her pregnancy, he was born in the North instead of at home. He grew up in a large house in the heart of Charleston, near the old mill pond now known as Colonial Lake. With his two younger sisters and friends, Maier would paddle the pond in small wooden boats. Charlestonians who could afford it spent summers at the beach for relief from the heat and humidity. The Triests would escape to Sullivan's Island, across the Cooper River from the city.

A graduate of The High School of Charleston, Maier attended the College of Charleston for a few years and then transferred to his father's alma mater, Columbia University, in New York City, close to relatives on both sides of the family. Upon graduation he went to work with his father and uncle in their family insurance, real estate, and auction business, Triest & Israel, on Broad Street in Charleston. Maier was twenty-six and had just married Miriam Neuberger of Augusta when his father died suddenly of a heart attack, thrusting upon him responsibility for managing the family's business and personal affairs.

Maier's great-grandparents, Joseph and Caroline Triest, had emigrated from the Kingdom of Bavaria with their son, the first Maier, around 1850. This Maier was thirty years old and a captain in the militia (Triest's Company, Beat 2) when the Civil War began. In January 1862 he enlisted in the Twenty-fourth South Carolina Volunteers, and a year later was promoted from sergeant major to regimental quartermaster sergeant. His job was to supply

the regiment with shoes, clothing, blankets, cooking utensils, and so forth. In 1869 he married German-born Hannah Reichman in Cincinnati and in 1871 both he and his father Joseph became American citizens in the South Carolina District Court.

Triest's service to the Confederacy was typical of German immigrants of the period, as was his family's allegiance to Reform Judaism and Beth Elohim. The second Maier Triest served as president of the congregation and president of Charleston's B'nai B'rith. He was a founder of AZA (*Aleph Zadik Aleph*)—B'nai B'rith's first youth chapter for boys in Charleston—southeastern district secretary for B'nai B'rith, and president of both the Hebrew Orphan and the Hebrew Benevolent Societies. In addition Maier was active in civic affairs. He chaired the Charleston County School Board,

belonged to the Elks Club and the Hibernian Society, served on the board of South Carolina Electric and Gas, and was a founder and board member of Home Federal Savings & Loan.

Later in life, Triest was a guest writer for the Charleston *News and Courier,* reporting on his travels to Canada and Europe.

Maier had one child, Maxine Anne Triest, and three grandchildren. Maxine's husband, Henry H. Freudenberg, was a Holocaust survivor who met Maxine when they were just eleven years old, at a dinner party at the Triest home.

Maier Triest died of cancer at the age of sixty-seven and was buried in the Coming Street cemetery.

Capital City

When Columbia was designated as the capital of South Carolina in 1786, seven Jewish men from Charleston were among the first to invest in town lots. The auction at which they bought the properties was conducted by Joseph Myers, merchant and member of Kahal Kadosh Beth Elohim. From Charleston and Camden came Jews of Sephardic and German descent, educated and well connected to the planter aristocracy and to Jewish merchants in the Atlantic maritime world. Most of Columbia's Jewish pioneers, including ten of the eleven men who founded the Columbia Hebrew Benevolent Society in 1826, were involved in business and trade, as their predecessors had been in Charleston.

Individual fortunes rose and fell in the speculative atmosphere of a frontier market town aspiring to be a capital city. A year after helping to found the Benevolent Society, Judah Barrett, for example, became the first Jew in Columbia to be elected to public office. He served two terms as a town warden, or city council man; within a few years, however, he had fallen in debt and departed for New Orleans.

Dr. Mordecai Hendricks DeLeon, son of the original South Carolina settlers, Jacob and Hannah DeLeon, built a lucrative medical practice among the Midlands elite and operated a small hospital that included "six wards for Negroes." In 1833 he was elected Columbia's intendant, or mayor, for the first of three straight terms. Like his good friend, South Carolina College president Thomas Cooper, DeLeon was an ardent "nullifier." His wife, Rebecca Lopez DeLeon, headed Columbia's Ladies Benevolent Society. Their three sons, David Camden, Edwin, and Thomas Cooper, all served the Confederacy. David Camden had earned the nickname "the Fighting Doctor" in the Mexican War. He had "fought under the flag," he said, lamenting, "Every star and stripe is dear to me," but when the time came to choose sides, he, like his brothers, offered his services to his new country, the Confederate States of America.

The careers of the DeLeon brothers, in medicine, diplomacy, and journalism, were shaped by the war. David Camden left the United States, first for Mexico and then for the territory of New Mexico, never to return. Edwin lost his diplomatic post for criticizing Secretary of State Judah Benjamin's efforts to persuade the European powers to ally with the South. T. C. DeLeon wrote two Civil War–era classics and won acclaim for penning the first American play to run more than a hundred performances on Broadway. As adults, all three brothers abandoned the Jewish faith. To paraphrase historian Jacob Rader Marcus, the third-generation DeLeons proved to be more southern than Jewish. ❧

CATALOGUE 132.

David Camden DeLeon (1816–1872),
by Solomon N. Carvalho, 1849.
The Jewish Museum.

~

La Belle Juive

Is it because your sable hair
Is folded over brows that wear
At times a too imperial air;

Or is it that the thoughts which rise
In those dark orbs do seek disguise
Beneath the lids of Eastern eyes;

That choose whatever pose or place
May chance to please, in you I trace
The noblest women of your race?

. . . .

You stroll the garden's flowery walks;
The plants to me are grainless stalks,
And Ruth to old Naomi talks.

Adopted child of Judah's creed,
Like Judah's daughters, true at need,
I see you mid the alien seed.

I watch afar the gleaner sweet;
I wake like Boaz in the wheat,
And find you lying at my feet!

My feet! Oh! If the spell that lures
My heart through all these dreams endures,
How soon shall I be stretched at yours!

—written for Rachel Lyons (1838-1930),
   Columbia-born daughter of Jacob Cohen
   Lyons and Louisa E. Hart Lyons, by Henry
   Timrod (1828–1867), "poet laureate of the
   Confederacy," and published in the *Charles-*
   ton Daily Courier, January 23, 1862.

CHAPMAN LEVY

ELIZA LEVY ANDERSON

CATALOGUE 51–54

Miniature portraits of Chapman Levy (1787–1849), ca. 1835; Eliza Levy Anderson (d. before 1839), ca. 1835; Sarah Moses Levy (d. 1839) and Chapman Levy as a youth, ca. 1798. Artists unknown. Chapman Levy miniature a gift of Thomas W. Crockett in honor of Loraine Crockett; Sarah Moses Levy, Chapman Levy as youth, and Eliza Levy Anderson miniatures gifts of Lane Dinkins. Jewish Heritage Collection, College of Charleston Library.

Born on the fourth of July 1787, in Camden, South Carolina, Chapman Levy studied law and was admitted to the bar in Columbia in 1806. A militia captain during the War of 1812, he served in both the state house and senate from Kershaw County. Attorney and legislator, soldier and master duelist, landowner and brickyard operator, Levy was a man of high profile and influence in his home state for thirty years before moving to Mississippi on the western frontier. Jewish by birth, he is listed in 1808 as an "incorporator" of the Camden Protestant Episcopal Church.

In 1820, Levy owned thirty-one slaves, twenty of whom were employed at his brickyard near Columbia Canal. These numbers, low compared to plantation slaveholdings, still made him the largest Jewish slaveholder of his era. He had a hand in many economic enterprises as a creditor and one-man banking operation in the days before organized banks. Active in the Masons, he served as "Worshipful Master" of Richmond Lodge No. 39, and probably helped found the Jewish burial society in 1822. The oldest surviving Jewish grave in Columbia belongs to his first wife, Flora, who died in 1823 after five years of marriage. He soon married a second time, but this marriage too ended with the premature death of his wife Rosina in 1828.

Levy gained notoriety for prosecuting William Taylor, the brother of Governor John Taylor, for murder. William Taylor had killed a man for "alleged improper intimacy with his wife." Levy lost the case; Taylor was acquitted. In his will, written in 1822, Taylor bequeathed to his wife "the full enjoyment & gratification of her unbounded Lust, her only Heaven," and instructed that he have no eulogy but a decent burial with "plenty to eat & drink of the best let none go away empty or dry."

An authority on the protocol of dueling, Levy was for many years, according to an upcountry physician, consulted "in every duel . . . fought in the upper part of South Carolina."

Levy returned to his hometown of Camden in the late 1820s and formed a law partnership with his lifelong friend, William McWillie. At the Nullification Convention of 1832, Levy argued vigorously against the right of a state to disobey a federal law. His legal work drew him to the western territories from which the Indians were being expelled and, in 1838, he and McWillie moved to Mississippi. Almost

SARAH MOSES LEVY
CHAPMAN LEVY AS YOUTH

immediately Levy was urged to run for Congress and five years later was nominated for governor on the Democratic ticket, but declined to run. (McWillie would later run for governor and win.) Levy died in 1849, at age sixty-two, and was buried at McWillie's plantation home, Kirkwood, in Mississippi.

~

By the late eighteenth century the demand for portraits had spread from the aristocracy to the mercantile and professional classes. Sarah Moses Levy, wife of Samuel Levy, poses in an elegant lace cap and collar and wears a miniature of her young son Chapman. The intriguing pair of portraits have stayed together for over two hundred years, a testament to the strength of the bond between mother and son. It seems likely that it was for his mother that the adult Chapman Levy had another miniature made shortly before leaving South Carolina for Mississippi.

Chapman's sister Eliza married Dr. Edward H. Anderson. The couple named one of their two children Chapman Levy Anderson, after her brother. Dressed in the conservative, refined style of the antebellum period, Eliza gazes at her viewers with a quiet beauty. Her black dress may indicate mourning or it may simply be her best dress. The ornate lace collar and jeweled belt buckle suggest the latter. Mourning, however, was a drawn-out affair in the nineteenth century. Some women who went into mourning at the death of a child or a husband never wore colors again; others would dress in black for a year, then return to normal attire. Mourning jewelry, such as a brooch containing a lock of hair of the dear departed, was commonly worn at the neck to signify bereavement and give solace to the mourner.

Although the artist who painted Eliza has not been determined, Camden-born Isaac B. Alexander is a possibility. Several images known to be his work resemble this portrait.

CATALOGUE 76.

Circular tray with Garden of Eden design, ca. 1810–1830. Collection of Rose Louise Rich Aronson.

For ten or fifteen years the brothers Lipman and Moritz Rich, with their wives Eva and Bertha, operated stores on Charleston's King Street. Observant Jews, originally from Neustadt, Posen, in Prussia, they landed in Charleston in the early 1850s and were drawn to the new "Polish" congregation just forming in the city. In April 1860, "L. Rich" was elected second

trustee of Brith Sholom. "P. Rich" (probably Lipman's son Philip, born in 1845) was elected secretary in 1865.

The 1860 census describes Lipman as a storekeeper, dealing in dry goods and clothing at 352 King Street, and Moritz as a merchant with a variety store on lower King—a site that would have been shelled on a daily basis during the wartime siege of the city. Moritz and Bertha had three children when the Civil War broke out, and soon would have two more, including a son, Philip, born in 1862. Lipman

and Moritz both served in the home guard. Several years after the war they moved west into the midlands of the state, looking for a new frontier. They settled first in St. Matthews, a cotton-trading town with a train station and a few Jewish families, about twenty miles from Columbia. They then moved on to the larger town of Orangeburg, which by the 1870s included a substantial community of German-born merchants, Jewish and gentile. In June 1873, the *Orangeburg News* published a list of fifty-six of the town's principal shopkeepers

CATALOGUE 118.

Hannah Jacobs Levi, artist unknown, ca. 1860. Collection of Sylvia Hanna Weinberg (Mrs. Julien Weinberg).

Hannah Levi was born Hannah Jekel (Jacobs) in Bavaria, on December 30, 1830. She arrived in Charleston, South Carolina, in 1853, and married Moses Levi, originally from the village of Bosenbach, Germany. The couple may have known each other in the Old Country and possibly were distant cousins. They were married in the home of Moses Winstock and his wife, Eva Leah Visanska. The son of Jacob Lövy, age forty-four, a butcher, and Johanna Grunewald, Moses had immigrated to America five years before Hannah. Amazingly the certificate announcing his birth at 7:00 A.M., August 11, 1827, survives; it was witnessed by a mason and a worker for town government, suggesting the family was solidly middle-class.

At the time Hannah arrived in South Carolina, Moses was running a store in Sumter. Under the provisions of their marriage contract, Moses gave his bride a settlement of two thousand dollars to be used for her benefit, not to be spent on household expenses. They stayed in Sumter for three years, then in 1856 moved to the new town of Manning, where they lived the rest of their lives.

Hannah and Moses had ten children, nine of whom survived to adulthood—David, Rosa (Weinberg), Mitchell, Ferdinand, Abe, Louis, Ellen (Iseman), Meyer, and Sallie (D'Ancona).

The Levis settled in Manning just as the town was established. They began a business, built a fine home, and made a fortune that was lost during the Civil War but rebuilt by the end of the century.

Like many German immigrants in the South, Moses Levi joined the Confederate army. He signed up as a private with the Sprott Guards, which later became Company I,

CATALOGUE 76 CONTINUED

and businessmen, giving their places of origin and their dates of arrival. Only seven were natives of Orangeburg, while seventeen gave Germany as their birthplace.

The younger Philip Rich married Rosa Platchek from Savannah. In 1894, this circular brass tray was used in the circumcision ceremony of their newborn son Lipman. While not originally made for that purpose, the object was sanctified by use. The tray has a heavy rolled edge. Its surface is decorated with a scene of Adam and Eve in the Garden of Eden —a repoussé design, hand-tooled by punching from the underside, then further worked by stippling. The double border in a loop-and-ball pattern was created by repeatedly hammering a small die or stamp to achieve a textured effect.

CATALOGUE 118 CONTINUED

Twenty-third Regiment, South Carolina Volunteers, commanded by Colonel Harry L. Benbow, and later served as regimental quartermaster. Taken prisoner on April 1, 1865, at the Battle of Five Forks during the last Federal attacks on Petersburg, Virginia, Levi was sent to the Point Lookout (Maryland) prison camp. There he managed to communicate with northern relatives and procure some things to sell. (Two of his sisters living in the North petitioned President Lincoln to parole him, but the request was not granted.) Levi opened a store in the sea of prison tents, employing W. H. Epperson and W. H. Cole as clerks at a salary of a plug of tobacco per week. According to his obituary in the *Manning Times* (February 1898), with his profits he was able to provide material comforts for himself and his comrades, and to help Colonel Benbow, who was a prisoner in a Union hospital in Washington, D.C.

Eight days after the Battle of Five Forks, General Robert E. Lee and the Army of Northern Virginia surrendered. Levi, however, was not released from prison until June 11, 1865. He and several friends walked back to Manning from Virginia. When he got to the edge of the yard, the story goes, he called for hot water, clean clothes, and a match to burn the clothes he was wearing.

Levi discovered that the considerable quantity of cotton his family had accumulated during the war had been burned when General Potter's army came through. Also consumed in the blaze were most of his buildings and virtually everything he owned. Losses for the town of Manning totaled about $103,000. Levi alone lost $40,000.

Both Moses and Hannah Levi had important buildings in Manning named after them. In 1899, the year after Moses died, the Manning Collegiate Institute was about to close because of indebtedness. Levi's family paid off the debt and provided operating funds for the school, which was renamed the Moses Levi Institute. The Levi family gave land and a thousand dollars, in memory of Hannah Levi, toward the building of Manning's first public library, which now houses the Clarendon County Archives.

CATALOGUE 115.

LEFT: Porcelain pitcher, inscribed "Royal Bayreuth Priv. 1784," Bavaria, ca. 1900. Collection of Rhetta Aronson Mendelsohn.

CATALOGUE 116.

Trolley bag of Henrietta Block Rich, United States, ca. 1910–1920. Collection of Rhetta Aronson Mendelsohn.

Lipman Rich, who in 1911 took Philip as his middle name in memory of his father, operated two stores in Orangeburg—an Army surplus store and a ladies' ready-to-wear shop. Soon after World War I ended, he married Henrietta Block from Camden. Among the treasured possessions she brought with her to Orangeburg were a porcelain pitcher and a well-wrought sterling silver trolley bag.

Made in Bavaria, the pitcher is decorated with a brown border that mimics a popular design from the 1820s and with a bucolic scene featuring cows, perhaps hand-painted in America. The trolley bag, so called because the inside is fitted for coins, calling cards, and face powder, has a hidden compartment for a photograph and is an exceptionally fine American piece. Made by the International Silver Company, it features an old-style pinned construction, a "brite-cut," hand-executed art deco design, a gold-washed interior, unusual sloping sides, and a handmade chain. The monogram on front and back reads "HB"—evidence that the bag belonged to Henrietta Block before her marriage to Lipman Philip Rich.

Henrietta Block was born in Camden, South Carolina, in 1891. Her father, Louis Leopold Block, from the Black Forest of Bavaria, was a cousin of Camden's Geisenheimer family. He arrived alone in the midlands town in the late

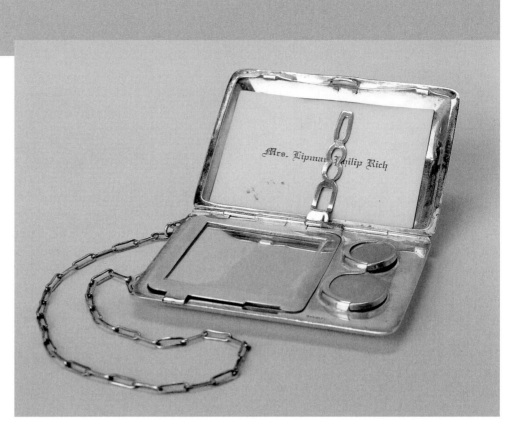

1880s, went into business with Jake and Gus Hirsch, and married their sister Rosa, six years his senior. Hirsch Brothers & Block grew into the biggest store in Camden.

Between 1895 and 1900, Rosa and Louis Block had three daughters: Bella, Henrietta, and Rosalie Carolyn. Less than two years after Rosalie's birth, Rosa died. Her place in the household was quickly assumed by another Rosa, Aunt Rosa Fried, who moved in to care for the girls and manage the help, who included a cook and a butler. When Aunt Rosa died in 1916, the girls' cousin Theresa Block came down from Brooklyn, New York, and took over the role of surrogate mother. Theresa soon met and married Herman Baruch, a first cousin of Bernard Baruch on his father's side and second cousin on his mother's.

Some ten or fifteen years after Henrietta wed and moved to Orangeburg, Lipman Rich's businesses fell victim to the Great Depression. He toyed with the idea of joining the New Deal's Works Projects Administration, but instead took a job as an insurance agent for Metropolitan Life. He later became a consultant to the company and retired about five years before his death in 1968. Henrietta lived another seventeen years, passing away in 1985. Lipman and Henrietta's one daughter, Rose Louise Rich Aronson, married and raised a family in Orangeburg—one of the town's few remaining Jewish families.

CATALOGUE 125 AND 126.

Wedding dress and trousseau trunk of Rebecca Winstock Rosenberg, late 19th century. Collection of Evelyn Rosenberg Gross-Brein.

Rebecca Winstock was born in 1860 of Polish immigrant parents who had married young and lived in London before coming to America in the 1840s. In 1854 the family moved to the upcountry town of Due West to escape the damp, feverish climate of Charleston. Abraham Rosenberg met Rebecca when he arrived from Poland in 1875. He worked in Abbeville in a cousin's store and later in Camden, where he served in Kershaw's Guard of the South Carolina Militia. In the fall of 1884 he moved to Greenwood and felt sufficiently established to ask for Rebecca's hand in marriage.

The Winstocks, Rosenbergs, and Visanskas exemplify the growing number of Jewish families from eastern Europe who, in the 1840s and 1850s, responded to persecution, conscription, and the deprivation of basic rights by immigrating to the United States. Extended kin resettled in America, some disembarking in Charleston and making their way inland. The first Winstock to show up in South Carolina was fourteen-year-old Ben, the youngest brother of the family, in 1838. His brothers followed, including Moses—who would become Rebecca's father—born in 1818 and said to have been dreaming of leaving Poland since he was twelve. In 1835 or 1836 he married Eva Leah Visanska, age seventeen. The couple had two children, Sam and Annie. Moses lived in London for three years and in 1842 boarded a ship in Liverpool and sailed to Charleston. Some four years later, Eva Leah, twice thwarted by shipwrecks, succeeded in crossing the Atlantic.

Winstock leapt into business, purchasing a wholesale jewelry concern that evolved into a peddler's supply company. City directories of 1852 and 1855 list him selling "fancy goods" on King Street. Hearing from peddlers about the cooler, drier climate of the upstate, Moses, who suffered from asthma, decided to check out prospects in the hamlet of Due West. He happened to stop at the graduation exercises of Erskine College and felt drawn to the young Presbyterian institution, which welcomed him. His fluency in Hebrew and facility with the Old Testament made him a valuable addition to the community.

The Winstocks, with their nephew and bookkeeper G. A. Visanska in tow, settled in Due West and had three more children—six in all. Moses built several brick stores on Main Street and a small home. By 1860, the year Rebecca was born, her parents were wealthy. Moses bought a 525-acre plantation five miles from Abbeville, known as the Winstock Place, where he planted cotton, corn, and other crops. The Winstock children were schooled at Miss Jones's in Abbeville, returning to the plantation only on the weekend.

Moses Winstock was reputed to be "excessively conscientious" toward his slaves. He sanctioned their marriages and went to great lengths to keep families together. Early in the Civil War he joined the South Carolina Reserves—he was forty years old when the state seceded—and reluctantly sent his family to Columbia for safety. Things did not turn out as he expected. On a Friday night, February 17, 1865, as Sherman's forces entered the city, the Winstocks sat down for their Sabbath meal. There was a knock on the door. The Union officers outside were invited in to dinner and joined the repast, but as dessert was completed they ordered the house burned down. The young children's "Mammy"—so the story goes—scooped up the silver flatware in the tablecloth and hid it under her skirts as she sat

in the yard comforting her charges. That night fire also consumed the warehouse where Moses stored his tobacco, coffee, rice, sugar, and cloth, which in claims for compensation submitted to a congressional court in 1871 were valued at $56,418.75.

The first Rosenbergs arrived in Abbeville in 1872 and, in association with Winstock's nephew G. A. Visanska, opened a store. Wounded in love by Rebecca Winstock's sister Cecilia, Wolfe Rosenberg sold his interest in the business to his cousin Philip and moved back to Europe. Philip, in turn, sent for his younger brother Abraham. Abraham arrived in 1875 and attended grammar school with the Winstock children, including Rebecca. Cecilia sent Philip packing too, but on his way back to Europe, a telegram from Visanska reached him in New York saying she had relented. They were married on October 27, 1885, just five months after Abraham married Rebecca.

The partnership of Philip Rosenberg and G. A. Visanska was highly successful. The two men eventually owned more than twenty buildings in Abbeville and some eight thousand acres of land in Abbeville and Greenwood counties. They were said to work a hundred mules and employ five hundred "Negroes." Visanska helped found the Abbeville Cotton Mill, and was its first secretary and later its president.

Meanwhile Moses Winstock, the Moses who had led his tribe through the wilderness to Due West two decades before, returned to Charleston. Through the 1870s and 1880s he is listed in the city directories as a tobacco and cigar merchant and "drummer." He lived first on St. Philip Street and later on George Street, near his son Israel, Charleston's first Jewish physician. Active in synagogue affairs, Moses served two terms as president of Brith Sholom, the Polish congregation started by his brother-in-law, Rabbi Hirsch Zvi Levine.

The Lost Cause

CHAPTER THREE

Be unto the Army of this Confederacy, as thou were of old, unto us,
thy chosen people. . . . Guide them O Lord of Battles, into the paths
of victory, guard them from the shaft and missile of the enemy.
Grant that they may ever advance to wage battle, and
battle in thy name to win!

—from "The Prayer of the C. S. Soldiers,"
the Rev. Max J. Michelbacher, rabbi of
Beth Ahabah Congregation (House of
Love), Richmond, Virginia

FIGURE 26. *Lieutenant Joshua Lazarus Moses
(1839–1865). Company C, Third (Palmetto)
Battalion, South Carolina Light Artillery.
Artist unknown. Courtesy of I. Harby and
Harriet C. Moses.*

Confederate Jews

Born to a Sephardic family in the West Indies, Judah P. Benjamin became the most highly placed Jew in the Confederacy. Benjamin spent his adolescence in Charleston and briefly attended Yale University in New Haven, Connecticut. He studied law privately and was admitted to the bar in New Orleans. He would have been the first Jewish U.S. Supreme Court justice, but he turned down an appointment offered to him by President Franklin Pierce in 1856.

Though he did not practice his religion or advocate Jewish causes, Benjamin was a lightning rod for anti-Semitic outbursts during the war. As secretary of war, he quarreled with the generals and questioned their strategies. As secretary of state, he outraged planters—he had been a successful sugar planter himself—by proposing to emancipate slaves who fought for the South, an offer designed to win French recognition of the Confederate States of America. Tennessee Senator Henry Foote, a notorious anti-Semite, referred to him as Judas Iscariot Benjamin. But Benjamin persisted, and as the war was coming to an end, he had Confederate President Jefferson Davis's ear.

Benjamin's notoriety has obscured the participation of thousands of other Jews on the Confederate side or, for that matter, on the Union side of the deadly conflict. In both South and North, Jewish men, out of deep feelings of belonging and wanting to belong, volunteered for military service in numbers disproportionate to their share of the population. Jewish women also were conspicuous in their display of loyalty and service to their native or adopted country.

Five Moses brothers from Sumter joined the Confederate ranks. Abraham Charles Myers from Georgetown, great-grandson of the first hazzan of Kahal Kadosh Beth Elohim, became quartermaster general of the Confederacy. Theodore Belitzer, a member of Beth Elohim and of the German Hussars, died on a prisoner-of-war ship. Maier Triest, originally from Bavaria, served as regimental quartermaster of the Twenty-fourth Carolina. E. W. Moïse raised a company called the Moïse Rangers and rode with the Seventh Confederate Cavalry. Marcus Baum, an orderly on the staff of General Kershaw in General Longstreet's army, was killed by friendly fire at the Battle of the Wilderness in 1864.

Jewish men were especially evident as combat physicians. Camden sent forth both David DeLeon, the first surgeon general of the Confederacy and, fresh out of medical school, Prussian-born Simon Baruch, a lowly assistant surgeon who, after the war, became president of the state medical society and chairman of the state board of health.

Jewish civilians contributed heavily to South Carolina's war chest. Charleston merchant Benjamin Mordecai donated ten thousand dollars for Governor Pickens

FIGURE 27. The Isabel, *by Edward McGregor, September 1848. Courtesy of the Maryland Historical Society.*

to use "for such purposes as will best advance the interests and honor of our noble commonwealth." Moses Cohen Mordecai's steamer, the *Isabel*, removed the federal defenders from Fort Sumter in April 1861 and became a blockade runner for the Confederacy. Operating out of Baltimore after the war, Mordecai's company brought home the bodies of South Carolina soldiers killed at Gettysburg, at no cost to their families. ✤

CATALOGUE 138.

Isabel Rebecca Lyons Mordecai (1804–1895), by Theodore Sidney Moïse, ca. 1835. Collection of Judith Tobias Siegel.

Born in Philadelphia, the only girl among Isaac and Rachel Cohen Lyons's six children, Isabel Rebecca grew up in Charleston. Her father was a native of Oberelsbach, Germany. He settled first in Philadelphia, where he met and married the daughter of Jacob Cohen, hazzan of the city's first synagogue, Mikveh Israel, before moving south around 1805. Early in the 1820s the family left Charleston and relocated in Columbia, where Isaac and his sons opened a grocery store at the corner of Richardson (Main) and Gervais Streets. In 1828 Isabel married future state senator Moses Cohen Mordecai, with whom she had eight children.

Isabel's brother Jacob Cohen Lyons married the daughter of Abraham Hart, Philadelphia's preeminent Jewish book publisher. Two other brothers became doctors: Isaac served as surgeon general of the Texas army; Joseph received his medical degree from the University of Pennsylvania. Another brother, Henry, made his mark in banking and politics. A director of the Commercial Bank of Columbia, a member of the Hebrew Benevolent Society, and a warden of the city for eight years, Henry Lyons was elected mayor of Columbia in 1850, the second Jewish man to attain this post.

CATALOGUE 137.

Medicine box of Moses Cohen Mordecai, 1865. The Charleston Museum.

M. C. Mordecai, importer of fruit, sugar, tobacco, and coffee, was Charleston's most prominent Jewish citizen in the decades before the Civil War. Born in 1804, son of David Mordecai and Reinah Cohen Mordecai, M. C. became, by the standards of his day, a shipping tycoon and a civic colossus. Elected to several offices at the city and state levels, he sat on more boards and committees than seems humanly possible. At various times he was vice president of the Charleston Ancient Artillery Society (1830–47), a member of the board of health (1833–36), captain of the Marion Artillery (1834), a member of the committee on civic improvements (1837), warden of police (1837), commissioner of markets (1837), a delegate to the Augusta Convention (1838), a director of the Southwestern Railroad Bank (1840–52), a commissioner of pilotage (1842–50), state representative (1845–46), state senator (1855–58), and director of the Gas Light Company (1848–56), the South Carolina Insurance Company (1848–56), and the Farmers' and Exchange Bank (1854–59).

First to raise his voice in the cause of disaster relief, Mordecai served on "The Committee in Relation to the Late Fire" (1838), established on his motion to the city council, to assist victims of the fire that destroyed 560 dwellings and businesses, some seventy of them owned or rented by Jews, and 600 outbuildings. In 1850 he sat on the committee for arrangements for the funeral of John C. Calhoun.

The next year Mordecai helped launch the *Southern Standard*, a newspaper that rejected the idea of separate state secession and promoted the path of cooperation in political affairs among the southern states. He himself owned fourteen slaves, while the average urban Jewish slaveholder in mid-century owned five. In 1834 he contracted to ship a cargo of slaves from Charleston to New Orleans. Though the weather was pleasant, the stars were shining brightly, and the captain was on deck at the time, the brig ran aground in the Bahamas. Mordecai blamed the captain who, he said, "did not care a damn for the slaves." Authorities in the Bahamas seized and liberated the captives, since Britain had abolished slavery in its territories. Seven of them made their way back to Charleston, where they were re-enslaved. Upon their return, Mordecai was sued for costs by the shipping agent, but the court found him not liable.

He and his wife, Isabel Lyons Mordecai, lived in a mansion on Meeting Street, south of Broad Street, near Saint Michael's Church. A close friend of Governor William Aiken, he may have persuaded the governor to excise passages offensive to Jews from the 1840 Thanksgiving speech authored by Aiken's predecessor, James Henry Hammond. Even

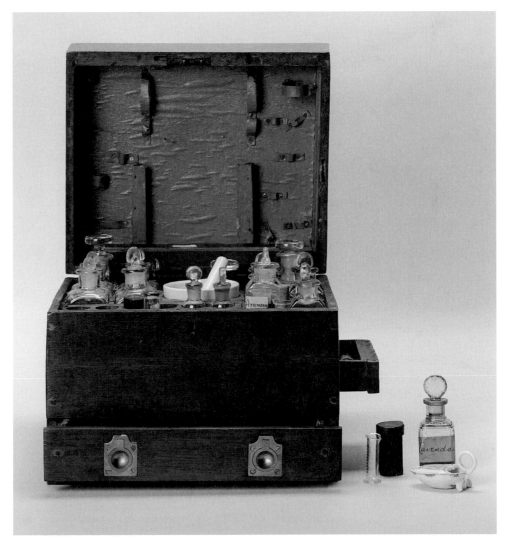

Hammond, who derided Mordecai's brother, Columbia merchant Isaac D. Mordecai, as "a miserable Jew," recognized M. C. as "a man of force and influence." In the debate over installing an organ in Beth Elohim's new building, he sided with the reformers in favor of the innovation. Upon the death of Joshua Lazarus in 1861, Mordecai became president of the congregation.

It was Mordecai's steamer, the *Isabel*, that transferred U.S. Army Major Robert Anderson and his men from Fort Sumter to the Union fleet following the opening bombardment of the Civil War. The *Isabel*, named for Mordecai's wife, afterwards became famous for breaking through the Yankee blockade of the coast and supplying Confederate forces.

In February 1865, when Sherman's troops marched out of Columbia, the capital smoldering behind them, the city council appointed Mordecai "food administrator" to help feed the starving citizens. Later that year he and twenty other community leaders, including his brother-in-law Jacob C. Lyons, were authorized to discuss South Carolina's return to the Union with President Andrew Johnson. Blind and broke from the war, the reluctant secessionist moved to Baltimore, leaving his son-in-law Edgar Marks Lazarus in charge of his business affairs in South Carolina.

M. C. Mordecai's pine medicine box contains some sixty-five objects, including glass bottles and stoppers, china spoons, mortars and pestles, mixing glasses, drinking straws, corkscrews, measuring devices, weights, medicines, poisons, liniment, tooth powder. His great-grandson Thomas Jefferson Tobias gave the box to The Charleston Museum in 1941; it was restored in 1978.

CATALOGUE 134.

Myer Buchanan Moses III (1833–1889), ambrotype, ca. 1862. Collection of Elizabeth Moses.

Myer Buchanan Moses is known in the family lore for his Civil War heroics. The oldest child of Montgomery Moses and Catherine Phillips Moses, Myer enlisted in Company D, Second South Carolina Infantry, three days before the shelling of Fort Sumter. His brother Henry Claremont Moses had joined the day before, and two cousins belonged to the same company. Two other brothers of Myer, Zalegman Phillips and Franklin J., also fought for the Confederate States of America.

Myer Moses served under the command of Camden lawyer Colonel Joseph B. Kershaw, whom he held in high regard. "There is not a man in [the regiment]," Sergeant Moses claimed, "who would not follow him to death." Moses participated in the protracted campaign in the Shenandoah Valley in 1864 where many of the Second South Carolina were captured and Kershaw's horse was killed. Retreating from a skirmish, Moses and Captain William C. Vance encountered a Federal detachment. According to Mac Wyckoff's history of the infantry, "The keen-witted Moses pretended he was a Yankee and demanded their surrender. Told that they were Federals, Moses acted overjoyed and urged them to 'catch those d——n rebels.' But when asked to what unit he belonged, he gave himself away, and was taken prisoner. Meanwhile,

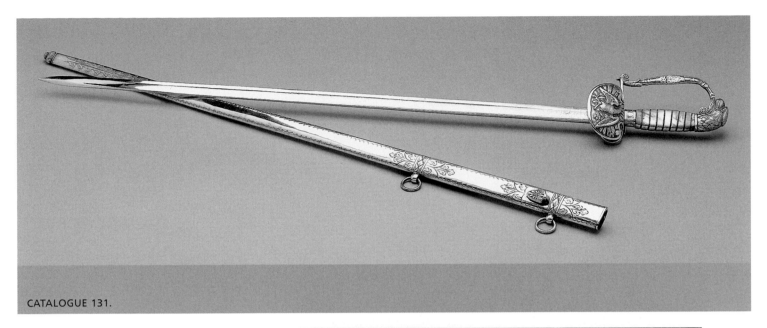

CATALOGUE 131.

Dress sword of Perry Moses, ca. 1840. Collection of I. Harby and Harriet C. Moses.

FIGURE 28. *Joshua Lazarus Moses (standing), Isaac Harby Moses (left), and Perry Moses, ca. 1861. Courtesy of Anne F. Jennings.*

Joshua Moses was killed at Fort Blakely, near Mobile, Alabama, in April 1865. Isaac Harby Moses saw action late in the war. A private in the Citadel Cadet Rangers, he was known as "Lord Shaftesbury" because of his bookish writing style. Perry Moses would become active in the Confederate Veterans and serve as commandant of his "Camp" in Sumter, South Carolina. He died in 1916.

CATALOGUE 134 CONTINUED

Vance had slipped off the horse and into the darkness."

Myer Moses never married. He was trained as a lawyer, but his nephew Herbert A. Moses did not recall him ever practicing. He did remember "Uncle Myer" making the rounds of relatives for his meals. "He was a good deal of a tease but good company," wrote his nephew in an unpublished memoir. Myer Moses III died at age fifty-eight in Sumter where he was born.

FIGURE 29. *Dr. Simon Baruch's field hospital in Gettysburg, Pa., July 5, 1863. Courtesy of the Confederate Relic Room and Museum.*

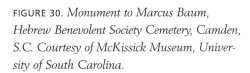

CATALOGUE 127.

The Last Council of War Meeting of Confederate President Jefferson Davis with his Military Chiefs and Advisors, by Wilbur George Kurtz, 1922. City of Abbeville, S.C.

Confederate President Jefferson Davis arrived in Abbeville, South Carolina, on May 2, 1865. Still hopeful that he could rally his troops, even after Lee's surrender, Davis summoned his field commanders and cabinet members to what would be the last Confederate council of war. They met in Major Armistead Burt's home. In Kurtz's painting, Secretary of State Judah Benjamin sits immediately to Davis's left. Davis is depicted here making his final plea to continue fighting. He was unsuccessful, however; at this meeting the Confederacy was dissolved and eight days later Davis would be captured by Federal forces in Georgia.

The mural painter Wilbur George Kurtz was born in Oakland, Illinois, in 1882, and educated at the Chicago Institute of Art. In 1939 he created murals for the New York World's Fair. Fascinated since youth by the Civil War, he was technical adviser to the movies *Gone with the Wind* and *Song of the South.*

FIGURE 30. *Monument to Marcus Baum, Hebrew Benevolent Society Cemetery, Camden, S.C. Courtesy of McKissick Museum, University of South Carolina.*

The inscription reads: "This shaft was erected to commemorate the life and death of Marcus Baum, born in Schwersenz, Prussia, on the 7th day of March, 1833. The sterling qualities of his nature were illustrated by his brief career, to which a glorious death in defense of his adopted country formed a fitting close. In the Battle of the Wilderness on the 6th May 1864 he fell at the side of his beloved chief, Gen. J. B. Kershaw, a martyr to the 'Lost Cause.' His bones now mingle with the dust upon that field of honor but his memory is enshrined in the hearts of those who esteem it a privilege to erect this humble memento."

Daughters of the Confederacy

Just as Jewish men, whether or not they supported secession, rallied around the Confederate flag once war was declared, Jewish women joined in perfect accord with their gentile sisters in their hatred of the enemy. Unable to meet the foe on the battlefield, they were constrained to stay at home, terrified that their sons and husbands would die, fearing imminent violation and the destruction of their way of life at the hands of Yankee invaders.

Jewish women had an advantage over Christian women in venting their frustrations. Confederate nurse Phoebe Pember understood Judaism in Christian terms and thus argued that forgiveness is Christian while Judaism permits vengeance. Jews, she rejoiced, were not required to turn the other cheek. In her diary, published after the war, Pember put it this way: "At last I lifted my voice and congratulated myself at being born of a nation, and religion that did not enjoin forgiveness on its enemies, that enjoyed the blessed privilege of praying for an eye for an eye, and a life for a life, and was not one of those for whom Christ died in vain, considering the present state of feeling. I proposed that till the war was over [my Christian friends] should all join the Jewish Church, let forgiveness and peace and good will alone and put their trust in the sword of the Lord and Gideon."

Phoebe Yates Levy Pember grew up on East Bay Street in Charleston, the fourth of seven children of Jacob Clavius and Fanny Yates Levy. The family was well-to-do. Her grandfather was a founder of Scottish Rite Masonry and a president of Beth Elohim, her father a treasurer of the congregation and a leading member of its reform faction. In 1848 the family moved to Savannah. Phoebe married Thomas Pember of Boston and was widowed at the age of thirty-three, when her husband died of tuberculosis.

During the war she got as close to the battle as a woman could. The first female administrator of Chimborazo hospital, just outside Richmond, Virginia, Pember daily had to fight the resentment army doctors and stewards felt toward a woman in a position of authority. For three years she worked at the hospital, the largest in the Western Hemisphere, during which time 76,000 wounded and sick soldiers passed through. She stayed at her post while Richmond was evacuated in 1865, even after the male nurses fled and the slave cooks defected. Following her patients to the hospital to which they were removed, she stayed on there until "all the sick were either convalescent or dead, and at last my vocation was gone."

After the war Jewish women took leading roles memorializing the Lost Cause. Octavia Harby Moses headed the campaign to erect a monument to the Confederate war dead of Sumter County. In 1869, she called a meeting to begin raising funds and was elected president of the "Ladies Monumental Association" (all the other officers were men), which purchased land on Washington Street between Liberty and Hampton Streets and laid a cornerstone in 1874. She was succeeded in the crusade by her daughter Rebecca Moïse, whose daughter Dulce declared she too had been "raised for the good of the Monument."

Octavia Harby was born in Charleston in 1823, daughter of Isaac Harby and Rachael Mordecai Harby. Orphaned at the age of six, she was raised by her father's sister, Caroline De Litchfield Harby. In 1839 she married Andrew Jackson Moses, seven years her senior, by whom she bore seventeen children, fourteen of whom lived to maturity. After the eleventh child her husband wrote in the family Bible, "Heaven spare her and make her the last one." But six more would follow, the last in 1866. Octavia confessed that it was her servants who made it possible—the family owned sixteen slaves in 1860—as she handed the babies over to a nurse who did everything for them. Her son Perry recalled that a nurse slept in his room and would wake him with a warm baked sweet potato.

Before South Carolina declared its independence, Octavia had advocated secession while her husband stood for the Union. At the outbreak of war he joined the home guard and, one by one, their five eldest sons went off to battle. Octavia threw herself into war work, organizing a sewing society to cut and make uniforms for the soldiers; sending off boxes of clothes and provisions; meeting every train with food and blankets; promoting entertainments for the troops; and assisting the Ladies Aid Association, whose members knitted socks, rolled bandages, raveled lint for dressing wounds, and solicited hospital supplies.

The day Lee surrendered to Grant at Appomattox, her eldest son, Joshua, was killed in action at Fort Blakely near Mobile. His brother Horace had been captured and his brother Perry wounded the day before.

When peace returned Octavia used the medium of poetry—she had been writing since she was twelve—to express her grief over her personal losses and the defeat of her beloved southland. In "An Exhortation" written in "the dark days 'After the War!'" she wrote:

> *Oh, Land of the South, be thy soil ever sacred!*
> *Enriched as it is by the blood of the brave,*
> *To thee our love, to thy foes our hatred,*
> *Thou birth-place of Heroes! Of Martyrs, the grave!*

CATALOGUE 139.

CATALOGUE 141.

Eleanor H. Cohen (1841–1874), by her brother Lawrence Cohen, ca. 1865. Collection of the Moses family.

"Columbia in Flames," *Harper's Weekly*, April 8, 1865. South Caroliniana Library, University of South Carolina.

Eleanor H. Cohen, daughter of Charleston pharmacist Philip Melvin Cohen and Cordelia Moïse Cohen, moved to Columbia with her family in pursuit of safety during the war. She was there when Sherman's army marched into the city in February 1865. Eleanor was engaged to be married in April, but her betrothed, Benjamin Mendes Seixas, was forced to leave Columbia as Sherman approached. "Oh! God, can I ever forget that day," Eleanor wrote in her diary. "Can time with Lethean draughts ever efface from my memory the deep sorrow, the humiliation, the agony of knowing we were to be under the Yankees, that our beloved flag was to be pulled down and the U.S.A. flag wave over the city."

The fires in Columbia, set by both sides, soon engulfed one-third of the city. As the inferno approached their neighborhood the Cohens fled, leaving behind their dearest possessions, "letters of loved absent ones, pictures of our precious relations, tokens and souvenirs of childhood." In a single night, the family was "brought from comparative wealth and luxury to abject poverty. . . . I never imagined I should be so near actual starvation."

It made Eleanor's "southern blood boil to see them [Yanks] in the streets!" She deplored the changes brought about by the war. "Slavery is done away with," she wrote. "I, who believe in the institution of slavery, regret deeply its being abolished. I am accustomed to have them wait on me, and I dislike white servants very much." She felt betrayed by the servants who left but pleased by Rose and Helen, who "were true," and by Lavinia, who gave them "cotton homespun and behaved like a friend."

Radicals and Redeemers

LEFT: FIGURE 31. *Franklin J. Moses Jr., ca. 1875. Courtesy of the South Carolina Historical Society.*

RIGHT: FIGURE 32. *Captain Edwin Warren Moïse, ca. 1862. Gift of Mr. and Mrs. Benjamin Moïse. Courtesy of the Sumter County Museum Archives.*

Edwin Warren Moïse epitomizes the fierce allegiance most Jewish South Carolinians felt for the Confederacy. Son of Abraham and Caroline Moses Moïse, he was born in Charleston in 1832 and brought up in Beth Elohim, where his father was a leader in the reform movement. At age fourteen, Edwin worked as a clerk and then went into his own business. In 1854 he married Esther Lyon of Petersburg, Virginia, and the next year moved to Columbus, Georgia, where he operated a flour mill, kept books, and studied law with his uncle Raphael J. Moses.

Though opposed to secession, once the Civil War began Moïse raised a company of "Partisan Rangers," or cavalry, at his own expense. Officially named the Moïse Rangers, the unit fought in North Carolina and Virginia, and teamed up with Major General Wade Hampton in 1864 in what came to be known as the

"Great Beefsteak Raid." When the South surrendered, Moïse settled in Sumter, where he built a law practice, went into politics, and wrote for the local newspaper. An ardent supporter of Hampton and a commander of the Red Shirts, an armed volunteer organization opposed to Radical Reconstruction, he was elected adjutant general of the state in the riotous 1876 election. To this day family members revere Moïse as a hero and continue to refer to him as "The General."

On the other side of the drama were three Reconstructionists with Jewish fathers and gentile mothers. Franklin J. Moses Jr. was governor of the state from 1872 to 1874, during the period white South Carolinians dubbed "Black Rule." Like his mother and his wife, Moses was a practicing Christian. His father, Franklin I. Moses Sr., came from a prestigious Jewish family and had been a distinguished lawyer and state senator from Sumter for twenty years before the war. The senior Moses served as chief justice of the state supreme court during Reconstruction, maintaining his reputation as an honest and competent jurist. The judge renounced neither Judaism nor his son.

When the Republican party rejected the younger Moses's bid for renomination as governor in 1874, friends in the legislature elected him circuit judge for the Sumter area. Edwin Moïse, who was practicing law in Sumter, threatened to shoot Moses if he ever came to town. Moses never did, because Governor David Chamberlain refused to issue the commission. In an attempt to distance themselves from the "Robber Governor," Moses family members changed their surnames to DeLeon and Harby. Reviled as a traitor to the South, and denounced for corruption, drug addiction, and consorting with blacks, Franklin Moses Jr. fled to the north and died in poverty in Worcester, Massachusetts, an apparent suicide.

Thomas W. and Francis Lewis Cardozo, champions of Negro education during Reconstruction, had a Sephardic father, Isaac N. Cardozo, who worked in the custom house and whose forebears were founders of Beth Elohim. Their mother, Lydia Williams, was known in the parlance of the time as a "free person of color." Educated in the city's self-supporting schools for free blacks, Francis was apprenticed out to learn carpentry, Thomas to a manufacturer of rice-thrashing machines. Francis Cardozo attended schools in Scotland and England and upon his return to the United States became minister of the Temple Street Congregational Church in New Haven, Connecticut. Thomas settled in New York with his mother and taught school in Flushing, where he met and married a fellow teacher.

At the end of the Civil War, even before peace was finalized, Thomas returned to Charleston to lead the American Missionary Association's efforts to assist the newly freed blacks, whom he described as "my oppressed brethren." In August 1865, after confessing to an affair with a student in New York, Thomas was replaced by his brother Francis as head of the association's Avery Institute in Charleston. Thomas went into the grocery business and eventually moved to Mississippi, where he returned to public life and was elected state superintendent of education in 1873. Three years later he resigned under threat of impeachment, and seems to have embezzled funds from Tougaloo College. He then vanishes from historical view.

Francis remained principal of Avery for three years. In the next decade he served as president of the South Carolina State Council of Union Leagues, a member of the South Carolina Constitutional Convention (1868), a trustee of the University of South Carolina (1869), secretary of state in the Scott administration (1868–72), and state treasurer in the Moses and Chamberlain administrations (1872–76). In contrast to the reputations of his brother Thomas and of the scalawag governor Franklin J. Moses Jr., Francis Cardozo's record was clean. ❧

A city of ruins, of desolation, of vacant houses, of widowed women, of rotting wharves, of deserted warehouses, of weed-wild gardens, of miles of grass-grown streets, of acres of pitiful and voiceful barrenness—that is Charleston.

—Sidney Andrews, *The South Since the War as Shown by Fourteen Weeks of Travel and Observation in Georgia and the Carolinas,* 1866 (originally published in the *Boston Advertiser,* September 4, 1865)

In the Wake of War

The impact of the war on Jewish society was, on the one hand, to impoverish a once-prosperous class of merchants and tradesmen and, on the other, to create economic openings for newcomers with energy and ambition. Columbia, as the capital of the state that led the rebellion, was singled out for punishment by General Sherman's army and suffered massive destruction. Portions of Charleston were reduced to rubble during three years of bombardment.

Jewish religious practice in South Carolina's cities was affected as well. Men had died, families had moved away, fortunes were ruined. In Columbia the Hebrew Benevolent Society, the center of Jewish life, had been destroyed. Moses Henry Nathan lost his home on Plain (Hampton) Street; he took shelter in the abandoned Columbia Female College and had to beg friends for food. Jacob C. Lyons, businessman and president of the Columbia Gas Works, had lived in the city since 1820. His house, the Gas Works, and four of his commercial properties were lost in the fire. After trying unsuccessfully to rebuild, he decided to leave Columbia. "Nothing was saved except some silver [we] had buried," his daughter recalled. "Soon after that my family moved to Philadelphia and none of us ever returned."

In Charleston, scarcity and social dislocation compelled Shearit Israel and Beth Elohim to set aside their differences and join in a single congregation. A six-year compromise was hammered out in 1866. The Portuguese minhag was reinstituted, in abbreviated form. The organ—which went up in smoke in Columbia, where it had been sent for safekeeping—would not be replaced, but a mixed choir of men and women was formed to sing in Hebrew and English. Old melodies cherished by the traditonalists and newer melodies preferred by the reformers both would be sung. No one but the hazzan would read from the Torah. A second day was added to holiday observances, for those who wanted it. The wall between the two cemeteries came down.

With the local economy shattered, congregants were hard pressed to pay their dues. Charles H. Moïse, Beth Elohim's first postwar president, was a wholesale grocer who styled himself "an enlightened Orthodox Jew." A man of his place and time, he was forced to resign due to financial embarrassments.

FIGURE 33. *Baruch family, ca. 1900. Left to right: Dr. Simon Baruch, his sons Hartwig and Sailing, his wife Isabelle Wolfe Baruch, his sons Herman and Bernard, Bernard's wife Annie Griffen Baruch. From Bernard Baruch,* Baruch: My Own Story, *following page 114.*

Newspaper columnist Dorothy Parker once remarked that two things confused her: the theory of the zipper and the exact function of Bernard Baruch. Perhaps South Carolina's most famous Jewish son, Bernard Mannes Baruch (1870–1965) became known as the "Park Bench Statesman" and "Adviser to Presidents." A graduate of New York's City College, he made a fortune on Wall Street by the age of thirty, then began a career of public service.

Baruch's father, Simon, who had immigrated to Camden following his landsmen Herman and Mannes Baum, served as a surgeon in the Confederate army. Bernard's mother, Isabelle Wolfe, was descended from Sephardim who had arrived in New York in the seventeenth century. When Bernard was eleven he moved with his parents and three brothers to New York City. In the postwar South, opportunities for education and professional advancement were scarce. Besides, Simon Baruch worried that the violence of everyday life, born of the white South's frustration and defeat, would affect his children. Yet the family remained staunchly pro-southern. Raised on the maxims of Robert E. Lee, Bernard Baruch remembered his father jumping up and giving the rebel yell whenever a band struck up "Dixie."

In 1918 Baruch was named to head the War Industries Board. The next year he attended the Versailles Peace Conference, conferring with President Woodrow Wilson on the economic terms of the treaty that ended World War I. An adviser to Franklin D. Roosevelt, Baruch also served in the Truman administration as counselor to fellow South Carolinian

CONTINUED ON PAGE 142

The Civil War came at a moment in South Carolina's Jewish history when the old Sephardic stock was dwindling. On the rise were Ashkenazim from central Europe, some who had been in America for a generation or two and some who had just disembarked. Herman and Max Furchgott, recent immigrants from Hungary, came to South Carolina to take advantage of frontier conditions created by the war. They arrived in Charleston at the end of 1865 and the next year opened a dry-goods store on the corner of King and Calhoun Streets.

Germanic names, common among Ashkenazim, sometimes masked a Sephardic lineage. For example, the Simon Baruchs of Camden, South Carolina, descended on their mother's side from a Portuguese family named Marques; the Pollitzers of Beaufort and Charleston traced their maternal line to the Kuhs, Sephardim who had settled in Prague in 1498. The Baruch and Pollitzer families were socially prominent, well educated, and ambitious, destined to produce famous sons and daughters. Buffeted by the storms of the Civil War, the families followed opposite trajectories.

Without forsaking their southern sympathies, the Baruchs relocated to New York City in 1881. The Pollitzers came south during the war to take advantage of a unique set of circumstances. Union forces had occupied the plantation strongholds around Port Royal Sound, near Beaufort, South Carolina, and had taken the unprecedented steps of confiscating thousands of acres of land and freeing the slaves, whose masters had fled during the Federal invasion in November 1861. Informed by coverage of events in the New York press, and sensing the vacuum created by the departure of cotton brokers and factors, who had bolted with the planters, Moritz Pollitzer brought his family, including five young children, to this

CONTINUED ON PAGE 143

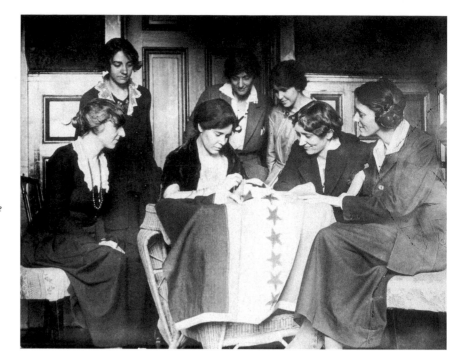

and Secretary of State James F. Byrnes. In 1946 Baruch was appointed as the American delegate to the United Nation's Atomic Energy Commission where he helped design policy for international atomic energy control.

Baruch used his fortune to endow a college at the City University of New York and to found Camden Hospital in his hometown. He returned regularly to South Carolina, where he entertained dignitaries at Hobcaw Barony, a coastal estate he pieced together from defunct rice plantations in Georgetown County.

ABOVE: FIGURE 34. *Anita Pollitzer with Alice Paul and others, sewing National Women's Party banner, ca. 1916. Courtesy of South Caroliniana Library, University of South Carolina.*

Three granddaughters of Moritz Pollitzer— children of his son Gustave Morris—became forceful advocates of women's suffrage and equal rights. Their mother, Clara, had graduated from Hunter College, and her experience there was influential in shaping her daughters' political ideas and activism. On their father's side they descended from an upper-class Prussian family with its own coat of arms. Moritz's brother Adolph, a brilliant musician, played as a child for Franz Joseph, emperor of Austria-Hungary, and performed Mendelssohn's Violin Concerto in the presence of the composer.

Moritz's son, Gus, born in New York in 1853, moved from Beaufort to Charleston at age sixteen and married Clara Kuh Guinzburg of Baltimore, daughter of a rabbi from Prague. Gus Pollitzer became a successful cotton factor in Charleston and, like his father, was accepted in the upper echelons of lowcountry society. He supported Wade Hampton's successful bid for governor in 1876, which brought an end to

carpetbag rule in the state. He was elected to the South Carolina Society in 1891, served as commissioner of the city hospital from 1895 to 1903, and was on the Committee on Reception for the South Carolina Inter-State and West Indian Exposition in 1901. He was a member of the school board for the city of Charleston, while his daughters were carving out careers as innovative educators and his son, Richard, was teaching pediatrics at the Medical College.

Carrie Pollitzer (1881–1974), the eldest daughter, pioneered the entry of women into the College of Charleston, beginning in 1918, when she raised $1,500 to provide for a women's lounge and a female supervisor for coeds. A graduate of Memminger Normal School and the South Carolina Kindergarten Training School, she also took courses at Harvard, Columbia, Cornell, the Universities of Michigan and Colorado, Wellesley, and Vassar.

After graduating from Columbia University, Mabel Pollitzer (1885–1979) returned to her high-school alma mater, Memminger Normal School, where she taught for forty years. There she headed the science department, organized the biology curriculum, and promoted programs in nutrition, health, and sex education. A champion of public libraries, Mabel helped

establish the collection that is now the Charleston County Public Library. She served as a trustee for the library, The Charleston Museum, and Kahal Kadosh Beth Elohim, the synagogue she and Carrie attended all their lives. As early as 1912, Mabel was agitating for women's right to vote. She later served as state chairman of the National Women's Party.

Like her older sisters, Anita Pollitzer (1894–1975) attended public and private schools in Charleston, graduating from Memminger in 1913. At Columbia University Teacher's College in New York she befriended fellow student and artist Georgia O'Keeffe. She later introduced O'Keeffe to photographer Alfred Stieglitz, and wrote a biography of her.

Leaving behind an early career in the art department at the University of Virginia, Anita Pollitzer devoted herself to women's rights through her work in the National Women's Party, which she went on to chair. For fifty years she crisscrossed the country to promote its causes, advocating the ratification of the Nineteenth Amendment, whose passage in 1920 gave women the right to vote, and helping to draft the Equal Rights Amendment in 1923.

new frontier. In a short time he became a successful cotton merchant and an agent for a cotton gin manufacturer. Though he did not become a planter himself, he accumulated extensive land holdings, valued at $15,700 in 1870. Technically a carpetbagger, that is, a Yankee who came south to profit from the upheavals of Reconstruction, Pollitzer nevertheless gained respect and authority in his adopted hometown.

In the period of flux that followed the Civil War, people were on the move. Whites and blacks, Jews and gentiles, were motivated by the desire to reconnect with their families, flee sites of destruction or return to rebuild, and find places for themselves in a depressed and volatile economy. Native South Carolinians were joined, after 1880, by a trickle of newcomers who had recently passed through either the Castle Island immigrant processing center in New York, predecessor to Ellis Island, or a smaller port of entry such as Baltimore, Maryland, or Galveston, Texas.

It is a truism of social history that in the competition for immigrants in the antebellum era, South Carolina and the South as a whole did not attract their share of new arrivals because of the presence of a massive enslaved workforce that drove down wages and stigmatized manual labor. Still, southern cities did manage to draw German, Irish, and other northern European mechanics, craftsmen, and construction workers to seasonal and sometimes permanent positions. After the war and the abolition of slavery, however, the immigrant flow to the South actually ebbed. A persistently low wage scale, predicated on Negro labor, was one source of discouragement. Another was the lack of industrial openings in the rural, single-crop economy.

Steps taken by the state to lure immigrants were largely futile. A Bureau of Immigration was established in 1882 under the aegis of the South Carolina Department of Agriculture to entice European workers. It sought to ease a perceived shortage of hands in upland cotton mills and to create a white majority in a state where more than half the people were black.

In 1883 South Carolina's foreign-born population stood at 7,686, down 2,300 from 1860. By 1890 the number had dropped to 6,270, by 1900 to 5,528. These numbers reflect a balance of out-migration over in-migration and could apply, more or less, to any southern state. Of more than 800,000 people who migrated to the United States in 1903, a mere seventy-three, or fewer than 1 percent of 1 percent, set their sights on the Palmetto State. South Carolina's Jewish population remained at about 2,500 individuals until 1907. Over the next ten years, however, the number almost doubled to 4,816 people. The consequences of this influx on the structure and leadership of the state's Jewish communities was profound. ❧

Figure 35. Keyserling family, Beaufort, S.C., 1915. Gift of Herbert and Harriet Keyserling. Courtesy of the Jewish Heritage Collection, College of Charleston Library.

William Keyserling came to the United States from Lithuania in 1888 at age nineteen and established himself with Macdonald, Wilkins and Company, a cotton ginnery and wholesale warehouse in Beaufort. Subsequently he sent for his four brothers, his mother, and his orphaned niece and nephew. The Keyserling brothers all became prosperous and prominent in their adopted home; one of their offspring would make his mark as an economist and architect of the New Deal.

In 1907 William Keyserling married Jennie Hyman, who had arrived in America at age five and was educated in New York City. Upon marrying William, she reluctantly left the glitter of the big city for a South Carolina backwater. William and Jennie's first child, Leon, spent his early years on St. Helena Island, east of the sleepy town of Beaufort, reading books with his mother and developing gifts of quick comprehension and remarkable memory. In 1917, at age nine, Leon moved with his parents and three siblings to town, where, in the tenth grade, he won an award for an essay entitled "A Bigger, Better, and More Beautiful Beaufort." A framed copy hung in his office and, after his retirement, at his home.

Leon attended Columbia University and Harvard Law School, then returned to Columbia to teach economics. He worked as chief legislative aid to New York Senator Robert F. Wagner and helped craft major New Deal economic and employment programs, including the National Industrial Recovery Act of 1933, the Social Security and National Labor Relations Acts of 1935, and the U.S. Housing Act of 1937.

From 1946 to 1953, he served on President Truman's Council of Economic Advisers and became its chairman. His interest in public policy continued after his retirement from government in 1953. During the 1970s he drafted the Humphrey-Hawkins Full Employment and Growth Act and the legislation establishing the Department of Housing and Urban Development. Upon his death in 1987, Massachusetts Senator Edward Kennedy cited Keyserling's "half century of tenaciously working to translate economic and social justice into everyday reality for every man, woman and child."

CHAPTER FOUR

Little Jerusalem

FIGURE 36. *Schoenberg family, Riga, Latvia, 1911. Courtesy of Lucille Bernice Schoenberg Greenly.*

Things from the Old Country

One reason Jewish boys and men fled the vast tract in western Russia called the Pale of Settlement was to avoid conscription into the czar's army, where they faced harsh discrimination and pressures to convert. Stretching from the Baltic Sea in the north to the Black Sea in the south, the Pale was the sole area in the czar's domains where Jews might live. Though not officially designated as the Pale until 1835, when Czar Nicolas gave the territory a name, restrictions had been in force since the late 1700s.

By 1880, the Pale was home to six million Jews. The assassination of Czar Alexander II in 1881 set off waves of persecution, to which hundreds of thousands of Jews responded by emigrating. Whether hailing from Poland, Lithuania, the Ukraine, Rumania, or Russia, inside or outside of the Pale, these refugees were known simply as Russian Jews. Within forty years, upwards of 2.5 million had boarded ships for America.

People migrated for a myriad of reasons besides the often-cited menace of conscription. Overpopulation made earning a living increasingly difficult. Jews were barred from schools and occupations, restricted in their movements, limited in all their civil and property rights. Murderous attacks called pogroms, often encouraged by local authorities, threatened their physical safety.

America offered the promise of a better life. Typically, immigrants gravitated toward family or countrymen who has come before. Charleston, South Carolina, with its old and illustrious Orthodox congregation and its warm climate, attracted substantial numbers of Russian Jews. The big jump occurred between 1907 and 1912 when the city's Jewish population more than doubled, growing from eight hundred to two thousand people. The neighborhood where the newcomers settled, north of Calhoun and west of King Streets, earned the name "Little Jerusalem."

These poorly shod, Yiddish-speaking immigrants filled the time-honored trades of peddler and small shopkeeper and invigorated the Orthodox tradition. The things they brought with them reflect what they valued most and regarded as essential to a good life. Generally, only the most durable and cherished items survived.

A carpenter's tools and Sabbath candlesticks may retain their functions and meanings in the New World. But as immigrants become acculturated, objects from Europe that cease to be used for the purposes they were intended are transformed into symbols of the past and heirlooms to bind the generations. A samovar that once made tea in Kaluszyn, for instance, may occupy a purely sentimental place on an end table in a St. Philip Street parlor where coffee is the drink of preference. ❧

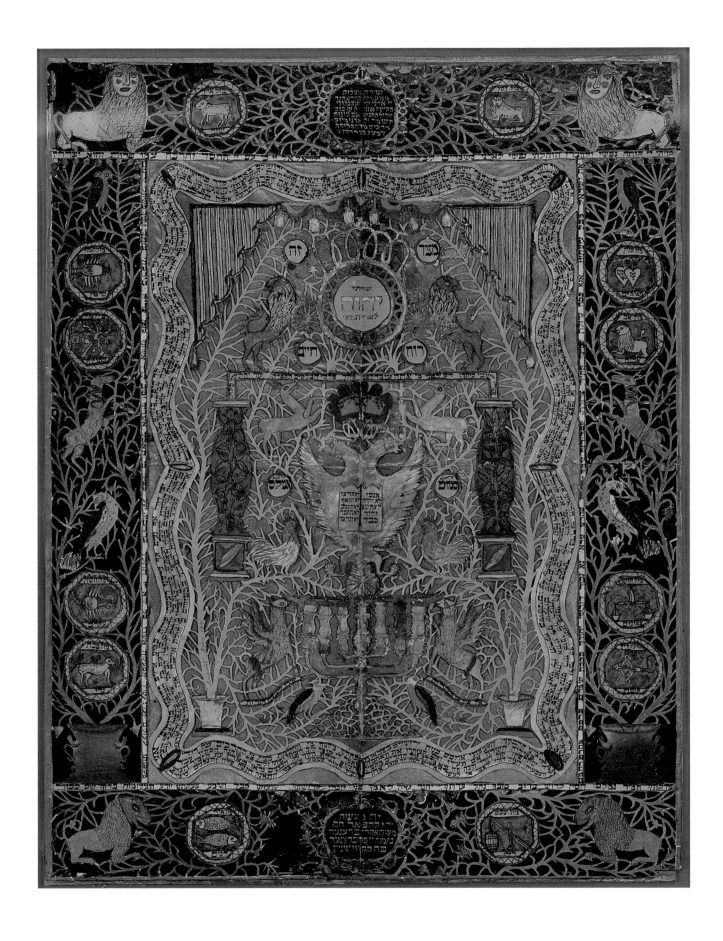

Mizrah, papercut made by Morris Aaron Brenner, Wisnicz, Austria-Hungary, 1887–1891. Collection of Susan H. Baker.

Morris Aaron Brenner was born in 1874 in the town of Wisnicz, in the Austro-Hungarian Empire. He began work on the papercut at age thirteen and completed it four years later. With little money for such extravagances as art supplies, Brenner used a piece of butcher paper, painted with dyes made from berries. The creation combines elements of two types of documents: the mizrah, meaning "east," a drawing or tapestry symbolizing hopes for the restoration of the Temple in Jerusalem, which is hung on the east wall of a house to indicate the direction to pray; and the *shivviti*, from the phrase "Shivviti Adonai l'negdi tamid" (I have set the Lord always before me, Psalm 16:8), frequently found on the bimah in a synagogue.

In the oval medallion at top center is the daily prayer, Shir Hama'Alot, taken from Psalm 130:1–5, "A Song of Ascents." Inside the border, around all four sides, runs a scroll containing eight chapters from the "Song of Songs." Around the edge of the scroll a single line of lettering quotes from the Psalms and the morning prayers. Just above the deer, flanked on the left and right by quotations from Psalm 145, are the words, "Know before whom you stand."

The six words circling the center section are kabbalistic symbols (emblems derived from a medieval theological approach to unlocking the secrets of scripture). The twelve ringed pictographs around the perimeter are the signs of the zodiac. Each of the animal figures conveys a distinct message: the rampant lions signify that "Judaism makes one's heart as strong as a lion." The deer proclaim, "I leap like a deer to stand in awe before you." The two eagles seem to have a double meaning. The first is the religious conviction that Judaism "makes one soar like an eagle." The second may refer to the double-headed eagle emblazoned in the royal crest of Austro-Hungarian Emperor Franz Joseph, who was known for his goodwill toward Jews. Morris Brenner's son Jerry says his father may have included the symbol as a patriotic gesture.

The oval medallion at center bottom is the "signature piece." It reads, "This is my creation of which I am very proud—Moshe Aaron Brenner, son of Josef Brenner, Wisnicz." On the branch of the tree growing out of the pot in the lower left quadrant is the date, in English, August 1891; the same date in Hebrew appears on the branch on the lower right. Jerry Brenner believes his father Morris may have penciled in these dates many years later.

Morris Brenner married Cecilia (Celie) Morowitz in Bremen, Germany, in 1899. A year later their first child, Ella, was born, and the next year the family immigrated to the United States. They lived on New York City's Lower East Side, where Moshe operated a used-clothing and junk business, as had the Morowitz family in Germany. The couple had seven more children. Four more girls, Henny, Sarah, Charlotte, and Gertrude, preceded three boys, two of whom lived to adulthood—Irving and Jerry (named for Josef, Moshe's father). Sarah, writing under the name Sydney Taylor, authored *All-of-a-Kind Family*, based on the life of the Brenner children growing up in New York. For a generation of Americans, the fictionalized Brenners came to represent the typical, if somewhat sanitized, eastern European Jews who turned the Lower East Side into a teeming ghetto.

The art of making cut-paper pictures and patterns is probably as old as paper itself. As a Jewish ceremonial art, it dates at least from the seventeenth century when papercuts were used to decorate Italian *ketubbot* (marriage contracts). A "people of the book," Jews are enjoined to demonstrate respect and deference for the written word by careful calligraphy and the embellishment of scriptural texts. The art of paper cutting was practiced by both Ashkenazim and Sephardim.

The Brenner papercut, carefully restored and framed, came to South Carolina with Charlotte Brenner and her husband Louis Himber, who moved from New Jersey to Spartanburg in their later years to be near their daughter, Susan Baker. It hangs today in the Baker home, displayed on an eastern wall, as required by tradition.

CATALOGUE 149.

Wicker suitcase, Poland, ca. 1920.
Collection of Sam and Mitzi Kirshtein.

In this suitcase Avraham Kirshtein packed what he needed to make the trip from Kaluszyn, Poland, to Charleston, South Carolina, in late autumn of 1920. Avraham, or Abe as he became known in America, and his brother Natan, or Nathan, were living in different towns in Poland and had received draft notices at the same time. Both were anxious to avoid long service in the Polish army. On a visit to Nathan and his wife to see their one-year-old son Max, Abe learned his brother was thinking of emigrating. "Avraham," Nathan's wife told him, "For the same money he can get two passports." They bribed an official, secured their passports, and set out for the train station in Warsaw.

"It was loaded with people dodging the draft," Nathan's son Max recounts, "and the government was checking all exits. Four out of the five exits were being checked thoroughly and my father and his brother had to select the right one, which they did. But to create more problems their youngest sister, who was fifteen years old at the time, had discovered that they were going to America and she ran through the station looking for them. 'Avramola!' she yelled, and 'Noota!'—that was their Jewish names—she says, 'Why are you leaving without coming to see me?'"

They finally boarded the train and got as far as Hamburg. Needing thirty-five dollars each for passage to America, they wired Mrs. I. M. Goldberg, in Charleston, South Carolina, one of three Kirshtein sisters already living in the United States. Though it was Shabbes, so the story goes, she went to the bank—banks were open on Saturday at that time—and she wired the money. The brothers continued on to Le Havre, booked passage on the *Lenox*, and arrived at Ellis Island on December 6. They reached Charleston exactly one week later, in time to celebrate the last night of Hanukkah in their new home.

CATALOGUE 77.

Hanukkiah, or Hanukkah menorah, Poland, ca. 1900. Collection of Sam and Mitzi Kirshtein.

Nathan's wife brought the menorah with her when she emigrated from Kaluszyn, the year after the Kirshtein brothers settled in Charleston. At their father's request, she gave the oil lamp to her brother-in-law Abe. Shortly before he died in 1992, Abe passed it on to his oldest son, Sam.

Many customs have evolved around the holiday of Hanukkah, the eight-day festival commemorating the victory of the Maccabees over the army of the Syrian tyrant Antiochus in 164 B.C.E. The most widely practiced ritual involves lighting a menorah or hanukkiah, an eight-branched candelabrum or oil lamp, with one light for each night and an additional one, the shammes or helper, to light the others. Lighting the candles recalls the original lamp for which there was enough oil to burn only one night. Miraculously it burned for eight. The illumination, which grows stronger each night, also symbolizes the increase of holiness as the festival reaches its fulfillment.

Gragger, Russia, late 19th century.
Collection of Shera Lee Ellison Berlin.

The *gragger* was brought to America by
Ezekiel Joseph Ellison, who got off the
boat in Baltimore, settled briefly
in Savannah, and arrived in
Charleston in 1883. Graggers, or
noisemakers, are used in the traditional Purim service to commemorate the rescue of the Jews of ancient
Persia from Haman, the king's chancellor, who sought to annihilate them in
the fifth century B.C.E. The Jews were
saved by the intercession of Esther, the
King's Jewish wife. Each time Haman is mentioned, children in the congregation twirl graggers to drown out his evil name.

CATALOGUE 157.

Letters in Yiddish, with cloth bag,
of Joseph Wolf Mark and his bride,
Lena Mae Banisch. Beaufort and
Burton S.C., and Russia, 1904–1912.
Collection of Rose Yospe Mark.

Joseph Wolf Mark, from Lithuania, arrived in
the United States on September 29, 1904. He
was twenty-eight years old, five foot five inches
tall, 148 pounds. He came to live in the Beaufort area with a sister. Rebuffed by his sweetheart in Russia, Mark began writing to her
younger sister, Lena Mae Banisch. Eight years
later Lena agreed to join him in South Carolina. She brought with her, in a crude linen
bag, the letters of their courtship.

Joseph and Lena were married in 1912 at
the home of her aunt and uncle, the Micha-
loves, in Asheville, North Carolina. Lena traveled by train from Asheville to Yemassee,
South Carolina, where she was met by Joseph's
chauffeur, Frankie Lawrence, who also worked

CONTINUED ON PAGE 152

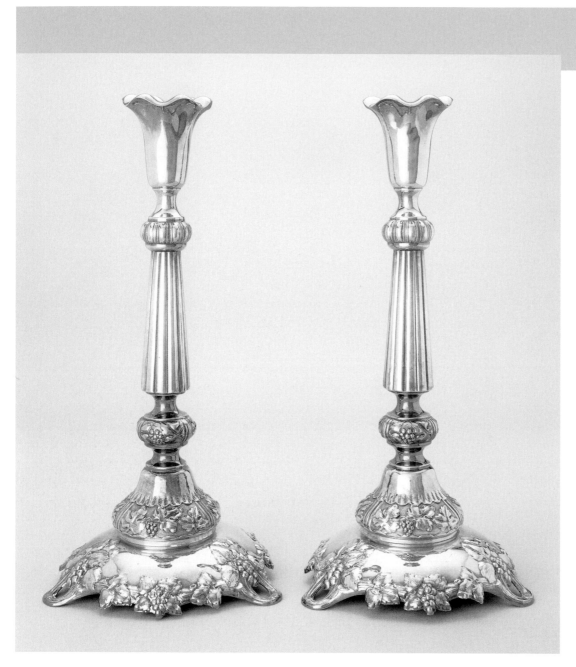

CATALOGUE 210.

Candlesticks belonging to Yocha Sobel Bolgla, Warsaw, Poland, ca. 1900. Collection of Sol and Sara Breibart.

CATALOGUE 157 CONTINUED

in the store. She had finished school and was well read, but she couldn't understand a word Frankie said to her. The Marks settled into the apartment above Joseph's dry-goods store in the crossroads settlement of Burton, five miles west of Beaufort. Their first child, Ada, was born in 1915, followed two years later by Ernest. Lena and the children moved into

Beaufort some time in the 1930s, when driving the youngsters to school in town became a burden. Joseph joined them in 1940 after his store in Burton was destroyed in a storm. The building had blown down on top of him and Frankie Lawrence pulled him out of the rubble.

CATALOGUE 158.

Bolgla address book, passports, and immigration documents, Poland, 1921. Gift of Sara Bolgla Breibart. Jewish Heritage Collection, College of Charleston Library.

Sara Bolgla (shown in inset, center, between mother, left, and brother) was eighteen months old when she left Brest-Litovsk, Poland, with her parents Abram Moshe (Morris) and Yocha

Sobel Bolgla, her five-year-old brother Hillel, grandmother Sheina Perel, and young uncle Leizor. The Bolglas sailed from Antwerp, their destination "the land of milk and honey, where the streets were paved with gold." The voyage was a nightmare. "What could be good about traveling steerage class," Sara recalls, "parents who could not speak English and were afraid to eat the food due to their obsession with keeping kosher?" Sara cried so much, no one wanted to come near her. "No

wonder you cried," her mother said. "We were afraid to let you eat the food."

Soon after reaching New York, the family received a telegram from Morris's father, who had gone ahead with his older brother to Augusta, Georgia, and opened a shoe store. Morris debated whether to rush to Augusta and set up a second shoe shop in space his father had rented for him, or to stay with his wife, who was approaching her ninth month of pregnancy. Yocha told him, "What will be

CONTINUED ON PAGE 154

Charleston's Uptown Jews

For fifty years, the center of Charleston's eastern European Jewish community was the neighborhood north of Calhoun and west of King Streets, a southern version of Manhattan's Lower East Side. Of the 2.5 million Jews who migrated to America between 1880 and 1924, the few thousand who came to Charleston, like their cousins in the North, were called "greeners" or "greenhorns." Men commonly started out as peddlers, then established small businesses on King Street, notably dry-goods, furniture, shoe-repair, and tailor shops; hardware, jewelry, and secondhand stores; mattress factories; groceries and delicatessens. At one time some forty stores on upper King Street were closed on Saturday, in observance of the Jewish Sabbath. Shopkeepers spoke Yiddish, kept their ledgers in Yiddish, and subscribed to Yiddish newspapers, *Der Forvertz*, *Der Tag*, or *Der Morgen Journal*. Though the *Forvertz*'s left-wing politics may have been alien to their experience, everyone loved reading *Bintel Briefs*, an advice column for immigrants.

Families would settle in apartments above their stores, then move into Charleston "single houses" along adjacent streets. They kept chickens and an occasional cow in their backyards. They used the services of *shohatim*, ritual slaughterers, and *mohalim*, who performed circumcisions. The men held prayer services above Zalkin's kosher meat market and behind Sam Solomon's wholesale jobbers. The women kept kosher homes.

The "uptown" Jews established a second Orthodox shul named Beth Israel, a *landsmannschaft* called the Kalushiner Society (many of the immigrants came from Kaluszyn, Poland, thirty miles northeast of Warsaw), and the Jewish Community

---

CATALOGUE 158 CONTINUED

with you, will be without you—you must go and get the business started."

Tucked in her baggage Yocha carried a pair of candlesticks and a small, hand-sewn address book, with names and addresses, most in English, and marginal notes in Yiddish, written mainly in her own hand. They included dozens of relatives and friends who had settled all over the United States: Abe Sobel, now living in San Francisco, who in the old country had made Persian-lamb caps for the Cossacks; Cousin Heyman in Savannah; Louis Wengrow in Blackville, South Carolina; Feinburg in Fitchburg, New York; Schereshevsky in Brooklyn; the Rosenthals in Milwaukee; Nathan Goldman in Chicago; the Sonenbergs in New York (in later years they would take Yocha to the Brestka Ball); and last but not least, the Joint

Distribution Committee, "20 Exchange Place, New York, America."

Thinking back on the experience, Sara Bolgla Breibart marvels at her mother's fortitude in "leaving home and relatives with very slim chance of ever seeing them again, traveling from New York to Augusta with three small children, one a new-born, and not even being able to speak the language."

Why were they willing to gamble on the great unknown? "My father's family was poor," Sara concludes. "When people are poor with very little opportunity to make life better, they are more willing to chance a change. So my father's family picked up and came. On the other hand, my mother's family was different. Her father, following the same pattern, came to this country, earned enough

money to send for his wife and children (my mother had two brothers), but my maternal grandmother would not go. She was ultra-Orthodox and came from a moderately well-to-do family, so things weren't bad enough for her to leave. And being so Orthodox, she would not go to a *treyf medinah* [a nonkosher country]. As a result, my father's family was spared the Holocaust, but my mother's family all perished. Would you call it luck—lucky to be poor?"

In Augusta, Morris and Yocha Bolgla opened their little store, first selling secondhand shoes, then new ones. They never became "a Saks or a Macy's," Sara reports, "but they made a respectable living—buying a house, educating their children to become professionals—and lived to a ripe old, comfortable age."

FIGURE 37. *Lilly Zalkin Bebergal in front of Zalkin's Meat Market, 535 King Street, Charleston, S.C., 1942. Courtesy of Robert Zalkin.*

During World War II, Americans were asked to save household items, such as paper and rubber, which were collected at designated stations to be reused for the war effort. The sign Lilly holds informs shoppers that Zalkin's kosher market is an official fat collection station, where housewives can turn in used cooking oils and grease to be recycled as explosives.

Center where boys, and some girls, attended heder, or Hebrew school. Eastern European Jews constituted a conspicuous minority, but not a majority, of the neighborhood. They lived next door to black Americans and immigrants from Greece, Italy, Germany, Ireland, and China. Serving a primarily African American clientele, uptown shopkeepers were more likely than downtown merchants to extend credit to black customers and let them try on clothes. Socially, the Orthodox Jews remained separate from the Reform "Deutscher" (German) downtown congregation, Kahal Kadosh Beth Elohim.

In the South as elsewhere, Jews of German extraction felt culturally superior to Jews from the *shtetlakh* (Jewish villages) and ghettoes of eastern Europe. In the spirit of Jewish charity, and in an effort to "uplift" the Russian Jews so as not to be tarnished by association with the greenhorns, the old-timers started classes to teach them English, hygiene, etiquette, and skills they would need to become citizens. The women of Beth Elohim founded the Happy Workers in 1889, which ran a sewing class for immigrant girls. The Charleston Section of the National Council

I'll tell you what I know about Kaluszyn, what my father told me about Kaluszyn. Friday night you were required to have the biggest meal you could have to usher in the Sabbath. And what they did to clean the house. When I came home on Friday, the house was sparkling clean. White tablecloth. Candles going. Just beautiful. You knew. No one had to tell you it was Shabbes. It was Shabbes.

—Samuel Appel (b. 1929,
    Charleston, S.C.)

Mrs. Banov would call on the women. Mrs. Banov, Mrs. Berlin, Mrs. Patla, Mrs. George Birlant, his mother—all from downtown. They would visit the greenhorn women, and the men would visit the men and give them advice about what to do, and who to buy from, and what kind of merchant, what you could sell, what you couldn't. They helped them with advice, you know. Not so much money, but advice. That's how they got started.

—Edna Ginsberg Banov
(b. 1908, Charleston, S.C.)

~

Our home was kosher, presided over by a colored woman named Agnes Jenkins, who came from the country and only had one job in her life and that was being my mother's cook . . . . One day you'd get a typical southern dinner of fried chicken and rice and okra gumbo, and the next day the appetizer would be pickled smoked salmon and then a bowl of lentil soup and then potato latkes or potato kugel or tsimmes.

—Saul Krawcheck
(b. 1926, Charleston, S.C.)

~

Having a cleaning person was very inexpensive in the South in those days. For two dollars, you could have a maid all week. And people want to know why we've had problems—there's been slavery here up until the time I was a little girl, you know.

—Lillie Goldstein Lubin
(b. 1923, Charleston, S.C.)

of Jewish Women, organized in 1906, tried to break down the immigrants' isolation and to work with the women of Brith Sholom and Beth Israel on common civic projects. Perhaps the most important help came informally, from members of eastern European families who had preceded them.

The transition of Russian Jews into Charleston was eased by the presence of an established, socially successful Jewish community. Strains between uptown and downtown Jews persisted, however, for two generations. Perhaps the most important infusion of southern culture came from a group of people descended from the first Carolinians—black servants hired to keep house, cook, and care for children, and black workers in the stores who handled stock, swept floors, delivered merchandise, and did everything but staff the counters and cash registers.

Even poor immigrants could afford maids, cooks, yardmen, and eventually men servants in the house. The black influence was particularly evident in language and foodways. The English dialect spoken by lowcountry white people was marked by the inflection and rhythm of Gullah, the African-American creole language that emerged on the Carolina coast. A creole cuisine following the kosher laws and utilizing local ingredients was created by black cooks standing at kitchen stoves with Jewish *bubbes* (grandmothers) giving directions. ❧

FIGURE 38. *Party for Carolee Rosen's first birthday, Asheville, N.C., 1931. Courtesy of Carolee Rosen Fox.*

TOP: FIGURE 39. *Opening day at Read & Dumas, 583 King Street (corner of Spring Street), Charleston, S.C., 1912. Courtesy of Rosemary Read Cohen.*

FIGURE 40. *E. Prystowsky & Sons ("Mike, Sam & Jake's"), 521 King Street, Charleston, S.C., ca. 1930. Courtesy of Arnold and Shirley Prystowsky.*

The Mazos' [delicatessen] was three or four doors up [from Zalkin's meat market]. Zucker had a furniture store a couple of doors next to us. Star Furniture Company was Max Zucker's father and that's Bubba Zucker's father also. Across the street—I remember when they came to Charleston—was the Siegels. They had a shoe-repair shop. They were cousins to the Oxlers who had a shoe-repair shop further up the street. Directly across the street from us was a candy store. All the [clothing stores and shoe stores] on King Street, I'd say 99 percent, were Jewish. Robinson had a bicycle shop up at the corner. Solomon had a bicycle shop halfway, next door to the Mazos.

[The Prystowskys] had Mike, Sam and Jake's, men's clothing. All the brothers were in the store. And across the street from them was Edward Kronsberg who had the five-and-dime store, Edward's. . . . On Saturday you couldn't buy a piece of furniture; you couldn't buy clothing. The stores were closed in Charleston. You couldn't buy anything on Saturdays. Of course, later on you could, but I'm talking about in the early thirties and late thirties. Seems like the war changed everything.

—Robert Zalkin (b. 1925, Charleston, S.C.)

CATALOGUE 166.

Telegram to E. Ellison in Savannah, Ga., April 26, 1883. Collection of Shera Lee Ellison Berlin.

Ezekiel J. Ellison came to Charleston in 1883 in response to an emergency telegram from G. Hoffman, the president of congregation Berith Shalom (Brith Sholom). Two shohatim in Charleston had been disabled, perhaps in a train accident. "Mr. Reuben broke his arm and Mr. Kaminsky his legs," the telegram said. "Come immediately by first train to take place as shohet. Answer by telegram when you will come."

The laws of kashrut, which regulate what Jews are permitted to eat and how certain foods must be prepared, require that animals be killed with one quick stroke of the knife against the throat. A man trained in this skill is known as a shohet. Because the Torah associates kashrut with holiness, and because the occupation of shohet is essential if a community is to keep kosher, the function is quasi-religious. In some cases, the slaughtering of animals is performed by the shammes, the cantor, or even the rabbi. Shohatim in the United States often were called "Reverend."

Reverend Ellison not only butchered meat for members of the congregation, but kept accounts for the shul. Reverend Feinberg, who succeeded Ellison, served as cantor and shohet. Rev. Alter Kirshtein, the older brother of Nathan and Abe Kirshtein, was caretaker as well as shohet of Beth Israel, the "Kaluszyner Shul" founded in 1911. Alter, which means "old" in Yiddish, was the oldest Kirshtein brother and deeply steeped in religion. "He was very, very religious, my *fetter* Alter, Uncle Alter," says his nephew Sam. He worked as shohet for Bakers' meat market on King Street, as well as for Beth Israel. "One time," Sam recalls, "the Bakers bought a freezer. My father Abe gave it to them at cost.

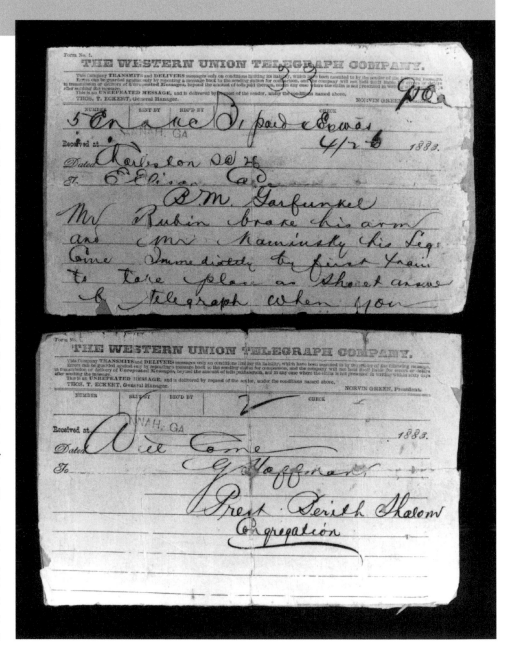

And the wife called us up [to say] that the freezer wasn't working. She was very upset and furious about that. We sent a crew over there, sent a serviceman. It wasn't even plugged in! That's how naive they were. I'm talking about worldly things."

CATALOGUE 164.

Shohet knife with sharpening stone and cloth used by Jake Kalinsky in Holly Hill, S.C., ca. 1920. Collection of Adrian and Ethel Kalinsky Kremer.

In 1912, at about fourteen years of age, Jake Kalinsky left Trestina, Poland, with his mother Ida and two sisters, bound for America. His father, Meyer, had come ahead and opened a little store in Holly Hill, South Carolina, fifty miles northwest of Charleston. The new arrivals stayed first in Charleston, and Jake learned to slaughter chickens in the ritually prescribed manner, a skill that would stand him in good stead in the frontier community to which the family was moving.

Soon they settled in Eutawville, where a few Jewish families, including relatives of the Kalinskys, were already living. Jake and his father would drive in a horse-drawn buggy seven miles to Meyer's shop in Holly Hill. Besides selling general merchandise, the Kalinskys went into the fur trade. They bought raccoon skins from local hunters, stretched them on the wall at the back of the store or in a shed behind their house, and sold the pelts to New York furriers.

In 1920 Jake married Minnie Friedman, who had arrived in America only months before. Debarking in Philadelphia on December 22, 1919, Minnie, with her mother and siblings, headed straight for Charleston. Like many eastern European Jewish immigrants, they followed the path blazed by their *mishpocha*, or relatives. Two older brothers, Sam and William, had come to the United States before 1910 and gained a foothold in Charleston thanks to their maternal kin, the Kareshes. Isaac, their father, arrived in 1914, expecting his wife and the other children to follow shortly. But World War I intervened, and it took five years for the family to reunite. When Mrs. Friedman and her children finally stepped off the train in Charleston, more than a hundred relatives and friends were there to meet them.

The Friedmans and Kalinskys knew each other in the Old Country, though Jake and Minnie were meeting for the first time. The young couple moved to Holly Hill and Jake went into business for himself. The trip to Charleston was arduous. Dry weather turned the dirt roads to deep sand; rain turned them to mud. Unable to depend on regular trips to Zalkin's meat market in the city, Jake used his shohet knife to provide the family with kosher meat. If a chicken did not die in a certain length of time, his daughter Ethel recalls, they would give it away. If it was deemed kosher, her mother Minnie would pluck the bird, lay it on a big board in the kitchen sink, and rub it with salt. Occasionally Jake traveled to the town of St. George, fifteen miles away, to slaughter chickens for Minnie's sister, Annie, who had married Louis Lourie and was raising a family of six children.

Once the roads to Charleston were paved and the family acquired a big refrigerator and freezer, the Kalinskys started buying kosher meat in Charleston and freezing it for later use. Sometime in the 1930s Jake's stint as a shohet came to an end.

I want you to imagine me, seven, eight years old. My mother always gave me ten cents for lunch. At that time I used to have a great love for delicatessen. My heart would go out to corned beef or salami—I'd die for it. One day I'm going through the line in school and I can't believe what I see. I see a sandwich that has pastrami in it, or what I thought was pastrami. So I paid my nickel for the sandwich and couldn't contain my joy. As I bit into the sandwich I realized it wasn't corned beef—it was ham. And I spit that sandwich out from my mouth. I threw the sandwich away, and my heart was full of terror. I thought that God was gonna get me 'cause I had eaten pork, eaten treyf. I immediately ran to the library, I hid in the library right after lunch, I stayed in that library the rest of that afternoon until school was out, then I ran home. I was terrified that God would strike me dead. Around two or three o'clock, which was my normal time to go to heder on George Street, I didn't want to go. I guess it was either suffer the consequences of God's wrath or my mother's wrath, and I took my chances with God. I walked to heder in terror. I thought God was going to kill me. It took me a few days to realize that God didn't have time, he didn't see me, so I was safe—but that's the mind-set of somebody who's accustomed to the Orthodox ways.

—Sam Liberman (b. 1926, Charleston, S.C.)

OPPOSITE: CATALOGUE 173–176.

Letters between Mamie Ellison and Jacob Karesh, Charleston and Bamberg, S.C., July 1898–August 1903. Collection of Barbara Karesh Stender.

"My Darling Beloved Mamie, Dearest one, The first Monday in our happy New Year"— so begins a love letter written in September 1898 by Jacob Leander Karesh, living in Bamberg, South Carolina, to his seventeen-year-old sweetheart in Charleston, Mamie A. Ellison. "Dearest Darling Beloved Jake," she writes in turn, filling him in on a dance given by the South Carolina Social Club over on Long Island and an upcoming moonlight excursion, events she longs to attend with him. She relays news of the young Jewish crowd, mentioning Jake Pearlstine, Morris Ellison, Mose, Mollie, Yank, and Rachel Karesh, the talk of the town now that she's engaged. Week after week, for almost five years, their correspondence continues, Mamie spicing her letters with enough romance to leave him on tenterhooks; Jake answering with serious declarations of love.

The couple married in 1903 and moved into a house at 8 Warren Street with Jacob's brother Abe and mother Kalie, widow of Israel Moses Karesh. Later they moved to their own place further down the street. After stints working as a clerk at Levin and Levy on King Street and a grocery on Wall Street, Jake opened a fish market. Every baby born in the neighborhood, as soon as the infant was a few days old, would be whisked down to the Karesh fish market. Jake would lay a fresh sheet of white wrapping paper in the huge scale, lay the baby on the paper, and announce the weight amidst a clamor of *mazel tovs.*

Births, britot milah (circumcisions), bar mitzvahs, weddings, funerals, and Jewish holiday celebrations were community social events. As in Europe, food played an important role. Mamie was well known as a cook, regularly serving, besides her seven children, numerous cousins and guests who gathered at her table. She catered kosher dinners for receptions and made special kosher cakes for weddings. Hiring extra hands for these large events, Mamie taught her black kitchen help how to cook "kosher-style," training that made them sought after by Jewish households around the city. The Karesh kitchen was always a beehive of activity, whether the occasion called for fifty baked chickens or fifty gallons of matzah ball soup.

Wedding photograph of Mamie Ellison Karesh, Charleston, S.C., 1903. Collection of Barbara Karesh Stender.

Dressed in the sweeping, long skirt and lacy, high-necked, billowy blouse in fashion at the turn of the century, Mamie strikes a regal pose for her wedding photograph taken at Clarke's Studio at 301 King Street. Coincidently, her seventh child, Karl Karesh, would open a men's clothing store three decades later at the same location.

Feather rose, Charleston, S.C., ca. 1905. Collection of Barbara Karesh Stender.

Mamie Ellison Karesh (1880–1934) wore this feather hatpin to shul on Friday nights. The rose, likely made from common duck feathers dyed purple to look exotic, could lend sophistication to a plain felt hat. Married Orthodox women cover their heads in synagogue. Wearing a hat, however, was not only a religious necessity but also a fashion statement. The women sat upstairs in the balcony, the men downstairs on the main floor. In general women did not know Hebrew and could follow the prayers only by rote, or in some cases in a special Yiddish-language siddur, or prayer book. The long services were punctuated by the rustle of skirts and patter of shoes as the women slipped in and out of the pews to catch some fresh air or tend to their children.

Flower pin in box, ca. 1890. Collection of Barbara Karesh Stender.

Jake's father presented his mother with this gold enameled pansy pin with diamond center and seed pearl stem. Israel Moses Karesh and Kalie Krawcheck both were born in Trzcianne, or Trestina, Russia (now Poland), about 1848, and with their two small sons immigrated to Charleston around 1873. Jacob was born in 1874, to be followed by another three children, Abe, Janie, and Eva Dora Karesh. Kareshes and Krawchecks had been coming to South Carolina since the 1850s and marrying other Kareshes and Krawchecks, as well as Pearlstines and Jacobses—kinsmen from the same shtetl in Russia. Marriages between cousins and landsmen, or people from the same part of the Old World, created networks of family and friends across the state.

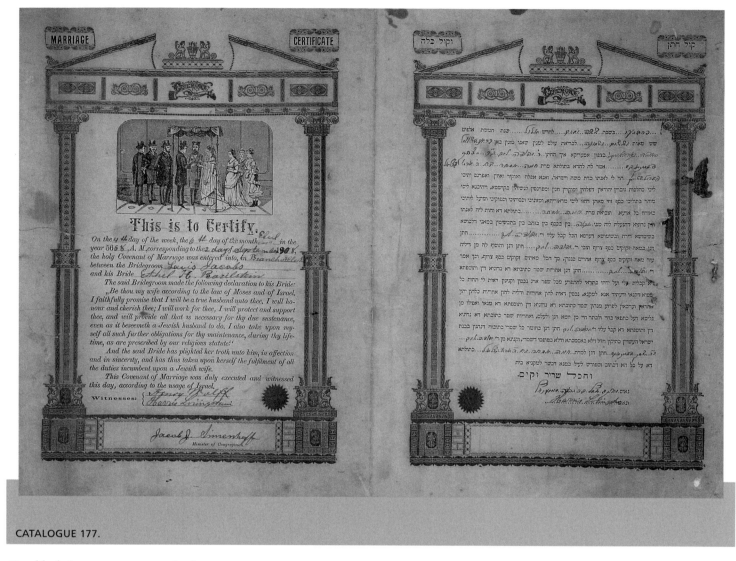

CATALOGUE 177.

Ketubbah (marriage contract) of Louis Jacobs and Ethel H. Pearlstine, Branchville, S.C., 1908. Gift of Ethel Pearlstine Jacobs. Brith Sholom Beth Israel.

Louis Jacobs and Ethel H. Pearlstine were married on September 2, 1908, in Branchville, South Carolina. (Pearlstine was misspelled Pearilstein on the *ketubbah*.) The bride and groom were cousins. A two-coach Southern Railway train was chartered to carry guests the sixty-five miles from Charleston, where many of their friends and relations lived. Rev. Jacob J. Simenhoff came from Brith Sholom to perform the ceremony.

The first generation of Pearlstines and Jacobses arrived in Charleston in the 1850s and were among the founders of the so-called Polish shul. Although family members fanned out across the state, opening stores in train-stop towns like Branchville, Bamberg, Ehrhardt, and St. Matthews, most kept their affiliation with Brith Sholom and observed Jewish rituals as best they could. The story is told that the night after the wedding Ethel's mother sat until dawn in the hall between two bedrooms to separate the bride and groom because the bride had been unable to go to the mikveh (ritual bath) in Charleston.

Louis and Ethel both were born in South Carolina, Louis in Charleston in 1878, Ethel in Branchville in 1886. Louis was the son of

Isaac and Jeanette Slager Jacobs. Ethel's mother was Rebecca Tobish Pearlstine. Her father, Louis Charles (L. C.) Pearlstine, died when she was three months old.

Ethel's grandfather, Tanchum (Tom or "Tonkle") Pearlstine came to Charleston in 1854 from Trestina with his eleven-year-old son, Isaac Moses (I. M). The rest of the family followed late the next fall, setting out in a covered wagon with straw at the bottom, padded with feather beds and pillows. The party included Tanchum's wife Janetta, in her mid-thirties, six of their children, ages three to eighteen, and her younger brother Isaac. Cold weather forced them to turn back; after Passover they tried again, crossing Germany and making their way to England, where all but two boarded a

FIGURE 41. *Brith Sholom men and boys choir, Charleston, S.C., ca. 1919. Gift of Joan G. Bovarnick, Eileen G. Goldfless, and Barbara G. Goodman. Courtesy of the Jewish Heritage Collection, College of Charleston Library.*

CATALOGUE 177 CONTINUED

sailing ship in Liverpool. Eleven weeks later they arrived in New Orleans.

Tanchum's daughter Lena was seven years old at the time; late in life she wrote down a shattering tale. On the voyage across the Atlantic, only the mate on the English ship spoke German. Janetta Karesh Pearlstine (also known as Jeanette or, later, Jane Esther) asked for some food to make soup or gruel, and the mate and captain gave her grain that had been mixed with rat poison. According to one version of the story the poison was administered deliberately, because the oldest sister, Fageh Etta, had resisted the captain's advances. Whether by design or accident, Fageh died that night, lying next to Lena; eleven-year-old Miriam Rose expired the next day about sunset. "A few minutes before she died," Lena recalled, "I saw my mother motion to those that were standing behind her to step back. As soon as they did, breath left my darling sister. My mother . . . wrapped her in a clean white sheet. Some of the men tied her on a board with a large rock on each end, put it on the railing of the ship, and shoved her overboard. I can see everything now, as then, after more than 75 years. The splash. I shall never forget, if I live to be a thousand years."

Lena's brother L. C. Pearlstine and uncle Isaac Karesh remained in Liverpool, where they worked as glaziers until they had raised enough money to pay for the ocean voyage. Upon arriving in America, Isaac, the son of Jacob and Rebecca Karesh, told immigration authorities his name was Yitzhak ben Yaakov, Isaac the son of Jacob, and was given the last name of Jacobs. In 1860 he married Jeanette Slager in Due West, South Carolina; they moved to Cincinnati at the start of the Civil War. Family legend claims that when Union recruiters came to the house to conscript him, Isaac hid under a bed. After the Confederate surrender, he peddled his way back to Charleston.

Tanchum Pearlstine just missed being hanged during the war. He manufactured buttons for the Confederacy, and also would go through the lines, selling and repairing leather equipment. One time he was suspected of being a spy and was brought before a Confederate officer. When the captain heard his voice, he called, "Is that you, Tom?" and he was released.

L. C. Pearlstine, Ethel's father, was stranded in New York, where he had gone to buy supplies for his leather work, when the war began. To get back to South Carolina, he trailed the Union forces, mending leather articles for the soldiers. Years later his granddaughter Cecile wanted to join the United Daughters of the Confederacy but held back because her mother told her that grandfather L. C. had followed the Northern army to get safely home.

Louis Jacobs and his father Isaac operated a hosiery and shoe store on King Street. The shop was closed on Shabbes. The Jacobses kept benches on the street for people to wait until Isaac (called "Jew Jacobs" by his black customers) opened the door after dark. One Saturday Louis decided to have a Mr. Greenberg open the store while he went to synagogue. The next Saturday Isaac was crossing King Street on his way to afternoon minyan, when from the corner of his eye he saw the door standing open—wide open. He turned around and walked into the shop, which was a hundred feet from front to back. He walked all the way to the back and then out the front. He didn't see Louis until the next morning.

"Lou," he said, "I see you got your store open on Shabbes."

Louis replied, "Yes. I need the business. I need to make more money."

His father said, "I don't care how much money you have, you'll never have enough. I'm not putting my foot in your store again."

Isaac later relented and worked the cash register in the store. He died at age seventy-six in 1915.

Louis and Ethel had eight children. Their descendants number thirty-two grandchildren, sixty-six great-grandchildren, and three great-great-grandchildren.

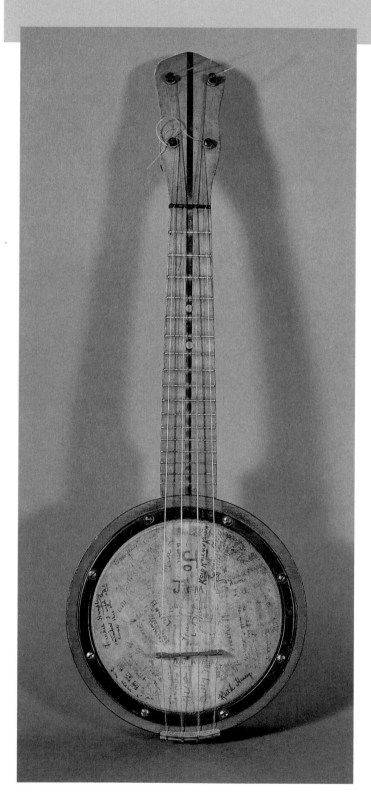

CATALOGUE 178.

Banjo ukelele, Columbia, S.C.,
ca. 1928. Collection of Sura Wolff Wengrow.

Rachel Pearlstine Wolff of Allendale, South Carolina, bought this banjo ukelele for her daughter Sura, during Sura's junior year at the University of South Carolina, when she and a group of friends at the university formed the "ukelele ladies." The friends performed on campus for groups such as the all-girl Euphrosynean Literary Society, of which Miss Wolff was a member, and the boys' Euphradian Society.

Most of the autographs on the "uke" came from members of the Arrow Social Club, an off-campus group of young Jewish people who met in private homes. Among the signers was a law student named Coleman Karesh, son of Rabbi David Karesh of Columbia's Beth Shalom synagogue. Coleman's signature is conspicuous because he signed his name in Hebrew and wrote next to it, in English, "Kool Coleman Karesh."

Wolff went out a few times with young Karesh, who would bring along his close friend and classmate Donald Russell. She enjoyed strolling on campus with "two boyfriends. . . . Students rarely had their own cars in those days," she recalls. "On dates we either went walking, sat on the benches on the Horseshoe (the trees were saplings then), on the steps of a college building, or on the dorm's long piazza." At her graduating voice recital, Coleman sent her red roses—she still has one rosebud framed under glass. (Coleman Karesh became a professor in the University of South Carolina's Law School in 1937 and taught there for thirty-five years. The law library is named for him. Donald S. Russell went on to become president of the university, then governor, United States senator, and a federal judge.)

Sura Wolff had led a sheltered life in her small hometown of Allendale. When she got to Columbia, she eagerly joined in college activities: the girls' glee club, the art club, and the student newspaper, *The Gamecock*. She took private voice lessons and tried her hand at tennis and field hockey.

When she first came to the university, Wolff lived in a small two-story house called the Annex. The following year she moved into the only girls' dorm on campus, known among some male students as "the chicken coop." There were two other Jewish girls in the dorm, but her closest friends were three non-Jewish girls. In their senior year the university allowed Greek sororities and fraternities on campus, and her friends joined a sorority. "We would like to ask you to join," they told her, "but they don't allow Jews!"

CHAPTER FIVE

Pledging Allegiance

FIGURE 42. *Confirmation at Beth Israel, Beaufort, S.C., 1926. From left: Lena Getz,*
Freda Lipsitz, Ethel Lipsitz, Samuel Leon Levin, Bethsheba Keyserling, Lena Schein,
Rosalyn Keyserling. Courtesy of Beth Israel Congregation.

New Departures

By World War I Jewish communities in Sumter, Camden, Spartanburg, Greenville, Aiken, and Beaufort had grown large enough to support synagogues. Meanwhile, access to gentile society had become more restricted. New Jewish immigrants from eastern Europe looked different from earlier arrivals. They spoke Yiddish or heavily accented English, wore long coats and hats, and rigorously observed Orthodox traditions. Acclimated, native-born Jews feared being tarred with the aliens' brush. Meanwhile the spread of racist doctrines based on a hierarchy of human types rationalized a nativist backlash against foreigners. Country clubs and certain fraternities and sororities barred Jews, who reacted by forming their own social groups, modeled on the organizations that kept them out.

A more self-conscious Jewish identity emerged. After 1906 the Charleston Section of the Council of Jewish Women, which had been founded in 1895, took an active role in integrating new immigrants. The women's auxiliary of Brith Sholom, South Carolina's first Ashkenazic congregation, built a Daughters of Israel Hall next door to the synagogue on St. Philip Street. In 1924 the Jewish Community Center opened around the corner. Jane Lazarus Raisin, wife of Beth Elohim's Rabbi Jacob Raisin, started up a branch of the progressive women's service organization Hadassah in the 1920s. The Charleston Chapter of Aleph Zadik Aleph (AZA), a fraternity for Jewish boys founded in 1931, sponsored social, educational, and charitable activities and athletic teams. AZA chapters sprang up in a number of South Carolina cities and members began attending regional, district, and national conventions. Social clubs—the Arrow Club and Yudedum in Columbia and the Key Klub in Charleston—held dances and functioned as matchmaking services.

Dan Lodge B'nai B'rith in Charleston dates from 1867. Revived around 1907, it brought together Reform and Orthodox Jews, and bridged the gap between old-timers and newcomers. By the 1920s immigrant Jews exceeded the native-born in most parts of the state. Recent immigrants began to run for and win the office of lodge president. B'nai B'rith lodges were organized in at least ten smaller communities, helping to unify Jews around an ethnic identity without regard to place of birth, date of arrival in America, or degree of observance.

Participation in parades and party politics integrated second-generation Jews into the larger community, while Jewish fraternities, clubs, athletic teams, religious and benevolent organizations set them apart in a parallel Jewish world. Jewish self-awareness between the world wars, in part a defensive response to anti-Semitism on the airwaves and in the press and in part a strategy for appearing as American as anybody else, gave rise to teams with names like "Jewish Juniors." Reuben Siegel, who lettered in five sports and was Clemson University's champion boxer, chose as his fighting name "Jew Boy Siegel." ❧

FIGURE 43. *Jewish Juniors champion basketball team, Charleston, S.C., 1927. Clockwise from upper left: Coach Albert Kohn, Albert Kaufman, Davie Collis, Rubin Goldin, Louis Rosen, (unidentified), (unidentified), Hymie Bebergal, Ben Epstein, Max Lerner, Jack Goldberg, Karl Karesh. Courtesy of Jack Lerner.*

CATALOGUE 179.

New Year's pop-up greeting card, ca. 1910.
Collection of Leonard B. Cohen.

The pop-up New Year's card, printed in Germany for the American market, was a prized possession of Hannah Jessie Horwitz Cohen. Born in Baltimore, Maryland, in 1900, Hannah lived most of her married life in the town of Latta, in the Pee Dee region of South Carolina. It is likely the New Year's card came from her favorite relative, her aunt Rose Rockowitz.

Hannah's grandparents had immigrated to America before 1900. They settled in Baltimore, attracted by its large Orthodox community. Her grandfather, Berel Laib Horwitz, had been born in Jerusalem, then moved to Latvia with his parents, where he married. Hannah's father, Louis B., a Hebrew teacher, died of pneumonia in March 1902, when Hannah was one-and-a-half years old. Her mother, Mary Caplan Horwitz, probably American-born, entrusted Hannah to Louis's sister Rose and her husband Abraham Rockowitz, who raised her in Baltimore along with their five daughters.

Hannah attended school through the seventh grade and then went to work as a secretary and bookkeeper at a wholesale food company in Baltimore. While she had limited formal education, she was a highly intelligent woman. She read the Bible and newspaper every day of her life. In 1923 she married Isadore Cohen, who had been born in Lithuania in 1896 and come alone to America at the age of fourteen. Settling in Baltimore, he earned enough money to send for his parents and younger brother and sister.

The story of the Cohens' move to South Carolina and their slow climb to success is typical of the small-town southern Jewish merchant. Working in Baltimore for two dollars and fifty cents a week, Isadore Cohen, his son Leonard reports, was looking for something better. Isadore's older brother, Harry, had been a peddler in the Pee Dee and suggested Isadore try his luck there. Harry gave Isadore five dollars, enough for a train ticket to Dillon, South Carolina. After working for a time in a store in nearby Latta, Isadore got a "stake" from the Baltimore Bargain House, which provided merchandise on credit to aspiring shopkeepers. He rented a small store in Latta (it was eleven feet wide) and went into business for himself. With help and encouragement from Hannah, he soon owned his own house and a more spacious store.

As supplier to Jewish dry-goods merchants, Baltimore was to the Southeast what New York was to the Northeast, and Cincinnati to the Midwest. The Cohens continued to buy their

CATALOGUE 179 CONTINUED

merchandise in Baltimore, noted for its men's clothing and good values. They catered mostly to rural people—farmers and tenant farmers—from the outlying communities, who did their shopping in Latta. Once the store became successful, Hannah stayed home and worked in the yard.

"My grandmother was a totally liberated woman," says Hannah's granddaughter Dona Cohen Guttler, "very unlike most grandmothers. She was definitely not a bubbe personality. I never knew her to have baked or cooked anything. She had help that did that because she simply had no interest in anything domestic. She was, however, devoted to the exterior and yard of her home. She almost always wore pants and covered her waist-length braided hair with a bandana and was outside almost every day. On more than one occasion, neighbors would call my dad at his store to tell him that his mother was on the roof of the house performing some chore such as cleaning the gutters. Since my grandmother was very strong willed, there was no 'talking her down'; she would come down when she was through with her project. She planted all types of flowers and trees in her yard. I recall picking up pecans from a giant pecan tree. She even had figs in a small garden."

Hannah was tiny, four foot eight inches tall and about eighty pounds in weight. A pretty woman with unwrinkled skin even in old age, she had no interest in fashion, but on her trips to Baltimore to visit Aunt Rose and Rose's daughters, she would buy high-quality apparel from her favorite store, Hutzler Brothers, often shopping in the children's department because she was so small.

Though not conventionally "domestic," Hannah was traditional in spiritual and religious matters. She kept her home "as close to kosher as possible," her granddaughter recalls. "I am certain that no treyf ever crossed her doorstep." Because there was no Hebrew teacher in Latta, Hannah arranged for her son Leonard to be trained and bar mitzvahed by Rabbi Israel Solomon at Camp Osceola, in Hendersonville, North Carolina.

CATALOGUE 184.

Lady Lafayette Hotel plate, Vernon Kilns, California, ca. 1938. Gift of Sam and Leona Novit Siegel. Jewish Heritage Collection, College of Charleston Library.

This commemorative plate, manufactured about 1938, was designed to promote the Lady Lafayette Hotel, Motor Court, and Grill in Walterboro, South Carolina. These and many other enterprises were founded and managed by a visionary, self-educated immigrant named Albert J. Novit.

In 1910, at twelve years of age, Albert Novit left the town of Kastrinaslav in the Ukraine with his mother, father, two brothers, and a sister, and arrived at Ellis Island, off the southern tip of Manhattan. The Novits (their name had been Novitsky in Russia) settled first on New York's Lower East Side. When Albert's brother Abe was transferred to Charleston, South Carolina, by his employer, Postal Telegraph, the family moved with him. Their father, Joseph, became the shammes, or caretaker, of Brith Sholom synagogue on St. Philip Street. The Novits lived in an adjoining building, on the first floor of which was the congregation's mikveh.

About 1918 Albert Novit moved from Charleston to Walterboro, where he married Bessie Zalin, whose family was already established as proprietor of Zalin's Department Store. He soon opened Novit's Department Store, occupying two adjoining storefronts across from the courthouse on Washington Street. He and Bessie initially lived in an apartment above the store. In the early 1930s, he moved the shop to the old Zalin's Department Store building down the same street and started a new, upscale ladies' shop, Novit's Fashion Shoppe, in the building that had housed his first store. He transformed the nineteenth-century brick building into a classic example of what is now called art deco.

Meanwhile, recognizing that the new north-south route from New York to Florida would pass through Walterboro, in 1927 he constructed the original building of what was to become the Lady Lafayette, "America's Most Unique Hotel." The hotel boasted freestanding cottages as well as rooms in a quaint, Old World-style main building. Within a few years he added the Lady Lafayette Grill, serving his traveling clientele "the finest food south of New York."

At the Lady Lafayette, Novit amassed the world's largest collection of miniature dog figures, all donated by guests. His eccentric ensemble won notoriety in more than six hundred publications, including *Life* and *Holiday*, and in the early 1940s was featured in a newsreel,

called "Strange As It Seems," distributed to movie theaters across the country. Before the heyday of chain stores, Novit opened branches of the Lady Lafayette Grill in Brunswick, Georgia, and Daytona Beach, Florida. The hotel and restaurant prospered until the mid-1950s, when Highway 301 bypassed Walterboro and killed the tourist trade.

Novit's Department Store was renamed Novit-Siegel Company when Sam Siegel of Anderson, South Carolina, married the Novits' daughter Leona and joined the firm. Novit-Siegel Company operated until Mr. Siegel's retirement in 1994. Novit's Fashion Shoppe closed a few years before that.

A. J. Novit had two brothers and one sister: Abe, Sam, and Miriam. Abe Novit established A. J. Novit Company, a restaurant supply house in Charleston. Sam Novit settled in Walterboro, where he became proprietor of Novit's Shoe Store. He drowned while fishing at Bennett's Point, at the southeastern tip of Colleton County. His widow, Frieda Levy Novit, ran the shoe store until the late 1970s, when she sold the business.

A. J. Novit was the classic self-made American. More secular and cosmopolitan than his brothers or sister, he dressed immaculately, prided himself on being well-read, and for years practiced perfecting his handwriting. His grandson Paul Siegel describes him as "patriotic to the extreme." He taught his daughter patriotic songs and enthusiastically supported war bond drives. Impressed with the American political model, he loved to talk politics and was active at all levels of the Democratic Party.

Putting his sense of civic duty into practice, Novit founded the Walterboro-Colleton County Chamber of Commerce and served as president for its first fifteen years. He headed the Department of Public Welfare for Colleton County and the Federal Housing Administration, and was a member of the local Board of Education and the South Carolina Pardon and Parole Board from its inception in 1942 until his death in 1962.

FIGURE 44. *Lady Lafayette float at Azalea Parade, Charleston, S.C., 1938. Courtesy of Sam and Leona Novit Siegel.*

Midlands Merchants

Jewish men who hailed from the German states, Prussia, Poland, and the Baltics peddled their notions and wares through South Carolina's Midlands in the 1840s and 1850s, learning to speak English along the way. Some acquired the means to open general merchandise stores, which came to serve as hubs of the farm economy. These merchants were well positioned to become middlemen in the crop lien system that took shape after the Civil War. The Witcovers, Hennigs, Baums, Blocks, Barnetts, Levis, and Weinbergs are just some of the families who furnished supplies to farmers against the sale of cotton at the end of the season, holding the land as collateral. If the crops failed, or if prices dropped below the cost of production, the merchants might acquire the land and become farmers in their own right.

FIGURE 45. *Barnett store, Sumter, S.C., 1904. Far left, B. J. Barnett; second from left, Henry D. Barnett Sr. Courtesy of Patty Levi Barnett (Mrs. Henry D. Barnett Jr.).*

When B. J. Barnett came [most likely from Estonia], he did like so many other Jews who landed in New York. He got himself together, ready to go out and be a business man, an entrepreneur. He got a pushcart, or whatever they pushed, and he became what they called a peddler. They usually headed south, those peddlers. All the Jews in the South—many of them—come from those people who came down as peddlers.

    He finally had enough money to buy some land, and he bought a place—we called it Manville. It's between here and Bishopville in Lee County. There was a swamp near there, and it was called the Scape O'er Swamp—means "escape over." Some slaves escaped over this swamp, so it's called Scape O'er Swamp. If you ever wanted to get Daddy mad—and we used to love to do that, needle

FIGURE 46. *Children of Shep and Sara Pearlstine. Clockwise from upper left: Sam, Leo, Hanna, Janet, Nathan (in Janet's lap), and J. T., St. Matthews, S.C., 1908. Courtesy of Marilyn Cohn Fine.*

Hoping to improve his health by leaving the sickly lowcountry, Sheppard Pearlstine, American-born son of I. M. Pearlstine and grandson of Tanchum Pearlstine, left Charleston in 1896 for the Midlands town of St. Matthews. There he opened a general store catering to the cotton trade, and in 1912 started a wholesale grocery business affiliated with his family's company in Charleston. He worked hard for I. M. Pearlstine & Sons, and for the good of the local community too. He served as alderman, member of the school board and the bank board, and an officer of the Masonic lodge. He was among those who lobbied the state legislature to create Calhoun County. In deference to "Mr. Shep," known as "the good shepherd of St. Matthews," several of his Christian friends walked out of a meeting called to organize a local chapter of the Ku Klux Klan and kept him posted about Klan activities.

Shep and his wife Sara raised a family of four boys and two girls. Though they did not keep kosher, the Pearlstines observed Jewish customs and maintained a membership at Brith Sholom. Their children later became members of Reform congregations, Tree of Life in Columbia and Beth Elohim in Charleston. The Pearlstines' daughter Hanna, who at the age of five attended Ethel Pearlstine and Louis Jacobs's wedding, is the oldest living descendent of Tanchum Pearlstine. In April 2002 she celebrated her ninety-ninth birthday.

him—you'd say, "You lived in the country. You lived on the swamp." "Certainly did not!" He'd say, "Why, we were the hub of everything out there!"

They ran the store that was the center of the community of the people that lived here, there, and yon, around Bishopville and on towards Sumter. It was sort of a commissary for the people on the farms, that would come into the store and get things that they needed, and then they would run an account which would be paid when the crop came in.

That was the gathering place, and they picked up their mail there. The oldest daughter, Minnie Barnett, she got her a little job as the postmistress at the store, and all the people in the rural area there came to that store to get their mail, so they knew the whole county. They knew everybody. They knew all the gossip and all the news and everything that was happening and going on. That's why Daddy'd get so mad if you wanted to get his goat—we loved to do that, you know. "Poppy, you was the hub of everything!"

My father was a cotton planter, and they had farms up at Dalzell Center, which is in this county. It's just about eight or nine miles up the road from [Sumter]. I used to ride out with him—he still rode in a buggy with a horse. He would go on a day's trip out to the farm and talk to the overseers, and talk about the planting and what was going on, and drive all over the fields, and on some days I was permitted to go with him. I will never forget those thrilling times. The other children never had that opportunity because cars came along, and after that he didn't use the horse and buggy anymore.

—Ruth Barnett Kaye (b. 1913, Sumter, S.C.)

Around the turn of the century, another group of Jewish peddlers and shop-keepers found their way to the Midlands and added a new element to Main Street. Try as they might, these Orthodox Jews from eastern Europe found it difficult to keep kosher and virtually impossible to close their stores on Saturday, the farmers' customary market day. Swimming in a heavily Protestant sea, Jewish people compromised with their environment, sometimes with hilarious results. The fact that these stories have passed into the genre of folk humor, however, suggests the lingering discomfort of having to make adjustments. The Sephardic proverb "A small-town Jew is half a Christian" speaks to the southern Jewish dilemma.

The neighbor across the street, she had seven children and she had the minister come to baptize them. While they were being baptized, I headed over there. Miz Violet told the minister, "There's a Jewish boy here, Mortie Cohen's coming over here, what do we do?" He said, "A little water won't hurt him." I was baptized.

—Mordecai (Mortie) Cohen
(b. 1917, St. Matthews, S.C.;
d. 2000, Charleston, S.C.)

FIGURE 47. *The Cohen family at the train station, St. Matthews, S.C., ca. 1910. Courtesy of Dorothy Gelson Cohen (Mrs. Mordecai Cohen).*

When I was a little girl, my best friend across the street went to the Baptist church, and they needed an extra angel for Christmas. "They need an extra one," Mother said. "Sure." So I was the extra angel in the Baptist church. We [also] sang at the Presbyterian church. I can sing "He Arose" with the best of them. That's the way it was in a small town.

—Ella Levenson Schlosburg
(b. 1920, Bishopville, S.C.)

Ella Levenson Schlosburg's father, Ephraim Zev (Frank) Levenson, dealt in mules and livestock in Bishopville, due east of Camden—a frontier for eastern European Jews at the turn of the century. Newcomers followed a route that took them from Bialystok to Baltimore to Bishopville, until there were some twenty-six Jewish families in the midlands town. For a time, the same Yiddishkeyt that flourished on Flatbush Avenue in Brooklyn appears to have bloomed in Bishopville. Mrs. Levenson baked hallah, made gefilte fish, tsimmes, and cherry wine, and lit candles to welcome the Sabbath. The family built a sukkah to celebrate the fall harvest and recall the desert wandering of the Hebrews during the Exodus.

[Dad] first started taking Sam out on the truck with him, and they'd go to the farmer's house early in the morning before the farmers went to the field—they were selling cows and horses and mules and they were trading—and always, when you went into a farmer's house: "Come to breakfast, come in and eat breakfast with us." So he went in and they were passing around big platters of grits, and this, that, and the other, and Sam—Daddy's putting on his plate, and put on Sam's plate, and Sam got a mouthful of something and he said, "Daddy, Daddy, what's this?" He had a mouthful of fatback and he didn't know what it was. My daddy turned to him and said, "Chew it and swallow."

—Ella Levenson Schlosburg

To Camden's German-Jewish old guard, Bishopville seemed like the Wild West. Carolyn Baruch, boarding a bus to go to Sunday school in Florence, was warned not to get off in Bishopville under any circumstances. When business came to a standstill in the Depression, most of Bishopville's Jewish families packed up and left. Some retraced their steps to Baltimore, landsman following landsman. Some moved on to other South Carolina towns and cities. Mrs. Levenson gave the community's Torah, candelabra, and books to Columbia's Beth Shalom.

I'm still kosher—I don't know if you know it—I'm a hundred percent kosher. And for forty-two years in Barnwell, I didn't ride on Friday night or on Shabbes. I'm not a fool, but I just wanted to keep up, and my sister Annie was the same way—that was Miss Lourie. But not my other sister, she didn't mind having meat on the table or milk. She'd buy kosher meat from Zalkin, but she would have milk with it. But not Annie nor I. We were the kosher ones in the family. We were very lucky, we were only twenty-eight miles from Augusta, and that was a very Orthodox city. We carried our children to AZA, BBG [B'nai B'rith Girls], and my son studied Hebrew for three summers in Augusta with the Smolen family.

—Libby Friedman Levinson
(b. 1909, Trestina, Poland; d. 2000,
Columbia, S.C.)

Textile Towns

Between 1880 and 1930, at a time when the Carolina upcountry was wielding the political power it had wrested from the lowcountry, Jewish populations in Spartanburg, Greenville, and Anderson more than quadrupled, thanks to an influx of eastern Europeans. Orthodox but beardless, Greenville's new Jews first held services in rented halls, then built Synagogue Beth Israel on Towne Street. Charles Zaglin, from Wilmington, North Carolina, became the community's shohet. Harris Bloom acted as religious lay leader and his son Julius as cantor. Most of the newcomers opened stores or worked as tradesmen, repairing shoes and watches. One family ran a barber shop, another a cigar factory. With the growth of a managerial sector in the textile industry, Greenville acquired a salaried class.

An unanticipated in-migration of Jews fleeing Hitler added dramatically to the Jewish communities of the Piedmont. Between 1937 and 1947, Greenville's Jewish population increased by more than 40 percent, from 183 to 260, while Spartanburg's jumped by 90 percent, from 98 to 170. Max Heller, who would go on to become mayor of Greenville from 1971 to 1979, was one of these refugees. Heller fled Austria in 1938 as the Nazis were closing in and came to Greenville to work in a shirt factory. The woman he would marry, Trude Schönthal, narrowly escaped from Vienna with her mother after the Nazis occupied Austria. It was nine months until they heard from Trude's father and nine months more until they saw him again.

I'm a born-again Jew, you have to remember that. I was born again in Greenville. Greenville became my home. The only thing I miss about Vienna was the music. That's the only thing, when I hear it. Yes, and the outdoor cafés. One reason you see those outdoor cafés, [when I became mayor] I said, "We have to have outdoor cafés in Greenville."

—Max Heller (b. 1919, Vienna, Austria)

Another refugee from Hitler's terror, Sandor Teszler came to America in 1948. Originally from Hungary, he had survived the war because his hosiery factories in Yugoslavia and Hungary could not operate without him. He stayed first on Long Island, in New York, where his brother already had settled eight years before, and established a small textile plant. Sandor's sons Otto and Andrew survived the war in Europe as well. Both enrolled at North Carolina State University in Raleigh, Otto in chemistry, Andrew in textile engineering. "In 1959," Teszler reports in his memoirs, "a new textile material appeared—double knit. Andrew got a call from a Mr. David Schwartz. 'You go to Europe and buy machines. You are starting a plant in Spartanburg.' Andrew went to Europe, bought machines, moved to Spartanburg, and in January of 1960, started the Butte knitting mill. It was a small little plant with 20,000 square feet; when he died in 1971 it was $1\frac{1}{2}$ million square feet and had become world famous."

While Andrew Teszler was introducing double-knit technology in Spartanburg, his father moved to North Carolina and started an innovation of his own. He opened a knitting mill in Kings Mountain, the first plant in the state with a racially integrated work force.

In 1969 Andrew joined the board of trustees of Spartanburg's Wofford College, a traditionally Methodist school. Without informing his father he donated money to build a new library, to be named after Sandor. In March 1971 the library was dedicated; six weeks later forty-year-old Andrew died. Sandor survived the death of both sons and his wife. He lived to be ninety-seven, taking classes at Wofford until the summer of 2000, when he quietly passed away. ❧

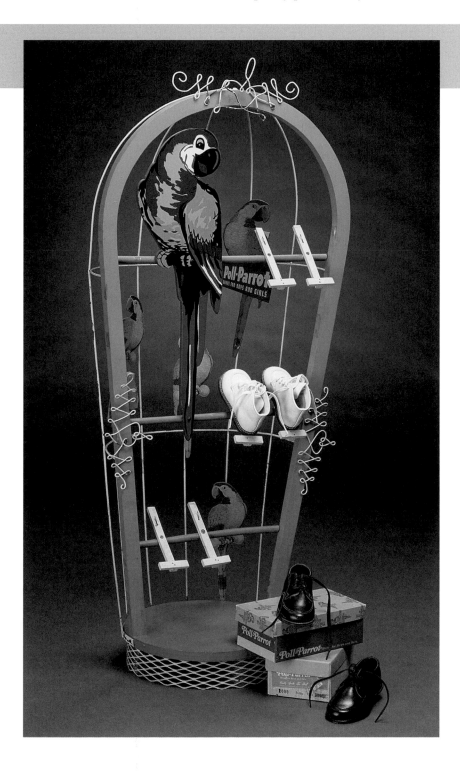

CATALOGUE 190.

Poll Parrot shoe display, mid-20th century. Collection of the Poliakoff family.

They loved this country. My mother had a picture of George Washington hanging in our house and a picture of Edison, 'cause she remembered when the electric lights first came. Those were her two heroes.

—Rosa From Poliakoff (b. 1914, Union, S.C.; d. 1999, Abbeville, S.C.)

CATALOGUE 192.

Pushke (charity box), inscribed "Charity for Jerusalem," ca. 1930. Collection of the Poliakoff family.

Poliakoff's dry-goods establishment opened for business on the square in the upcountry town of Abbeville in 1900. Its founder, David Poliakoff, came to America from Russia in 1896 and peddled first on foot and then by wagon in South Carolina. On February 19, 1900, at age twenty-five, he launched his store on the site where John C. Calhoun had practiced law. (Calhoun, a senator from South Carolina and vice president of the United States under John Quincy Adams and Andrew Jackson, was a staunch defender of slavery and states' rights in the age of abolition.) Sixteen months later Poliakoff became a citizen, an event heralded by a headline in the local paper, "He Is One of Us Now." His marriage to Elka Rachel Axelrod, his sweetheart from Minsk, Russia, was editorialized by the *Abbeville Medium* as "the wisest act of his life."

The couple had five sons and a daughter, and sent them all to college. The boys attended the University of South Carolina. Daughter Eva went to Agnes Scott College in Decatur, Georgia. She roomed with Rosa From of Union, South Carolina, whose father, like hers, was an immigrant and small-town storekeeper. In 1940 Rosa married Eva's brother Myer, the designated heir to the Abbeville business. After Myer died in 1986, Rosa ran the store until her death, five months short of its hundredth anniversary. Poliakoff's closed its doors for good in August 2000.

In its century-long history, Poliakoff's catered to a clientele that extended across the upcountry and over the Savannah River to Georgia. A town institution, Poliakoff's was a popular destination for generations of farmers and their families who came to buy hats, clothes, and shoes. Served by salesgirls trained by the Poliakoff women, and enticed by colorful merchandise displays supplied by manufacturers such as Poll Parrot shoes, customers found "not only the leading lines of the country but a varied and complete stock of clothing and ready-to-wear for men and women, dry goods, gents furnishings and every other item a modern department store stocks for the demands of the trade" (*The Press and Banner* and *Abbeville Medium*, November 4, 1937).

A small tin *pushke,* in which Rachel Poliakoff saved a few coins every week to send to Jerusalem, represents the persistence of the value of *tzedakah,* or giving, as well as support for a Jewish homeland in Palestine. In contrast to the silver-plated almsbox from Charleston, dated 1820, the Poliakoff pushke reflects the humble origins of the eastern European immigrants.

The World Wars

Most Jewish South Carolinians who went to war in 1917 could trace their roots to people who had come to America after 1880. The tombstones of the Civil War soldiers in the state's Jewish cemeteries mark the graves of southern patriots to whom they were not related. In effect, by joining the fight against the Kaiser alongside other young men from South Carolina, Jewish soldiers took a giant step toward solidifying their acceptance as citizens of their state and country. Identification with the ideals and struggles of the past might forever be out of reach, but participation in the wars of the twentieth century would create a shared heritage and a bulwark against forces of intolerance that have haunted the United States until recent times.

FIGURE 48. Huppah *for the wedding of Hilda Hennig and David Alexander Cohen, Darlington, S.C., October 17, 1918. Courtesy of David J. Cohen.*

The wedding of Hilda Hennig and David Alexander Cohen, First Lieutenant, U.S. Army, was scheduled to take place in Darlington on October 17, 1918, with a formal dinner to follow. But when the lethal flu epidemic that was circling the globe broke out in South Carolina, the couple's plans changed. The ceremony and reception were moved outdoors because people were prohibited from congregating in groups indoors. The Hennigs' yard, recently filled with bales of cotton, was draped in patriotic bunting, with a Star of David gracing the makeshift huppah. *The meal described in the printed menu was never served.*

ABOVE: FIGURE 49. *Julius H. Bloom (front row, second from left), Company A, First Battalion, 118th Infantry Regiment, Thirtieth Division, at Camp Sevier, Greenville, S.C., ca. 1917. Courtesy of Jack L. Bloom.*

My father was born in 1893 in Bialystok, Poland, and came to this country with his parents and brothers and sisters, going first to Columbia and then to Greenville. . . . He entered military service on October 9, 1917, and trained at Camp Sevier, just outside Greenville. He served as a soldier in the 118th Infantry Regiment, known as the Butler Guards, which saw service in the Confederate Army in the War of Northern Aggression. It agreed to rejoin the Union after "we" proved "our" fighting ability. The Thirtieth Division engaged in heavy combat against Germany in northern France and Belgium. . . . My father participated until he was severely wounded on October 8, 1918. He was hospitalized over six months—wounded by shrapnel. After he recovered, my parents were married—on August 19, 1919, as a matter of fact.

—Jack L. Bloom (b. 1920, Washington D.C.; raised in Greenville, S.C.)

LEFT: FIGURE 50. *Fannie Jolles Farbstein with her sons, Casper and Abe, Athens, Ga., 1918. Courtesy of Stanley Farbstein.*

World War II "changed everything," says Robert Zalkin, army veteran and son of Charleston's kosher butcher. Mobilization began in South Carolina in the 1930s and brought a level of prosperity the state had not experienced since before the Civil War. Thousands of soldiers and sailors passed through the port. "The only business in the city was on King Street," recalls Fannie Appel Rones, whose parents ran a furniture store on upper King. "There was no business off of King Street, so it was jam-packed. You had to stand in line for everything, stand in line for the movies, stand in line to eat, stand in line for everything. People started making money."

Besides reviving the economy, the war altered Jewish social life forever. Fort Jackson in Columbia, Fort Croft near Anderson, Shaw Air Force Base in Sumter, the Navy Base in Charleston—wherever servicemen were stationed and trained, the Jewish men among them were wined, dined, and entertained by local Jewish families, many with eligible daughters. In Charleston especially, Jewish girls had their pick of beaus. After the war, some soldiers returned and married their sweethearts. Others never came back. ❧

The war years came and it changed the life of a young girl in Charleston. We had fellows bursting in here from the army, the navy, the marines, the air corps, and they all wanted girlfriends. Before the war was over, every girl had a husband or boyfriend waiting for her—never mind the Charleston boys.

—Lillie Goldstein Lubin (b. 1923, Charleston, S.C.)

~

I think there wasn't a Jewish officer, sailor, coast guard, army guy, even air force, that did not come into [Laufer's kosher] restaurant to eat. And a lot of those fellows met Charleston girls and they got married.

—Helen Laufer Berle (b. 1923, Charleston, S.C.)

~

The [soldiers] were facing a terrible war. Some of them felt they would never come back; it was something that grew on the girls for those four years. They didn't know what was happening, and every year it was more and more serious. We started to see refugees come into the town from Germany, and it changed the tone.

—Lillie Goldstein Lubin

FIGURE 51. *Lieutenant Allen A. Rosenblum in his fighter plane "Rosey the Riveter," Seventy-eighth Fighter Group of the Eighth Air Force, England, ca. 1944. Courtesy of Raymond and Sandra Lee Rosenblum.*

Of Blessed Memory

In 1945, American Jews constituted the largest, most affluent, and politically influential Jewish community in the world. South Carolinians shared with their compatriots the dilemma of reconciling belief in God and in themselves as a "chosen people" with God's apparent abandonment of the Jews to the Nazis. To the descendants of people who had emigrated from areas in Europe where millions perished, the tragedy struck home.

Sabbath eve, my mother, may she rest in peace, would bless the candles in five brass candlesticks. Before this, of course, would be the regimen of cleaning and polishing, in order to get the brass to gleam. She would rub two bricks together to obtain a kind of brick powder, which was a wonderful polishing agent. This was what she used on the candlesticks, and it was far more effective than the chemical polishes in use today. I have already mentioned earlier my Friday afternoon errands to the candle-maker. When I got back home with the candles, my mother was ready: Dressed in her long Sabbath gown with a new cloth on her head, her face clean and shining with a joyous light in her eyes—all finished with her hard day's work. The floors had been swept and covered with clean yellow sand, everything in the house was immaculate. Her hands shielding her eyes, she recited the blessing over the candles. For all of us children, it became Sabbath at that moment.

—Yehoshua Katzovitch, "Old Kryvitsh Lights up in my Memory," *Kryvitsh: A Yzkor Book,* 1976

LEFT: FIGURE 52. *Katzovitch family, Kryvitsch, Poland, July 1927. Courtesy of Dale Rosengarten.*

This photograph was made in the shtetl of Kryvitsch, not far from Vilna (then in Poland) in July 1927, to commemorate the visit of a daughter of the Katzovitch family after twenty years in America. Ida Katzoff had left home in 1907 and followed her fiancé Isaac to New York. They married and settled in Brooklyn where they tried their hand at running a dry-goods store, a delicatessen, a succession of movie theaters—whatever they could do to make a living. In 1920 their youngest child, Trudy, was born; later that year Ida's husband Isaac died. To pay for the trip to Europe for herself and her

two youngest daughters, Ida agreed to pick up a small parcel of diamonds in Belgium on the way back to New York. She smuggled the jewels past customs in a special belt hidden under her corset.

Trudy recalls the summer clearly, and the circumstances under which the photograph was taken. "Somebody showed up one day. I guess they told us ahead of time that it was going to happen, because everybody got their best bib and tucker out. Then this photographer who had a camera on a stand, rolled out these rugs. I have one picture in which the clapboards of the house show [behind the] backdrops that he stood up against the house. . . . You could kill them for putting this stuff in front of the house and not letting us see the architecture."

Ida, or Chaya, as her family would have called her, sits in the center of the group flanked by her parents. Trudy sits cross-legged on the floor at her mother's knee, and her older sister Martha stands second from the right in the back row.

At the end of the summer when the three Americans returned home, Trudy got off the boat speaking Yiddish. Among the family left behind, only Ida's parents, who died before Hitler came to power, and her brother Yehoshua, or Szaie (third from the left in the front row), who spent the war years in a labor camp in Siberia, escaped death at the hands of the Nazis.

Candlesticks tell us where people come from. Ornate or plain, tall or short, crafted of silver, brass, or ceramic, candlesticks are often the most important objects a Jewish person owns, things that would not get left behind. There are stories of people in Europe plucked from their homes and transported to the Nazi death camps, who took with them bread and candlesticks. In a more hopeful vein, people have crossed oceans and continents, on their way to new homes, with candlesticks tucked in their sacks and suitcases. How else could they welcome Shabbat?

The lighting of candles ushers in that special guest, the Sabbath, and with it a day of rest, reflection, and prayer. No ceremony equals the lighting of candles for transmitting the essence of Jewish culture. Mothers teach their daughters how to say the prayers over the lighting of candles. Observant fathers lay aside their work. Observant sons stop their games and sports.

To mark the *yahrzeit*, or anniversary of a death, observant Jews light a special candle that burns for twenty-four hours and is believed to provide light in the next world. Always, when the deceased person's name is mentioned, it is followed by "*alav* (or *aleha*) *ha-shalom*," peace be upon him or her. In English one says "of blessed memory."

Since World War II, every yahrzeit candle lit to keep alive the memory of a loved one recalls as well the millions of children, women, and men murdered in the Holocaust. Ninety percent of American Jews are descended from eastern European families who were targeted for destruction. What Jewish person in Aiken or Columbia, Spartanburg or Charleston does not have a grandfather whose cousin's

FACING: CLOCKWISE:

CATALOGUE 209.

Candlesticks, ca. 1890–1900. Collection of George and Bertha Breibart.

CATALOGUE 151.

Candlesticks, Poland, 1879. Collection of Margi Levinson Goldstein.

CATALOGUE 211.

Candlesticks, Lithuania, ca. 1860. Collection of Harriet Hirschfeld Keyserling.

CATALOGUE 74.

Candlesticks, Poland, mid-19th century. Collection of Allan and Sophia Payeff Sindler.

FIGURE 53. *Renee Fuchs (later Fox) and her brother Michael arriving in New York, January 1947. Photograph by Hebrew Immigrant Aid Society. Courtesy of Pincus Kolender.*

children never set out for America but remained in some city or shtetl of the Pale and met a terrible fate? Coming to grips with the catastrophic loss of life was not a quick or spontaneous process. Survivors were not eager to talk, and few people wanted to listen. The slow integration of survivors into society has made it possible to retrieve their stories.

After the war we went back to Kaluszyn because we were trying to get our flour mill back, which the Germans took. That was the family business. My parents were killed in Kaluszyn, my grandmother, my aunts, my uncles—everybody. The home was torn apart but the mill was operating. We were trying to get it back. But the government had already come and said, "No, you can't get it back because it's too big. We got to nationalize it."

So we said, "Let's go into the post office and see, maybe, maybe somebody wrote a letter." The postman who knew us from before the war said there was a letter from the United States. My mother had a sister who went to Palestine in 1936. She knew the address of the Zuckers in Charleston, so she wrote to them and they wrote right to us. We didn't even know them— they left Poland before I was even born. We made contact and in a little while they said, "If you want to come to the United States we could help you."

We came on Thanksgiving Day in 1949. Late in the evening on Wednesday we came to New York. The seas were so rough—twelve days on the boat—it was November, in the fall. I'll never forget. I was very seasick and pregnant and with a small child, and my husband came into the cabin and he said, "Come on the deck. Let me show you something." And we came on the deck—after so many days, sea and sky, sea and sky, we saw the panorama of New York. But it was too late to unload us. Thursday was Thanksgiving so they couldn't unload us— it was a holiday. So they gave us the first dinner, Thanksgiving dinner, on the boat. The dinner was so delicious but we didn't know why—we thought because they're welcoming us to New York. We didn't know it was Thanksgiving. Then on Friday they unloaded us and Saturday we were in Charleston.

—Paula Kornblum Popowski
(b. 1923, Kaluszyn, Poland)

CHAPTER SEVEN

Palmetto Jews

By the end of World War II, America's place in world Jewry had changed dramatically. Only ten years earlier, 65 percent of the world's Jews lived in Europe. Now more than half lived in the United States. Thus the Holocaust had the inadvertent effect of thrusting America into a leadership role in Jewish affairs. Whether in the arena of denominational debate, or support for the new State of Israel, Jews in postwar America set the pace.

I remember [the Depression] when people worked for a dollar a day. I remember when people would come and ask you for a box to bury a baby in. I remember bartering a bushel of corn for a pair of shoes. Those were tough days. Hope they never happen again, terrible.

But we stayed in business. My father closed, had to close up in '29 or '30 and he reopened. He opened stores in Latta and Dillon. Isadore Blum, his partner, opened a store in Rowland [North Carolina] and we've been here ever since. When I came in the store, this side was a drug store. Later years we opened it up and took the wall out and made a double store.

I've seen so many changes in retailing, so much has happened in merchandising. We've had the advent of outlets, discounters, shopping malls, better highways for people to travel. Families working days and taking nights off to go shopping, where the small towns can't stay open at night. You had the Wal-Marts to come in. You had the Jmarts, the Kmarts, and all the rest of them. It's just a different ball game altogether.

You don't compete with them. You try to sell service, sell credit, help on credit, and sell only tip-top merchandise. Don't try to sell the same socks and shoes that they sell; [carry] some brand that they don't have. Of course they've got practically everything. That's the only hope for a small retailer. It's come down to a mom and pop deal. You take all the expenses out of it and you cut everything you can and do it all yourself. You won't find many small Jewish merchants over the state; when you travel around, you won't find a whole lot. . . . Because so many of the children don't want to come back to the small towns, into their own business. These doctors and Indian chiefs and CPAs. Neither one of my boys want any part of this as far as that goes.

—Moses Kornblut (b. 1915, Latta, S.C.)

In many ways, South Carolina was a microcosm of the nation. As elsewhere, the class of Jewish merchants had begotten a generation of lawyers, doctors, accountants, and college teachers, who shifted the Jewish economic niche away from retail business. With the rest of the white American mainstream in cities across the country, urban Jews abandoned the old neighborhoods and moved to the suburbs—a migration that coincided with the first stirrings of the civil rights movement. The suburbs became the desirable place to live, and people quickly accustomed themselves to driving in their automobiles wherever they wanted to go. Walking to work, to school, to shopping, and even to synagogue became for many a thing of the past.

Charleston's Jews gravitated to the northwest section of the city, near Hampton Park, forsaking the old single houses of "Little Jerusalem" for houses with front yards, driveways, and, eventually, air-conditioning. Deliberately "modern," Jewish suburbanites were the driving force behind the Conservative movement in congregational life. Conservative Judaism, a self-described compromise between tradition and change, was not a new idea. Its sudden growth was spurred by Jewish veterans who had seen how Jews practiced their faith in other places. They wanted to drive to shul, indeed they could get to shul only by driving, which Jewish law prohibits on the Sabbath and High Holy Days. And they wanted to sit next to their wives in synagogue. But like the Orthodox, they continued to wear tallisim and yarmulkes and to pray mainly in Hebrew.

In Charleston, the Conservative impulse originated among the Orthodox. In 1943, Brith Sholom hired a new rabbi, Solomon D. Goldfarb, the first graduate of the Jewish Theological Seminary to hold a pulpit in South Carolina. His position as a Conservative rabbi in an Orthodox synagogue was an anomaly. During his tenure the congregation began using a Conservative prayer book and holding late Friday evening services at which men and women sat together. In April 1947, 125 members formally petitioned to make these changes permanent, and asked that the word "traditional" be substituted for "orthodox" in the first article of Brith Sholom's constitution. At a special meeting in July, the resolution was defeated by a vote of 100 to 72. Within a month, the dissidents, including most of synagogue's officers, formed a new congregation, Emanu-El. Seven years later, Brith Sholom and its Orthodox rival Beth Israel merged. Taking the fittings and furniture from its old quarters on St. Philip Street, the Big Shul moved into the Little Shul's new and larger Moorish edifice on Rutledge Avenue.

Emanu-El, South Carolina's first Conservative congregation, met initially in an army chapel that was relocated to the postwar Jewish neighborhood in Charleston's northwest section, and later built a new house of worship on the same property. When the community migrated west of the Ashley River, Emanu-El followed; in 1975 the synagogue acquired land and four years later dedicated its new sanctuary. Smaller Orthodox congregations in Columbia, Greenville, and Spartanburg likewise responded to changes in the residential patterns and social aspirations of their members by becoming Conservative and moving out of the downtown neighborhoods in which their immigrant founders had settled.

I was here for the dedication of [Emanu-El's] building on Gordon Street. . . . The city was changing; it was right in the middle of the 1950s when the whole segregation and integration issue was red hot. It was a daily issue here in Charleston. It wasn't just a minor discomfort. . . . When I preached a sermon, I had to think very carefully about trigger words. The Jewish community was vulnerable at that point. It was small. You know, on one side the black community was threatening to boycott Jewish stores if they didn't take this position. Yet on the other hand, white citizen groups were saying, "Well, wait a minute, you've been here five generations, how come you don't think the same way as we do?" It was an interesting experience for me to learn how to be definite about things, yet at the same time not to create problems for the people who I'm supposed to serve. . . .

I would speak [to] Kiwanis or I'd speak [to] church groups. They would ask, "What do you Jews believe about segregation?" I would never say how Jews feel about segregation because I knew [some] Jews believe differently than [others]. I would say, "I can't tell you what Jews believe about segregation because I haven't interviewed every Jew. But I'll tell you what Judaism thinks about segregation. . . . Probably Moses was about the same shade as some of the people you are now sending into separate schools, so I can tell you that as a professing Jew I cannot accept segregation."

—Gerald Isaac Wolpe (b. August 7, 1927, Boston, Mass.), rabbi of Synagogue Emanu-El, Charleston, 1955–1958

~

When I was president of Emanu-El, some of the members decided they'd like to have an organ. There are Conservative synagogues who have organs. I think it's beautiful—as I said, I don't care about classical music, but I think organ music in a synagogue is nice, to sing to it. I said, "We'll have a vote and see how the congregation feels." Well, the vote was ninety for it and eighty-nine against, so the ninety for it said, "We won." I said, "No, you didn't win, not with me. You'll never put an organ there as long as I'm president. I'm not going to be president of a synagogue, and we're going to have ninety people on one side and eighty-nine on the other side. When I get out of office, you can do anything you want to." They never brought it up after that.

—William Ackerman (b. 1915, California, Pa.; d. 1999, Charleston, S.C.), president of Synagogue Emanu-El, 1961–1962

~

[The change from Orthodox to Conservative at Beth Shalom in Columbia] was just so subtle you weren't too much aware of it. You just sort of drifted into the ways of the world, so to speak. When you could come downstairs and sit across the aisle from the men, that was a big change. Then, of course, when we got together with the men and sat together it just evolved. You just accepted it and you weren't surprised, but there were people who resented seeing women on the bimah. Some religious men in this shul walked out on it, but I notice now that they come in and they stay. . . . I remember the first time I was up on the bimah. I was asked to go up and

open the ark. I just felt like I didn't have the right to be up there. I didn't feel good enough to be up there. It was so ingrained in me . . . till I was just shaking and trembling in my boots.

—Emma Bogan Lavisky Bukatman (b. 1906,
　　Coatesville, Pa.; d. 1999, Columbia, S.C.)

~

The synagogue that I grew up in [Beth Shalom] was Orthodox; although women sat downstairs, they were segregated. . . . When I came back to Columbia in 1972, women were still all on one side. There was more English in the service—I did not remember any English in the service up to that point. I prefer to hear the Hebrew because it's what I remember from my childhood. In 1972, when this synagogue was built, the seating was together, but the service was still all men. When I was president of the Sisterhood in 1975 I was asked to go up there and read a prayer in English. I think I was the first female who went up to the bimah. The ark was not open at that point. They still would not allow a woman to be up there with the ark open. . . .

I was honored to be asked the first Saturday morning that they let women participate in the services to have an aliyah and go up and say the prayer before the Torah reading. Now, since I don't read Hebrew I had to practice very hard. The first person up there was a young woman who had been the agitator of the whole thing, and the second one up there was me. And here were all these little old men who had gotten up and walked out all those years ago, but because it was me, because they had known me all my life, they helped me. They showed me what to do and they all kissed me when I got through. Now since that time we have a lot of women who participate. I will tell you another little something. They would say, "Okay, we count women in the minyan," but they wouldn't start service until ten men were there. They'd say, "We're counting you. We're counting you." But they wouldn't start until ten men were there.

—Belle Lavisky Jewler
　　(b. 1936, Columbia, S.C.)

The same forces that launched the construction of suburban synagogues, with their expanded range of social and cultural functions, transformed an unassuming urban institution into a hub of community life. In Charleston, the Jewish Community Center had provided, since the 1920s, a place for Jewish youth to meet, play sports, and take Hebrew classes. During World War II, the center hosted dances and social events for Jewish GIs passing through Charleston. Building on its wartime alliance with the Jewish Welfare Board and on its success in bringing together young Jewish men and women with different synagogue affiliations, the Jewish Community Center in the postwar years became a unifying force in a diverse and geographically dispersed community. In 1959 the center purchased twenty-five acres of land west of the Ashley River, and seven years later moved into a spacious new facility serving a membership of fifteen hundred. Sports, camps, youth clubs, cultural and civic programs—activities once spread among a variety of organizations—now clustered on the modern campus of Charleston's JCC.

Columbia soon followed suit in what was, indeed, a national trend. Leadership in some cases came from northerners who had landed in the South as a consequence of the population shake-up that occurred during World War II. Charleston's

Jewish Community Center owed its expansiveness, for example, largely to the energy and vision of Nat Shulman, a young man from New Jersey who embraced an ethic of social service that extended beyond the boundaries of the Jewish community. With the infusion of new people and new ideas, southern Jewish culture became less insular and also less distinctive than it had been in the past.

Greater Charleston's first shopping center, Pinehaven, was built on the site of a former tuberculosis sanitarium—the air around pine trees was thought to be good for the lungs—by the Kronsberg brothers, originally from Tilghman's Island, North Carolina. Pennsylvania-born attorney William Ackerman transformed a cabbage patch into the shopping mall and subdivision of South Windermere, complete with a residential clientele who bought new houses in a maze of winding streets around a hub called Confederate Circle, known to locals as "the Bagel." It was said that when Bill Ackerman lifted his rod, the waters of the Ashley parted and the Jews crossed to the other side.

> *When we opened the new store, [Edward's] was the most modern building in town. That was 1947. We gave a thousand orchids to the first thousand ladies that came in on opening day. The flowers were flown in from wherever they came from. I remember going with somebody to the airport, and in those days the airport wasn't much, to pick them up. It was a little glass vial with an orchid in it. And that was the biggest thing that happened in Charleston that year, for people, black and white, to stand together to receive their purple orchid, when we opened that store.*
>
> —Avram Kronsberg (b. 1936, Charleston, S.C.)

The emergence of a Jewish professional and corporate class provided a reason for the younger generation to stay, or to resettle after college, in the cities and suburbs. Higher education became available to women, who began to have alternatives to keeping house, teaching, or working in the family store. While they lagged behind their northern sisters, Jewish women joined their southern gentile counterparts in breaking down the barriers against women in the workplace.

When the sons and daughters of successful shopkeepers leave home, no one is left to mind the store. Jewish life in small towns begins to die out. Congregations dwindle; synagogues go up for sale. The last foothold for small-town Jews is the cemetery, which ironically was the first real estate their forebears purchased in such places as Georgetown, Beaufort, Sumter, and Camden. While South Carolina's larger cities gain population from the movement out of the small towns, these cities themselves suffer an out-migration of ambitious young people to regional hot spots such as Charlotte and Atlanta, and to the even more glittering Los Angeles and New York.

At the same time, mild winters and a robust economy are luring Jews to Sunbelt states from the wider world. Immigrants from the Snowbelt and the Rustbelt, from the former Soviet Republics, the Middle East, and South Africa, can be found in many southern congregations. An infusion of population, Jewish and gentile, is returning the South to the fertility and ferment, culturally speaking, of the eighteenth century..

Today, every McDonald's restaurant from Waycross, Georgia, to Lynchburg, Virginia, serves bagels as well as biscuits for breakfast. As Jewish foods, holidays, and slang are absorbed into American culture, what deeper manifestations of cultural exchange are taking place? Will Jewish retirees who settle in Sun City, South Carolina, come to look more like their peers in Palm Beach and Miami, or like the older Jewish families of Beaufort?

We're trying to keep this little community together. It's difficult. When you look around, it breaks your heart to look at some of our members who are getting up in age who are not well and when we lose one, it's just like part of us is going. And we're having a rather difficult time in bringing in young people. Unfortunately, we don't have a lot of Jewish people coming into Beaufort and if they're here we don't know about them because they don't want to be known.

I grew up knowing I would always marry Jewish. . . . For some reason or other [my children] never went with Jewish people. . . . We had wonderful young Jewish girls here, but when it came to dating, they knew the boys too well. Joe Young's family, when he saw he had six children, they were growing up and they weren't exposed to very many Jewish people, he picked up the whole family, gave up his business and moved to Jacksonville, Florida. Every one of them married Jewish. We couldn't pick ourselves up and move and maybe we didn't instill enough in them. I was always a worker in our little congregation, they knew that. They went to services. They went to the High Holidays and they went for their lessons, but beyond that, you know, I can't blame them. I guess I have to be at fault too.

They had always come to us and we'd say, "Are you that in love?" And of course they were, and I cannot and will never alienate my children. I could have said, "No, you're not marrying." But I know that barrier would have gone up. It would have killed them and it would have killed Ernest and I. I didn't think about myself first, I was thinking about them, because I always wanted them to be able to come to us.

—Rose Yospe Mark (b. 1927, Baltimore, Md.), first female president of Beth Israel congregation, Beaufort, 1997–present

A people in motion, Jewish immigrants are propelled by waves that continue to radiate from the cataclysm of the Holocaust. "In Ukraine is the Holocaust today," a woman, speaking in newly learned English, told a Shabbat audience at Columbia's Beth Shalom. This firsthand perception may explain why Jews from Michigan and Ohio feel the regrets of exile more than people from abroad. There are bound to be tensions between the "come-heres," as the newcomers are called, and the old Jewish families of Charleston, who, like old gentile families, eat rice and cherish their ancestors. Yet in the postmodern era, distinctions among Jews of varied ancestry—Sephardic, German, eastern European—have dimmed in significance. Whether you are a seventh-generation American or just off the boat no longer carries as much weight.

Furthermore, in tangible ways, the upstarts are revitalizing their communities and making it easier to be a Jew in South Carolina. Bar and bat mitzvahs, more elaborate than weddings, are standard fare in synagogues and temples. Memberships of Conservative congregations are growing. *Habad* and Hebrew day schools have sprouted in Myrtle Beach, Columbia, and Charleston, welcoming families that run the gamut from Lubavitcher to agnostic. Reform congregations in South Carolina as elsewhere are gravitating toward more traditional observance, seen in the wearing of skullcaps by some and the infusion of Hebrew into services. "The Jews are taking over the temple," Charleston attorney Morris Rosen told his son Robert with wry humor, while other worshipers welcome the return to customs abandoned more than a hundred years ago.

South Carolina's Jews today are as much "a portion of the people" as they were in the early 1800s when Isaac Harby penned the phrase. They believe in pluralism and democracy, in the pursuit of opportunity and the survival of Judaism. The State of Israel has become a focal point for their philanthropy and pilgrimages. Israel is the place where Jewish people have regained a reputation for militarism and tilling the soil—values much appreciated in a South that once experienced military defeat and has not forgotten its rural roots. To most Jews, the State of Israel is a source of pride and a place of refuge, but caring about its well-being also entails a measure of pain and grief, like watching a child caught in some terrible strife.

Israel represents the present and the future, not the past, which until recently nobody wanted to talk about. In a turnaround from the post–World War II years, when the wounds inflicted on Jewish consciousness by the Nazis were too raw to be touched, the children of Holocaust survivors have spearheaded the movement to memorialize, publicize, and teach the history of the *Shoah*, a development not without its skeptics in the Jewish community.

> *Growing up I'd be a Jewish southerner, but now I'm a southern Jew. I've definitely changed. I have to just look at the history of my family and what happened to us in Germany. I have to look at that lesson. We were Germans, we were Jewish Germans, and it just didn't work. No matter who you were, if you were Jewish, [if] your grandmother was Jewish, they kicked you out or they killed you. So I have to look at that experience and always remember that I'm Jewish first—that I am first and foremost Jewish.*
>
> —Larry W. Freudenberg
> (b. 1959, Charleston, S.C.)

One hundred and fifty years ago, Jews in the South could aptly be called Jewish southerners, that is, southerners who happened to be Jewish. At the dawn of the twenty-first century, they are more likely to see themselves as southern Jews, Jews who happen to live in the South. Still, historical patterns that have long distinguished Jews in the South from Jews in the North persist. The proportion of southerners who are Jewish remains small, less than half of one percent in South Carolina, while membership in synagogues remains at twice the American average. Southern Jews reflect the mores of their church-going neighbors. Attitudes about providing Jewish education and combating anti-Semitism reveal stronger than average identification with the Jewish heritage. A recent survey conducted by the Charleston Jewish Federation finds that an exceptionally high percentage of Jewish households have mezuzahs on their doorposts, and an exceptionally low number indulge in Christmas trees.

Another persistent pattern, even among urban Jews, is a nostalgia for the era of peddlers and small-town merchants. As "Fiddler on the Roof" paints shtetl life through the rose-colored lenses of a later generation, so southerners imagine the small-town experience to be more pastoral than it actually was.

The typical Jewish merchant in Charleston no longer runs a modest shop on upper King Street, but rather owns an upscale men's store, jewelry or dress shop, boutique or antique business downtown. The days when the majority of Jewish families employed full-time black household help also are over. After raising generations of young Jewish children and keeping kosher kitchens, black nannies and cooks are no longer the norm. Still, as in all prolonged cultural encounters, influences of language and cuisine linger. To a great extent, the caste structure also persists. The racial etiquette of the Old South is more deeply rooted in the lowcountry of South Carolina than in many parts of the region. But the Old South has bequeathed, along with injurious deprivations and delusional notions of superiority, the decent values of family, friendship, amiability, and love of the outdoors.

At an early age I knew I was no Dixiecrat and God knows, no Republican. What did matter? Was there any connection to be made between the world of which I was a part and the pronouncements of Amos in the Old Testament? Let justice roll down as waters, and righteousness as a mighty stream. On Fridays, we were sermonized on Israel and the Holocaust. . . . It seems that we recognize no other injustices. Even as we read the liberating message of the Passover story it did not seem to matter that people of color were third class citizens in our midst with separate public waiting rooms and toilets, unpaved streets, substandard homes that drew the line of separation from the white majority. And what unspoken irony that blacks identified in the role of modern day Jewish slaves while white society, Jew and Gentile alike, were left to rule as the Egyptians. These and other vestigial remnants of slavery and racism poisoned generations of youth, regardless of how forward-looking our families may have been.

At some point, the question was inescapable.

—Rick Cagan (b. 1951, Newark,
    N.J.; raised in Florence, S.C.)

The roles Jews have played in the battles to desegregate the South are complex and changing. In states like Mississippi, where local Jews came face to face simultaneously with Jewish freedom riders and Ku Klux Klan terrorists, the natives tried to distance themselves from the Yankee agitators. Michael Schwerner and Andrew Goodman, two Jewish New Yorkers who, with James Chaney, were murdered in Neshoba County, Mississippi, in 1964, were not heroes to Delta Jews. In South Carolina in the 1960s, where the struggle was less organized and overt, Jews tended to keep a low profile. Across the region, however, southern Jews have voted more like northern Jews than like white southern gentiles. Forty years later, in the battle over the Confederate flag, southern Jews lean strongly to the "take it down" side and many espouse liberal points of view on subjects of social equity and race relations.

Perhaps the chief distinction shared by Jews in the Old South cities of Charleston, Savannah, New Orleans, and Richmond is a status and sense of security that owe a lot to the early presence of a Jewish elite. For gentiles of Jewish descent, the Jewish branch of the family tree may be the loftiest lineage they can claim. There is little motive to conceal one's Jewish roots. Only half jokingly do some of the Ravenels of South Carolina allege their name was Abravenel before the Inquisition. History counts in the South more than elsewhere in our young country. And history works in favor of Palmetto Jews. ❧

Photo Essay by Bill Aron

October 17–November 1, 2000
Courtesy of the Jewish Heritage Collection,
College of Charleston Library

FIGURE 54. *Greenville Army and Navy Store*
Jeff Zaglin, proprietor. Greenville, S.C.

FIGURE 55. *Three generations of sportsmen*
Bob Lyon with sons Robert, Michael, and David and grandsons Craig
and Ross. Spartanburg, S.C.

FIGURE 56. *D. Poliakoff Department Store*
Elaine Poliakoff Fenton, Edward Poliakoff, and Doris Poliakoff Feinsilber.
Established in 1900 by their Russian immigrant grandfather, David
Poliakoff, the store closed permanently in August 2000. Abbeville, S.C.

FIGURE 57. *Palmetto Pigeon Plant*
Wendell M. Levi Jr. and his twin sister Patty Levi Barnett. Founded in 1923 by their father, attorney and naturalist Wendell Levi Sr., and his partner, engineer Harold Moïse, the plant today is the largest squab farm in the world. Sumter, S.C.

FIGURE 58. *Temple Sinai*
Robert A. Moses in the temple's sanctuary, noted for its remarkable
stained-glass windows featuring biblical scenes. Sumter, S.C.

FIGURE 59. *Allan Sindler*
At work in his studio on a new piece of sculpture. Camden, S.C.

FIGURE 60. *Hebrew Benevolent Society Cemetery*
Left to right: Harold M. Aronson, Rose Louise Aronson, Carolyn Baruch
Levenson, Ella Levenson Schlosburg, Deborah Baruch Abrams, Ann
Briskin Baum, Bernie Baum, Cheryl Baum, Garry Baum, Faye
Lamanski Levinson, and Arnold Levinson. Camden, S.C.

FIGURE 61. **Sisterhood members preparing the oneg Shabbat in the
synagogue kitchen at Tree of Life**
*Left to right: Catherine Weiner, Libby Paul, Julie Strauss, Sarah Strauss,
Mary Helen Baum. Columbia, S.C.*

FIGURE 62. *Construction site for Iceland U.S.A.*
Jeff Selig, Alan Kahn, and Jerry Kline. Irmo, S.C.

FIGURE 63. **South Carolina Supreme Court**
David I. Bruck, "death row" defense attorney. Columbia, S.C.

FIGURE 64. *Columbia Jewish Day School*
Students light the Shabbat candles at Beth Shalom Synagogue.
Columbia, S.C.

FIGURE 65. *Lubavitcher Chabad (Orthodox day school)*
Rabbi Doron Aizenman, director. Myrtle Beach, S.C.

FIGURE 66. *Avram Aizenman reciting the morning prayers*
Myrtle Beach, S.C.

FIGURE 67. *Jerusalem Restaurant*

*A glatt kosher Israeli restaurant, with owners Nina and Yossi (Joseph)
Elmalih, and Nina's nieces, Hanni Logasy and Hanni Zohar. Myrtle
Beach, S.C.*

FIGURE 68. *Mah-jongg game at Beth Israel*
Lucille Bass Lipsitz, Rose Yospe Mark, Corinne S. Hagood, and Celia
Pinosky Lipson in the social hall of the synagogue. Beaufort, S.C.

FIGURE 69. ***Kahal Kadosh Beth Elohim***
Friday night service celebrating the 250th anniversary of the congregation.
Charleston, S.C.

FIGURE 70. **Coming Street Cemetery**
Sol Breibart, historian of Kahal Kadosh Beth Elohim and caretaker of the
cemetery. Charleston, S.C.

214

FIGURE 71. *St. Philip Street*
The "uptown crowd" in their old neighborhood. Charleston, S.C.

FIGURE 72. *West Ashley Minyan House (prayer house)*
Members of Charleston's congregation Brith Sholom Beth Israel at a
satellite synagogue in suburban South Windermere. Charleston, S.C.

FIGURE 73. **Addlestone Hebrew Academy**
Students and faculty of Charleston's Hebrew day school, run by Brith
Sholom Beth Israel, gathered under the Angel Oak. Johns Island, S.C.

FIGURE 74. *Ziff family*
On the piazza of Stephen and Julie Ziff's house on Legare Street.
Charleston, S.C.

FIGURE 75. **Russian Jewish émigré musicians**
Alexander Agrest, Marina Agrest, and Rozolita Agrest. Charleston, S.C.

FIGURES 76–78. *Charleston Police Chief Reuben Greenberg*

In the uniform of the Fifty-fourth Massachusetts Voluntary Infantry,
Co. I, Civil War reenactors, on the South Battery; in his office on Lock-
wood Drive; and in his yarmulke and tallit, at Conservative Synagogue
Emanu-El. Charleston, S.C.

Catalogue of Exhibition Items

SECTION ONE *First Families*

1. Jonas Phillips (1736–1803)

Charles Willson Peale (1741–1827)
United States, ca. 1800
Oil on canvas, 39 × 34 in.
American Jewish Historical Society

2. Myer Moses II (1779–1833)

Artist unknown
Ca. 1820
Oil on canvas, 24 × 20 in.
Collection of Sally B. Drake

3. Esther Phillips Moses (Mrs. Myer Moses II) (1778–1845)

Artist unknown
Ca. 1820
Oil on canvas, 26 × 20 in.
Collection of Sally B. Drake

4. Myer Moses II

Artist unknown
Ca. 1840
Quarterplate daguerreotype, 3 ½ × 3 in.
(3 ¾ × 3 ¼ in. case)
Collection of the Moses family

5. Esther Phillips Moses (Mrs. Myer Moses II)

Artist unknown
Ca. 1840 after ca. 1820 painting (cat. 3)
Quarterplate daguerreotype, 3 ½ × 3 in.
(3 ¾ × 6 ½ in. case open)
Collection of the Moses family

6. Montgomery Moses (1808–1886)

P. Prescott
United States, 1858
Oil on canvas, 37 × 32 in.
Collection of the Moses family

7. Mary Olivia Lucas Harby (Mrs. George Washington Harby) (d. 1834)

Artist unknown
Ca. 1830
Oil on canvas, 35 ½ × 30 ½ in.
Collection of the Moses family

8. Rebecca Elias Israel (Mrs. Morris Israel) (1839–1896)

Artist unknown
Ca. 1885
Oil on canvas, 37 × 32 in.
Collection of Larry Freudenberg

9. Caroline Goldstein Belitzer (Mrs. Isaac Belitzer) (1822–1899)

Artist unknown
Ca. 1860
Oil on canvas, 36 ½ × 30 ½ in.
Collection of Carolee Rosen Fox

10. Louis Mann

Attributed to Solomon N. Carvalho
(1815–1894)
United States, 1865
Oil on canvas, 31 ½ × 26 ½ in.
Collection of Mrs. William Mann Price

11. Mrs. Louis Mann

Attributed to Solomon N. Carvalho
(1815–1894)
United States, 1865
Oil on canvas, 31 ½ × 26 ½ in.
Collection of Mrs. William Mann Price

12. Caroline "Caro" Agnes Moïse Lopez (Mrs. J. L. Lopez) (1854–1885)

Theodore Sidney Moïse (1808–1885)
United States, February 1876
Oil on canvas, 42 × 37 in.
Collection of Mary Kohn Strasburger

13. *The Fundamental Constitutions of Carolina, July 21, 1669*

Charleston, S.C., undated edition
Paper and ink, bound in leather,
13 ½ × 8 ½ in.
Private collection

14. *Naturalization of Simon Valentine, Mercht: an alien of the Jewish Nation, May 26, 1697* (facsimile)

Paper and ink, 18 ½ × 14 ¼ in.
South Carolina Department of Archives
and History

15. *The Ambush of Francis Salvador, August 1, 1776* (Diorama)

Robert N. S. Whitelaw
Charleston, S.C., 1970 (restored 2002)
Mixed media, 12 × 28 ½ × 26 ¼ in.
Kahal Kadosh Beth Elohim

16. Grant of arms of the Salvador
    family (with case)

College of Heralds
England, 1745
Grant: Parchment, ink, and watercolor,
    23 × 25 in. Case: Leather, wood, paper,
    and brass, 22 × 5 × 2 ½ in.
Special Collections, College of Charleston
    Library

17. Mordecai Cohen (1763–1848)

Theodore Sidney Moïse (1808–1885)
United States, ca. 1830
Oil on canvas, 30 × 20 in.
Carolina Art Association/Gibbes Museum
    of Art
Charleston, South Carolina

18. Nathan Nathans (1782–1854)

N. F. Wales (active 1803–1815)
United States, 1814
Oil on canvas, 29 ½ × 25 ½ in.
Collection of Judith Tobias Siegel

19. Mordecai Manuel Noah
    (1785–1851)

John Wesley Jarvis (1780–1840)
United States, ca. 1820
Oil on canvas, 30 × 26 in.
Congregation Shearith Israel

20. Henry Lyons (1805–1858)

Artist unknown
Ca. 1850
Oil on canvas, 36 × 32 in.
Collection of Sandy Luce

21. Sixteenth Degree Prince of
    Jerusalem Masonic patent, issued
    to Thomas Napier (facsimile)

Charleston, S.C., July 20, 1803
Paper and ink, 18 ½ × 11 in.
Ancient and Accepted Scottish Rite

22. Prayer book written by Emanuel
    de la Motta (1760–1821)

Charleston, S.C., 1820
Leather, paper and ink, 7 ½ × 6 ½ in.
American Jewish Historical Society

23. Writing desk
Ca. 1800–1830
Mahogany with brass inlay,
    7 ½ × 20 × 11 in.
Collection of the Moses family

24. Desk set with ink stand belonging
    to Henry M. Phillips

James Dixon and Sons
Ca. 1835
Silver and glass, 12 ½ × 9 ½ × 8 in.
Collection of the Moses family

25. *The Gordian Knot or Causes
    and Effects*

Isaac Harby (1788–1828)
Charleston, S.C.: G. M. Bounetheau, 1810
Paper and ink, with leather binding,
    7 ½ × 4 ½ in.
Temple Sinai Archives

26. *Alberti*

Isaac Harby
From *The Miscellaneous Writings of the Late
    Isaac Harby*
Charleston, S.C.: James S. Burges, 1829
Paper and ink, with leather binding,
    8 ½ × 5 ½ in.
Temple Sinai Archives

27. Cashbook of Isaac Harby's
    Academy

Charleston, S.C., January 1819–May 1820
Paper and ink, 8 × 6 ½ in.
Collection of Anita Moïse Rosefield
    Rosenberg

28. Prayer book manuscript

Isaac Harby
Charleston, S.C., 1825
Paper and ink, 8 ¼ × 4 ¾ in.
Temple Sinai Archives

29. *Biblia Hebraica*

Amsterdam, 1667
Paper and leather, 8 × 5 ½ in.
Collection of I. Harby and Harriet C. Moses

30. Baruch D'Ancona

Artist unknown
Holland, ca. 1821–1825
Watercolor on ivory, 4 ¾ × 4 in.
Collection of Wendell M. Levi Jr.

31. Hannah DeFrece D'Ancona

Artist unknown
Holland, ca. 1821–1825
Watercolor on ivory, 4 ¾ × 4 in.
Collection of Wendell M. Levi Jr.

32. Medical diploma awarded to
    Jacob D'Ancona

Amsterdam, April 13, 1753
Parchment and ink, 15 × 23 in.
Collection of Nina D'Ancona Weinberg

33. Medallion of Jacob D'Ancona

Amsterdam, ca. 1760
Cast metal, 2 in. (diameter)
Collection of Nina D'Ancona Weinberg

34. Leah Lazarus Cohen (Mrs. Mordecai
    Cohen) (1778–1844)

John Canter (1782–1823)
Charleston, S.C., ca. 1820
Oil on canvas, 30 × 26 in.
Carolina Art Association/Gibbes Museum
    of Art

35. Abraham Alexander Sr.
    (1743–1816)

Attributed to Lawrence Sully (1769–1804)
United States, ca. 1795
Watercolor on ivory, 3 ½ × 2 ¼ in.
Carolina Art Association/Gibbes Museum
    of Art

36. Order of prayers for Rosh
    Hashanah and Yom Kippur

Abraham Alexander Sr.
Charleston, S.C., 1805
Paper and ink, Morocco leather binding with
    gold gilding, 5 ½ × 3 ¾ in.
Special Collections, Emory University
    Library

37. Myer Moses II [?]

J. Wood (ca. 1778–1830)
United States, ca. 1810
Watercolor on ivory, 3 × 2 in.
Collection of the Moses family

38. Jacob DeLeon (1764–1828)

John Ramage (ca. 1748–1802)
United States, 1789
Oil on ivory, 2 × 1 ¾ in.
American Jewish Historical Society

39. Phebe Yates Lazarus (Mrs. Joshua Lazarus) (1794–1870)

Amélie Dautel D'Aubigny (ca. 1796–1861)
France, ca. 1840
Watercolor on ivory, 10 ¾ × 8 ¾ in.
   (4 ¾ × 3 ½ in. image)
Gift of Mrs. Edgar M. Lazarus
Carolina Art Association/Gibbes Museum
   of Art

40. Joshua Lazarus (1796–1861)

Amélie Dautel D'Aubigny (ca. 1796–1861)
France, ca. 1840
Watercolor on ivory, 10 ¾ × 8 ¾ in.
   (5 × 3 ¾ in. image)
Gift of Mrs. Edgar M. Lazarus
Carolina Art Association/Gibbes Museum
   of Art

41. Emma Lazarus (1798–1865)

Amélie Dautel D'Aubigny (ca. 1796–1861)
France, ca. 1840
Watercolor on ivory, 10 ¾ × 8 ¾ in.
   (5 × 3 ¾ in. image)
Gift of Mrs. Edgar M. Lazarus
Carolina Art Association/Gibbes Museum
   of Art

42. "Settlement Previous to the Marriage of Mr. Joshua Lazarus and Miss Phebe Yates, dated 27th October, 1835" (facsimile)

Liverpool, England
Paper, ink, wax and ribbon, 24 × 27 ¾ in.
Collection of Judith Tobias Siegel

43. "Post Nuptial Settlement in Pursuance of Antenuptial Contract, Joshua Lazarus to Benjamin D. Lazarus and Philip Phillips, dated 13th April 1836" (facsimile)

Charleston, S.C.
Parchment, paper, ink, wax, and ribbon,
   26 × 32 ¼ in.
Collection of Judith Tobias Siegel

44. Abraham Moïse (1736–1809)

Artist unknown
Ca. 1790
Watercolor on ivory, 2 ½ × 2 in.
Collection of Mary Kohn Strasburger

45. Isaac DeLyon (b. 1739)

Possibly Pierre Henri (1760–1822)
Ca. 1790
Watercolor on ivory, 2 ½ × 2 ½ in.
Kahal Kadosh Beth Elohim

46. Judith DeLyon Cohen (Mrs. Moses Cohen) (1748–1816)

Possibly Pierre Henri (1760–1822)
Ca. 1790
Watercolor on ivory, 4 × 2 in.
Kahal Kadosh Beth Elohim

47. Daniel Hart (d. 1811)

Artist unknown
Ca. 1800
Watercolor on ivory, 3 ½ × 2 ½ in.
Collection of David Hart Crum

48. David Lopez (1750–1811)

After a miniature painted ca. 1801
Ambrotype, 5 ½ × 5 ¾ in. (frame)
Collection of Judith Tobias Siegel

49. Isaac Clifton Moses (1781–1834)

Artist unknown
Ca. 1815
Ink and watercolor on paper, 8 ¾ × 7 ¾ in.
Collection of I. Harby and Harriet C. Moses

50. Arabella Solomons Phillips (Mrs. Zalegman Phillips) (1786–1826)

Artist unknown
Ca. 1805
Watercolor on ivory, 5 × 7 ¾ in. (case open)
Collection of Dr. Andrena E. Ray

51. Chapman Levy (1787–1849)

Artist unknown
Ca. 1835
Watercolor on ivory, 3 ½ × 3 in.
Gift of Thomas W. Crockett in honor of
   Loraine Crockett
Jewish Heritage Collection, College of
   Charleston Library

52. Sarah Moses Levy (Mrs. Samuel Levy) (d. 1839)

Artist unknown
Ca. 1798
Watercolor on ivory, 2 ½ × 1 ¾ in.
Gift of Lane Dinkins
Jewish Heritage Collection, College of
   Charleston Library

53. Chapman Levy as a youth

Artist unknown
Ca. 1798
Watercolor on ivory, 3 × 2 ¼ in.
Gift of Lane Dinkins
Jewish Heritage Collection, College of
   Charleston Library

54. Eliza Levy Anderson (Mrs. Edward H. Anderson) (died before 1839)

Artist unknown
Ca. 1835
Watercolor on ivory, 3 ¼ × 2 ¾ in.
Gift of Lane Dinkins
Jewish Heritage Collection, College of
   Charleston Library

55. John M. Hirsch (1801–1874)

Solomon N. Carvalho (1815–1894)
Charleston, S.C., 1844
Watercolor on ivory in case, 3 ½ × 2 ½ in.
Gift of Willard Hirsch
Carolina Art Association/Gibbes Museum
   of Art

56. Mourning pin

Ca. 1840

Gold, enamel, and hair, 2 1/2 × 2 in.

Private collection

57. Adeline Cohen Phillips (Mrs. Isaac Phillips) (1839–1906)

Artist unknown

Ca. 1860

Oil on canvas, 27 1/2 × 23 3/4 in.

Collection of Charles Whitehead

58. Isaac Phillips (1836–1889)

Artist unknown

Ca. 1860

Oil on canvas, 27 1/2 × 23 3/4 in.

Collection of Charles Whitehead

59. Dr. Joseph Robert Solomons (1824–1887)

Artist unknown

Ca. 1857

Oil on canvas, 40 × 35 in.

Collection of Virginia Moïse Rosefield and Anita Moïse Rosefield Rosenberg

60. Emma Solomons Harby (Mrs. Horace Harby) (1847–1913)

Artist unknown

Ca. 1880

Oil on canvas, 39 1/2 × 34 1/2 in.

Collection of Virginia Moïse Rosefield and Anita Moïse Rosefield Rosenberg

61. Tea service of Samuel Hart and Esther Ezekiel Hart

Charles Fox II (active 1822–1840)

London, ca. 1832

Silver

Sugar bowl: 6 1/4 × 5 1/2 × 8 in.

Creamer: 9 × 4 × 5 3/4 in.

Coffee pot: 9 1/2 × 6 × 10 in.

Tea pot: 7 × 7 × 11 in.

Collection of David Hart Crum

62. Tea service milk pitcher belonging to Marx E. Cohen

G. K. Childs

Philadelphia, ca. 1835

Silver, 7 1/2 × 6 3/4 × 4 1/2 in.

Collection of the Moses family

63. Lazarus family rice spoon

Ca. 1830

Silver, 2 1/4 × 12 in.

Private collection

64. Lazarus family cake knife

Attributed to Wood and Hughes

New York, ca. 1850

Silver, 1 3/4 × 12 1/2 in.

Private collection

SECTION TWO *This Happy Land*

65. Kahal Kadosh Beth Elohim exterior (facsimile)

John Rubens Smith (1775–1849)

1812

Paper and ink, 18 × 21 1/2 in. (framed)

Courtesy of Stephen and Julie Ziff

Original in collection of the Library of Congress

66. Kahal Kadosh Beth Elohim interior

Solomon N. Carvalho (1815–1894)

1838

Oil on canvas, 38 × 33 in.

Kahal Kadosh Beth Elohim

67. Prayer book for the New Year and Day of Atonement, belonging to the Rodriguez Rivera family

Amsterdam, 1717

Paper and ink, leather-covered wood, and metal clasp, 6 1/4 × 4 1/4 in.

Kahal Kadosh Beth Elohim

68. Charity box with hinged cover

Inscribed: "This Almsboxe belongeth to the Synagogue of Kahal Kadosh of Charleston in South Carolina"

United States, early 19th century

Silver-plated, 5 3/4 × 5 1/2 × 4 1/2 in.

Collection of Michael Jesselson

69. Wimpel

1849

Undyed cotton and paint, 6 × 129 in.

Gift of Mordenai Raisin Hirsch and Rachel M. Raisin

Jewish Heritage Collection, College of Charleston Library

70. Havdalah spice box

Warsaw, Poland, ca. 1810–1830

Silver, 8 × 2 × 2 in.

Private collection

71. Tefillin with bag

Russia, ca. 1890

Tefillin: leather and parchment, 1 1/2 × 2 × 1 1/2 in.

Bag: cotton velvet, 5 × 6 in.

Collection of Paul Wexler

72. Mizrah presented to Agnes and Joseph A. Volaski on their wedding, May 6, 1890

Mordecai Judah Patla (ca. 1852–1925)

Charleston, S.C., 1890

Paper and ink, gold gilt, and metal, 24 1/2 × 19 1/2 in.

Brith Sholom Beth Israel

73. Pair of temple menorahs

19th century

Brass, 22 × 17 1/2 × 7 and 22 1/4 × 16 3/4 × 7 in.

Collection of Lucille Finger Powers

74. Candlesticks

Poland, mid-19th century

Silver, 12 1/2 × 4 3/4 × 4 3/4 in. (each)

Collection of Allan and Sophia Payeff Sindler

75. Kiddush cup of Aaron Lazarus

Tiffany, ca. 1850
Silver, 8 × 3 ¼ × 3 ¼ in.
Private collection

76. Circular tray with Garden of Eden design

Ca. 1810–1830
Brass, 15 ½ in. (diameter)
Collection of Rose Louise Rich Aronson

77. Hanukkiah, or Hanukkah menorah

B. Buch
Warsaw, Poland, ca. 1900
Silver-plated, 9 ¼ × 11 ¼ × 2 ½ in.
Collection of Sam and Mitzi Kirshtein

78. Megillah

Poland, ca. 1900
Parchment, ink, and wood, 21 × 71 ½ in.
Collection of Sam and Mitzi Kirshtein

79. Gragger

Russia, late 19th century
Wood, 9 ½ × 12 in.
Collection of Shera Lee Ellison Berlin

80. Torah

Russia, ca. 1750
Velum and wood, 37 × 31 ½ × 7 in.
Beth Shalom Synagogue

81. Yad

Russia
Cast metal, 20 ½ × 1 ½ in.
Beth Shalom Synagogue

82. "Minutes of the Board of Trustees of Kahal Kadosh Beth Elohim"

Charleston, S.C., September 20, 1838–
    September 4, 1843
Paper, ink, and leather, 15 ½ × 10 ½ in.
Kahal Kadosh Beth Elohim Manuscript
    Archives, College of Charleston Library

83. Sugar or sweetmeat bowl

Inscribed: "Presented to the Cong. Beth
    Elohim by Josh. A. Lazarus, AM 5601"
David Bell
England, ca. 1777
Silver, 6 in. (height) × 4 ½ in. (diameter)
Kahal Kadosh Beth Elohim

84. Hymnal belonging to B. D. Lazarus

Charleston, S.C.: Levin and Tavel, 1842
Paper and ink, 6 ¾ × 4 ¼ in.
Kahal Kadosh Beth Elohim

85. Hebrew Orphan Society book of minutes

Charleston, S.C., February 19, 1850–
    May 6, 1862
Paper, ink, and leather, 14 ½ × 18 ½ in.
Kahal Kadosh Beth Elohim Manuscript
    Archives, College of Charleston Library

86. Hebrew Benevolent Society seal

Faith Murray
Charleston, S.C., 1967
Painted wood, 17 in. (diameter)
Kahal Kadosh Beth Elohim

87. *Fancy's Sketchbook*

Penina Moïse (1797–1880)
Charleston, S.C.: J. S. Burges, 1833
Paper and ink, 6 ½ × 4 ¼ × ½ in.
Collection of Daniel Ravenel

88. "Facts for You and Me"

An educational card game used by
    Penina Moïse
Ca. 1867
Fifty-four question-and-answer cards:
    3 × 2 in. (each)
Booklet: 5 ½ × 3 in.
Box: 1 ¼ × 7 ¼ × 3 ¼ in.
Kahal Kadosh Beth Elohim

89. *Hours of Devotion: A Book of Prayers and Meditations for the Use of the Daughters of Israel, during Public Service and at Home, for all Conditions of Woman's Life*

New York: J. Rosenbaum, 1889, translated
    from the German *Stunden der Andacht* by
    M. Mayer
Paper and ink, 7 ¼ × 4 ¾ in.
Collection of Conie Spigel Ferguson

90. *The Sabbath School Companion* (facsimile)

Volume 1, No. 2, February 1895
Paper and ink, 12 × 9 ½ in.
Kahal Kadosh Beth Elohim Manuscript
    Archives, College of Charleston Library

91. Rabbi Hirsch Zvi (Margolis) Levine notebook

Charleston, S.C., 1852
Paper and ink, 6 ¼ × 7 ½ in.
Collection of Carol Kaminsky

92. Isaiah Moses (1772–1857)

Theodore Sidney Moïse (1808–1885)
United States, ca. 1835
Oil on canvas, 37 ½ × 34 in.
Collection of Cecil A. Alexander

93. Rebecca Isaiah Moses (née Phillips) (Mrs. Isaiah Moses) (1792–1872)

C. W. Uhl
United States, 1843
Oil on canvas, 38 ½ × 34 in.
Collection of Henry A. Alexander Jr.

94. *Avenue at The Oaks, Goose Creek*

Elizabeth O'Neill Verner (1883–1979)
Charleston, S.C., ca. 1940
Pastel on silk, 31 ½ × 36 ½ in.
Carolina Art Association/Gibbes Museum
    of Art

95. Survey plat of The Oaks (facsimile)

Based on a survey by William Brailsford
South Carolina, 1817
Paper, ink, and watercolor, 18 × 23 ½ in.
South Carolina Historical Society

96. Israel Solomons (1847–1854)

Artist unknown
Ca. 1850
Oil on canvas, 22 × 19 in. (oval)
Collection of Henry A. Alexander Jr.

97. Album quilt made for Eleanor
Israel Solomons (née Joseph)
(Mrs. Israel Solomons) (1794–1856)

Various contributors, blocks fabricated
1851–1854
Pieced and appliquéd chintz and calico, on
muslin, 102 × 113 in.
Collection of Cecil A. Alexander

98. Loan document between Israel
Solomons, Abram Alexander, and
Abram Otolengui (facsimile)

Charleston, S.C., May 15, 1814
Paper and ink, 16 ½ × 13 ½ in.
Collection of Henry A. Alexander Jr.

99. Pearl arrow pin of
Rebecca Isaiah Moses

Mid-19th century
Pearls and silver, 1 ¼ × ¼ × ¼ in.
Collection of Judith Weil Shanks

100. Watch fob or locket of Judah
Touro Moses, son of Levy J. Moses
and Adeline Moses

Ca. 1870
Rose gold-plated metal and photographs,
1 ¾ × 1 × ¼ in. (fob)
Collection of Judith Weil Shanks

101. Sarah Moses Alexander (Mrs.
Aaron Alexander) (1813–1892)

Artist unknown
Mid-19th century
Opalotype, 6 ¼ × 9 ½ in.
Collection of Judith Tobias Siegel

102. Goblet of Levy J. Moses

1855
Silver repoussé, 7 ¼ × 4 ¼ in.
Collection of Judith Weil Shanks

103. Baby cap

Cecilia Moses Solomons
South Carolina, ca. 1840
Cotton, 8 × 3 ¾ × 3 ¾ in.
Collection of Judith Weil Shanks

104. Triest family Bible

Ca. 1853
Paper and ink, 11 ¾ × 9 ½ in.
Collection of Maxine Triest Freudenberg

105. Toys belonging to Maier Triest

Ca. 1910
Tin and paint
Clarinet clown and cat: 8 × 9 × 4 ¼ in.
Hornblower in car: 6 ¾ × 7 × 3 ¾ in.
Collection of Maxine Triest Freudenberg

106. Rabbi Solomon Raphael Kuh

Jos. Bindeles
United States, 1849
Pencil and watercolor, 21 × 16 ½ in.
Collection of William S. and Peggy Pollitzer

107. Paisley shawl belonging to
Caroline Kuh Guinzburg

Ca. 1860
Silk and wool, 125 × 64 ½ in.
Collection of William S. and Peggy Pollitzer

108. Cup given to Emil Pollitzer at
his brit milah, ca. 1850

Inscribed: "To Emil Pollitzer from his spon-
sors, Mr. and Mrs. H. Greenhood"
United States, mid-19th century
Silver, 7 × 3 ½ × 3 ½ in.
Collection of William S. and Peggy Pollitzer

109. Souvenir cup from the South
Carolina Inter-State and West
Indian Exposition

Charleston, S.C., 1901–1902
Glass, 4 × 3 ¼ in.
Brith Sholom Beth Israel

110. Bound booklet for a banquet in
honor of the President of the
United States

Charleston, S.C., April 8, 1902
Paper and ink, 8 ½ × 6 ¾ in.
South Carolina Historical Society

111. Getta Silberman (Mrs. James J.
Klein) (1837–1886)

Ca. 1857
Photograph framed in union case,
5 × 8 ¼ in. (open)
Collection of Lucille Finger Powers

112. Apothecary bottles, mortar and
pestle, and measuring cup from
J. J. Klein drugstore (1845–1938)

Glass and ceramic
Small bottle: 4 ¼ × 1 ¼ × ¾ in.
Medium bottle: 4 ½ × 2 × 1 in.
Large bottle (2): 5 ¼ × 2 × 1 in.
Small glass: 2 ¾ in. (height) × 2 ¼ in.
(diameter)
Mortar: 1 ¾ in. (height) × 2 ¾ in. (diame-
ter)
Pestle: 2 ¾ × ¾ in.
Collection of Lucille Finger Powers

113. Metal box and contents including
photograph of John Marcus Klein
(1858–1927)

Ca. 1900
Various materials, 5 ½ × 12 × 8 ½ in. (box)
Collection of Lucille Finger Powers

114. *The Linah C. Kaminski*

Capt. S. E. Woodbury
E. Mikkelson, 1885
Tempera, ink, and pencil on paper,
23 × 29 in.
Collection of Michael and Virginia Prevost

115. Porcelain pitcher

Inscribed: "Royal Bayreuth Priv. 1784"
Bavaria, ca. 1900
Painted porcelain, 4 ¾ × 5 × 4 in.
Collection of Rhetta Aronson Mendelsohn

116. Trolley bag of Henrietta Block
     Rich (Mrs. Lipman Philip Rich)

United States, ca. 1910–1920
Silver, 3 ½ × 3 × ½ in.
Collection of Rhetta Aronson Mendelsohn

117. Miniature prayer book belonging
     to Rosa Fried (1838–1916)

Germany, 1841
Paper and ink, with leather binding,
     3 ¼ × 2 ¼ × 2 ¼ in.
Collection of Rose Louise Rich Aronson

118. Hannah Jacobs Levi
     (Mrs. Moses Levi)

Artist unknown
Ca. 1860
Graphite on paper, 33 ¼ × 29 ½ in.
Collection of Sylvia Hanna Weinberg
     (Mrs. Julien Weinberg)

119. Candlesticks of Dora Witcover

1858–1860
Brass, 11 × 4 × 4 in. (each)
Collection of Alexander Cohen

120. Dinner menu and invitation for
     the wedding of Hilda Hennig and
     David Alexander Cohen

Darlington, S.C., October 17, 1918
Menu: Paper and ink, with silk cord and
     tassel, 8 ½ × 10 ¾ in. (open)
Invitation: Paper and ink, 6 × 6 ½ in.
Gift of David A. Cohen Jr.
Jewish Heritage Collection, College of
     Charleston Library

121. Food hamper

Late 19th century
Coiled fiber, 10 ½ × 15 × 8 in.
Collection of Evelyn Rosenberg Gross-Brein

122. Passover Haggadah

Ca. 1900
Paper and ink, 8 × 5 in.
Collection of Evelyn Rosenberg Gross-Brein

123. Candelabra belonging to Eva Leah
     and Moses Winstock

Wurttemberg Silver Plate Co.
Geislingen, Germany, ca. 1880
Silver-plated, 19 ¾ × 16 ¾ × 3 in.
Collection of Jenny Rosenberg

124. Mezuzah

Ca. 1885
Brass, 4 × ½ in.
Collection of Evelyn Rosenberg Gross-Brein

125. Wedding dress of Rebecca
     Winstock Rosenberg

South Carolina, 1885
Silk and cotton, 74 × 56 × 26 in.
Collection of Evelyn Rosenberg Gross-Brein

126. Trousseau trunk of Rebecca
     Winstock Rosenberg

Late 19th century
Wood and metal, 21 ½ × 28 ½ × 17 in.
     (closed)
Collection of Evelyn Rosenberg Gross-Brein

SECTION THREE *The Lost Cause*

127. *The Last Council of War Meeting
     of Confederate President Jefferson
     Davis with his Military Chiefs and
     Advisors*

Wilbur George Kurtz (1882–1967)
United States, 1922
Oil on canvas, 67 × 128 in.
City of Abbeville, S.C.

128. Judah P. Benjamin (1811–1884)

Adolph Rinck (1811–1875)
United States, 1853
Oil on canvas, 48 × 39 in.
The Historic New Orleans Collection

129. Confederate currency

B. Duncan, Engraver
Columbia, S.C., 2nd Series, June 2, 1862
Paper and ink, 2 ¾ × 6 ¼ in.
South Carolina State Museum

130. Confederate currency

Keating and Ball, Engravers
February 17, 1864
Paper and ink, 3 × 7 ¼ in.
South Carolina State Museum

131. Dress sword of Perry Moses

Ca. 1840
Silver with mother-of-pearl inlay,
     2 × 35 ½ × 4 ½ in.
Collection of I. Harby and Harriet C. Moses

132. David Camden DeLeon
     (1816–1872)

Solomon N. Carvalho (1815–1894)
United States, 1849
Oil on canvas, 11 ¾ × 10 ¾ in.
Gift of the William Wolman Foundation
The Jewish Museum

133. Andrew Jackson Moses
     (1815–1877)

Artist unknown
Ca. 1840
Oil on canvas, 37 × 32 ¼ in.
Collection of Mr. and Mrs. Thomas M.
     Bultman

134. Myer Buchanan Moses III
     (1833–1889) in early Confederate
     uniform

George S. Cook
Ca. 1862
Ambrotype, 3 ¾ × 6 ½ in. (open)
Collection of Elizabeth Moses

135. Civil War captain's uniform,
     Company H, South Carolina
     Calvary

Ca. 1862
Wool, felt, and brass
Tunic: 36 × 24 in.
Pants: 40 ½ × 17 in.
McKissick Museum, University of South
     Carolina

136. Southern Cross of Honor
     awarded to B. D. Lazarus

Designed by Mrs. Erwin and
   Mrs. Sarah E. Gabbett
Ca. 1865
Metal, 2 × 1 ½ in.
Private collection

137. Medicine box of
     Moses Cohen Mordecai

November, 1865
Pine, brass, china, glass, poplar top, cardboard,
   tin, and paper, 10 × 12 ½ × 10 ½ in.
Gift of Thomas J. Tobias
The Charleston Museum

138. Isabel Rebecca Lyons Mordecai
     (Mrs. Moses Cohen Mordecai)
     (1804–1895)

Theodore Sidney Moïse (1808–1885)
United States, ca. 1835
Oil on canvas, 38 × 33 in.
Collection of Judith Tobias Siegel

139. Eleanor H. Cohen (Mrs. Benjamin
     Seixas) (1841–1874) (facsimile)

Lawrence Cohen
United States, ca. 1865
Pencil on paper, 12 × 10 in.
Collection of the Moses family

140. Diary kept by Eleanor H. Cohen
     (facsimile)

Columbia and Charleston, S.C., Richmond,
   Va., 1865–1866
Pencil or ink on paper, 6 × 4 in.
Collection of the Moses family

141. "Columbia in Flames" (facsimile)

Harper's Weekly, April 8, 1865
Paper and ink engraving, 10 ½ × 16 ¼ in.
South Caroliniana Library, University of
   South Carolina

142. Octavia Harby Moses
     (Mrs. Andrew Jackson Moses)
     (1823–1904)

Artist unknown
Ca. 1840
Oil on canvas, 37 × 32 ¼ in.
Collection of Mr. and Mrs. Thomas M.
   Bultman

143. *A Mother's Poems*

Octavia Harby Moses
Privately published, South Carolina, 1915
Paper and ink, with gilded cloth cover,
   9 ¾ × 6 ½ in.
Collection of Anita Moïse Rosefield Rosenberg

144. Campaign banner of
     Franklin J. Moses Jr.

South Carolina, 1872
Cotton and ink, 43 × 46 ½ in.
McKissick Museum, University of South
   Carolina

145. Top hat of Franklin J. Moses Jr.

Ca. 1870
Beaver skin, 6 ½ × 11 ½ × 10 in.
South Carolina State Museum

146. Paperweight

Inscribed: "F. J. Moses, Jr."
Ca. 1870
Marble, 5 × 9 × 1 in.
South Carolina State Museum

147. Adjutant General (Col.) Edwin
     Warren Moïse (1832–1903)

Charles Masen Crowson (1916–1973)
United States, 1940
Oil on canvas, 35 × 30 ½ in.
Sumter County Museum

148. Plantation desk belonging to
     Edwin Warren Moïse

United States, early to mid-19th century
Wood, 64 × 54 × 35 in.
Collection of William and Michele Harritt

SECTION FOUR *Little Jerusalem*

149. Wicker suitcase

Poland, ca. 1920
Wicker with hasp locks, 8 ½ × 21 × 13 in.
Collection of Sam and Mitzi Kirshtein

150. Samovar

Russia, ca. 1880
Brass, 20 × 15 × 14 ½ in.
Collection of Allan and Sophie Payeff
   Sindler

151. Candlesticks

Poland, 1879
Silver, 13 × 5 ¼ × 5 ¼ in. (each)
Collection of Margi Levinson Goldstein

152. Master Shoemaker's Certificate
     of Isaac Oberman

Andreev Village, Russia, 1905
Paper and ink, backed with linen,
   16 × 20 in.
Collection of Ethel Oberman Katzen

153. Bankas

Poland, ca. 1910
Glass, 2 × 1 ½ × 1 ½ in. (each)
Gift of Helen Laufer Dwork Berle
Jewish Heritage Collection, College of
   Charleston Library

154. Cigarette case

Russia, 1915
Silver, ¾ × 3 ¾ × 2 ¼ in.
Collection of Clara Helfer

155. Mandolin and case, with
     Cyrillic letters

Russia, late 19th century
Wood, metal and mother-of-pearl inlay,
   24 ½ × 6 × 7 ½ in. (mandolin),
   25 ½ × 9 ¼ × 9 ½ in. (case)
Private collection

156. Handmade wood plane

Late 19th century
Wood and metal, 6 × 17 × 3 in.
Private collection

157. Letters in Yiddish, with cloth bag, wedding invitation, and photographs of Joseph Wolf Mark and his bride, Lena Mae Banisch (partial facsimile)

Beaufort and Burton, S.C., and Russia, 1904–1912
Paper and ink, photographs, and linen
Linen bag: 8 ½ × 2 ¾ × 2 ¾ in.
Letters and photographs of various sizes
Collection of Rose Yospe Mark

158. Bolgla address book, passports, and immigration documents

Poland, 1921
Paper and ink
Address book: 5 ⅝ × 7 ¾ × ⅛ in. (open)
Gift of Sara Bolgla Breibart
Jewish Heritage Collection, College of Charleston Library

159. Mizrah

Morris Aaron Brenner (1874–1962)
Wisnicz, Austria-Hungary, 1887–1891
Papercut painted with natural dyes, 31 ½ × 25 ½ in.
Collection of Susan H. Baker

160. Minutes of the meetings of the Brith Shalom Congregation

Charleston, S.C., April 23, 1922– April 7, 1935
Paper and ink, with cloth cover, 14 ¼ × 8 ¾ in.
Brith Sholom Beth Israel Manuscript Archives, College of Charleston Library

161. Beth Israel Congregation book of minutes in Yiddish and English

Charleston, S.C., October 3, 1926– November 29, 1942
Paper and ink, with cloth cover, 14 ¼ × 8 ¾ in.
Brith Sholom Beth Israel Manuscript Archives, College of Charleston Library

162. Notice of the price of High Holy Day seats at Beth Israel Synagogue (facsimile)

Charleston, S.C., August 28, 1933
Paper and ink, 3 ¼ × 5 ½ in.
Collection of Ethel Oberman Katzen

163. Invitation to circumcision (facsimile)

Charleston, S.C., August 5, 1913
Paper and ink, 3 ¼ × 5 ½ in.
Collection of Ethel Oberman Katzen

164. Shohet knife with sharpening stone and cloth used by Jake Kalinsky in Holly Hill, S.C.

Ca. 1920
Metal, bone, stone, and cotton
Knife: 8 × 1 × ½ in.
Stone: 1 ¾ × 7 ¾ × ¾ in.
Cloth: 15 × 21 ¼ in.
Collection of Adrian and Ethel Kalinsky Kremer

165. Jake Kalinsky with mother and sisters

Trestina, Poland, ca. 1912
Framed photograph, 8 ¾ × 6 ½ in.
Collection of Adrian and Ethel Kalinsky Kremer

166. Telegram to E. Ellison in Savannah, Ga.

Charleston, S.C., April 26, 1883
Paper and ink, two sheets, 5 ½ × 8 ½ in. (each)
Collection of Shera Lee Ellison Berlin

167. Drain board for koshering meat

United States, ca. 1944
Wood, 22 × 13 ½ × ¾ in.
Collection of Sura Wolff Wengrow

168. Noodle cutter

Germany, ca. 1930
Metal and wood, 8 × 7 × 13 ¼ in.
Collection of Renée Hoffman Steinberg Levin

169. Passover Haggadah

United States, 1938
Distributed by Maxwell House Coffee Company, through I. M. Pearlstine and Sons
Paper and ink, 6 ½ × 4 ¾ in.
Collection of Sura Wolff Wengrow

170. Candlesticks

Lithuania, ca. 1914
Brass, 3 ¼ × 1 ½ × 1 ½ in. (each)
Collection of Sidney and Helen Silver

171. Passover matzah cover

Ca. 1920
Printed satin and muslin, 15 × 15 in.
Collection of Rabbi David J. and Barbara Radinsky

172. Passover kiddush cup

Ca. 1920
Glass, 4 ¼ × 2 × 2 in.
Collection of Rabbi David J. and Barbara Radinsky

173. Letters between Mamie Ellison and Jacob Karesh (facsimile)

Bamberg and Charleston, S.C., July 1898–August 1903
Paper and ink, 7 × 5 in. (each)
Collection of Barbara Karesh Stender

174. Wedding photograph of Mamie Ellison Karesh

Charleston, S.C., 1903
Hand-tinted photograph, 4 ¾ × 4 in.
Collection of Barbara Karesh Stender

175. Feather rose

Charleston, S.C., ca. 1905
Duck feathers, 2 ½ × 6 × 3 in.
Collection of Barbara Karesh Stender

176. Flower pin in box

Ca. 1890
Gold with enamel overlay, set with a single diamond and seed pearls
Pin: 1 in. (diameter); box: 2 ¾ × 1 ¾ in.
Collection of Barbara Karesh Stender

177. Ketubbah of Louis Jacobs
and Ethel H. Pearlstine

Branchville, S.C., 1908
Paper and ink, 17 × 10 ¾ in.
Gift of Ethel Pearlstine Jacobs
Brith Sholom Beth Israel

178. Banjo ukelele

Columbia, S.C., ca. 1928
Wood, metal, and hide, 2 ½ × 7 × 20 ¾ in.
Collection of Sura Wolff Wengrow

SECTION FIVE *Pledging Allegiance*

179. New Year's pop-up card

Ca. 1910
Paper and ink, 8 × 5 × 8 in. (open)
Collection of Leonard B. Cohen

180. Scrapbook for the Charleston
Section of the Council of Jewish
Women (facsimile)

Charleston, S.C., 1906–1964
Paper and photographs,
16 ½ × 24 ½ × 1 ½ in. (open)
Gift of the Council of Jewish Women,
Charleston Section
Jewish Heritage Collection, College of
Charleston Library

181. Photograph album of
Ben Keyserling

Beaufort, S.C., ca. 1928–1940
Paper and photographs with cloth cover,
5 ¾ × 9 ¾ × 1 ¾ in.
Collection of Rosalyn Keyserling Taratoot

182. Darlington, S.C., high school
football jersey given to Andrew
Cohen, 1974

United States, ca. 1974
Cotton with blue stencil, 29 × 51 in.
Gift of Alexander A. Cohen
Jewish Heritage Collection, College of
Charleston Library

183. Aleph Zadik Aleph (AZA)
athletic jersey belonging to
Harold Lurey, Greenville, S.C.

Goldsmith Sports Equipment
United States, ca. 1938
Cotton, 22 × 49 ½ in.
Gift of Ann Lurey
Jewish Heritage Collection, College of
Charleston Library

184. Lady Lafayette Hotel plate

Vernon Kilns
California, ca. 1938
Glazed ceramic with transfer design,
10 ½ in. (diameter)
Gift of Sam and Leona Novit Siegel
Jewish Heritage Collection, College of
Charleston Library

185. Cash register from the L. Lourie
Department Store ("Lourie's") in St.
George, S.C.

National Cash Register Company
Dayton, Ohio, ca. 1915
Brass, wood, enamel, and glass,
59 × 35 ¼ × 20 ¾ in.
Collection of the Lourie family

186. Poliakoff store ledger

Abbeville, S.C., 1901
Paper and ink, 12 × 7 ½ in.
Collection of the Poliakoff family

187. American flag

United States, early 20th century
Cotton, 43 ½ × 70 ½ in.
Collection of the Poliakoff family

188. Star Brand chairs

United States, mid-20th century
Wood and metal, 32 × 62 × 22 in.
Collection of the Poliakoff family

189. Shoe bench

United States, mid-20th century
Wood, 16 × 25 × 15 in.
Collection of the Poliakoff family

190. Poll Parrot shoe display

United States, mid-20th century
Metal, wood, wire, and paper,
39 × 18 × 11 in.
Collection of the Poliakoff family

191. Poll Parrot display figure

United States, mid-20th century
Plastic, metal, and paint, 16 ¾ × 5 ¼ × 5 in.
Collection of the Poliakoff family

192. Pushke (charity box)

Inscribed: "Charity for Jerusalem"
United States, ca. 1930
Metal and paint, 3 ¼ × 3 ½ × 2 ¼ in.
Collection of the Poliakoff family

193. World War I Purple Heart,
awarded to Julius Bloom, 1918

Bailey, Banks and Biddle, Co.
Philadelphia, ca. 1914–1918
Metal and fabric, 3 ½ × 1 ½ in.
Gift of Jack L. Bloom
Jewish Heritage Collection, College of
Charleston Library

194. World War I window flag for war
service

United States, ca. 1914–1918
Cotton, 61 × 34 in.
Collection of Evelyn Rosenberg Gross-Brein

195. World War I Red Cross arm band,
headgear and apron worn by Nina
Moïse

United States, ca. 1914–1918
Cotton
Armband: 4 × 15 ½ in.
Headgear: 18 × 24 in.
Apron: 16 ½ × 29 in.
Temple Sinai Archives

196. *Abridged Prayer Book for Jews in the Army and Navy of the United States,* issued to Edwin Strauss Pearlstine

Philadelphia: The Jewish Publication Society of America, 1917
Paper and ink, with cloth cover, 6 1/4 × 4 in.
Collection of Gerald and Jane Pearlstine Meyerson

197. *Abridged Prayer Book for Jews in the Armed Forces of the United States,* issued to Isaac Jacobs

New York: Jewish Welfare Board, 1941
Paper and ink, with cloth cover,
5 1/4 × 3 1/2 in.
Gift of Ruth Bass Jacobs (Mrs. Isaac Jacobs)
Jewish Heritage Collection, College of Charleston Library

198. World War II foot locker and memorabilia belonging to Dr. Abraham Ellis Poliakoff

Ca. 1939–1945
Wood, metal, and paper,
14 × 33 1/2 × 19 1/2 in. (foot locker)
Collection of the Poliakoff family

199. World War II Army Air Corps uniform of Gerald Meyerson

United States, ca. 1943–1946
Wool blend
Dress jacket: 31 1/4 × 29 1/2 in.
Pants: 41 × 29 in.
Collection of Gerald and Jane Pearlstine Meyerson

200. World War II army hat and military regalia of Jerome Schwartz

Hat: Luxemberg Military and Civilian Tailors
New York, ca. 1941–1945
Wool and leather, 4 1/4 × 11 × 10 1/2 in.
Regalia (framed): United States, ca.
1941–1945
Various materials, 8 × 12 in.
Collection of Jerome Schwartz

201. World War II pilot helmet and belt of Harold M. Aronson

United States, ca. 1941–1944
Helmet: leather and wool, 9 × 11 1/4 in.
Belt: cotton and metal, 26 1/4 × 3 in.
Collection of Michael Patrick Kelly

202. Nazi helmet confiscated by Louis Wolff

Germany, ca. 1940
Metal and leather, 6 × 8 1/2 × 10 1/2 in.
Collection of Sura Wolff Wengrow

SECTION SIX *Of Blessed Memory*

203. Memorial album for Moshe Yidel Gelbart

Poland, 1935
Paper and photographs, with black satin cover, 5 × 4 1/2 in.
Gift of Ralph G. Geldbart
Jewish Heritage Collection, College of Charleston Library

204. Candlesticks

Ebenezer Coker or Elizabeth Cooke
London, 1766 and 1768
Silver, 10 × 4 1/2 × 4 1/2 in. (each)
McKissick Museum, University of South Carolina

205. Candlesticks

Russia, ca. 1770–1790
Brass, 9 3/4 × 3 3/4 × 4 in. (each)
Collection of Moshe and Stacey Radinsky

206. Candlesticks

Lithuania, ca. 1867
Silver, 13 3/4 × 5 × 5 in. (each)
Collection of Mrs. William Mann Price

207. Candlesticks

Lithuania, late 19th century
Brass, 10 × 5 1/2 × 5 1/2 in. (each)
Collection of Shera Lee Ellison Berlin

208. Candlesticks

B. Henneberg
Warsaw, Poland, 1901
Silver-plated, 14 1/2 × 5 1/2 × 5 1/2 in. (each)
Collection of Marlene Alfred Addlestone

209. Candlesticks

Ca. 1890–1900
Silver, 12 1/4 × 4 3/4 × 4 3/4 in. (each)
Collection of George and Bertha Breibart

210. Candlesticks

Warsaw, Poland, ca. 1900
Silver, 15 1/2 × 7 1/4 × 7 1/4 in. (each)
Collection of Sol and Sara Breibart

211. Candlesticks

Lithuania, ca. 1860
Brass, 15 1/2 × 7 1/4 × 7 1/4 in. (each)
Collection of Harriet Hirschfeld Keyserling

212. Candlesticks

Russia, 1896
Brass, 10 × 4 × 4 in. and
9 1/2 × 3 1/4 × 3 1/4 in.
Collection of the Poliakoff family

213. Candlesticks

Lithuania, ca. 1870
Brass, 9 1/2 × 3 1/2 × 3 1/4 in. (each)
McKissick Museum, University of South Carolina

214. Candlesticks

Poland, late 19th century
Silver, 14 × 6 × 6 in. (each)
Collection of Bernard and Norma Rae Solomon Karesh

215. Candlesticks

Warsaw, Poland, late 19th century
Silver, 14 × 5 × 5 in. (each)
Collection of Ruth Bazerman ❧

Contributors' Biographies

BILL ARON is best known for his photographs documenting Jewish communities around the world. *From the Corners of the Earth*, with an introduction by Chaim Potok, includes images from the Soviet Union, Cuba, Jerusalem, New York, and Los Angeles. Since 1989, Aron has been collaborating with the Museum of the Southern Jewish Experience, in Mississippi, on a project depicting Jewish life in the Deep South. A volume drawing from this work, *Shalom Y'all: Images of Southern Jewish Life in America*, will be published in 2002. Aron's photographs can be found in numerous public and private collections, including the Museum of Modern Art, the International Center for Photography, the Jewish Museum, the Chicago Art Institute, the Boston Museum of Fine Arts, the Skirball Museum, the Museum of American Jewish History, the Israel Museum, and the Museum of the Diaspora.

JACK BASS has authored or coauthored seven books about the American South, including *The Orangeburg Massacre*, a narrative account of the 1968 shooting of students at South Carolina State College by highway patrolmen, and *Taming the Storm*, a biography of Judge Frank M. Johnson Jr., which won the 1994 Robert F. Kennedy Book Award grand prize. The son of immigrant Jewish parents, Bass grew up in the town of North, South Carolina. Capping a distinguished career in journalism, he studied at Harvard University as a Nieman Fellow. He received a Ph.D. in American studies from Emory University, and in 1999 he joined the College of Charleston faculty as professor of humanities and social sciences.

ELI N. EVANS is the author of *The Provincials: A Personal History of Jews in the South*, *Judah P. Benjamin: The Jewish Confederate*, and *The Lonely Days Were Sundays: Reflections of a Jewish Southerner*. Born and raised in Durham, North Carolina, he earned degrees from the University of North Carolina and Yale Law School. Evans served in the United States Navy and worked as an aide and speech writer in President Lyndon Johnson's administration. Currently he is president of the Charles H. Revson Foundation in New York City. In 2001 he was elected to the American Academy of Arts and Sciences.

JENNA WEISSMAN JOSELIT is visiting professor of American studies at Princeton University. A scholar of the American Jewish experience, her books include *Our Gang: Jewish Crime and the New York Jewish Community, 1900–1940*; *New York's Jewish Jews: The Orthodox Community in the Interwar Years*; and *The Wonders of America: Reinventing Jewish Culture, 1880–1950*, which won the National Jewish Book Award in history. Her most recent work is *A Perfect Fit: Clothes, Character, and the Promise of America*. Joselit writes a monthly column on material culture and American Jewish life for the *Forward*.

DEBORAH DASH MOORE, professor of religion at Vassar College, specializes in twentieth-century American Jewish history. Her first book, *At Home in America: Second Generation New York Jews*, explores how the children of immigrants created an ethnic world that blended elements of Jewish and American culture into a dynamic urban society. *To the Golden Cities: Pursuing the American Jewish Dream in Miami and L.A.* follows the post–World War II migration of Jews to sunny south Florida and California. Moore's other books include *B'nai B'rith and the Challenge of Ethnic Leadership* and the award-winning two-volume *Jewish Women in America: An Historical Encyclopedia*, which she edited with Paula Hyman. Recently published is *Cityscapes: A History of New York in Images*, co-edited with Howard B. Rock. Moore is currently working on a study of Jewish GI's during the Second World War.

DALE ROSENGARTEN is curator of the Jewish Heritage Collection at the College of Charleston. Since 1995 she has been recording oral history interviews, collecting archival materials, and coordinating research for *A Portion of the People: Three Hundred Years of Southern Jewish Life*. Born and raised in New York, she earned a B.A. from Radcliffe College and a Ph.D. in the history of American civilization from Harvard University. Her previous publications include the exhibition catalogue *Row Upon Row: Sea Grass Baskets of the South Carolina Lowcountry*, produced by McKissick Museum.

THEODORE ROSENGARTEN, a native of Brooklyn, New York, is a teacher, writer, and community activist. He holds a B.A. in American studies from Amherst College and a Ph.D. in the history of American civilization from Harvard University. Author of *All God's Dangers: The Life of Nate Shaw*, winner of the National Book Award for contemporary affairs, and *Tombee: Portrait of a Cotton Planter*, winner of the National Book Critics Circle Award for best biography, Rosengarten was named a MacArthur Fellow in 1989.

Glossary

The language of foreign terms and literal translations are given parenthetically after the word. Spellings of Hebrew and Yiddish words follow the *Encyclopedia Judaica*, but without marks denoting pronunciation, such as *ḥ*, often rendered as *ch*. Terms not in common English usage appear in italics upon first occurrence in the text.

adjunta (Spanish) Governing council of a Sephardic congregation.

alav or **aleha ha-shalom** (Hebrew, "Peace be upon him [her]") Phrase traditionally spoken when mentioning the name of a deceased person.

Aleph Zadik Aleph (AZA) Jewish fraternal boys' club organized by B'nai B'rith in 1923. The name is derived from letters of the Hebrew alphabet. See B'nai B'rith.

aliyah (Hebrew, "ascend") The honor of being called to read from the Torah in synagogue.

ark (Latin, "box") An enclosure in a synagogue for the Torah scrolls.

Ashkenazi (Hebrew, "native of Germany"), pl. **Ashkenazim** Jews from central and eastern Europe, distinguished from the Sephardim by their religious rituals, customs, foods, and pronunciation of Hebrew. Until the twentieth century, the primary language of the Ashkenazim was Yiddish. See Sephardi.

bankas (Yiddish) Medicinal glass cups heated and applied to the skin to draw blood to the surface, formerly used to treat a variety of illnesses.

bar mitzvah (Aramaic and Hebrew, "son of the commandment") Coming-of-age ceremony marking a Jewish boy's acceptance, at age thirteen, of responsibility for carrying out the commandments of the Torah.

bat mitzvah (Hebrew, "daughter of the commandment") Coming-of-age ceremony marking a Jewish girl's acceptance, at age twelve, of responsibility for carrying out the commandments of the Torah.

Beth Israel (Hebrew, "House of Israel") Congregation founded in Beaufort, South Carolina, in 1905. Also the name of congregations in Greenville and Charleston. Charleston's Beth Israel, known locally as the "Little Shul" or the "Kaluszyner Shul," was founded in 1911; in 1954, it merged with Brith Sholom, the "Big Shul." See Kaluzsyn.

Beth Shalom (Hebrew, "House of Peace") Congregation founded in Columbia, South Carolina, in 1906.

Biblia Hebraica (Latin) Hebrew Bible.

bimah (Hebrew, "high place") Raised platform in a synagogue where the Torah is placed for reading and from which prayer services are led.

B'nai B'rith (Hebrew, "Sons of the Covenant") Oldest and largest Jewish service and fraternal organization in America, founded in New York in 1843.

bodek (Hebrew, "examiner") Official who inspects the shohet's knives to determine if they are free from nicks and sufficiently sharp; also checks slaughtered animals to see if their internal organs are clear. See shohet.

brit milah (Hebrew, "covenant of circumcision"), pl. **britot milah** Ceremony of circumcision performed on the eighth day of a Jewish boy's life. "Brit" is the Serphardic pronounciation, "bris" the Ashkenazic, and "brith" the Americanized.

Brith Sholom (Hebrew, "Covenant of Peace") Originally spelled Berith Shalome, the first Ashkenazic congregation in South Carolina, founded in Charleston, ca. 1854.

bubbe (Yiddish) Grandmother.

cantor Synagogue official who leads the congregation in prayer; the chief singer of the liturgy. See hazzan.

Conservative Judaism Movement rooted in the nineteenth-century dissatisfaction with the Reform approach to reconciling tradition and change. First known as "Historical Judaism," it opposes extreme changes in traditional observances, while accepting secular scholarship on sacred texts and allowing certain modifications of Jewish law to accommodate the demands of modern life.

converso (Spanish, "convert"), or **anusim** (Hebrew, "those compelled") A Jew forced to convert to Christianity under pain of persecution or death. Also referred to as marrano (Portuguese, "swine").

crypto-Jew Convert who outwardly professes another religion but inwardly adheres to Judaism.

Emanu-El (Hebrew, "God with us") South Carolina's first Conservative synagogue, founded in Charleston in 1947.

etrog (Hebrew) A yellow citrus fruit similar in appearance to a lemon, identified as "the fruit of a goodly tree," carried in procession during the celebration of Sukkot. According to legend, the etrog, also called "the apple of Paradise," may have been the forbidden fruit eaten by Adam in the Garden of Eden.

feme covert (Old French, "woman covered") A married woman.

feme sole (Old French, "woman alone") An unmarried woman; spinster, divorcée, or widow.

fetter (Yiddish) Uncle.

gefilte fish (Yiddish) Chopped fish, usually a mixture of white fish, pike, and carp, mixed with minced onion, egg, and seasoning, and boiled; ordinarily served cold.

get (Hebrew) Bill of divorce.

glatt (Yiddish, "smooth") **kosher** Refers to food prepared in strict adherence to the laws of kashrut; strictly kosher. See kashrut, kosher.

goldene medinah (Hebrew) Golden land; usually refers to America.

goy (Hebrew), pl. **goyim** Non-Jew, gentile.

gragger (Yiddish) Noisemaker used in the Purim service to drown out the name of Haman, wicked chancellor of the king of Persia. See megillah, Purim.

habad, or **chabad** Acronym for the Hebrew "hokhmah" (wisdom), "binah" (understanding), and "da'at" (knowledge); the name of the Hasidic movement founded by Rabbi Shneur Zalman (1745–1812); synonymous with Lubavitch, the town in Byelorussia where the movement developed. See Hasidism, Lubavitcher.

Haggadah (Hebrew) Text read during the Passover seder recounting the story of the Exodus. See Passover, seder.

halahkah (Hebrew) Collective body of the laws and ordinances not written down in the Jewish scriptures but based on an oral interpretation of them.

halizah (Hebrew) Biblically prescribed ceremony (Deuteronomy 25:9–10) performed when a man refuses to marry his brother's childless widow, enabling her to remarry.

hallah, or **challah** (Hebrew, "loaf of bread") Special braided egg-bread eaten on the Sabbath.

Hanukkah, or **Chanukah** (Hebrew) Eight-day festival starting on the twenty-fifth day of the Jewish month of Kislev commemorating the rededication of the Temple at Jerusalem that followed the Maccabees' victory over the Syrians in 165 B.C.; also called the "Festival of Lights." See hanukkiah, Maccabees.

hanukkiah (Hebrew) Eight-branched menorah with a ninth candle, called a shammes or helper, used to light the others. The hanukkiah is lit to recall the miracle that took place at the time of the Maccabees, when a one-day supply of oil found in the desecrated Temple lasted eight days. See Hanukkah, Maccabees, shammes.

Hasidism (Hebrew, from hasid, "the pious") Revivalist movements that have appeared three times in the course of Jewish history, most recently in eastern Europe in the eighteenth century. Synonomous today with ultraorthodoxy, contemporary Hasidism was originally regarded as religiously liberal because of its emphasis on a pure spirit over study of the Talmud and on getting close to God through joy. See habad, Lubavitcher.

havdalah (Hebrew, "separation") Ceremony at the end of the Sabbath separating the Holy Day from the rest of the week, or at the end of a holiday marking the passage from sacred to profane.

hazzan, or **chazan** (Hebrew), pl. **hazzanim** Person who leads the congregation in prayer. See cantor.

heder, or **cheder** (Hebrew, "room") School for teaching the basics of the Hebrew language and Jewish religious observance.

High Holy Days, or **High Holidays** The period encompassing Rosh Hashanah and Yom Kippur, at the start of the new year in the Jewish calendar. See Rosh Hashanah, Yom Kippur.

Holocaust (Greek, "the destruction of life by fire") Since the 1950s the term has been applied primarily to the Nazi regime's attempted annihilation of the Jews of Europe. Six million Jews—two out of every three living at the time in Europe—were murdered as part of a systematic genocide. Millions of other people also were killed because of their ethnicity, culture, political ideas, sexual orientation, or physical or mental handicaps. See Shoah.

huppah, or **chuppa** (Hebrew) Wedding canopy under which a man and woman are married.

hutzpah, or **chutzpah** (Hebrew) Insolence, shamelessness.

kabbalah, or **cabala** (Hebrew, "received tradition") Jewish mystical traditions that attempt to discover the hidden meanings of scripture. Kabbalistic, or cabalistic, pertaining to those traditions.

kaddish (Aramaic, "consecration") Prayer in praise of God recited as part of the daily service, and by mourners and those observing yahrzeit. See yahrzeit.

Kahal Kadosh Beth Elohim (Hebrew, "Holy Congregation House of God") Congregation organized in Charleston, South Carolina, in 1749.

Kaluszyn Town near Warsaw, Poland. Between 1880 and 1950, a small stream of Jews from Kaluszyn immigrated to Charleston, South Carolina, where they founded the Kalushiner Society for landsman, and formed the core of Beth Israel congregation. See landsman, Beth Israel.

kashrut (from the Hebrew, "kasher," "fit" or "proper") Jewish dietary laws derived from the book of Leviticus. See kosher, treyf.

ketubbah (Hebrew, "document"), pl. **ketubbot** Marriage contract stipulating a husband's obligations to his wife.

kiddush (Hebrew, "sanctification") Blessing recited over wine on the eve of the Sabbath or a festival.

kittel (Yiddish from German) White robe worn as a shroud, and by the Orthodox during High Holiday services.

kosher (Yiddish from Hebrew, "kasher") Ritually fit for use; especially food that conforms to Jewish dietary laws. See kashrut, treyf.

kugel (Yiddish, "ball") Crusty baked pudding made of potatoes or noodles.

Ladino Judeo-Spanish dialect spoken by Sephardic exiles in the Ottoman empire and Greece.

landsman (Yiddish from German, "countryman") A fellow Jew from the same town or district in eastern Europe.

landsmannschaft (German) Organization of countrymen. See landsman.

latkes (Yiddish from Russian, "patch") Potato pancakes traditionally eaten during Hanukkah.

Lubavitcher Follower of the Lubavitch branch (named for a Byelorussian town meaning "town of brotherly love") of the Hasidic movement. See habad, Hasidism.

Maccabees Followers of Judah, son of Mattathias, who rebelled against Syrian rule in the second century B.C.E. See Hanukkah.

mahzor (Hebrew, "cycle") Special prayer book for the High Holy Days and festivals.

matzah, or **matzoh** (Hebrew) Unleavened bread eaten during Passover to commemorate the flight of the Hebrews from Egypt. See Passover, seder.

mazel tov (Hebrew, "good luck") "Congratulations."

megillah (Hebrew, "scroll") Commonly refers to the book of Esther that tells the story of the deliverance of the Jews from a massacre planned by the Persian king's chancellor Haman. In slang, it has come to mean a very long story. See Purim.

menorah (Hebrew) Candelabrum with seven branches, a traditional symbol of Judaism; a menorah with eight branches and a shammes, or helper candle, is used during the festival of Hanukkah. See hanukkiah, shammes.

mezuzah (Hebrew, "doorpost") Parchment scroll inscribed with biblical passages, placed in a case, and attached to the doorpost of a house.

mikveh (Hebrew, "collection," especially of water) Bath in which Orthodox Jews immerse themselves for ritual purification, as before the Sabbath or following menstruation.

Mikveh Israel (Hebrew, "Gathering of Israel") Eighteenth-century Sephardic synagogue founded in Philadelphia. Mikve Israel, an alternate spelling, is the name of the first Jewish congregation in Savannah, Georgia, established in 1733.

minhag (Hebrew) Custom or observance considered to be as binding as law; the form and content of the Jewish liturgy.

minyan (Hebrew, "number") Group of ten Jewish men, the minimum required for holding prayer service or reading from the Torah; the Reform and Conservative movements include women as well.

mishpocha (Yiddish), **mishpahah** (Hebrew) Family, relatives.

mizrah, or **mizrach** (Hebrew, "east") Plaque placed on an eastern wall indicating the direction in which to pray.

mohel (Hebrew), pl. **mohalim** Official who performs the rite of circumcision.

oneg Shabbat (Hebrew, "joy of Sabbath") Social gathering after Friday night services customary among Conservative and Reform congregations.

Orthodox Judaism Beliefs and practices of Jews for whom the strict observance of Jewish law is inseparable from faith. The term came into use in the nineteenth century to describe Jews opposed to Reform.

Pale of Settlement Twenty-five provinces of czarist Russia where Jews were permitted permanent residence.

parnas (Hebrew, "leader") Chief synagogue official, originally vested with both religious and administrative functions; subsequently an elected lay leader, the president of a congregation.

Passover (from Hebrew, Pesah or Pesach) Festival commemorating the Exodus of the Hebrew people from Egypt nearly 3,300 years ago. See Haggadah, matzah, seder.

Purim (Hebrew, "lots") Festive holiday commemorating the rescue of the Jews from the villain Haman, chancellor to the King of Persia, through the intercession of Esther, in the fifth century B.C.E. See gragger, megillah.

pushke (Yiddish from Slavic origin) Box used to collect money for charity.

rabbi (Hebrew, "my master") Spiritual head of a Jewish community; a Jewish teacher or leader.

reb, rebbe (Yiddish, "rabbi") Applied generally to a teacher or Hasidic rabbi.

Reform Judaism Movement that arose in the nineteenth century in both Europe and the United States to modernize Judaism through changes in rituals and practice.

Rosh Hashanah (Hebrew, "head of the year") The Jewish New Year, celebrated on the first and second days of the month of Tishri (September–October).

seder (Hebrew, "order") Passover ceremony commemorating the Exodus from Egypt, observed by reading the Haggadah on the eve of the first day and, in most Diaspora communities, on the second night of the holiday as well. The Passover seder includes symbolic foods, prayers, songs, and a festive meal. See Haggadah, matzah, Passover.

sefer (Hebrew), pl. **seferim** Scroll or book. Sefer Torah is Hebrew for "Scroll of the Law."

semikhah, or **semicha** (Hebrew, "laying," or "leaning" of the hands) Ordination conferring the title "rabbi" and authorizing the ordained to interpret Jewish law and settle disputes.

Sephardi (Hebrew, "native of Spain"), pl. **Sephardim** Jews of Spanish and Portuguese extraction. Following their expulsion in the fifteenth century, the Iberian Jews settled around the Mediterranean, the Balkans, western Europe, and the Americas. See Ashkenazi.

Shabbes (Yiddish), **Shabbat** (Hebrew) Sabbath; the Jewish day of rest, from sundown Friday until sundown Saturday.

Shaddai (Hebrew) The Almighty, one of the names of God.

shammes (Yiddish), **shammash** (Hebrew, "one who serves") Caretaker of a synagogue; also, candle used to light the other eight candles of a Hanukkah menorah. See hanukkiah.

Shearith Israel (Hebrew, "Remnant of Israel") New York's first Jewish congregation, founded in 1654. A congregation of the same name, spelled Shearit Israel, was established in Charleston by the traditionalists who broke away from Kahal Kadosh Beth Elohim in 1840.

sheitl (Yiddish) Wig worn by married Orthodox women as a sign of modesty.

Shema Yisrael (Hebrew, "Hear, O Israel!") First words of the prayer proclaiming the oneness of God, the central creed of Judaism.

Shir Hama'Alot (Hebrew, "A Song of Ascents") Daily prayer taken from Psalm 130:1–5.

shivviti, or **sheviti** (Hebrew) From the verse "Shivviti Adonai l'negdi tamid" (I have set the Lord always before me), Psalm 16:8; a plaque often located on the synagogue bimah.

Shoah (Hebrew, "chaos, destruction, catastrophe") Term widely used in Israel and increasingly used in the United States to denote the murder of the Jews by the Nazis. See Holocaust.

shohet (Hebrew), pl. **shohatim** Ritual slaughterer trained in the Jewish manner of killing food animals as quickly and painlessly as possible.

shtetl (Yiddish), pl. **shtetlakh** Small Jewish town or Jewish enclave within a town in eastern Europe.

shul (Yiddish) Synagogue.

siddur (Hebrew) Prayer book; among Ashkenazim, the volume containing the daily prayers (in distinction to the mahzor containing those for the festivals).

snoga (Portuguese) Synagogue.

sukkah (Hebrew) Temporary structure with a roof of leafy boughs, straw, and so forth, built for Sukkot to commemorate the tabernacles of the Exodus. See Sukkot.

Sukkot (Hebrew, "booths") The Feast of Tabernacles celebrating the fall harvest and commemorating the desert wandering of the Hebrews during the Exodus. See sukkah.

synagogue Jewish house of worship, from a Greek word meaning "place where people come together."

tallit, or **tallis** (Hebrew, "cloak"), pl. **tallisim** Four-cornered prayer shawl with fringes or tassels (zitzit) at each corner.

Talmud (Hebrew, "teaching"), adj. **talmudic** Collection of writings constituting Jewish civil and religious law; it consists of two parts, the Mishnah (text) and Gemara (commentary).

tefillin (Hebrew) Small leather boxes containing biblical passages, one worn on the left forearm (or, if left-handed, on the right arm) and one on the forehead during weekday morning prayers.

Temple Sinai Congregation in Sumter, South Carolina, organized in 1881 as the Sumter Society of Israelites.

Torah (Hebrew, "learning," "law") The five books of Moses, also called the Pentateuch, containing the foundation of Jewish law and practice.

Tree of Life Congregation organized in Columbia, South Carolina, in 1896.

treyf, **trayf**, or **terefah** (Hebrew) Not kosher; especially food not prepared according to Jewish dietary laws. See kashrut, kosher.

treyf medinah (Hebrew) Nonkosher country.

tsimmes (Yiddish) A kind of carrot stew.

tzedakah (Hebrew) Righteousness, charity.

wimpel, or **wimple** (German) Cloth binder wound around Torah scrolls. Beginning in Germany in the seventeenth century, it became customary to make Torah binders upon the birth of a child, sometimes from the swaddling cloth in which an infant boy was wrapped during his circumcision.

yad (Hebrew, "hand") Special pointer used while reading from the Torah. A yad traditionally tapers at one end to a hand with an outstretched finger.

yahrzeit (Yiddish, "year time") Anniversary of a death, observed with prayer and memorial candles.

yarmulke (Yiddish) or **kippah** (Hebrew) Skullcap worn by Jewish males in synagogue and by the observant at all times.

Yehudishkeit (from Yehudah, Yiddish for Jew) Jewishness.

yeshivah, or **yeshiva** (Hebrew) School for Talmudic study; seminary for the training of Orthodox rabbis. Contemporary **yeshivot** (pl.) in America offer instruction in secular as well as sacred subjects.

Yiddish Judeo-German; a High German language with vocabulary borrowed from Hebrew and the Slavic languages, written in Hebrew letters, and spoken mainly by Jews from eastern and central Europe.

Yiddishkeyt Yiddish culture, Jewishness.

Yom Kippur (Hebrew) Day of Atonement, solemn fast day observed on the tenth day of the Jewish month of Tishri.

Bibliography

Sources on Southern Jewish History, with an emphasis on South Carolina

The archival section of this selected bibliography lists a wide range of repositories in South Carolina and major collections elsewhere in the region. Synagogue archives are not listed, though they are an important resource. When designing a research project on Jewish history, it is worth checking not only synagogues but county historical societies, Jewish federations, public libraries, museums, college and university archives, and state, county, and municipal records for primary materials. The richest veins of all may be found in private collections. Books and periodicals itemized below include basic works on American Jewish history, selected regional and state studies, and a comprehensive list of titles on South Carolina Jewry.

Archival Collections

American Jewish Archives, Cincinnati, Ohio

American Jewish Historical Society, New York, New York

Beth Ahabah Museum and Archives, Richmond, Virginia

Calhoun County Museum, St. Matthews, South Carolina

Camden Historical Society Archives, Camden, South Carolina

Charleston County Public Library, South Carolina Room, Charleston, South Carolina

Charleston Library Society, Charleston, South Carolina

The Charleston Museum, Charleston, South Carolina

College of Charleston Library, Special Collections, Charleston, South Carolina (includes the manuscript and oral history archives of the Jewish Heritage Collection)

Darlington County Historical Commission, Darlington, South Carolina

Georgia Historical Society, Savannah, Georgia

Gibbes Museum of Art, Charleston, South Carolina

Goldring/Woldenberg Institute of Southern Jewish Life, Jackson, Mississippi

Kahal Kadosh Beth Elohim Museum, Charleston, South Carolina (manuscript archives housed at the College of Charleston Library, Special Collections)

Louisiana State Museum, New Orleans, Louisiana

Museum of the Southern Jewish Experience, Utica, Mississippi

New-York Historical Society, New York, New York

Sanford L. Ziff Jewish Museum of Florida, Miami Beach, Florida

South Carolina Department of Archives and History, Columbia, South Carolina

South Carolina Historical Society, Charleston, South Carolina

South Caroliniana Library, University of South Carolina, Columbia, South Carolina

Southern Historical Collection, University of North Carolina, Chapel Hill, North Carolina

Sumter County Historical Museum and Genealogical and Historical Research Center, Sumter, South Carolina

Temple Sinai Archives, Sumter, South Carolina

Touro Infirmary Archives, New Orleans, Louisiana

Tulane University, New Orleans, Louisiana

Virginia Historical Society, Richmond, Virginia

Virginia State Library, Richmond, Virginia

William Breman Jewish Heritage Museum, Atlanta, Georgia

Williams Research Center, Historic New Orleans Collection, New Orleans, Louisiana

Winthrop University Archives and Special Collections, Rock Hill, South Carolina

Books, Dissertations, and Pamphlets

Abbot, Belle Kendrick. *Leah Mordecai*. New York: Sheldon & Co., 1875.

Abrams, Morris B. *The Day Is Short, An Autobiography*. New York: Harcourt Brace Jovanovich, 1982.

Alexander, Henry A. *Notes on the Alexander Family of South Carolina and Georgia, and Connections*. Atlanta: Henry A. Alexander, 1954.

Altschuler, David, ed. *The Jews of Washington, D.C.: A Communal History Anthology*. Chappaqua, N.Y.: Jewish Historical Society of Greater Washington, 1985.

American Jewish Art and History in the South, 1697–1900: An Exhibition. Charleston, S.C.: Carolina Art Association, 1964.

Apte, Helen Jacobus. *Heart of a Wife: The Diary of a Southern Jewish Woman*. Edited by Marcus D. Rosenbaum. Wilmington, Del.: Scholarly Resources, Inc., 1998.

Aron, Bill. *Shalom Y'all: Images of Southern Jewish Life in America*. Edited by Vicki Reikes Fox with Bill Aron and Marcie Cohen Ferris. Chapel Hill, N.C.: Algonquin Books, 2002.

Ashkenazi, Elliott. *The Business of Jews in Louisiana, 1840–1870*. Tuscaloosa: University of Alabama Press, 1988.

Ashkenazi, Elliott, ed. *The Civil War Diary of Clara Solomon: Growing Up in New Orleans, 1861–62*. Baton Rouge: Louisiana State University Press, 1995.

Atherton, Lewis E. *The Southern Country Store, 1800–1860*. Baton Rouge: Louisiana State University Press, 1949.

Bailey, N. Louise, Mary L. Morgan, and Carolyn R. Taylor. *Biographical Directory of the South Carolina Senate, 1776–1985*. 3 vols. Columbia: University of South Carolina Press, 1986.

Banov, Leon. *As I Recall: The Story of the Charleston County Health Department*. With illustrations by John Lee (Johnson) and historical notes by Joseph I. Waring. Columbia, S.C.: R. L. Bryan, 1970.

Barkai, Abraham. *Branching Out: German-Jewish Immigration to the United States, 1820–1914*. New York: Holmes & Meier, 1994.

Baruch, Bernard. *Baruch: My Own Story*. New York: Henry Holt & Co., 1957.

———. *The Public Years*. New York: Holt, Rinehart & Winston, 1960.

Baum, Charlotte, Paula Hyman, and Sonya Michel. *The Jewish Woman in America*. New York: New American Library, 1976.

Bauman, Mark K., and Berkley Kalin, eds. *The Quiet Voices: Southern Rabbis and Black Civil Rights, 1880s to 1900s*. Tuscaloosa: University of Alabama Press, 1997.

Ben-Ur, Aviva. "The Exceptional and the Mundane: A Biographical Portrait of Rebecca (Machado) Phillips (1746–1831)." In *Women and American Judaism*, edited by Pamela S. Nadell and Jonathan D. Sarna. Hanover, N.H.: Brandeis University Press by University Press of New England, 2001.

Berman, Myron. *Richmond's Jewry, 1769–1976: Shabbat in Shockoe*. Charlottesville: University Press of Virginia, 1979.

Bern, Ronald L. *The Legacy*. New York: Mason/Charter Publishers, Inc., 1975.

Bingham, Emily Simms. "Mordecai: Three Generations of a Southern Jewish Family, 1780–1865." Ph.D. diss., University of North Carolina at Chapel Hill, 1999.

Birmingham, Stephen. *The Grandees: America's Sephardic Elite*. New York: Harper & Row, 1971. Reprint, New York: Syracuse University Press, 1997.

———. *"Our Crowd": The Great Jewish Families of New York*. New York: Harper & Row, 1967.

———. *"The Rest of Us": The Rise of America's Eastern European Jews*. Boston: Little, Brown, 1984.

Blatt, Solomon. *The Bridge Builder: Solomon Blatt Reflects on a Lifetime of Service to South Carolina*. Edited by George D. Terry and Catherine Wilson Horne. Columbia: McKissick Museum, University of South Carolina, 1986.

Blau, Joseph L., and Salo W. Baron, eds. *The Jews of the United States, 1790–1840: A Documentary History*. 3 vols. Jacob R. Schiff Library of Jewish Contributions to American Democracy Series. New York: Columbia University Press, 1963. Reprint, New York: Columbia University Press, 1969.

Blumberg, Janice R. *One Voice: Rabbi Jacob Rothschild and the Troubled South*. Macon, Ga.: Mercer University Press, 1985.

Braude, Ann. "The Jewish Woman's Encounter with American Culture." In *Women and Religion in America*. Vol. I., *The Nineteenth Century*, edited by Rosemary Radford Ruether and Rosemary Skinner Keller. San Francisco: Harper & Row, 1981.

Breibart, Solomon. *Articles on the Southern Jewish Experience in the Journals of the American Jewish Historical Society and the American Jewish Archives*. Valdosta, Ga.: Southern Jewish Historical Society, 1986.

———. *The Rev. Mr. Gustavus Poznanski: First American Jewish Reform Minister*. Charleston, S.C.: Kahal Kadosh Beth Elohim, 1979.

———. *Some Places in Charleston, S.C. of Jewish Interest*. [1995.] Rev. ed. Charleston, S.C.: Kahal Kadosh Beth Elohim, 2001.

Brilliant, Richard. *Facing the New World: Jewish Portraits in Colonial and Federal America*. New York: Prestel, 1997.

Brith Sholom Beth Israel: 130th Anniversary, 30th Anniversary Merger, January 13, 1985, 20 Teveth, 5745. Charleston, S.C.: [Brith Sholom Beth Israel], 1985.

Brownell, Blaine A., and David R. Goldfield, eds. *The City in Southern History: The Growth of Urban Civilization in the South*. Port Washington, N.Y.: Kennikat Press, 1976.

Butler, Pierce. *Judah P. Benjamin*. Philadelphia: George W. Jacobs & Co., 1907.

Buxton, Julian Thomas, Jr. "Franklin J. Moses, Jr.: The Scalawag Governor of South Carolina." Honor's thesis, Princeton University, 1950.

Cardozo, Isaac N. *A Discourse Delivered in Charleston (S.C.) on the 21st of Nov. 1827 Before the Reformed Society of Israelites for Promoting True Principles of Judaism According to Its Purity and Spirit*. Charleston, S.C.: James S. Burges, 1827.

Cardozo, Jacob N. *A Plan of Financial Relief. Addressed to the Legislature of Georgia and Confederate States Congress*. Atlanta: J. H. Seals and Co.'s Power Press, 1863.

———. *Reminiscences of Charleston*. Charleston, S.C.: J. Walker, 1866.

Carvalho, Solomon N. *Incidents of Travel and Adventure in the Far West, Etc*. New York: Derby and Jackson, 1857. Reprint, edited and with an introduction by Bertram W. Korn, Philadelphia: Jewish Publication Society, 1954.

Cauthen, John K. *Speaker Blatt: His Challenges Were Greater*. Columbia, S.C.: R. L. Bryan Co., 1965.

Coburn, Randy Sue. *Remembering Jody*. New York: Carroll & Graf, 1998.

Cohen, Edward. *The Peddler's Grandson: Growing Up Jewish in Mississippi*. Jackson: University Press of Mississippi, 1999.

Cohen, Martin A., and Abraham J. Peck, eds. *Sephardim in the Americas: Studies in Culture and History*. Tuscaloosa: University of Alabama Press, 1993.

Cohen, Naomi, W. *Encounter with Emancipation: The German Jews in the United States, 1830–1914*. Philadelphia: Jewish Publication Society of America, 1984.

Cohn, Edward L., ed. *The Isaac Harby Prayerbook*. Columbia, S.C.: R. L. Bryan, 1974.

Coit, Margaret L. *Mr. Baruch*. Boston: Houghton Mifflin Co., 1957.

Commemoration Book of Dedication: Synagogue Emanu-El: The Story of the First Conservative

Synagogue of South Carolina, 1947–1957. Charleston, S.C.: [Emanu-El] Dedication Committee, 1957.

Conroy, Pat. *Beach Music.* New York: Doubleday, 1995.

Cowett, Mark. *Birmingham Rabbi: Rabbi Morris Newfield and Alabama, 1895–1940.* University, Ala.: University of Alabama Press, 1986.

Cunningham, H. H. *Doctors in Gray: The Confederate Medical Service.* Baton Rouge: Louisiana State University Press, 1958.

The Dedication Book of the New Synagogue Emanu-El: The Story of the First Conservative Synagogue of South Carolina, 1947–1980. Charleston, S.C.: [Emanu-El] Dedication Committee, 1980.

Dedication of Beth Israel Synagogue, Charleston, South Carolina. Charleston, S.C.: [Beth Israel], 1948.

DeLeon, Edwin. *Thirty Years of My Life on Three Continents.* London: Ward and Downey, 1890.

DeLeon, Thomas Cooper. *Belles, Beaux, and Brains of the '60s.* New York: G. W. Dillingham, 1901. Reprint, New York: Arno Press, 1974.

———. *Four Years in Rebel Capitals: An Inside View of Life in the Southern Confederacy, from Birth to Death.* Mobile, Ala.: Gossip Printing Co., 1890.

Demoff, Allison L. "Strategies of an Independent Woman: The Life of Phoebe Pember." Honor's thesis, College of William and Mary, 1993.

Diner, Hasia R. *A Time for Gathering: The Second Migration, 1820–1880.* Baltimore: Johns Hopkins University Press, 1992.

Dinnerstein, Leonard. *Antisemitism in America.* New York: Oxford University Press, 1994.

———. *The Leo Frank Case.* New York: Columbia University Press, 1968. Reprint, Athens: University of Georgia Press, 1987.

———, and David M. Reimers. *Ethnic Americans: A History of Immigration.* 1975. 4th ed. New York: Columbia University Press, 1999.

———, and Mary Pallson, eds. *Jews in the South.* Baton Rouge: Louisiana State University Press, 1973.

Dobkowski, Michael N. *The Tarnished Dream: The Basis of American Anti-Semitism.* Westport, Conn.: Greenwood Press, 1979.

Dobrinsky, Herbert C. *A Treasury of Sephardic Laws and Customs: The Ritual Practices of Syrian, Moroccan, Judeo-Spanish and Spanish and Portuguese Jews of North America.* 1986. Rev. ed. New York: Yeshiva University Press, 1988.

Doyle, Don. H. *New Men, New Cities, New South: Atlanta, Nashville, Charleston, Mobile, 1860–1910.* Chapel Hill: University of North Carolina Press, 1990.

Drago, Edmund Lee. *Initiative, Paternalism, and Race Relations: Charleston's Avery Normal Institute.* Athens: University of Georgia Press, 1990.

Dryer, Richard E. "The Culture, Practice and Ideals of an Early Nineteenth Century Southern Acculturated Congregation as Reflected in the Minutes of Congregation Beth Elohim, South Carolina, 1838–1842." Term paper, Hebrew Union College–Jewish Institute of Religion, 1955.

Dumenil, Lynn. *Freemasonry and American Culture, 1880–1930.* Princeton, N.J.: Princeton University Press, 1984.

Early American Jewish Portraiture. New York: American Jewish Historical Society, 1952.

Edens, Ruth J. *"It Takes a Heap O' Livin'": The Families of the Sumter County Museum Home.* Sumter, S.C.: Sumter County Museum, 1996.

Edgar, Walter. *South Carolina: A History.* Columbia: University of South Carolina Press, 1998.

Edgcomb, Gabrielle Simon. *From Swastika to Jim Crow: Refugee Scholars at Black Colleges.* Malabar, Fla.: Krieger, 1993.

Elovitz, Mark H. *A Century of Jewish Life in Dixie: The Birmingham Experience.* University, Ala.: University of Alabama Press, 1974.

Elzas, Barnett A. *A Century of Judaism in South Carolina.* Charleston, S.C.: YMHA, 1904. Originally published in the Centennial Edition of the *Charleston (S.C.) News and Courier,* May 1904.

———. *[The 1820] Constitution of the Hebrew Congregation of Kaal Kadosh Beth-Elohim or House of God. Charleston, S.C. MDCCCXX.* Charleston, S.C.: Daggett Printing Co., 1904.

———. *Documents Relative to a Proposed Settlement of Jews in South Carolina in 1748.* Charleston, S.C.: The Daggett Printing Co., 1903.

———. *A History of Congregation Beth Elohim of Charleston, S.C., 1800–1810.* Charleston, S.C.: Daggett Printing Co., 1902.

———. *Jewish Cemeteries at Columbia, S.C.* Charleston, S.C.: n.p. 1910.

———. *Jewish Cemeteries of Congregation Berith Shalome at Charleston, S.C.* Charleston, S.C.: n.p., 1910.

———. *Jewish Cemetery at Camden, S.C.* Charleston, S.C.: n.p., 1910.

———. *Jewish Cemetery at Georgetown, S.C.* Charleston, S.C.: n.p., 1910.

———. *Jewish Marriage Notices from the Newspaper Press of Charleston, 1775–1906.* New York: Bloch Publishing Co., 1917.

———. *The Jews of South Carolina: A Record of the First Naturalization in the Province.* Charleston, S.C.: Daggett Printing Co., [1903].

———. *The Jews of South Carolina From the Earliest Time to the Present Day.* Philadelphia: J. B. Lippincott Co., 1905. Reprint, Spartanburg, S.C.: Reprint Co., 1983.

———. *Joseph Salvador: Jewish Merchant Prince who Came to South Carolina.* Charleston, S.C.: Daggett Printing Co., [1903?].

———. *Leaves from My Historical Scrapbook.* Charleston, S.C.: n.p., 1907.

———. *New Jewish Cemetery of K. K. Beth Elohim at Charleston, S.C.* Charleston, S.C.: n.p., 1910.

———. *Old Jewish Cemeteries of Charleston, S.C. A Transcript of the Inscriptions on Their Tombstones, 1762–1903.* Charleston, S.C.: Daggett Printing Co., 1903.

———. *The Organ in the Synagogue: An Interesting Chapter in the History of Reform Judaism in America.* Charleston, S.C.: Daggett Printing Co., 1902.

Epstein, Helen. *Children of the Holocaust: Conversations with Sons and Daughters.* New York: Bantam Books, 1979.

Epstein, Howard V. *Jews in Small Towns: Legends and Legacies.* Santa Rosa, Calif.: Vision Books International, 1997.

Evans, Eli. N. *Judah P. Benjamin: The Jewish Confederate.* New York: The Free Press, 1988.

————. *The Lonely Days Were Sundays: Reflections of a Jewish Southerner.* Jackson: University Press of Mississippi, 1993.

————. *The Provincials: A Personal History of Jews in the South.* 1973. Rev. ed. New York: Simon & Schuster, 1997.

Ezekiel, Herbert T., and Gaston Lichtenstein. *The History of the Jews of Richmond from 1769 to 1917.* Richmond, Va.: H. T. Ezekiel, 1917.

Ezratty, Harry A. *500 Years in the Jewish Caribbean: The Spanish and Portuguese Jews in the West Indies.* Baltimore: Omni Arts, Inc., 1971.

Faber, Eli. *Jews, Slaves, and the Slave Trade: Setting the Record Straight.* New York: New York University Press, 1998.

————. *Slavery and the Jews: A Historical Inquiry.* New York: Hunter College of the City University of New York, 1995.

————. *A Time for Planting: The First Migration, 1654–1820.* Baltimore: Johns Hopkins University Press, 1992.

Faust, Drew Gilpin. *Mothers of Invention: Women of the Slaveholding South in the American Civil War.* Chapel Hill: University of North Carolina Press, 1996.

Fein, Isaac M. *The Making of an American Jewish Community: The History of Baltimore Jewry from 1773 to 1920.* Baltimore: Jewish Historical Society of Maryland, 1985.

Feingold, Henry L. *A Time for Searching: Entering the Mainstream, 1920–1945.* Baltimore: Johns Hopkins University Press, 1992.

Field, Carter. *Bernard Baruch: Park Bench Statesman.* New York: McGraw-Hill Co., 1944.

Ford, Francis A. *Civil War Sutlers and Their Wares.* New York: T. Yogeloff, 1969.

Forman, Seth Adam. "The Unbearable Whiteness of Being Jewish: Black Americans in the Jewish Mind, 1945–1972." Ph.D. diss., State University of New York at Stony Brook, 1996.

Fox, William L. *Lodge of the Double-Headed Eagle: Two Centuries of Scottish Rite Freemasonry in America's Southern Jurisdiction.* Fayetteville: University of Arkansas Press, 1997.

Frank, Fedora Small. *Beginning on Market Street: Nashville and Her Jewry, 1861–1901.*

Nashville, Tenn.: Jewish Community of Nashville, 1976.

————. *Five Families and Eight Young Men: Nashville and Her Jewry, 1850–1861.* Nashville, Tenn.: Tennessee Book Co., 1962.

Freehling, William W. *Prelude to Civil War: The Nullification Controversy in South Carolina, 1816–1836.* New York: Harper & Row, 1966.

Freudenberg, Larry, ed. *The Source: A Guide Book to Jewish Life.* 1993. 2d ed. Charleston, S.C.: Charleston Jewish Federation, 1995.

Freund, Miriam K. *Jewish Merchants in Colonial America.* New York: Behrman's Jewish Bookhouse, 1939. Reprint, West Orange, N.J.: Behrman House, Inc., 1986.

Friedman, Saul S. *Jews and the American Slave Trade.* New Brunswick, N.J.: Transaction Publishers, 1998.

Gergel, Belinda, and Richard Gergel. *In Pursuit of the Tree of Life: A History of the Early Jews of Columbia and the Tree of Life Congregation.* Columbia, S.C.: Tree of Life, 1996.

Ginsberg, Louis. *Chapters on the Jews of Virginia, 1658–1900.* Petersburg, Va.: Privately printed, 1969.

————. *History of the Jews of Petersburg, 1789–1950.* Petersburg, Va.: Privately printed, 1954.

Glazer, Nathan. *American Judaism.* 1957. 2d ed. Chicago: University of Chicago Press, 1989.

Golden, Harry L. *Jewish Roots in the Carolinas: A Pattern of American Philo-Semitism.* Greensboro, N.C.: Deal Print Co., 1955.

————. *Our Southern Landsman.* New York: G. P. Putnam, 1974.

Golden Anniversary: Daughters of Israel Auxiliary of the House of Peace Synagogue: 1917–1967. [Columbia, S.C.: House of Peace Synagogue, 1967].

Golden Anniversary: House of Peace Synagogue, Beth Shalom Congregation: 1908–1958. Columbia, S.C.: Beth Shalom Synagogue, 1958.

Golden Reflections: Looking Forward through the Past, 50th Anniversary, the Charleston Jewish Community Center, 1945–1995. Charleston, S.C.: Charleston Jewish Community Center, 1995.

Goldman, Judy. *The Slow Way Back.* New York: William Morrow & Co., 1999.

Goodman, Abram Vossen. "A Jewish Peddler's Diary." In *Critical Studies in American Jewish History,* edited by Jacob R. Marcus. Vol. 1. Cincinnati: American Jewish Archives, 1971.

————. "South Carolina from Shaftesbury to Salvador." In *Jews in the South,* edited by Leonard Dinnerstein and Mary Pallson. Baton Rouge: Louisiana State University Press, 1973.

Goran, Lester. *This New Land.* New York: New American Library, 1980.

Grant, James. *Bernard M. Baruch: The Adventures of a Wall Street Legend.* New York: Simon and Schuster, 1983.

Gratz, Rebecca. *Letters of Rebecca Gratz.* Edited by David Philipson. Philadelphia: Jewish Publication Society of America, 1929.

Greb, Gregory Allen. "Charleston, South Carolina, Merchants, 1815–1860: Urban Leadership in the Antebellum South." Ph.D. diss., University of California, San Diego, 1978.

Green, Henry Alan, and Marcia Kerstein Zerivitz. *Jewish Life in Florida: A Documentary Exhibit from 1763 to the Present.* Coral Gables, Fla.: Mosaic Inc., 1991.

Greenberg, Mark I. "Creating Ethnic, Class, and Southern Identity in Nineteenth-Century America: The Jews of Savannah, Georgia, 1830–1880." Ph.D. diss., University of Florida 1997.

Greenberg, Reuben, with Arthur Gordon. *Let's Take Back Our Streets!* Chicago: Contemporary Books, 1989.

Greene, Harlan. "Charleston, South Carolina." In *Hometowns, Gay Men Write About Where They Belong,* edited by John Preston. New York: Dutton, 1991.

————. "What She Gave Me: My Mother Regina and History." In *A Member of the Family: Gay Men Write About Their Families,* edited by John Preston. New York: Dutton, 1992.

————. *Why We Never Danced the Charleston.* New York: St. Martin's/Marek, 1984.

Greene, Melissa Fay. *The Temple Bombing.* Reading, Mass.: Addison-Wesley, 1996.

Gregorie, Anne King. *History of Sumter County, South Carolina.* Sumter, S.C.: Library Board of Sumter County, 1954.

Groce, George C., and David H. Wallace. *The New-York Historical Society's Dictionary of*

Artists in America, 1564–1860. New Haven: Yale University Press, 1957.

Gross, Theodore L., ed. *The Literature of American Jews.* New York: Macmillan, 1973.

Grossman, Grace Cohen, with Richard Eighme Ahlborn. *Judaica at the Smithsonian: Cultural Politics as Cultural Model.* Washington, D.C.: Smithsonian Institution Press, 1997.

Grusd, Edward E. *B'nai Brith: The Story of a Covenant.* New York: Appleton-Century, 1966.

Gurock, Jeffrey S., ed. *American Jewish History.* 8 vols. New York: Routledge, 1998.

———. *American Jewish History—A Bibliographic Guide.* Washington, D.C.: Anti-Defamation League, 1983.

Ha Levi-Mordeki, Rebekah. *I Wish with a Rhythm of Song: Poems.* New York: H. Harrison, 1936.

Hagedorn, Leah Elizabeth. "Jews and the American South, 1858–1905." Ph.D. diss., University of North Carolina at Chapel Hill, 1999.

Hagy, James W. *This Happy Land: The Jews of Colonial and Antebellum Charleston.* Tuscaloosa: University of Alabama Press, 1993.

Harap, Louis. *The Image of the Jew in American Literature: From Early Republic to Mass Immigration.* Philadelphia: Jewish Publication Society, 1974.

Harby, Isaac. *A Discourse Delivered in Charleston (S.C.) on the 21st of Nov. 1825 Before the Reformed Society of Israelites for Promoting True Principles of Judaism According to Its Purity and Spirit on Their First Anniversary.* Charleston, S.C.: A. E. Miller, 1825.

———. *The Gordian Knot; or Causes & Effects, a Play in Five Acts.* Charleston, S.C.: G. M. Bounetheau, 1810.

Harris, Melvin A. *The Columbia Hebrew Benevolent Society.* Columbia, S.C.: Columbia Hebrew Benevolent Society, 1947.

Harris, Ray Baker. *Eleven Gentlemen of Charleston: Founders of the Supreme Council, Mother Church of the World, Ancient and Accepted Scottish Rite of Freemasonry.* Washington, D.C., 1959.

Harris, Woodrow Wilson, Jr. "The Education of the Southern Urban Adult: Charleston, South Carolina, and Savannah, Georgia,

1790–1812." Ed.D. diss., University of Georgia, 1979.

Heinze, Andrew R. *Adapting to Abundance: Jewish Immigrants, Mass Consumption, and the Search for American Identity.* New York: Columbia University Press, 1990.

Hennig, Helen. *August Kohn: Versatile South Carolinian.* Columbia, S.C.: Vogue Press, 1949.

———. *The Tree of Life.* Columbia, S.C.: Tree of Life Congregation, 1945.

Herd, E. Don, Jr. *The South Carolina Upcountry, 1540–1980: Historical and Biographical Sketches.* 2 vols. Greenwood, S.C.: Attic Press, 1981–82.

Hermann, Isaac. *Memoirs of a Veteran Who Served as a Private in the 60's in the War Between the States.* Atlanta: Byrd Printing Company, 1911.

Hersch, Virginia. *Storm Beach.* Boston: Houghton, Mifflin, 1933.

Hertzberg, Arthur. *The Jews in America: Four Centuries of an Uneasy Encounter.* New York: Simon & Schuster, 1989.

Hertzberg, Steven. *Strangers within the Gate City: The Jews of Atlanta, 1845–1915.* Philadelphia: Jewish Publication Society of America, 1978.

Hinchin, Martin I. *Fourscore and Eleven: A History of the Jews of Rapides Parish [La.], 1828–1919.* Alexandria, La.: Privately printed, 1978.

Hirsch, Benjamin. *Hearing a Different Drummer: A Holocaust Survivor's Search for Identity.* Macon, Ga.: Mercer University Press, 2000.

Hirschfelder, Arlene B. *Photo Odyssey: Solomon Carvalho's Remarkable Western Adventure, 1853–54.* New York: Clarion Books, 2000.

Hoch, J. Hampton. *The History of Pharmacy in South Carolina.* Charleston, S.C.: n.p., 1951.

Hollis, Daniel Walker. *University of South Carolina.* 2 vols. Columbia: University of South Carolina Press, 1951–56.

Howe, Irving, with the assistance of Kenneth Libo. *World of Our Fathers.* New York: Harcourt Brace Jovanovich, 1976. Reprint, New York: Galahad Books, 1994.

Hyman, Paula E., and Deborah Dash Moore, eds. *Jewish Women in America: An Historical*

Encyclopedia. 2 vols. New York: Routledge, 1997.

Hymns Written for the Service of Hebrew Congregation Beth Elohim of Charleston, S.C. Charleston, S.C.: Levin and Tavel, 1842.

Hymns Written for the Use of Hebrew Congregations. Charleston, S.C.: Congregation Beth Elohim, 1856.

Jacobs, Tzvi. *From the Heavens to the Heart.* Morristown, N.J.: T. Jacobs, 2000.

Jewish Art and Culture in Early America: May 21–June 3, 1981. Kahal Kadosh Beth Elohim. Charleston, South Carolina, and Temple Beth-Or, Montgomery, Alabama. Charleston, S.C.: Piccolo Spoleto, 1981.

Jewish Population Study for Charleston, S.C.: 1997/1998. Charleston, S.C.: Charleston Jewish Federation, 1998.

Jews and Georgians: A Meeting of Cultures: 1733–1983. Atlanta: Atlanta Jewish Federation, [1983].

"The Jews of Charleston." In *The Souvenir Book of the Bicentennial (1750–1950): The Story of the Celebration of the Bicentennial of the Charleston Jewish Community, November 19 through November 26, 1950.* Charleston, S.C.: Bicentennial Committee, 1951. First published in *Charleston (S.C.) News and Courier,* March 25, 1950.

Jick, Leon A. *The Americanization of the Synagogue, 1820–1870.* Hanover, N. H.: Brandeis University Press by University Press of New England, 1976.

Joselit, Jenna Weissman. *The Wonders of America: Reinventing Jewish Culture, 1880–1950.* New York: Hill and Wang, 1994.

Joyner, Charles. "A Community of Memory: Assimilation and Identity among the Jews of Georgetown." In *Shared Traditions: Southern History and Folk Culture.* Urbana: University of Illinois Press, 1999.

Kaganoff, Nathan M., and Melvin I. Irofsky, eds. *Turn to the South: Essays on Southern Jewry.* Charlottesville: University of Virginia Press, 1979.

Kahal Kadosh Beth Elohim Symagogue, 250th Anniversary. Charleston, S.C.: Congregation Beth Elohim, 1999.

Kanter, Kenneth A. "Isaac Harby—Dramatist and Playwright." Term paper, Hebrew Union College–Jewish Institute of Religion, 1979.

Karp, Abraham J. *Golden Door to America: The Jewish Immigrant Experience.* New York: Penguin Books, 1977.

———. *A History of the Jews in America.* Northvale, N.J.: J. Aronson, 1997. Originally published as *Haven and Home: A History of the Jews in America.* New York: Schocken Books, 1985.

———. *Mordecai Manuel Noah: The First American Jew.* New York: Yeshiva University Museum, 1987.

———, comp. *The Jewish Experience in America: Selected Studies from the Publications of the American Jewish Historical Society.* 5 vols. Waltham, Mass.: American Jewish Historical Society, 1969.

Keyserling, Harriet. *Against the Tide.* Columbia: University of South Carolina Press, 1998.

Keyserling, Herbert. *Doctor K.* Beaufort, S.C.: Privately published by the author, 1999.

King, William L. *The Newspaper Press of Charleston, S.C.* Charleston, S.C.: E. Perry, 1872.

Kleeblatt, Norman L., and Gerard C. Wertkin. *The Jewish Heritage in American Folk Art.* New York: Universe Books, 1984.

Kohn, August. *Essay of Mr. August Kohn.* Charleston, S.C.: n.p., 1907. Pamplet reproduces the essay "The Possibility of Jewish Immigration to the South," which Mr. Kohn read before annual meeting of the International Order of B'nai B'rith, April 14, 1907.

Kohn, Douglas. "Two Paths of Nineteenth Century Synagogue Reform: Charleston and Philadelphia." Prize essay, Hebrew Union College–Jewish Institute of Religion, 1986.

Kole, Kaye. *The Minis Family of Georgia, 1733–1992.* Savannah, Ga.: Georgia Historical Society, 1992.

Korn, Bertram Wallace. *American Jewry and the Civil War.* Philadelphia: Jewish Publication Society of America, 1957. Reprint, New York: Atheneum, 1970.

———. *The Early Jews of New Orleans.* Waltham, Mass.: American Jewish Historical Society, 1969.

———. *Eventful Years and Experiences: Studies in Nineteenth Century American Jewish History.* Cincinnati: American Jewish Archives, 1954.

———. *German-Jewish Intellectual Influences on American Jewish Life, 1824–1972.* B. G. Rudolph Lecture Series. Syracuse, N.Y.: Syracuse University Press, 1972.

———. *Jews and Negro Slavery in the Old South, 1789–1865.* Elkins Park, Pa.: Reform Congregation Keneseth Israel, 1961.

———. *The Jews of Mobile, Alabama, 1763–1841.* Cincinnati: Hebrew Union College Press, 1970.

Lavender, Abraham D., ed. and comp. *A Coat of Many Colors: Jewish Subcommunities in the United States.* Westport, Conn.: Greenwood, 1977.

Leavey, Jane D. *Creating Community: The Jews of Atlanta from 1845 to the Present.* Atlanta: Atlanta Jewish Federation, 1994.

Leiman, Melvin M. *Jacob Cardozo: Economic Thought in the Antebellum South.* New York: Columbia University Press, 1966.

LeMaster, Carolyn Gray. *A Corner of the Tapestry: A History of the Jewish Experience in Arkansas, 1820s-1990s.* Fayetteville: University of Alabama Press, 1994.

Leon, Louis. *Diary of a Tar Heel Confederate Soldier.* Charlotte, N.C.: Stone Publishing Co., 1913.

Levasseur, Auguste. *Lafayette in America in 1824 and 1825; or Journal of a Voyage to the United States.* Translated by John D. Godman. 2 vols. Philadelphia: Carey & Lea, 1829. Reprint, New York: Research Reprints, 1970.

Levin, Alexandra Lee. *Dare to Be Different: A Biography of Louis H. Levin of Baltimore, A Pioneer in Jewish Social Service.* New York: Block Publishing Company, 1972.

Levitan, Tama. *Fransis Salvador.* Bruklin, Nu York [Brooklyn, N.Y.]: 1949.

Levy, B. H. *Savannah's Old Jewish Community Cemeteries.* Macon, Ga.: Mercer University Press, 1983.

Levy, David. *Service of the Sanctuary for the Sabbath and Festivals, Arranged for the Use of Congregation Beth Elohim.* New York: M. Thalmessinger, 1879.

Lewis, Selma S. *A Biblical People in the Bible Belt: The Jewish Community of Memphis, Tennessee, 1840s–1960s.* Macon, Ga.: Mercer University Press, 1998.

Lewisohn, Ludwig. *Mid-channel: An American Chronicle.* New York: Harper & Brothers, 1929.

———. *Upstream: An American Chronicle.* New York: The Modern Library, 1926.

———. *What Is this Jewish Heritage?* New York: Schocken Books, 1964.

Liberles, Robert. "Conflict over Reforms: The Case of Congregation Beth Elohim, Charleston, South Carolina." In *The American Synagogue,* edited by Jack Wertheimer. New York: Cambridge University Press, 1987.

Libo, Kenneth, and Irving Howe. *We Lived There Too.* Marek, N.Y.: St. Martin's Press, 1984.

Lindemann, Albert S. *The Jew Accused: Three Anti-Semitic Affairs (Dreyfus, Beilis, Frank), 1894–1914.* New York: Cambridge University Press, 1991.

Lipson-Walker, Carolyn. "'Shalom Y'All': The Folklore and Culture of Southern Jews." Ph.D. diss., Indiana University, 1986.

Loeb, John Langeloth, and Frances Lehman Loeb, with Kenneth Libo. *All in a Lifetime: A Personal Memoir.* New York: John L. Loeb, 1996.

London, Hannah R. *Miniatures of Early American Jews.* Springfield, Mass.: The Pond-Ekberg Co., 1953.

———. *Portraits of Jews by Gilbert Stuart and Other Early American Artists.* New York: W.E. Rudge, 1927. Reprint, Rutland, Vt.: Charles E. Tuttle Co., 1969.

Mackey, Albert Gallatin. *The History of Freemasonry in South Carolina, from Its Origin in the Year 1736 to the Present Time.* Charleston, S.C.: Walker, Evans and Cogswell Co., 1936.

Marcus, Jacob Rader. *The American Jew, 1585–1990: A History.* Brooklyn, N.Y.: Carson Publishing, 1995.

———. *The American Jewish Woman, 1654–1980.* New York: KTAV Publishing House, 1981.

———. *American Jewry: Documents, Eighteenth Century.* Cincinnati: Hebrew Union College Press, 1959.

———. *The Colonial American Jew, 1492–1776.* 3 vols. Detroit: Wayne State University Press, 1970.

———. *Early American Jewry, 1655–1790.* 2 vols. Philadelphia: Jewish Publication Society of America, 1951–53. Reprint, New York: Ktav Publishers House, 1975.

———. *The Jew and the American Revolution.* Cincinnati: American Jewish Archives, 1974.

———. *Memoirs of American Jews 1755–1865.* 3 vols. Philadelphia: Jewish Publication Society of America, 1955–56.

———. *To Count a People: American Jewish Population Data, 1585–1984.* Lanham, Md.: University Press of America, 1990.

———. *United States Jewry, 1776–1985.* 4 vols. Detroit: Wayne State University Press, 1989–1993.

———, comp. *Critical Studies in American Jewish History.* 3 vols. Cincinnati: American Jewish Archives, 1971.

———, ed. *The American Jewish Woman: A Documentary History.* New York: KTAV Publishing House, 1981.

———, and Judith M. Daniels, ed. *The Concise Dictionary of American Jewish Biography.* 2 vols. Brooklyn, N.Y.: Carlson Publishing, 1994.

Marinbach, Bernard. *Galveston: The Ellis Island of the West.* Albany: State University of New York Press, 1983.

McGraw, Eliza Russi Lowen. "The Country of the Heart: Twentieth-Century Representations of Southern Jewishness." Ph.D. diss., Vanderbilt University, 2000.

Meade, Robert Douthat. *Judah P. Benjamin: Confederate Statesman.* New York: Oxford University Press, 1943.

Melnick, Ralph. *The Life and Work of Ludwig Lewisohn.* 2 vols. Detroit: Wayne State University Press, 1998.

———, comp. *The Wendell Mitchell Levi Library and Archives: A Catalog of Its Holdings.* Charleston, S.C.: College of Charleston Library Associates, 1979.

Meyer, Isidore S., ed. *The American Jew in the Civil War: Catalog of the Exhibit of the Civil War Centennial Jewish Historical Commission.* New York: American Jewish Historical Society, 1962.

Meyer, Michael A. "German-Jewish Identity in Nineteenth-Century America." In *Toward Modernity: The European Jewish Model,* edited by Jacob Katz. New Brunswick, N.J.: Transaction Books, 1987.

———. *Response to Modernity: History of the Reform Movement in Judaism.* New York: Oxford University Press, 1988.

Miller, Randall M., and George E. Pozzetta, eds. *Shades of the Sunbelt: Essays on Ethnicity, Race, and the Urban South.* New York: Greenwood Press, 1988.

Mirvis, Tova. *The Ladies Auxiliary.* London: Picador, 2000.

Mittelman, Karen S., ed. *Creating American Jews: Historical Conversations about Identity.* Philadelphia: National Museum of American Jewish History, 1998.

Mizrahi, Judith. *Seven Hundred and Three American Sephardim: Diversity within Cohesiveness.* New York: Gemini Books, 1993.

Moïse, Harold. *The Jewish Cemetery at Sumter, S.C.: A Transcription of the Names and Dates on the Tombstones, 1874–1912.* Sumter, S.C.: n.p., 1942.

———. *The Moïse Family of South Carolina: An Account of the Life and Descendants of Abraham and Sarah Moïse Who Settled in Charleston, South Carolina, in the Year 1791 A.D.* Columbia, S.C.: R. L. Bryan, 1961.

Moïse, Lucius Clifton, Abraham Moïse, and Isaac Newton Cardozo. *Biography of Isaac Harby, with an Account of the Reformed Society of Israelites of Charleston, S.C., 1824–1833.* Columbia, S.C.: R. L. Bryan Co., 1931.

Moïse, Penina. *Fancy's Sketch Book.* Charleston, S.C.: J. S. Burges, 1833.

———. *Secular and Religious Works of Penina Moïse, with Brief Sketch of Her Life.* Complied and published by Charleston Section, Council of Jewish Women. Charleston, S.C.: Nicolas G. Duffy, 1911.

Moore, Deborah Dash. *To the Golden Cities: Pursuing the American Jewish Dream in Miami and L.A.* Cambridge: Harvard University Press, 1996.

Moses, Octavia Harby. *A Mother's Poems: A Collection of Verses.* Sumter, S.C.: Privately printed, 1915.

Nelson, Jack. *Terror in the Night: The Klan's Campaign Against the Jews.* New York: Simon & Schuster, 1993.

Newsome, Yvonne DeCarlo. "A House Divided: Conflict and Cooperation in African American-Jewish Relations." 2 vols. Ph.D. diss., Northwestern University, 1991.

O'Brien, Michael, and David Moltke-Hansen, eds. *Intellectual Life in Antebellum Charleston.* Knoxville: University of Tennessee Press, 1986.

O'Keeffe, Georgia. *Lovingly, Georgia: The Complete Correspondence of Georgia O'Keeffe and Anita Pollitzer.* Edited by Clive Giboire, with an introduction by Benita Eisler. New York: Simon & Schuster, 1990.

Ornish, Natalie. *Pioneer Jewish Texans: Their Impact on Texas and American History for Four Hundred Years, 1590–1990.* Dallas: Texas Heritage Press, 1989.

Pearlstine, Jeanette Felsenthal. "An Editorial." In *The Souvenir Book of the Bicentennial (1750–1950): The Story of the Celebration of the Bicentennial of the Charleston Jewish Community, November 19 through November 26, 1950.* Charleston, S.C.: Bicentennial Committee, 1951.

Pember, Phoebe Yates. *A Southern Woman's Story: Life in Confederate Richmond.* New York: G. W. Carleton & Co., 1879. Reprint, edited by Bell Irvin Wiley, Wilmington, N.C.: Broadfoot Publishing, 1991.

Pettus, Louise, and Ron Chepesiuk. "Happyville, South Carolina." In *The Palmetto State: Stories from the Making of South Carolina.* Orangeburg, S.C.: Sandlapper Publishing, 1991.

Pettus, Mildred Louise. "European Immigration to South Carolina, 1881–1908." Master's thesis, University of South Carolina, 1954.

Petuchowski, Jakob J. *Prayerbook Reform in Europe: The Liturgy of European Liberal and Reform Judaism.* New York: World Union for Progressive Judaism, 1968.

Philipson, David. *The Reform Movement in Judaism.* 1907. New and rev. ed. New York: The Macmillan Company, 1931. Reissue of 1931 revised edition, with an introduction by Solomon B. Freehof, New York: Ktav Publishing House, 1967.

Pickard, Kate E. R. *The Kidnapped and the Ransomed: The Narrative of Peter and Vina*

Still after Forty Years of Slavery. Syracuse, N.Y.: William T. Hamilton, 1856. Reprint, with an introductory essay on Jews in the anti-slavery movement by Maxwell Whiteman, Philadelphia: Jewish Publication Society of America, 1970.

Pinckney, Henry L., and Abraham Moïse. *A Selection from the Miscellaneous Writings of the Late Isaac Harby, Esq., Prefixed with a Memoir of His Life.* Charleston, S.C.: James S. Burges, 1829.

Plaut, Gunther W. *The Rise of Reform Judaism.* New York: World Union for Progressive Judaism, 1963.

Proctor, Samuel, and Louis Schmier, eds., with Malcolm Stern. *Jews of the South: Selected Essays from the Southern Jewish Historical Society.* Macon, Ga.: Mercer University Press, 1984.

Raisin, Jacob S. *Centennial Booklet: Commemorating the Introduction of Reform Judaism in America at Kahal Kadosh Beth Elohim at Charleston, S.C. Organized 1750.* Charleston, S.C.: [K. K. Beth Elohim], 1925.

Reed, John Shelton. *The Enduring South: Subcultural Persistence in Mass Society.* Lexington, Mass.: Lexington Books, 1972.

———. *One South: An Ethnic Approach to Regional Culture.* Baton Rouge: Louisiana State University Press, 1982.

Reekie, Clara, Ralph Calhoun, and Richard L. Ruehrwein. *Kaminski House Museum.* Greendale, Ind.: Creative Company, 1996.

Renick, Timothy D. "Solomon Blatt: An Examination into the Conservative Racial Views of a Jewish Politician in the Deep South 1937–1986 with an accompanying guide to the Solomon Blatt papers." Master's thesis, University of South Carolina, 1989.

Rezneck, Samuel. *The Story of an American Jewish Family Since the Revolution: A History of the Family of Jonas Phillips.* Washington, D.C.: University Press of America, 1980.

———. *Unrecognized Patriots: The Jews in the American Revolution.* Westport, Conn.: Greenwood Press, 1975.

Reznikoff, Charles, and Uriah Z. Engelman. *The Jews of Charleston: A History of an American Jewish Community.* Philadelphia: Jewish Publication Society of America, 1950.

Rogers, George C., Jr. *A History of Georgetown County, South Carolina.* Columbia, University of South Carolina Press, 1970. Reprint, Spartanburg, S.C.: Reprint Co., 1990.

Rogoff, Leonard. *Homelands: Southern Jewish Identity in Durham and Chapel Hill, North Carolina.* Tuscaloosa: University of Alabama Press, 2001.

Rogow, Faith. *Gone to Another Meeting: The National Council of Jewish Women, 1893–1993.* Tuscaloosa: University of Alabama Press, 1993.

Rosen, Robert N. *Confederate Charleston: An Illustrated History of the City and the People during the Civil War.* Columbia: University of South Carolina Press, 1994.

———. *The Jewish Confederates.* Columbia: University of South Carolina Press, 2000.

———. *A Short History of Charleston.* 1982. Rev. ed. Columbia: University of South Carolina Press, 1997.

Rosenthall, William A. "Jewish Artists in Early Charleston." In *Jewish Art and Culture in Early America.* Charleston, S.C.: Piccolo Spoleto, 1981. First published in *KKBE Bulletin*, September 1981, 16–18.

Rosenwaike, Ira. *On the Edge of Greatness: A Portrait of American Jewry in the Early National Period.* Cincinnati: American Jewish Archives, 1985.

Rothschild, Janice O. *As But a Day: The First Hundred Years, 1867–1967.* Atlanta: Hebrew Benevolent Congregation, The Temple, 1967.

Rubenovitz, Herman H., and Mignon L. Rubenovitz. *The Waking Heart.* Cambridge, Mass.: Nathaniel Dame and Company, 1967.

Rubenstein, Aryeh. "The Beginnings of the Reform Movement in American Judaism." Ph.D. diss., Hebrew University, 1973.

Rubin, Louis D., Jr. *The Golden Weather.* New York: Atheneum, 1961. Reprint, Baton Rouge: Louisiana State University Press, 1995.

———. *Surfaces of a Diamond.* Baton Rouge: Louisiana State University Press, 1981.

Rubin, Saul Jacob. *Third to None: The Saga of Savannah Jewry, 1733–1983.* Savannah, Ga.: Congregation Mikve Israel, 1983.

Rutledge, Anna Wells. *Artists in the Life of Charleston.* Philadelphia: American Philosophical Society, 1949.

The Sabbath Service and Miscellaneous Prayers Adopted by the Reformed Society of Israelites. Charleston, S.C.: J. S. Burges, 1830. Reprint, by Barnett A. Elzas, New York: Bloch Publishing Company, 1916.

Sachar, Howard M. *A History of the Jews in America.* New York: Alfred A. Knopf, 1992.

Salvaterra, David L. "Becoming American: Assimilation, Pluralism, and Ethnic Identity." In *Immigrant America: European Ethnicity in the United States,* edited by Timothy Walch. New York: Garland Publishing, 1994.

Salzman, Jack, and Cornel West, eds. *Struggles in the Promised Land: Toward a History of Black-Jewish Relations in the United States.* New York: Oxford University Press, 1997.

Samuel, Stuart Montagu, and Lucien Wolf. *The History and Genealogy of the Jewish Families of Yates and Samuel of Liverpool.* Edited, with an introduction, additions, and notes by Lucien Wolf. London: Mitchell and Hughes, Printers, 1901.

Sarna, Jonathan D. *The Americanization of Jewish Culture, 1888–1988.* Philadelphia: Jewish Publication Society, 1989.

———. *Jacksonian Jew: The Two Worlds of Mordecai Noah.* New York: Holmes & Meier, 1981.

———, ed. *The American Jewish Experience.* New York: Holmes & Meier, 1986.

———, Benny Kraut, and Samuel K. Joseph, eds. *Jews and the Founding of the Republic.* New York: Markus Wiener, 1985.

Schappes, Morris U. *The Jews in the United States: A Pictorial History, 1654 to the Present.* New York: Citadel Press, 1958.

———, ed. *A Documentary History of the Jews in the United States 1654–1875.* 1952. 3d ed., rev., New York: Schocken Books, 1971.

Schmier, Louis, ed. *Reflections on Southern Jewry: The Letters of Charles Wessolowsky, 1878–1879.* Macon, Ga.: Mercer University Press, 1982.

Schoener, Allan. *The American Jewish Album, 1654 to the Present.* New York: Rizzoli, 1983.

Schultz, Debra L. "'We Didn't Think in Those Terms Then': Narratives of Jewish Women in the Southern Civil Rights Movement, 1960–1966." Ph.D. diss., The Union Institute, 1995.

Schwarz, Jordan A. *The Speculator, Bernard M. Baruch in Washington, 1917–1965.* Chapel Hill: University of North Carolina Press, 1981.

[Seixas, Eleanor Cohen.] "The Diary of Eleanor Cohen Seixas: Columbia, South Carolina, 1865–1866." In *Private Pages: Diaries of American Women, 1830s–1870s,* edited by Penelope Franklin. New York: Ballantine Books, 1986.

The Sephardic Journey, 1492–1992. New York: Yeshiva University Museum, 1992.

Severens, Martha R. *The Miniature Portrait Collection of the Carolina Art Association.* Edited by Charles L. Wyrick Jr. Charleston, S.C.: Carolina Art Association, Gibbes Art Gallery, 1984.

Shapiro, Edward S. *A Time for Healing: American Jewry since World War II.* Baltimore: Johns Hopkins University Press, 1992.

Shapiro, Henry D., and Jonathan D. Sarna, eds. *Ethnic Diversity and Civic Identity: Patterns of Conflict and Cohesion in Cincinnati since 1820.* Urbana: University of Illinois Press, 1992.

Shpall, Leo. *The Jews of Louisiana.* New Orleans: Steeg Printing & Publishing Co., 1936.

Shumway, Harry Irving. *Bernard M. Baruch, Financial Genius, Statesman and Adviser to Presidents, with a foreword by James F. Byrnes and an appendix by Bernard M. Baruch.* Boston: L. C. Page & Co., Inc., 1946.

Silberstein, Laurence J., and Robert L. Cohn, ed. *The Other in Jewish Thought and History: Constructions of Jewish Culture and Identity.* New York: New York University Press, 1994.

Silverstein, Alan. *Alternatives to Assimilation: The Response of Reform Judaism to American Culture, 1840–1930.* Hanover, N.H.: Brandeis University Press by University Press of New England, 1994.

Simkins, Francis Butler, and Robert Hilliard Woody. *South Carolina during Reconstruction.* Chapel Hill: University of North Carolina Press, 1932.

Simms, William Gilmore, ed. *The Charleston Book: A Miscellany in Prose and Verse.* Charleston, S.C.: S. Hart, 1845. Reprint, with a new introduction and biographical notes by David Moltke-Hansen and bibliographical notes by Harlan Greene, Spartanburg, S.C.: Reprint Co., 1983.

Simonhoff, Harry. *Jewish Notables in America, 1776–1865: Links of an Endless Chain.* New York: Greenberg, 1956.

———. *Jewish Participants in the Civil War.* New York: Arco, 1963.

———. *Saga of American Jewry, 1865–1914: Links of an Endless Chain.* New York: Arco, 1959.

Simons, Howard. *Jewish Times: Voices of the American Jewish Experience.* New York: Anchor Books, Doubleday, 1988.

Smith, William Atmar. *Leon Banov, M.D., and Public Health in Charleston.* Columbia, S.C.: R. L. Bryan Co., 1968.

Sollors, Werner, ed. *The Invention of Ethnicity.* New York: Oxford University Press, 1989.

Solomon Nunes Carvalho: Painter, Photographer, and Prophet in Nineteenth Century America. Baltimore: The Jewish Historical Society of Maryland, 1989.

Sorin, Gerald. *A Time for Building: The Third Migration, 1880–1920.* Baltimore: Johns Hopkins University Press, 1992.

South Carolina Department of Agriculture, Commerce and Immigration. *South Carolina: The Garden of America.* Columbia, S.C.: South Carolina Department of Agriculture, Commerce and Immigration, [1905].

Speizman, Morris. *The Jews of Charlotte.* Charlotte, N.C.: McNally and Loftman, 1978.

Spruill, Julia Cherry. *Women's Life and Work in the Southern Colonies.* Chapel Hill: University of North Carolina Press, 1938. Reprint, with a new introduction by Anne Firor Scott, New York: W. W. Norton & Co., 1972.

Stein, Kenneth A. *History of Ahavoth Achim Congregation, 1887–1977.* Atlanta: Standard Press, 1978.

Stern, Malcolm H. *Americans of Jewish Descent.* Special Publications of the National Genealogical Society, no. 20. Washington, D.C.: National Genealogical Society, 1978. First published in *National Genealogical Society Quarterly* 46, no. 2 (1958).

———. *Americans of Jewish Descent: A Compendium of Genealogy.* Cincinnati, Ohio: Hebrew Union College Press, 1960. Reprint. New York: KTAV Publishing House, 1971.

———. "The 1820s: American Jewry Comes of Age." In *A Bicentennial Festschrift for Jacob Rader Marcus,* edited by Bertram Wallace Korn. Waltham, Mass.: American Jewish Historical Society, 1976.

———. *Tracing Your Jewish Roots.* Cincinnati, American Jewish Archives, 1977.

———, comp. *The First American Jewish Families: 600 Genealogies, 1654–1988.* 1978. 3d ed., updated and rev. Baltimore: Ottenheimer Publishers, 1991.

Stern, Steve. *Lazar Malkin Enters Heaven.* New York: Viking, 1987.

Sturhahn, Joan. *Carvalho: Artist, Photographer, Adventurer, Patriot—Portrait of a Forgotten American.* Merrick, N.Y.: Richwood Publishing Co., 1976.

Suberman, Stella. *The Jew Store: The Story of a Family Business in God's Country.* Chapel Hill, N.C.: Algonquin Press, 1998.

Sussman, Lance J. "Isaac Harby, Leadership, and Liturgy of the Reformed Society of Israelites, 1824–1833: a Reevaluation." Term paper, Hebrew Union College–Jewish Institute of Religion, 1979.

Synagogue Emanu-El: 50 Years, 1947–1997. [Charleston, S.C.: Synagogue Emanu-El, 1997].

Tannenbaum, Karen. *The Louries of South Carolina.* Columbia, S.C.: privately printed, 1991.

Tarshish, Allan. *A Bi-Centennial Anniversary in Charleston.* Cincinnati: Union of American Hebrew Congregations, 1950.

———. "The Charleston Organ Case." In *The Jewish Experience in America,* edited by Abraham J. Karp. New York: KTAV Publishing House, 1969.

Teszler, Sandor. *The Memoirs of Sandor Teszler.* Spartanburg, S.C.: Wofford College, 1991.

Tetterton, Beverly, Helen F. Solomon, JoAnn Folger. *History of the Temple of Israel, Wilmington, North Carolina, 1876–2001.* Wilmington, N.C.: [Temple of Israel], 2001.

Tindall, George Brown. *The Ethnic Southerners.* Baton Rouge: Louisiana State University Press, 1976.

Tobias, Thomas J. *The Hebrew Benevolent Society of Charleston, S.C. Founded 1784, the Oldest Jewish Charitable Society in the United States: An Historical Sketch.* Charleston, S.C.: The Society, 1965.

———. *The Hebrew Orphan Society of Charleston, S.C. Founded 1801: An Historical Sketch*. Charleston, S.C.: The Society, 1957.

———. *Historical Diorama: Francis Salvador (1747–1776)*. Klutznik Exhibit Hall, B'nai Brith Building, Washington, D.C., [1970].

———. *Tombstones That Tell Stories: The Historic Coming Street Cemetery of Congregation Beth Elohim, Charleston, S.C.* Rev. ed. Charleston, S.C.: Kahal Kadosh Beth Elohim, 2000.

Turitz, Leo E., and Evelyn Turitz. *Jews in Early Mississippi*. Jackson: University Press of Mississippi, 1983. Reprint, Jackson: University Press of Mississippi, 1995.

Twenty-five Years of Jewish Life: 1939–1964, 5700–5725. Dillon, S.C.: Ohav Shalom Congregation, [1965].

"Uncle Billy: The First Carrier." In *Centennial Edition: The News and Courier*. Charleston, S.C.: [News and Courier], 1903.

Urofsky, Melvin I. *Commonwealth and Community: The Jewish Experience in Virginia*. Richmond, Va.: Virginia Historical Society and Jewish Community Federation of Richmond, 1997.

Wade, Richard C. *Slavery in the Cities: The South, 1820–1860*. New York: Oxford University Press, 1964.

Ward, Patricia Spain. *Simon Baruch: Rebel in the Ranks of Medicine, 1840–1921*. Tuscaloosa: University of Alabama Press, 1994.

Waring, Joseph I. *A History of Medicine in South Carolina*. 3 vols. Charleston, S.C.: South Carolina Medical Association, 1964–71. Reprint, Spartanburg, S.C.: Reprint Co., 1971.

Watson, Charles S. *Antebellum Charleston Dramatists*. Tuscaloosa: University of Alabama Press, 1976.

Weiner, Hollace Ava. *Jewish Stars in Texas*. College Station: Texas A & M University Press, 1999.

Wertheimer, Jack. *The American Synagogue: A Sanctuary Transformed*. New York: Cambridge University Press, 1987.

White, William Lindsay. *Bernard Baruch: Portrait of a Citizen*. New York: Harcourt, Brace & Co., 1950. Reprint, Westport, Conn.: Greenwood Press, 1970.

Whitfield, Stephen J. *Voices of Jacob, Hands of Esau: Jews in American Life and Thought*. Hamden, Conn.: Archon Books, 1984.

Whiteman, Maxwell. *Copper for America: The Hendricks Family and a National Industry, 1755–1939*. New Brunswick, N.J.: Rutgers University Press, 1971.

Williams, Arthur V. *Tales of Charleston, 1930s*. Charleston, S.C.: College of Charleston Library, 1999.

Wilson, Charles Reagan, ed. *Religion in the South*. Jackson: University Press of Mississippi, 1985.

———, and William Ferris, eds. *Encyclopedia of Southern Culture*. Chapel Hill: University of North Carolina Press, 1989.

Winegarten, Ruthe, and Cathy Schecter. *Deep in the Heart: The Lives and Legends of Texas Jews, a Photographic History*. Austin, Tex.: Eakin Press, 1990.

Wise, Isaac Mayer, *Reminiscences*. Translated and edited by David Phillipson. 1901. 2d ed. New York: Central Synagogue of New York, 1945.

Wolf, Edwin, and Maxwell Whiteman. *The History of the Jews of Philadelphia from Colonial Times to the Age of Jackson*. Philadelphia: Jewish Publication Society of America, 1956.

Wolf, Simon. *The American Jew as Patriot, Soldier, and Citizen*. Chicago: Levytype Co., 1895.

Woodman, Harold D. *King Cotton & His Retainers: Financing & Marketing the Cotton Crop of the South, 1800–1925*. Lexington: University of Kentucky Press, 1968.

Woodward, C. Vann. *Tom Watson: Agrarian Rebel*. New York: Oxford University Press, 1963.

———, ed. *Mary Chesnut's Civil War*. New Haven: Yale University Press, 1981.

———, and Elisabeth Muhlenfeld, eds. *The Private Mary Chesnut: The Unpublished Civil War Diaries*. New York: Oxford University Press, 1984.

Woolf, Maurice. "Joseph Salvador, 1716–1786." *Transactions of the Jewish Historical Society* (London) 21 (1968): 104–37.

Wycoff, Mac. *A History of the 2nd South Carolina Infantry, 1861–1865*. Fredericksburg, Va.: Sergeant Kirkland's Museum and Historical Society, 1994.

Yaschik, Henry. *From Kaluszyn to Charleston: The Yaschik Family in Poland, Argentina, and South Carolina*. Charleston, S.C.: Privately published by the author, 1990.

Young, Mel, ed. *Last Order of the Lost Cause: The True Story of a Jewish Family in the "Old South," Raphael Jacob Moses, Major, C.S.A., 1812–1893*. Lanham, Md.: University Press of America, 1995.

Zola, Gary Phillip. *Isaac Harby of Charleston, 1788–1818*. Tuscaloosa: University of Alabama Press, 1994.

Journal, Magazine, and Newspaper Articles

Abbreviations

AHR   *American Historical Review*
AJA   *American Jewish Archives*
AJH   *American Jewish History*
AJHQ   *American Jewish History Quarterly*
CJJ   *Charleston Jewish Journal*
GHQ   *Georgia Historical Quarterly*
JAEH   *Journal of American Ethnic History*
JAH   *Journal of American History*
JAJHS   *Journal of the American Jewish Historical Society*
JHSSC   Jewish Historical Society of South Carolina
JSH   *Journal of Southern History*
KKBE   Kahal Kadosh Beth Elohim
PAJHS   *Publications of the American Jewish Historical Society*
SCHM   *South Carolina Historical Magazine*
SJH   *Southern Jewish History*
SJHS   Southern Jewish Historical Society

"The Ancestry of the Children of Henry Phillips Moses and Charlotte Virginia Emanuel." *The Saint Charles* 1 (January 1935): 83–105.

Appel, Sam. "As Time Goes By—Notes on a Trip Back Home." *Atlanta Jewish Georgian*, March–April 1998, 30-31.

Ashkenazi, Elliot. "Jewish Commercial Interests between North and South: The Case of the Lehmans and the Seligmans." *AJA* 43 (spring/summer 1991): 24–39.

Baruch, Simon. "Bernard Baruch's Father Recounts His Experiences As a Confederate Surgeon." *Civil War Times Illustrated* 4, no. 6 (1965): 40–47.

———. "The Heroic Death of Marcus Baum." *Confederate Veteran* 22 (April 1914): 170.

———. "A Surgeon's Story of Battle and Capture." *Confederate Veteran* 22 (December 1914): 545–48.

Bass, Alice Cabaniss. "Southern Exposure." *Hadassah Magazine,* April 1991, 32–35.

Bauman, Mark K., and Arnold Shankman. "The Rabbi as Ethnic Broker: The Case of David Marx." *JAEH* 2 (September 1983): 51–68.

Berlin, Ira, and Herbert G. Gutman. "Natives and Immigrants, Free Men and Slaves: Urban Workingmen in the Antebellum American South." *AHR* 88 (December 1983): 1175–1200.

Berman, Elizabeth Kessin. "Transcendentalism and Tradition: The Art of Solomon Nunes Carvalho." *Jewish Art* 16/17 (1990/1991): 65–81.

Berthoff, Rowland T. "Southern Attitudes Toward Immigration, 1865–1914." *JSH* 17 (August 1951): 328–60.

"Beth Elohim Temple of Jewish Congregation Here Is Dedicated at Services Last Sunday." *Georgetown (S.C.) Times.* February 23, 1950.

Blu, Karen I. "Varieties of Ethnic Identity: Anglo-Saxons, Blacks, Indians, and Jews in a Southern County." *Ethnicity* 4 (1977): 263–86.

Brande, Dorothea. "Mr. Lewisohn Interprets America." *American Review* 2 (December 1933): 189–98.

Breibart, Solomon. "Beth Elohim and the Earthquake." *KKBE Bulletin,* October 1986, 4–5.

———. "Beth Elohim's Second Organ." *KKBE Bulletin,* January 1986, 3.

———. "BSBI Celebrates 140th Anniversary," Parts 1 and 2. *CJJ,* April 1995, 17; May 1995, 16.

———. "Charleston Jewish Service Men in World War II." Parts 1 and 2. *CJJ,* June 1995, 15; August 1995, 16.

———. "Charleston Jews and the Earthquake of 1886." *CJJ,* March 1994, 18.

———. "Chronology of the Jewish Congregations of Charleston, S.C." *CJJ,* December 1993, 18.

———. "The Community Reflecter." *CJJ,* September–October 1993, 32.

———. "A Courageous Stand." *CJJ,* November 1994, 18.

———. "David Lopez, Builder." *KKBE Bulletin,* March 1991, 8–9.

———. "Forerunners of the Charleston Jewish Community Center." Parts 1–4. *Charleston Jewish Community Center Talk,* January 1980, 16; April 1980, 19; May 1980, 11, 23; and June 1980, 8.

———. "Francis Salvador, Revolutionary War Martyr." *CJJ,* July 1996, 18.

———. "The Jewish Cemeteries of Charleston." *CJJ,* January 1994, 18.

———. "KKBE: The Transition from Orthodox to Reform." *JHSSC Newsletter,* Fall 1999, 3–6.

———. "A Long-Unknown Congregation." *CJJ,* February 1994, 18.

———. "Louis M Shimel, First JCC President." *CJJ,* February 1995, 18.

———. "Some Charleston Jews in Law Enforcement." *CJJ,* April 1996, 22.

———. "The Status of Women in KKBE to 1920." *KKBE Bulletin,* April 1984, 3–4.

———. "The Synagogues of Kahal Kadosh Beth Elohim, Charleston." *SCHM* 80 (July 1979): 215–35. Revised and published as *The Synagogues of Kahal Kadosh Beth Elohim.* Charleston, S.C.: Kahal Kadosh Beth Elohim, 1999.

———. "This Synagogue is Our Temple." Parts 1–4. *KKBE Bulletin,* March 1980, 3; April 1980, 3; May 1980, 3; June 1980, 4–5.

———. "Two Jewish Congregations in Charleston, S.C., before 1791: A New Conclusion." *AJH* 69 (March 1980): 360–63.

———. "Women Who Made a Difference," Parts 1–5. *CJJ,* April 1994, 28; June 1994, 22; July 1994, 21, 22; October 1994, 18.

"B'rith Sholom Beth Israel Synagogue Receives Charter." *Charleston (S.C.) News and Courier,* October 10, 1954.

Bunker, Gary L., and John Appel. "'Shoddy,' Anti-Semitism and the Civil War." *AJH* 82 (1994): 43–72.

Cardozo, Jacob N. "The Congregation Beth Elohim." *Occident* 9 (1851–1852): 311–22.

Carvalho, Solomon N. "The Congregation Beth Elohim of Charleston." Parts 1 and 2. *Occident* 9 (1851–1852): 203–8, 354–65.

Chaplin, George. "Beth Elohim Hallowed Ground in Southern Jewish History. *Charleston (S.C.) Post and Courier,* October 17, 1999.

Chyet, Stanley. "Ludwig Lewisohn in Charleston (1892–1903)." *AJHQ* 54 (March 1965): 296–322.

———. "Ludwig Lewisohn: The Years of Becoming." *AJA* 11 (October 1959): 125–47.

———. "The Political Rights of the Jews in the United States: 1776–1840." *AJA* 10 (April 1958): 14–75.

Click, Carolyn. "Jewish Society's Oldest Member to be Honored." *Columbia (S.C.) State,* April 4, 1998.

Cline, Scott. "Jewish-Ethnic Interactions: A Bibliographical Essay." *AJH* 77 (September 1987): 135–54.

"The Congregation of Shearith Israel of Charleston." *Occident* 5 (1847–1848): 49–50.

Dauber, Leonard G., M.D. "David Camden DeLeon, M.D.: Patriot or Traitor." *New York State Journal of Medicine* 70 (1970): 2927–33.

Davis, Mary Katherine. "The Feather Bed Aristocracy: Abbeville District in the 1790's." *SCHM* 80 (April 1979): 136–55.

Dean, Andrea Oppenheimer. "Dixie Diaspora." *Preservation* 52, no. 4 (2000): 52–59.

DeLaMotta, Jacob. "The Congregations of Charleston." Parts 1 and 2. *Occident* 1 (1843–1844): 600–4; 2 (1844–1845): 26–28.

"DeLaMotta, Jacob" (obituary). *Occident* 3 (1845–1846): 59–66.

DeLeon, Perry M. "Military Record of the DeLeon Family and of Captain Perry M. DeLeon." *PAJHS* 50 (June 1961): 332–34.

Dinnerstein, Leonard. "A Neglected Aspect of Southern Jewish History." *AJHQ* 61 (summer 1971): 52–68.

———. "A Note on Southern Attitudes Toward Jews." *Jewish Social Studies* 32 (January 1970): 43–49.

———. "Southern Jewry and the Desegregation Crisis, 1954–1970." *AJHQ* 62 (March 1973): 231–41.

Dunn, Richard S. "The English Sugar Islands and the Founding of South Carolina." *SCHM* 72 (April 1971): 81–93.

Eckman, Julius. "Beth Elohim Congregation of Charleston, South Carolina." *Occident* 10 (1852–53): 134–44.

Elzas, Barnett A. "Jewish Merchants in Charleston in the Revolutionary Era." *Charleston (S.C.) News and Courier,* ca. 1903.

———. "New Material on the First Reform Movement in America." *American Hebrew* (literary supplement) 80 (December 7, 1906): iv.

———. "A Triumph of Tolerance." *Charleston (S.C.) News and Courier,* ca. 1902.

Engelman, Uriah Z. "Jewish Education in Charleston, South Carolina during the Eighteenth and Nineteenth Centuries." *PAJHS* 42 (1952–1953): 43–67.

———. "Jewish Statistics in the U.S. Census of Religious Bodies (1850–1936)." *Jewish Social Studies* 9 (1947): 127–74.

"An Era Passes: Jewish Communities Dying in Dixie." *Columbia (S.C.) State,* September 29, 1991.

"Examination of the Pupils of the School for Instruction of Jewish Youth, Charleston, S.C." *Occident* 4 (1846–1847): 207–8.

"Examination of the Society for the Instruction of Jewish Doctrine." *Occident* 3 (1845–1846): 136–43.

"Examination of the Society for the Instruction of Jewish Doctrines, at Charleston, S.C." Parts 1 and 2. *Occident* 5 (1847–1848): 260–61, 308–10.

Fagin, N. Bryllion. "Isaac Harby and the Early American Theater." *AJA* 8 (January 1956): 3–13.

Farley, M. Foster. "The Mighty Monarch of the South: Yellow Fever in Charleston and Savannah." *Georgia Review* 27 (spring 1973): 56–70.

Ferris, Marcie Cohen. "'From the Recipe File of Luba Cohen': A Study of Southern Jewish Foodways and Cultural Identity." *SJH* 2 (1999): 129–64.

———. "Matzah Ball Memories in the Jewish South." *JHSSC Newsletter,* Fall 2001, 6–8.

"Fifty-Sixth Anniversary of the Hebrew Benevolent Society of Charleston, S.C." *Occident* 6 (1848–1849): 41–48.

Fleming, Walter L. "Immigration to the Southern States." *Political Science Quarterly* 20 (June 1905): 276–97.

Forman, Seth. "The Unbearable Whiteness of Being Jewish: Desegregation in the South and the Crisis of Jewish Liberalism." *AJH* 85 (June 1997): 121–42.

Foulkes, Roland A. "Hortense Powdermaker's *After Freedom:* Making Sense of the Conundrum of Black/Jewish Relations in American Anthropology and Society." *Western Journal of Black Studies* 18, no. 4 (1994): 231–43.

Friedenberg, Albert M. "A List of Jews Who Were Grand Masters of Masons in Various States of This Country." *PAJHS* 19 (1910): 95–100.

Friedenwald, Herbert. "Note Relative to Jews Keeping Their Stores Open on Sundays in the District of Charleston, S.C." *PAJHS* 5 (1897): 202ff.

Friedland, Eric L. "The Sabbath Service and Miscellaneous Prayers of the Reformed Society of Israelites." *Hebrew Abstracts* 15 (1974): 130–32.

Friedman, Lee M. "Jacob Mears and Simon Valentine of Charleston, South Carolina." *PAJHS* 41 (September 1951): 77–82.

Fuchs, Lawrence H. "Comment: 'The Invention of Ethnicity': The Amen Corner." *JAEH* 12 (fall 1992): 53–58.

Gans, Herbert J. "Comment: Ethnic Invention and Acculturation, A Bumpy-Line Approach." *JAEH* 12 (fall 1992): 42–52.

Gergel, Belinda F. "The Israelites of Columbia, South Carolina: The Development of an Antebellum Jewish Community." In *Proceedings of the South Carolina Historical Association.* Columbia, S.C.: South Carolina Historical Association, 1996.

Gilman, Samuel. "Harby's Discourse on the Jewish Synagogue." *North American Review* 23 (July 18, 1826): 67–79.

Goldfield, David. "A Sense of Place: Jews, Blacks, and White Gentiles in the American South." *Southern Cultures,* no. 1 (1997): 58–79.

Greenberg, Mark I. "Becoming Southern: The Jews of Savannah, Georgia, 1830–70." *AJH* 86 (March 1998): 55–75.

———. "Savannah's Jewish Women and the Shaping of Ethnic and Gender Identity, 1830–1900." *GHQ* 82, no. 4 (1998): 751–74.

Gutmann, Joseph. "Jewish Participation in the Visual Arts of Eighteenth and Nineteenth Century America." *AJA* 15 (April 1963): 21–57.

Hagy, James W. "The Death Records of Charleston." *SCHM* 91 (January 1990): 32–44.

———. "From the Crimea to Charleston: The Career of Columbus DaVega." *KKBE Bulletin,* February 1989. Reprinted in *SJHS Newsletter,* Fall 1989, [3].

———. "Her 'Scandalous Behavior': A Jewish Divorce in Charleston, South Carolina, 1788." *AJA* 41 (fall/winter 1989): 185–98.

Hamrick, Tom. "Carolina's First Jewish Patriot." *Sandlapper,* March 1971, 15–16.

Handlin, Oscar. "Our Unknown American Jewish Ancestors: Fact and Myth in History." *Commentary,* February 1948, 104–10.

"Hebrew Benevolent Society of Charleston, South Carolina." *Occident* 16 (1858–1859): 571–89.

"Hebrew Society for the Instruction of Jewish Youth in Charleston." *Occident* 3 (1845–1846): 94–96.

Hecht, Arthur. "Abraham Cohen: Deputy Postmaster at Georgetown, S.C. (1789–1800)." *PAJHS* 48 (March 1959): 177–93.

Hemperly, Marion R. "Federal Naturalization Oaths, Charleston, South Carolina, 1790–1860." Parts 1 and 2. *SCHM* 66 (April 1965): 112–24; (July 1965): 183–92.

Hendrick, Bill "Jews in the Confederacy." *Atlanta Journal-Constitution,* January 7, 2001.

Higham, John. "Integrating America: The Problem of Assimilation in the Nineteenth Century." *JAEH* 1 (fall 1981): 7–25.

———. "Social Discrimination against Jews in America, 1830–1930." *PAJHS* 47 (September 1957): 1–33.

Horan, Martin. "Grave Encounters: The Jews of Georgetown." *Pawley's Island (S.C.) Lowcountry Companion,* July 17, 2001.

Hühner, Leon. "Francis Salvador, a Prominent Patriot of the American Revolution." *PAJHS* 9 (1901): 107–22.

———. "The Jews of South Carolina from the Earliest Settlement to the End of the American Revolution." *PAJHS* 12 (1904): 39–61.

———. "Some Additional Notes on the History of the Jews of South Carolina." *PAJHS* 19 (1910): 151–56.

"The Israelites of South Carolina." *Occident* 12 (1854–1855): 496–510.

Jervey, Elizabeth H. "Planters and Patriarchy: Charleston, 1800–1870." *JSH* 46 (February 1980): 45–72.

———, comp. "Marriage and Death Notices from the State Gazette of South Carolina, of Charleston, South Carolina." *South Carolina Historical and Genealogical Magazine* 51 (April 1950): 97–102.

"The Jewish Community at Georgetown, S.C." *JHSSC Newsletter,* spring 2001, 3.

"Jewish People in Georgetown Date Back Before Revolution." *Georgetown (S.C.) Times,* February 9, 1956.

"Jewish Population." *American Jewish Year Book* 27 (1925–26): 382.

"Jewish Statistics—The United States—Table by States." *American Jewish Year Book.* (1906–7): 128.

Joyner, Charles. "The Jews of Georgetown: Acceptance and Contributions." *Georgetown (S.C.) Times,* May 23, 1984.

———. "The Jews of Georgetown: Assimilation, Growing Power." *Georgetown (S.C.) Times,* May 30, 1984.

Kabakoff, Jacob. "The Tombstone of the Reverend Moses Cohen." *AJA* 17 (April 1965): 77–79.

Kaplan, Jeffrey. "A Glimpse of BSBI Circa 1920." *Brith Sholom Beth Israel Messenger,* February 1983, 5–7.

Kaye, Ira. "The Turks (Alice in Sumterland)." *New South* 18 (June 1963): 9–14.

———. [A. Schwarzlieber, pseud.]. "A Kaddish for Whom?" *New South* 1 (October 1964): 9–10, 15.

King, Spencer B., Jr., ed. "Fanny Cohen's Journal of Sherman's Occupation of Savannah, Georgia." *GHQ* 41 (December 1957): 407–16.

Klebaner, Benjamin Joseph. "Public Poor Relief in Charleston, 1800–1860." *SCHM* 55 (October 1954): 210–20.

Kohler, Max J. "Isaac Harby, Jewish Religious Leader and Man of Letters." *PAJHS* 32 (1931): 35–53.

———. "Phases in the History of Religious Liberty in America, with Special Reference to the Jews." *AJHQ* 11 (1903): 53–73.

Kohut, George Alexander. "A Literary Autobiography of Mordecai Manuel Noah." *PAJHS* 5 (1897): 113–21.

Korn, Bertram W. "Factors Bearing upon the Survival of Judaism in the Antebellum Period." *AJHQ* 53 (June 1964): 341–51.

———. "The Jews of the Confederacy." *AJA* 13 (April 1961): 3–90.

———. "Judah P. Benjamin as a Jew." *PAJHS* 38 (March 1949): 153–71.

Krause, P. Allen. "Rabbis and Negro Rights in the South, 1954–1967. *AJA* 21 (April 1969): 20–47.

Leeser, Isaac. "The Appeal Case of the Charleston Congregation." Parts 1–4. *Occident* 3 (1845–1846): 615–26; 4 (1846–1847): 50–55, 103–6, 157–62.

———. "The Jews in the United States—1848." *AJA* 7 (January 1955): 82–84.

———. "The Quo Warranto Case at Charleston." *Occident* 2 (1844–1845): 166.

Lelyveld, Arthur J. "Ludwig Lewisohn: In Memoriam." *AJA* 17 (April 1965): 109–13.

Levenson, Dorothy. "Simon Baruch: A Confederate Surgeon Comes North." *Montefiore Medicine* 3 (fall 1978): 9–17.

Levin, Nathaniel. "Address Delivered Before the Society for the Instruction of Jewish Youth, in Charleston, S.C., on the Anniversary of the Society, February, 1842." *Occident* 1 (1843–1844): 162–74.

———. "The Congregation 'Beth Elohim,' Charleston, S.C." *City of Charleston Yearbook, 1883.* Charleston, S.C.: The News and Courier Presses, 301–16. See addendum, *City of Charleston Yearbook, 1884.* Charleston: 280–81.

———. "The Jewish Congregation of Charleston." Parts 1–4. *Occident* 1 (1843–1844): 336–42, 384–90, 434–40, 491–96.

Levinson, Arlene. "Different Lives in a Different Region: They're Really Not Southerners." *Present Tense* 10, no. 2 (1983): 44–49.

Levy, Jacob C. "The Reformed Israelites." *Southern Quarterly Review* (April 1844): 312–60.

Lewis, David Levering. "Parallels and Divergencies: Assimilationist Strategies of Afro-American and Jewish Elites from 1910 to the Early 1930's." *JAH* 71 (December 1984): 543–64.

Libo, Kenneth. "The Moseses of Montgomery: The Saga of a Jewish Family in the South." *Alabama Heritage* 36 (spring 1995): 18–25, 49.

Lindo, Moses. "An Account of a New Die from the Berries of a Weed in South Carolina." *Philosophical Transactions* 53 (1763): 238–39.

Logan, Mary. "They Called It the Borough: Former Merchant Recalls 50 Years of Retail Business on Front Street." *Georgetown (S.C.) Times,* February 9, 1995.

Malone, Bobbie. "New Orleans Uptown Jewish Immigrants: The Community of Congregation Gates of Prayer, 1850–1860." *Louisiana History* 32 (summer 1991): 239–78.

Marcus, Jacob Rader. "Jews and the American Revolution: A Bicentennial Documentary." *AJA* 27 (November 1975): 103–269.

———. "From the Archives: Jew Who Refused Supreme Court Seat." *Boston Jewish Advocate,* January 13, 1972, sec. 2, p. 3.

———. "The Periodization of American Jewish History." *PAJHS* 47 (March 1958): 125–33.

———, ed. "Isaac Harby on Religious Liberty: A Letter to Secretary of State James Monroe." *AJA* 7 (January 1955): 68–72.

Marcuson, Isaac. "Two Unknown Historic Candelabra from K.K. Beth Elohim of Charleston, S.C." *PAJHS* 23 (1915): 186–87.

Marks, Henry, and Marsha Kass. "Jewish Life in Alabama: The Formative Stages." *Alabama Heritage* 36 (spring 1995): 6–13.

Mays, Amanda. "Rubin Fights Injustice with Action." *Columbia (S.C.) State,* June 23, 1997.

Melnick, Ralph. "Billy Simons: The Black Jew of Charleston." *AJA* 32 (April 1980): 3–8.

Menard, Russell R. "New Directions in the Study of Slavery." *JAEH* 19 (summer 2000): 82–84.

Mesinger, Jonathan S. "Reconstructing the Social Geography of the Nineteenth-Century Jewish Community from Primary Statistical Sources." *AJH* 72 (March 1983): 354–68.

Miller, Randall M. "The Enemy Within: Some Effects of Foreign Immigrants on Antebellum Southern Cities." *Southern Studies* 24 (spring 1985): 30–53.

Moïse, Charles H. "Charleston." *Occident and American Jewish Advocate* 24 (September 1866): 266–71.

Moore, Lawrence R. "Religion, Secularization, and the Shaping of the Culture Industry in Antebellum America." *American Quarterly* 41 (June 1989): 216–42.

Morgan, David T. "Judaism in Eighteenth Century Georgia." *GHQ* 58 (spring 1974): 41–54.

Moses, Robert A. "A Sephardic Story." *JHSSC Newsletter*, Fall 1999, 9.

Munday, Dave. "Beth Elohim Poised for Major Expansion." *Charleston (S.C.) Post and Courier*, October 17, 1999.

———. "Birthday Bash: Charleston Jews Celebrate 250 Years of Growth." *Charleston (S.C.) Post and Courier*, October 17, 1999.

———. "Reform Rabbis Embrace Traditional Conversion Guidelines." *Charleston (S.C.) Post and Courier*, Charleston, July 15, 2001.

Nielsen, J.V., Jr. "Dedication Set Thursday for New Synagogue." *Charleston (S.C.) News and Courier*, August 20, 1956.

Noah, Mordecai Manuel. "Ararat Address." *PAJHS* 21 (1913): 230–52.

"Old Billy" (from the *San Francisco Weekly Gleaner*). *AJA* 15 (April 1963): 3–5.

Oppenheim, Samuel. "The Jews and Masonry in the United States Before 1810." *PAJHS* 19 (1910): 1–94.

"Ottolengui, Abraham" (obituary). *Occident* 8 (1850–1851): 528–30.

Passamaneck, Stephen M. "Morris Goldsmith: Deputy United States Marshal." *AJA* 46 (spring/summer 1994): 63–100.

Peck, Abraham J. "That Other 'Peculiar Institution': Jews and Judaism in the Nineteenth-Century South." *Modern Judaism* 7 (February 1987): 99–114.

Pessen, Edward. "How Different from Each Other Were the Antebellum North and South." *AHR* 85 (December 1980): 1119–49.

Petrusak, Frank, and Steven Steinert, "The Jews of Charleston: Some Old Wine in New Bottles." *Jewish Social Studies* 38, no. 3–4 (1976): 337–46.

Philipson, David. "The Progress of the Jewish Reform Movement in the United States." *Jewish Quarterly Review* 10 (1897): 52–99.

Phillips, N. Taylor. "Family History of the Rev. David Mendez Machado." *PAJHS* 2 (1894): 45–61.

Phillips, Philip. "Southern Unionist: A Memoir." *Commentary* 21 (1956): 41–52.

"The Poetry of Aaron Moses." Transcribed by Lani Florian. *JHSSC Newsletter*, Spring 2000, 7.

"Polish Immigrant in 1854 Founded the Orthodox Temple of Judaism Here." *Charleston (S.C.) News and Courier*, October 15, 1934.

Powers, Mary V. "The Salvador Grant of Arms." *PAJHS* 40 (March 1951): 215–20.

Pressley, Sue Anne. "Southern Jews Close Up Shop: Small-Town Traders Go the Way of Main Street." *Washington Post*, May 23, 1999.

Proctor, Samuel. "Jewish Life in New Orleans, 1718–1860." *Louisiana Historical Quarterly* 40, no. 2 (1957): 110–32.

Rabinowitz, Howard N. "Nativism, Bigotry, and Anti-Semitism in the South." *AJH* 72 (March 1988): 437–51.

"Rebecca Cohen Loses Her Baby." *AJA* 31 (April 1979): 67–68.

"Rev. Mr. Poznanski." *Occident* 2 (1844–1845): 210–12.

"Rev. Mr. Rosenfeld's Address at Charleston." *Occident* 5 (1847–1848): 75–79.

"Rev. S. Jacob of Charleston." *Occident* 10 (1852–1853): 461–62.

"Rev. Solomon Jacobs, of Charleston." *Occident* 11 (1853–1854): 271.

Robertson, Tatsha. "A Southern Exodus: As Jewish Population Declines, a Culture Departs Dixie." *Boston Globe*, May 5, 2001.

Rogoff, Leonard. "Is the Jew White? The Racial Place of the Southern Jew." *AJH* 85 (September 1997): 195–230.

Rosen, Robert. "Jews Thrived throughout the South." *Charleston (S.C.) Post and Courier*, October 17, 1999.

Rosenfeld, Jacob. "Discourse Delivered by the Rev. Jacob Rosenfeld, at the Consecration of the Orthodox Synagogue, Charleston, S.C., on Friday the 1st Day of Elul, 5607, 13th of August, 1847." *Occident* 5 (1847–1848): 325–36.

———. "The Proposed Assembly. Letter from Rev. Jacob Rosenfeld of Charleston." *Occident* 6 (1848–1849): 563–65.

Rosenwaike, Ira. "An Estimate and Analysis of the Jewish Population of the United States in 1790." *PAJHS* 50 (September 1960): 23–68.

———. "The Jewish Population of the United States as Estimated from the Census of 1820." *AJHQ* 53 (December 1963): 131–78.

Roth, Cecil, ed. "A Description of America, 1785—A Letter from Joseph Salvador." *AJA* 17 (April 1965): 27–33.

Rousey, Dennis C. "Aliens in the WASP Nest: Ethnocultural Diversity in the Antebellum Urban South." *JAH* 79 (June 1992): 152–64.

Rubin, Hyman, Sr. "Rubin's Reminiscences." *Columbia (S.C.) Jewish News*, 1990–1997.

Rudisill, Hillyer. "Simon Baruch, M.D." *Baruch Number, Library Bulletin of the Medical College of South Carolina* Special number (September 1944).

Salley, A. S. "The Fundamental Constitutions of Carolina." *Proceedings of the South Carolina Historical Association* (1934): 25–47.

Saltzman, Rachelle. "Shalom Y'all." *Southern Exposure* 11, no. 5 (1983): 28–36.

"Salvador Marker Unveiled." *The Greenwood (S.C.) Index-Journal*, July 16, 1960.

Sarna, Jonathan D. "The Impact of the American Revolution on American Jews." *Modern Judaism* 1 (1981): 149–60.

———. "Jewish Community Histories: Recent Non-Academic Contributions." *JAEH* 6 (fall 1986): 62–70.

———. "The Spectrum of Jewish Leadership in Ante-Bellum America." *JAEH* 1 (spring 1982): 59–67.

Schmier, Louis. "For Him the 'Schwartzers' Couldn't Do Enough: A Jewish Peddler and his Black Customers Look at Each Other." *AJH* 73 (September 1983): 39–55.

Schwarz, Christopher. "Bagels and Barbeque: Yankees Flooding South Find Their Preconceptions 'Ain't Necessarily So,'" *The Greenville (S.C.) News*, June 21, 1992.

Shankman, Arnold. "Happyville, the Forgotten Colony." *AJA* 30 (April 1978): 3–19.

"Shearith Israel Congregation, Charleston." *Occident* 12 (1854–1855): 258–59.

Silver, Helen Schneider. "Charleston." *Hadassah Magazine*, April 1987, 32–35.

Silverman, Jason H. "Ashley Wilkes Revisited: The Immigrant as Slaveholder in the Old South." *Journal of Confederate History* 7 (1991): 123–35.

Simonhoff, Harry. "Tolerance in Carolina in 1697." *Chicago Jewish Forum* 25 (winter 1966–67): 147–51.

Stern, Malcom H. "Charleston's First Jews." *Southern Jewish Historical Newsletter*, Fall 1988, [3–4].

———. "New Light on the Jewish Settlement of Savannah." *AJHQ* 52 (March 1963): 169–99.

———. "Portuguese Sephardim in the Americas." *AJA* 44 (spring/summer 1992): 141–78.

———. "Reforming of Reform Judaism—Past, Present, and Future." *AJHQ* 63 (December 1973): 111–37.

———. "South Carolina Jewish Marriage Settlements 1785–1839." *National Genealogical Society Quarterly* 66 (June 1978): 105–11.

Stumpf, Stuart Owen. "Implications of King George's War for the Charleston Mercantile Community." *SCHM* 77 (July 1976): 161–88.

———. "South Carolina Importers of General Merchandise, 1735–1765." *SCHM* 84 (January 1983): 1–10.

"Sunday Laws in South Carolina." *Occident* 5 (1847–1848): 593–99.

"Sunday Laws in South Carolina: Review of Judge O'Neal's Opinion." *Occident* 6 (1848–1849): 36–39.

"Sunday School Anniversary at Charleston, South Carolina." *Occident* 12 (1854–1855): 253–57.

"Synagogue to Celebrate Its 150th Year." *Columbia (S.C.) State*, March 16, 1991.

Tarshish, Allan. "The Charleston Organ Case." *AJHQ* 54 (June 1965): 411–49.

Thomas, John Peyre, Jr. "The Barbadians in Early South Carolina." *South Carolina Historical and Genealogical Magazine* 31 (April 1930): 75–92.

Tobias, Thomas J. "Charles Town in 1764." *SCHM* 67 (April 1966): 63–74.

———. "Joseph Tobias of Charleston: Linguister." *PAJHS* 49 (September 1959): 33–38.

———. "The Many-Sided Dr. De La Motta." *AJHS* 52 (March 1963): 200–19.

———. "This Cemetery We Rededicate." *AJHQ* 53 (June 1964): 352–70.

"Token of Respect to Rev. Mr. Poznanski." *Occident* 8 (1850–1851): 249–55.

Toll, William. "Jewish Families and the Intergenerational Transition in the American Hinterland." *JAEH* 12 (winter 1993): 3–34.

Trillin, Calvin. "U.S. Journal: Charleston, South Carolina, the Blacks, the Jews, and the Bird Lovers." *New Yorker*, December 15, 1981, 101–7.

Valentine, Samuel. "Consecration of the 'Beth Chayim' of the Congregation 'Shearith Israel,' Charleston, S.C." *Occident* 15 (1857–1858): 479–84.

"Violation of Sunday Laws at Charleston." *Occident* 4 (1846–1847): 588–96.

Versola, Rhesa. "Area Immigrant Works to Make Life Easier for Soviet Jews." *Charleston (S.C.) Post and Courier*, May 26, 1992.

Waddell, Gene. "An Architectural History of Kahal Kadosh Beth Elohim, Charleston." *SCHM* 98 (January 1997): 6–55.

Weinberg, Sylvia Hanna. "The Jewish Influence in Clarendon County." *JHSSC Newsletter*, Spring 2001, 5–7, 11.

Weissbach, Lee Shai. "East European Immigrants and the Image of Jews in the Small-Town South. *AJH* 85 (September 1997): 231–62.

Wenger, Beth S. "Jewish Women of the Club: The Changing Public Role of Atlanta's Jewish Women (1870–1930)." *AJH* 76, no. 3 (1987): 311–33.

White, Gayle. "The Dwindling—Empty Stores, Silent Temples: The Rural South's Jewish Culture Is Dying." *Atlanta Journal-Constitution*, March 31, 1991.

Whitfield, Stephen J. "Blood and Sand: The Jewish Community of South Florida." *AJH* 82, no. 1–4 (1994): 73–96.

———. "The Braided Identity of Southern Jewry." *AJH* 77 (March 1988): 363–87.

———. "Commercial Passions: The Southern Jew as Businessman." *AJHQ* 71 (March 1982): 342–57.

Williams, Oscar R., Jr. "Historical Impressions of Black-Jewish Relations Prior to World War II." *Negro History Bulletin* 40, no. 4 (1977): 728–31.

Wilson, Zane. "Community of Memory: Jewish Community Plays an Important Part in the History of Georgetown." *Myrtle Beach (S.C.) Sun News*, January 16, 1994.

Woodward, Carol. "Montmorenci Colony Enjoyed Two-Year Success." *Aiken Standard*, July 1989.

Woody, Robert H. "Franklin J. Moses, Jr.: Scalawag Governor of South Carolina, 1872–74." *North Carolina Historical Review* 10 (April 1933): 111–32.

Zola, Gary P. "Southern Rabbis and the Founding of the First National Association of Rabbis." *AJH* 85 (December 1997): 353–72.

———. "Why Study Southern Jewish History?" *SJH* 1 (1998): 1–21.

Acknowledgments

Exhibition Staff and Consultants

PROJECT DIRECTOR Lynn Robertson

CURATOR Dale Rosengarten

PROJECT MANAGER Jason E. Shaiman

RESEARCH CURATOR FOR FINE ARTS
Barbara Karesh Stender

ASSOCIATE CURATORS Noelle Rice, Judith
Alexander Weil Shanks, Jay Williams

PROJECT EDITOR Theodore Rosengarten

EXHIBITION DESIGNER Benjamin Hirsch

GRAPHIC DESIGNER Pat Callahan

MUSEUM CURATORIAL AND DESIGN STAFF
Alice Bouknight, Pam Chumney, Dwayne
Clark, Mary Evans, Brandy Hamilton, Stu
Heebner, Todd Heebner, Kathy Hilliard,
Sara Markusich, Peggy Nunn, Scott Peek,
Linn Rogers, Nathan Stalvey, Karen Swager,
Saddler Taylor

RESEARCH ASSISTANTS James Buxton, Michael
S. Grossman, Tara Kelly, Elizabeth Moses,
Barbara Schwartz

PHOTOGRAPHERS Bill Aron, Gordon Brown,
Brian Dressler, Richard Gehrke, Stephen
Halperson, Jay Leviton, Rick Rhodes,
William Struhs, Marlene Znoy

"PALMETTO JEWS" PHOTO PRODUCTION CREW
John Reynolds, Sheila Rodin-Novak, Heather
Webb

AUDIO PRODUCERS Marcus D. Rosenbaum,
Alice Winkler

VIDEO PRODUCERS Steven A. Channing, Paul
Keyserling, Bill Pendergraft

WEBSITE DESIGNER Karen Beidel

CONSULTING SCHOLARS Jack Bass, Solomon
Breibart, Jenna Weissman Joselit, Charles
Joyner, Daniel C. Littlefield, Deborah Dash
Moore, Robert N. Rosen, Jonathan D. Sarna,
Jason Silverman, Stephen J. Whitfield

**PUBLIC PROGRAM, DESIGN, AND EDUCATION
CONSULTANTS** Rick Black, Susan Craig,
Rebekah Farber, Darcie Fohrman, Selden K.
Smith, Margaret B. Walden

CONSERVATORS
Carol Aiken, Baltimore, Md.
Terry Boone, University Park, Md.
Alfred Crabtree, Charleston, S.C.
Craig Crawford, Columbia, S.C.
Judith Eisenberg, New York, N.Y.
Mary L. Ekroos, Trappe, Md.
Holly Herro, Columbia, S.C.
Marie Hollings, Charleston, S.C.
M. Cynthia Hughes, Baltimore, Md.
Marion Hunter, Charleston, S.C.
Elizabeth Ingber, Bayside, N.Y.
Beth McLaughlin, Asheville, S.C.
Virginia Newell, Columbia, S.C.
Catherine Rogers, Charleston, S.C.
Wendell Snapp, Columbia, S.C.

Archival, Historical, and Curatorial Advisers

Henry A. Alexander Jr., Eugene, Ore.
Sharon Bennett, The Charleston Museum,
    Charleston, S.C.
Sandy Berman, Jewish Community Archives,
    William Breman Museum, Atlanta, Ga.
Annette Blum, College of Charleston
    Library, Charleston, S.C.
Doris Bowman, Smithsonian Museum of
    American History, Washington, D.C.
Beverly Brannan, Library of Congress, Wash-
    ington, D.C.
Barbara Brannon, University of South Caro-
    lina Press, Columbia, S.C.
Nic Butler, South Carolina Historical Society,
    Charleston, S.C.
James Carolina, Georgetown Public Library,
    Georgetown, S.C.
Cecilia Chin, National Portrait Gallery,
    Washington, D.C.
Susan Dick, Georgia Historical Society,
    Savannah, Ga.
Michael Feldberg, American Jewish Histori-
    cal Society, New York, N.Y.
Marcie Cohen Ferris, Washington, D.C.
Valerie Fry, Georgia Historical Society,
    Savannah, Ga.
Belinda Gergel, Columbia College, Colum-
    bia, S.C.
Mary Giles, Catholic Diocese of Charleston,
    Charleston, S.C.
Benjamin Goldberg, Charleston, S.C.
Harlan Greene, Charleston County Public
    Library, Charleston, S.C.
Mark I. Greenberg, University of South
    Florida, Tampa, Fla.
Michael Grunberger, Hebraic Section,
    Library of Congress, Washington, D.C.
Jayne Guberman, Jewish Women's Archives,
    Brookline, Mass.
James W. Hagy, Oviedo, Fla.

Jan Heister, The Charleston Museum, Charleston, S.C.

Steve Hoffius, Charleston, S.C.

Arturo de Hoyos, The Supreme Council (Mother Council of the World), Ancient and Accepted Scottish Rite of Freemasonry, Southern Jurisdiction, Washington, D.C.

Mandi Johnson, Georgia Historical Society, Savannah, Ga.

Tom Johnson, South Caroliniana Library, University of South Carolina, Columbia, S.C.

Cathy Kahn, Touro Infirmary Archives, New Orleans, La.

Nancy Katzoff, New-York Historical Society, New York, N.Y.

Katrina Lawrimore, Kaminski House, Georgetown, S.C.

Jane Leavey, William Breman Museum, Atlanta, Ga.

Charles Lesser, South Carolina Department of Archives and History, Columbia, S.C.

Chris Loeblein, The Charleston Museum, Charleston, S.C.

Angela Mack, Gibbes Museum of Art, Charleston, S.C.

Karen Mittelman, National Endowment for the Humanities, Washington, D.C.

Alexander Moore, University of South Carolina Press, Columbia, S.C.

Cindy Pease, Kaminski House, Georgetown, S.C.

Peggy Pearlstein, Hebraic Section, Library of Congress, Washington, D.C.

Kevin Profitt, American Jewish Archives, Cincinnati, Ohio

Jane Przybysz, San Jose Museum of Quilts and Textiles, San Jose, Calif.

Ellie Siekiewicz, Washington, D.C.

Ellen Smith, American Jewish Historical Society, Waltham, Mass.

Roberta Sokolitz, Charleston, S.C.

Phillip Solomons, Savannah, Ga.

Gary Stanton, Mary Washington College, Fredericksburg, Va.

Mark Tabbert, Museum of Our National Heritage, Lexington, Mass.

George D. Terry, University of South Carolina, Columbia, S.C.

Nan Tournier, Charleston, S.C.

Steven D. Tuttle, South Carolina Department of Archives and History, Columbia, S.C.

Gene Waddell, College of Charleston Library, Charleston, S.C.

Merikay Waldvogel, Knoxville, Tenn.

Chrissy Wilson, Mississippi Department of Archives and History, Jackson, Miss.

Zinnia M. Willits, College of Charleston Library, Charleston, S.C.

Deborah Wright, Avery Research Center, Charleston, S.C.

Shelly Zegart, Louisville, Ky.

Marcia Zerivitz, Sanford L. Ziff Jewish Museum of Florida, Miami, Fla.

Gary Zola, American Jewish Archives, Cincinnati, Ohio

Community Advisers and Volunteers

Deborah Baruch Abrams
Ditty Abrams
Mikail Agrest
Mark Antman
Sam Appel
Gerry Sue Arnold
Susan H. Baker
Leah Barkowitz
Garry Baum
Peter and Doris Baumgarten
Shera Lee Ellison Berlin
Cydney Berry
Paul and Jean Birnbaum
Jack L. Bloom
Sara Breibart
Marilyn Brilliant
David and Beverly Bruck
Abby Bryan
Leah F. Chase
Eileen Chepenik
Elaine Epstein
Stanley B. Farbstein
Brian Keith Faudman
Marilyn C. Fine
Phyllis Firetag
Carolee R. Fox
Larry W. Freudenberg
Helen L. Goldman
Alwyn O. Goldstein
Martin and Harriet Goode
Ezra and Riki Greenspan

Evelyn Rosenberg Gross-Brein
Dona Cohen Gutter
L. Eden Harvey
Mordenai R. Hirsch
Rabbi Anthony D. Holz
Ruth Bass Jacobs
Janice Kahn
Ruth K. Kaplan
Sam and Mitzi Kirshtein
Michael Kogan
Herbert and Harriet Keyserling
Harold J. Kornblut
Adrian and Ethel Kremer
Carolyn Baruch Levenson
Rabbi Theodore Levy
Joseph J. Lipton
A. M. (Mick) Lourie
Susan Lourie
Rose Y. Mark
Rhetta A. Mendelsohn
Jane P. Meyerson
Robert A. Moses
Joseph Nussbaum
Neda Nussbaum
Mordecai Persky
Edward Poliakoff
Marsha Poliakoff
Gerald and Arline Polinsky
William S. Pollitzer
Harry Price
Shirley Prystowsky
Rabbi David J. Radinsky
Rachel M. Raisin
Fannie Appel Rones
Meyer Rosen
Anita Moïse Rosenfield Rosenberg
Sandra Lee Rosenblum
Rabbi William A. Rosenthall
Maizie-Louise Rubin
Rose Rubin
Gail Rubinstein
Betty Rau Santandrea
Hugo Schiller
Ella L. Schlosburg
Laz Schneider
Philip Schneider
Norton and Mindelle Seltzer
Randi Serrins
Paul and Jayne Siegel
Allan and Sophia (Skip) Sindler
Jania Sommers

Aron and Karen Tannenbaum
Irene Taradash
Bernard and Rosalyn Keyserling Taratoot
Peter Wagner
Sadie B. Want
Sylvia Hanna Weinberg
Arnold Wengrow
Sura Wolff Wengrow
Jeff Zaglin

Sponsoring Institutions

McKissick Museum, College of Liberal Arts,
    University of South Carolina
    Lynn Robertson, Director

The College of Charleston Library
    David J. Cohen, Dean of Libraries
    Marie Hollings, Head of Special Collections

The Jewish Studies Program at the College
of Charleston
    Martin Perlmutter, Director

Jewish Historical Society of South Carolina
    Isadore E. Lourie, Founding President
    Klyde Robinson, Past President
    Richard M. Gergel, Past President
    Jeffrey Rosenblum, Past President
    Robert N. Rosen, President

Major Contributors

National Endowment for the Humanities
Bank of America
College of Charleston
University of South Carolina
Jewish Historical Society of South Carolina
Jerry and Sue Kline
Maurice Amado Foundation
Jesselson Foundation
Harriet and Herbert Keyserling
Ron and Anne Krancer
Institute of Museum and Library Services
State Historical Records Advisory Board
Brand Foundation
Benedict Rosen
South Carolina Humanities Council
Jerry and Anita Zucker Family Endowment
    Fund, Community Foundation
John and Frances Loeb Foundation
Helena Rubinstein Foundation
Joseph J. Miller Foundation
Lucius J. Littauer Foundation
Marilyn and Marshall Butler Foundation
William Price Fund, Spartanburg County
    Foundation

Hadassah International Institute for Research
    on Jewish Women, Brandeis University
South Carolina Department of Parks,
    Recreation, and Tourism
Southern Jewish Historical Society
Fern Karesh Hurst
Saul Alexander Foundation
Barnet Family Foundation
Robert and Nancy Lyon
Sam and Regina Greene Family Fund
Irving Sonenshine
Jack Alterman
Atelier 4

Index